THE WAR
WENT
ON

CONFLICTING WORLDS
New Dimensions of the American Civil War
T. Michael Parrish, Series Editor

THE WAR WENT ON

RECONSIDERING
the LIVES *of* CIVIL WAR
VETERANS

EDITED BY
Brian Matthew Jordan
AND
Evan C. Rothera

Louisiana State University Press
Baton Rouge

Published by Louisiana State University Press
Copyright © 2020 by Louisiana State University Press
All rights reserved
First printing

DESIGNER: Michelle A. Neustrom
TYPEFACE: Adobe Caslon Pro

Portions of the essay by Adam H. Domby are adapted from
*The False Cause:Fraud, Fabrication, and White Supremacy in Confederate
Memory* (Charlottesville: University of Virginia Press, 2020)
and appear here with permission.

Portions of the essay by Zachery Fry are adapted from
A Republic in the Ranks: Loyalty and Dissent in the Army of the Potomac
(Chapel Hill: University of North Carolina Press, 2020).

Cataloging-in-Publication Data are available at the Library of Congress.

ISBN 978-0-8071-71981 (cloth) — ISBN 978-0-8071-73046 (pdf) — ISBN
978-0-8071-73053 (epub)

In Memory of J. Gary Dillon (1929–2018)—BMJ

For Kelsey and Ian—ECR

CONTENTS

III. THE MULTIVOCALITY OF CIVIL WAR VETERANHOOD

ACKNOWLEDGMENTS

IT WAS AN ABSOLUTE delight to publish this book with Louisiana State University Press. We would like to thank Mike Parrish for his commitment to this project. Mike supported our vision and understood what we hoped to accomplish from the very beginning. Rand Dotson of LSU Press also deserves our thanks for his efforts to shepherd this book into print. George Roupe, our copy editor, offered many good suggestions about polishing the manuscript. We would also like to thank the talented cast of contributors to this volume for their insightful and pioneering essays. Working with this group of historians was immensely rewarding, and we hope this is but the first of many collaborations. We were fortunate to cut our historical teeth under the tutelage of Allen C. Guelzo, who deserves our thanks. We would also like to recognize and thank our dissertation advisers, David Blight, Bruno Cabanes, Mark Neely, and Amy Greenberg. Their guidance, good sense, and wisdom have made us better scholars; this book is a small token of our appreciation for their efforts.

THERE ARE CERTAIN people who come into your life and change it forever. For two decades, I was privileged to call J. Gary Dillon my friend. As a young boy, Gary had crisscrossed the Midwest in search of the last survivors of Lincoln's armies. Growing up, I had the good fortune to listen to Gary reminisce about "his veterans." His eyes sparkled—and occasionally, tears would well up behind his unusually thick lenses—whenever he remembered the "Boys in Blue." With fondness, Gary recalled his trip to Wauseon, Ohio, to meet with "Uncle Dan" Clingaman, who had attended the 1938 Blue-Gray reunion in Gettysburg. Gary recollected his attendance at a birthday party for the centenarian Alvin Smith, Ohio's last surviving African American Civil War veteran. But he cherished above all else his two rail journeys to Duluth, Minnesota, where he finally met his venerable old pen pal Albert Woolson—the very last survivor of the Union armies. The power of those encounters would never be effaced; even in later years, as Gary's hair turned to snow and his powers of recollection dimmed, he could still recall with precision Woolson's address: 215 ½ East Fifth Street. To know Gary was to know those veterans. He provided a living link to the Grand Army of the Republic—a sobering reminder that the Civil War wasn't so long ago. Gary passed away on October 22, 2018, at the age of eighty-nine. In gratitude for our remarkable friendship and in loving memory of a life well lived, I dedicate this volume to him.

—B. JORDAN

MIDWAY THROUGH THIS project I left Penn State to take up a position at Sam Houston State University. As I moved from central Pennsylvania to Texas, I spent a great deal of time thinking about community and family. At Penn State, I benefited from a remarkable community of scholars including Mark Neely, Amy Greenberg, Bill Blair, Annie Rose, Carol Reardon, Dan Letwin, Nan Woodruff, Gary Cross, and the late Tony Kaye. This immensely talented and generous group of historians taught me a great deal about what it means to be a historian and how to be an effective teacher, a good departmental citizen, and a productive member of the academy. It is my privilege to call them mentors and friends. My family members, too numerous to name individually, have celebrated with me during the good times, commiserated with me during the not so good times, and supported me through thick and thin. Quite simply, I could not have achieved what I have without their love and support. Two of my oldest friends, Emily Flyntz and Casey Nitsch, and a new friend, David H. Green, helped me through a difficult time. In a larger sense, therefore, I dedicate this book to everyone—family, friends, mentors, and students—who helped make me who I am today. Specifically, however, I dedicate it to Kelsey and Ian. It is my gift to my sister and new brother as they build a life for themselves and work to make a better world.

—E. ROTHERA

THE WAR
WENT
ON

Introduction

EVAN C. ROTHERA & BRIAN MATTHEW JORDAN

T HIS IS A BOOK about Civil War veterans. It is a book about messy, non-linear, and complicated transitions from war to peace. It is about guerrillas who could never quite demobilize; wounded veterans who found themselves objects of pity, scorn, and state surveillance; and ex–prisoners of war who believed their experiences did not fit into the arc of sectional reconciliation and the emerging sanitized narrative of the US Civil War. In sum, it is about people who passed through a profoundly disorienting experience and spent the rest of their lives trying to put the pieces back together. While some succeeded, others did not. The contributors to this volume analyze a rich cross section of veteran stories and highlight the ways in which scholars might continue to explore the postwar lives of Johnny Reb and Billy Yank.

For the most part, the contributors to this volume are neither senior scholars nor specialists working on veterans; instead, we solicited contributions from scholars equipped to discuss how various subfields might speak to or engage with veteran studies. The contributors approach veterans from some oblique angles, but they nonetheless provide innovative, surprising, and often unconventional answers to old questions. While paying close attention to the stories of veterans themselves, the contributors note the development of veteran studies and offer suggestions about how the literature could develop in the future. As a result, many of the essays highlight bodies of sources that scholars have either overlooked or minimized.

Four major themes run throughout many—although not all—pieces in this volume. First, many contributors critique Gerald F. Linderman's famous "hibernation thesis." In his important study of soldier motivations, *Embattled Courage: The Experience of Combat in the American Civil War*, Linderman contended that, for about fifteen years after the war, veterans slipped into a sort of "hibernation" because the scalding experience of war left them dazed and disillusioned.[1] But more than a few essays in this volume illustrate that many veterans did not hibernate at all. Rather than shrinking into self-imposed reverie, veterans inserted themselves (and often rather forcefully) into the important political debates of the day. In the immediate postwar years, veterans drew on their authority in two ways. First, they became involved in electoral politics at the local, state, and federal level. Some veterans retained their affection for "Little Mac" (General George McClellan), Horatio Seymour, and the Democratic Party. Other veterans, however, became radicalized by war and supported Radical Republicans in their contest with Andrew Johnson. Prominent veterans such as Daniel E. Sickles, Benjamin F. Butler, and John A. Logan, among others, abandoned the Democratic Party, their prewar political home, and became ardent Radical Republicans. Many veterans followed their lead and campaigned for Ulysses S. Grant in 1868, while denouncing Seymour's alleged copperheadism.[2] Second, veterans used their authority to reject Secretary of State William H. Seward's cautious approach toward the French Intervention. They deplored French emperor Napoleon III's attempt to overthrow Benito Juárez, the democratically elected president of Mexico.[3] They pushed the government to take a more bellicose stand toward the French violation of the Monroe Doctrine. In other words, in an alleged period of hibernation, many veterans stayed active and alert. Their actions demonstrated the important relationship between veterans and politics, as well as ways in which they used their authority as veterans to engage with political questions.[4]

Veterans resisted the siren song of hibernation in still other ways. Frank James, a member of William Clarke Quantrill's band of guerrillas, apparently hoped to make a smooth transition from bushwhacker to civilian. However, his transition to peace involved robbery and murder. This led some people to brand James an outlaw and others to romanticize him as a social bandit who refused to submit to a tyrannical government. Ex–prisoners of war refused to allow the nation to forget their experiences in hellholes like Andersonville.[5] Their narratives emphasized rebel cruelty and barbarity and did not seem the work of men who went quiescent for fifteen years. Veterans gathered themselves into fraternal organizations like the Grand Army of the Republic (GAR).[6] They prodded the government to make good on Lincoln's promises in his second inaugural address.[7] They erected monuments and memorial halls across the nation and wrote and performed plays extolling the Won Cause. In the late

1870s, periodicals such as the *National Tribune* magnified veteran voices and influence. These newspapers created space for veterans to rehash battles and campaigns, dole out praise and criticism, and commune with fellow veterans around a giant, albeit imagined, campfire.

Still, this volume eschews generalization, refusing to shoehorn veterans into stereotypes—a problem that plagues much existing literature in the field. Though some veterans refused to hibernate, others did—either unable or unwilling to return to their prewar communities. Many of these ex-soldiers went west, either as individuals or in groups.[8] In "veteran colonies" in the Dakotas and elsewhere, men sought stillness and space from turbulent political and social questions. These veterans consciously rejected politics and strove to avoid the great questions of the day.[9]

Second, many of the contributors analyze the creation of various types of communities. Veterans often created networks of mutual support in regions where they were not particularly popular, such as Union veterans in postwar Arkansas. African American veterans, fighting against the rising tide of reconciliation and Jim Crow segregation, defiantly maintained an emancipationist vision of Abraham Lincoln and the US Civil War. In addition, some black veterans demanded and earned places for themselves, as well as their wives and children, in state soldiers' homes. Veterans promoted the construction of memorial halls because they provided space for many different community organizations and events. Memorial halls contained a meeting room for the local Grand Army of the Republic post, displays of war relics, venues for other fraternal and social organizations, and spaces for theater and oratory. These spaces thus reinforced links between veterans and members of their towns and cities. Veterans created communities by performing plays extolling their sacrifices and castigated rebels for attempting to destroy Lincoln's "last best, hope of earth."[10]

Through their memory work—disseminating ex–prisoner of war narratives or fighting about the particulars of the battle of Cedar Creek, for instance—veterans also created and reinforced a sense of community. Further, when applying for pensions, veterans had to call on local people and former comrades to testify about their health and the effects of the war. Political divisions easily created gulfs within communities and unraveled pension applications. Union veterans in Arkansas often failed in their pension applications because of prejudiced testimony from former rebels. Dissenters in North Carolina, on the other hand, who did not support the rebel war effort and often did not fight, managed to secure Confederate pensions. Communities even praised some dissenters at the time of their deaths as good Confederate veterans.

Third, the pieces in this volume emphasize the multivocality of veteran experiences. While some veterans readjusted to civilian life with little difficulty, others struggled mightily to return to civilian routines. Some veterans found political activism rewarding and served their communities in ways large and small. Other veterans felt alienated by their experiences and believed that they no longer fit in with the folks at home. More than a few veterans snubbed sectional reconciliation or pursued rapprochement with their former enemies on their own terms. Understanding how or why veterans behaved in certain ways requires far more than a thumbnail sketch of their wartime service. Furthermore, the varied nature of veteran experiences validates Laura de Mello e Souza's observation that "beneath the single face of Clio lies a hidden mosaic of individual adventures, which may be recovered."[11]

Fourth and finally, these essays confirm that veterans proved exceptionally attentive to history. Veterans and nonveterans alike understood that the Civil War was a powerful and transformative experience, even if they quarreled among themselves about causes, consequences, and niggling details. Yet historians have not always been attentive to how veterans, particularly on the winning side, shaped history. An old military history adage suggests, "the winners forget and go about their business, while the losers spend the rest of their lives remembering and explaining their, or their ancestors', exploits, motives, and failures."[12] In the case of the US Civil War, veterans on both sides engaged in memory work by forging and contesting hegemonic narratives such as the Lost Cause and the Won Cause. Veterans argued with former foes and the people who fought alongside them about the specifics of battles, campaigns, and leaders. Veterans put a great deal of emphasis on historical truth and explained that they looked to the future to make sure bias and fallacy did not creep into analyses of the war. In addition, most veterans did their best to make sure their experiences—even if out of line with the mood of the postwar nation—appeared in the historical record. In sum, veterans worked to ensure that succeeding generations remembered and understood their sacrifices, as well as the history of the conflict more generally.

THE VOLUME OPENS with Zachery A. Fry's "'Let Us Everywhere Charge the Enemy Home': Army of the Potomac Veterans and Public Partisanship, 1864–1880." Fry surveys veteran political activity from Abraham Lincoln's reelection in 1864 to James A. Garfield's election in 1880. Historians have long contended that the soldier vote in 1864 sealed Lincoln's reelection bid. However, in line with recent work by Jonathan W. White, Fry analyzes diversity of sentiment among veterans. Some veterans favored Lincoln, but others supported Little Mac, despite George Pendleton and the peace platform.[13] Soldiers backed U. S. Grant over Horatio Seymour in 1868 and over Horace Greeley in 1872, but some had soured on the Republican Party by 1876. For Fry, the election of 1880 proves an important moment because Republican James A. Garfield faced Democrat Winfield Scott Hancock, the commander of the Union's 2nd Corps at Gettysburg. Republicans could not "wave the bloody shirt" as vigorously against Hancock as they did against Seymour; many soldiers switched party allegiances to vote for their old commander. After 1880, Fry argues, veterans generally prioritized pension reform over partisanship.

Evan C. Rothera's essay examines a different brand of veteran political activity. Whereas Fry charts domestic political activism, Rothera analyzes international affairs, specifically the French Intervention. In 1861, Mexico concluded a destructive civil war, and President Benito Juárez suspended foreign debt payments. Great Britain, France, and Spain seized the Veracruz Customs House to service their debts. However, Britain and Spain left when they realized Emperor Napoleon III of France wanted to re-create a French empire in the New World. Although a Mexican army stalled the French at Puebla on May 5, 1862, French troops seized Mexico City a year later, and Napoleon installed Ferdinand Maximilian of Austria as Emperor Maximilian I of Mexico. In response to this gross violation of the Monroe Doctrine, Secretary of State William H. Seward pursued a conciliatory policy. Rothera demonstrates how veterans, ranging from U. S. Grant to largely unknown actors, challenged Seward and invoked their authority as veterans to direct US foreign policy.

The following two essays complement Rothera's focus on the United States / Mexico borderlands by discussing other segments of the western United States. Many veterans moved to Iowa, Kansas, and Nebraska, but Kurt Hackemer's "Civil War Veteran Colonies on the Western Frontier" offers fine-grained analysis of veteran colonies in the Dakotas. He explains how prospective groups solicited members, took advantage of Republican economic policies, gathered subscriptions, and created new settlements. In addition, Hackemer offers a different position on the hibernation thesis than most of the other contributors. He discovers, through newspaper research, that the colonies tended to eschew politics. Hackemer considers this logical because many of the veterans in the colonies came from one of the "Three Hundred Fighting Regiments."[14] Thus they had more exposure to trauma. In other words, veterans deliberately created communities of like-minded men and sought tranquility to recuperate from the trauma of war. Matthew Christopher Hulbert's "The Trials of Frank James: Guerrilla Veteranhood and the Double Edge of Wartime Notoriety" builds on his significant previous work about guerrillas.[15] Hulbert employs Frank James as a case study to analyze how guerrillas reintegrated—or not— into everyday life. James apparently believed he could make a seamless transition from guerrilla to veteran at the end of the war. However, his postwar career involved several robberies and murders, and his transition to peace did not occur until the 1880s with acquittals by juries of his peers in Missouri and Alabama. Frank James's war continued long after 1865 and opens up, Hulbert asserts, a series of important questions about guerrilla veteranhood.

Sarah Handley-Cousins's and Angela M. Riotto's pieces continue the analysis of problematic veteranhood. Handley-Cousins's "Speaking for Themselves: Disabled Veterans and Civil War Medical Photography" opens with the striking account of Rowland Ward, who suffered a terrible wound: a shell fragment tore off his lower jaw. Ward's pension application, however, differed from so many others because it included a photograph of his injuries. Handley-Cousins employs photography as a way to discuss the relationship of veterans to the state.[16] This period saw the development of the US medical profession. Officials attempted to recover specimens from the war, a practice that intensified but did not end with the US Civil War.[17] Specimens often included images of disabled veterans, some of which might have been made without the veteran's permission. In sum, veterans had an ambivalent relationship with the state; while many received pensions, others found their wounds placed on display for public consumption. Riotto's essay examines captivity narratives written in the seven decades following the war. Prisoner of war experiences differed dramatically from those of their fellow soldiers and did not always fit neatly into emerging narratives of the conflict. Some ex-prisoners wrote venomous narratives that pulled no punches and exposed rebel cruelty. Others, as the decades passed, softened their language and massaged their accounts to conform to growing sectional reconciliation. While Riotto echoes Hulbert and Handley-Cousins in her attention to problematic veteranhood, she also raises another important issue: history and memory. Ex–prisoners of war felt, with some justification, that their stories would not make it into the histories of the war, or, perhaps more problematically, that only flawed versions would be included. Thus they did their best to disseminate their stories.

Ex–prisoners of war were not the only veterans fretting that they would not make it into the history books. Riotto's analysis anticipates Steven E. Sodergren's and Jonathan A. Noyalas's discussions of similar concerns among other veterans with more conventional wartime experiences. Sodergren's "'Exposing False History': The Voice of the Union Veteran in the Pages of the *National Tribune*" makes excellent use an important veteran newspaper. Sodergren carefully analyzes how Union veterans fought and refought their old battles and campaigns. He also discusses their ideas about education and the persistent concern, echoed by many rebel veterans as well, that the other side was winning the history wars. Sodergren contends that veterans saw their work as embracing a larger purpose: the search for truth. As one veteran put it, "Truth is a Krupp gun, before which Falsehood's armor, however thick, cannot stand."[18] Noyalas's essay, a focused case study analyzing the memory of the Shenandoah Valley Campaign of 1864, serves as an excellent follow-up to Sodergren's essay. Noyalas pays careful attention to memory battles, but he spends more time on the vicious quarrels among men who fought on the same side. Indeed, both Sodergren and Noyalas ask scholars to revisit an old question: Who wrote the history of the Civil War? Although the South clearly won the peace, with the overthrow of Reconstruction and the imposition of Jim Crow, people on both sides wrote the histories of the conflict, and veterans played a critical role in this process.

Jonathan D. Neu and Tyler Sperrazza consider some of the same discussions about history and memory, but from different perspectives. Neu's "A Building Very Useful: The Grand Army Memorial Hall in US Civic Life, 1880–1920" analyzes veteran efforts to build memorial halls, which Neu distinguishes from monuments. Many veterans, he contends, preferred memorial halls. In addition to providing meeting space for the local GAR post, or posts, and an area to display war relics, memorial halls also housed other community organizations. Thus they proved to be a way for communities to celebrate veterans while providing communal space. Memorial halls endured long after veterans died and, in a different manner than monuments, perhaps, helped people remember veteran struggles and sacrifices. Sperrazza's "Veterans at the Footlights: Unionism and White Supremacy in the Theater of the Grand Army of the Republic" builds on Neu's contribution by thinking about another type of communal space: theaters. Sperrazza discusses veteran plays and how they often struck a discordant note in an era of burgeoning sectional reconciliation. Veteran plays offered a Manichean view of the Civil War: brave, noble, self-sacrificing, and virtuous northerners and vile, contemptible, and sadistic southerners. Furthermore, some of the plays Sperrazza analyzes took place in the memorial halls Neu describes. Sperrazza also probes veteran attitudes toward African Americans. Perhaps not surprisingly, he finds that most of them internalized the white supremacist attitudes of their society, with the occasional exception.

In the past fifteen years, scholars have produced important treatments of African American veterans.[19] Matthew D. Norman's essay and Kelly D. Mezurek's contribution build on this scholarship and offer compelling discussions of black veterans. Norman analyzes black veteran attitudes toward Abraham Lincoln. African Americans such as H. Ford Douglas, not to mention many white abolitionists, thought little of Lincoln during the 1850s. However, many changed their tune dramatically after 1863, when Lincoln's Emancipation Proclamation and the dramatic efforts of the freed people helped transform a war for union into a war for union and emancipation. African Americans maintained an emancipationist memory of the US Civil War well into the twentieth century, and they did so against powerful forces such as Jim Crow segregation, sectional reconciliation, and racial violence. Interestingly, as Mezurek illustrates, African Americans sought and received places in state soldiers' homes throughout the Midwest. Mezurek never denies the systematic and pervasive racism African American veterans faced in the postbellum period. However, by foregrounding black veterans who insisted on the right to live in soldiers' homes and received the same benefits, services, burials, and headstones as white veterans, she illuminates the diverse array of black veteran experiences and complicates recent studies of the Midwest that emphasize the racism and violence of the region.[20] To be sure, in an era correctly labeled the nadir of US race relations, many white veterans and nonveterans did not approve of integrated soldiers' homes or celebrating an emancipationist memory of the conflict. However, both Norman and Mezurek demonstrate how African Americans insisted on securing the benefits of their service and refused to subscribe to narratives that minimized their participation or whitewashed the war.

The next two essays take readers out of the northern states and into rebeldom. Rebecca Howard's "Lost to the Lost Cause: Arkansas's Union Veterans" analyzes Union veterans, both white and African American, in Arkansas. Interestingly, the GAR flourished in Arkansas in the 1880s and veterans often took stridently emancipationist stands in the midst of sectional reconciliation. Howard attributes these tendencies to the ways Reconstruction unfolded in Arkansas and postwar migration of northerners to Arkansas. She illustrates the problems, as well as the opportunities, of living cheek to jowl with former enemies once the fighting ceased. Adam H. Domby's "Loyal Deserters and the Veterans Who Weren't: Pension Fraud in Lost Cause Memory" offers a detailed discussion of dissenters in North Carolina. At various points, people's ideology changed dramatically based on what seemed most remunerative. Dissenters emphasized Unionism when asking the Southern Claims Commission for reimbursement. However, as the decades passed, other dissenters claimed Confederate pensions, despite their lack of approval of the so-called Confederacy and their active efforts to harm the rebel war effort. Domby offers a powerful lesson about the Lost Cause: it erased southern dissent while facilitating Unionist claims to rebel pensions. Thus people disloyal to a disloyal experiment became, at the end of their lives, loyal to disloyalty. Both Howard and Domby complicate analysis of loyalty and dissent and echo Edward L. Ayers that more work is necessary to understand the complexities of the subject.[21]

Brian Matthew Jordan's "Veterans in New Fields: Directions for Future Scholarship on Civil War Veterans" closes the volume. Jordan surveys the scholarly literature on veterans and describes both positive developments and a few shortcomings. In addition, he outlines a few directions for future research. Taken in conjunction with the suggestions found throughout the rest of the volume, Jordan reveals that, for all the ink that has been spilled on veterans, there is still a great deal more historians could profitably say about them. Indeed, it is the hope of the editors that the essays in this volume will spark some of those conversations.

NOTES

1. Gerald Linderman, *Embattled Courage: The Experience of Combat in the American Civil War* (New York: Free Press, 1987). See also David W. Blight, *Race and Reunion: The Civil War in American Memory* (Cambridge, MA: Harvard University Press, 2001). For recent challenges to the hibernation thesis see Brian Matthew Jordan, *Marching Home: Union Veterans and Their Unending Civil War* (New York: Liveright, 2014), and Jordan, "The Hibernation That Wasn't: Rethinking Union Veterans Immediately after the Civil War," *Journal of the Civil War Era* 5, no. 4 (December 2015): 484–503.

2. For a new study of Horatio Seymour see William C. Harris, *Two against Lincoln: Reverdy Johnson and Horatio Seymour, Champions of the Loyal Opposition* (Lawrence: University Press of Kansas, 2017). For analysis of copperheadism see Frank L. Klement, *The Copperheads in the Middle West* (Chicago: University of Chicago Press, 1960); Frank L. Klement, *The Limits of Dissent: Clement L. Vallandigham and the Civil War* (Lexington: University Press of Kentucky, 1970); Frank L. Klement, *Dark Lanterns: Secret Political Societies, Conspiracies, and Treason Trials in the Civil War* (Baton Rouge: Louisiana State University Press, 1984); Jennifer L. Weber, *Copperheads: The Rise and Fall of Lincoln's Opponents in the North* (New York: Oxford University Press, 2006); and Stephen E. Towne, *Surveillance and Spies in the Civil War: Exposing Confederate Conspiracies in America's Heartland* (Athens: Ohio University Press, 2015).

3. See Alfred J. Hanna and Kathryn A. Hanna, *Napoleon III and Mexico: American Triumph over Monarchy* (Chapel Hill: University of North Carolina Press, 1971); Thomas D. Schoonover, *Dollars over Dominion: The Triumph of Liberalism in Mexican–United States Relations* (Baton Rouge: Louisiana State University Press, 1978); Patrick J. Kelly, "The North American Crisis of the 1860s," *Journal of the Civil War Era* 2, no. 3 (September 2012): 337–68; and Don H. Doyle, *The Cause of All Nations: An International History of the American Civil War* (New York: Basic Books, 2015).

4. The classic study of Union veterans and politics remains Mary Dearing, *Veterans in Politics: The Story of the G.A.R.* (Baton Rouge: Louisiana State University Press, 1952).

5. See William Best Hesseltine, ed., *Civil War Prisons* (Kent, OH: Kent State University Press, 1962), and Benjamin G. Cloyd, *Haunted by Atrocity: Civil War Prisons in American Memory* (Baton Rouge: Louisiana State University Press, 2010).

6. See Stuart McConnell, *Glorious Contentment: The Grand Army of the Republic, 1865–1900* (Chapel Hill: University of North Carolina Press, 1992), and Barbara A. Gannon, *The Won Cause: Black and White Comradeship in the Grand Army of the Republic* (Chapel Hill: University of North Carolina Press, 2011).

7. Abraham Lincoln, second inaugural address, March 4, 1865.

8. Richard White, *The Republic for Which It Stands: The United States during Reconstruction and the Gilded Age, 1865–1896* (New York: Oxford University Press, 2017), 146–47, discusses how Hamlin Garland's father, a veteran of the Union army, moved his family several times after the US Civil War.

9. See Reid Mitchell, *The Vacant Chair: The Northern Soldier Leaves Home* (New York: Oxford University Press, 1993), and William Deverell, "Redemption Falls Short: Soldier and Surgeon in the Post–Civil War Far West," in *Civil War Wests: Testing the Limits of the United States,* ed. Adam Arenson and Andrew R. Graybill (Berkeley: University of California Press, 2015), 139–57.

10. Abraham Lincoln, "Annual Message to Congress," December 1, 1862, in *Collected Works of Abraham Lincoln*, ed. Roy P. Basler (New Brunswick, NJ: Rutgers University Press, 1953), 5:537.

11. Laura de Mello e Souza, *The Devil and the Land of the Holy Cross: Witchcraft, Slavery, and Popular Religion in Colonial Brazil* (Austin: University of Texas Press, 2003), 219.

12. Don E. Alberts, *The Battle of Glorieta: Union Victory in the West* (College Station: Texas A&M University Press, 1998), 185n9.

13. Jonathan W. White, *Emancipation, the Union Army, and the Reelection of Abraham Lincoln* (Baton Rouge: Louisiana State University Press, 2014).

14. See William F. Fox, *Regimental Losses in the American Civil War, 1861–1865* (Albany, NY: Albany Publishing, 1889).

15. See Matthew Christopher Hulbert, *The Ghosts of Guerrilla Memory: How Civil War Bushwhackers Became Gunslingers in the American West* (Athens: University of Georgia Press, 2016).

16. Her discussion of the power of photographs is reminiscent of Mark E. Neely Jr.'s analysis of photographs of Andersonville survivors in *The Civil War and the Limits of Destruction* (Cambridge, MA: Harvard University Press, 2007).

17. See, for example, Cameron B. Strang, "Violence, Ethnicity, and Human Remains during the Second Seminole War," *Journal of American History* 100, no. 4 (March 2014): 973–94.

18. See Sodergren, "'Exposing False History,'" in this volume.

19. See Donald R. Shaffer, *After the Glory: The Struggles of Black Civil War Veterans* (Lawrence: University Press of Kansas, 2004); Elizabeth A. Regosin and Donald R. Shaffer, *Voices of Emancipation: Understanding Slavery, the Civil War, and Reconstruction through the U.S. Pension Bureau Files* (New York: New York University Press, 2008); Richard M. Reid, *Freedom for Themselves: North Carolina's Black Soldiers in the Civil War Era* (Chapel Hill: University of North Carolina Press, 2008); Gannon, *The Won Cause*; Kelly D. Mezurek, *For Their Own Cause: The 27th United States Colored Troops* (Kent, OH: Kent State University Press, 2016); and Douglas R. Egerton, *Thunder at the Gates: The Black Civil War Regiments That Redeemed America* (New York: Basic Books, 2016).

20. See, for example, Brent M. S. Campney, *This Is Not Dixie: Racist Violence in Kansas, 1861–1927* (Urbana: University of Illinois Press, 2015); Christopher Phillips, *The Rivers Ran Backward: The Civil War and the Remaking of the American Middle Border* (New York: Oxford University Press, 2016); and Matthew E. Stanley, *The Loyal West: Civil War and Reunion in Middle America* (Urbana: University of Illinois Press, 2017).

21. Edward L. Ayers, "Loyalty and America's Civil War," 49th Annual Fortenbaugh Memorial Lecture, Gettysburg, PA, Gettysburg College, 2010.

I

REJECTING
HIBERNATION

"Let Us Everywhere Charge the Enemy Home"

Army of the Potomac Veterans and Public Partisanship, 1864–1880

ZACHERY A. FRY

I N MARCH 1866, a series of published resolutions from the Union veterans' group the Soldiers' and Sailors' League fumed that Robert E. Lee must "answer to the charge of treason." As the leader of rebel forces in the Virginia theater, Lee had committed "treachery to God for wantonly violating the obligations of his oath" and thus deserved "the reward of a traitor." The veterans called attention to their own sacrifices during the war and, in calling for a harsh and unforgiving Reconstruction, demanded justice for their fallen comrades. Nearly a year after Appomattox, therefore, Union veterans continued to assail the defeated foe, the black-and-white letters of newspaper print having replaced salvoes of lead.[1]

Two broad innovations in Civil War literature have dominated the field in recent years. The first and perhaps most significant is the so-called dark turn. Historians of this school have increasingly emphasized the war's destructive effects on its participants (both physical and psychological), on the national culture, and even on the country's landscape itself.[2] The second trend is a steady growth in the recognition of a "long Civil War" in which the actual military struggle between 1861 and 1865 was only the most dramatic and conventional phase.[3] Using the political experiences of wartime and postwar Union veterans, this essay offers insights for both historiographical trends.

Historians have traditionally viewed Union veterans through an emphasis on social and political history, including the lengthy campaign for pensions and civil service positions.[4] Recent works have changed tack to focus on the traumatic cultural effects the war itself had on the difficult readjustment to civilian life, in the process highlighting the chasm between veterans and ordinary civilians in the postwar North.[5] Neither approach appreciates the central role returning Union soldiers played in the raging partisan issues of Reconstruction. Veterans used the process of political organization and mobilization to replicate their wartime service, in large part because their time in uniform had been characterized by a constant spirited debate over loyalty. While Democratic veterans convened to oppose radical measures that would revolutionize the vanquished South, Republican veterans and their allies quickly came to oppose anyone who would uproot the gains they had fought for and gained under Lincoln's leadership. As years went on, both sides appealed to the soldier's hallowed place in the national political culture to cast the veteran as the true guardian of civic virtue.[6]

THE FIRST UNION VETERANS to exert influence on national politics actually mobilized during the height of the war itself. By autumn 1864, thousands of men who had hung up the blue uniform rather than reenlist at the end of their terms of service participated in the presidential contest between Abraham Lincoln and former Army of the Potomac commander George McClellan. The crucial election witnessed Lincoln reaching broadly for northern support in a "National Union" Party that joined Republicans with like-minded pro-administration War Democrats. McClellan's candidacy, decided after an awkward convention struggle dominated by the Democratic Party's peace faction, left a weakened standard bearer hoping to capitalize on the vote of an army that had once revered him. By 1864, the Army of the Potomac had therefore become an arena for competing views of political loyalty. On one side were those who endorsed the Republican message and the administration's policies as a wartime imperative.[7] On the other side, maligned by many soldiers because of the Democratic Party's peace activism, were those who stuck to a conservative message that valued the Constitution and individual liberty in a white man's republic.[8]

Men returning from the front lines threw themselves into political activity across the North, Democrats and Republicans working in their wartime social circles to form paramilitary campaign clubs. Pro-Republican generals, some of them in the army still and others having left, mobilized former subordinates and enlisted men to prove to the nation that the Army of the Potomac had escaped the shadow of Little Mac. In New York, for example, Abner Doubleday,

Dan Sickles, Daniel Butterfield, and other Republican-leaning figures formed the Veteran Union Club, specifically mirroring the more inclusive title of Lincoln's National Union Party and meeting weekly at Cooper Union, where the rail-splitter himself had famously impressed eastern Republicans in 1860.[9]

Outside New York, Republican veterans relied more heavily on junior officers to do the heavy lifting of political mobilization. In Philadelphia, to oppose the McClellan Old Guard, former colonel Peter C. Ellmaker of the city's 119th Pennsylvania took command of the "First Battalion" of the Union Campaign Club (UCC). Ellmaker had made a name for himself and his regiment by publicly opposing an autumn 1863 effort by Army of the Potomac commander George G. Meade to honor McClellan with an army-wide testimonial of support.[10] By 1864, Ellmaker worked with fellow Pennsylvanians John F. Glenn of the "Birney Zouaves," Thomas F. B. Tappan of the 4th Reserves, DeWitt Clinton Baxter of the "Fire Zouaves," and Turner G. Morehead of the 106th Regiment.[11] As many as thirty-five hundred veterans eventually united under the UCC banner, resolving in the inaugural meeting at Sansom Street Hall on September 12 to settle "finally and forever" the conflict's root cause of slavery. Thanking the state's Republicans for allowing absentee voting in the field, the UCC also made emotional appeals to voters of the Keystone State. Former lieutenant Lemuel Reeves of the 12th Corps resolved, for instance, that the harshest rebuke of "traitors at home" would have come from the thousands of fallen martyrs on Army of the Potomac battlefields.[12] The UCC mimicked the old Wide Awakes of 1860 in organizing a series of torchlight parades to intimidate the opposition and inspire followers. Aligning with the city's powerful Union League, Army of the Potomac veterans of every rank marched through the city bearing lanterns adorned with powerful political messaging. "Robert, I will not hurt you too much; I will fight you gentlemanly," proclaimed one sarcastic transparency, while another (reported soon afterward in the *Philadelphia Press*) mocked McClellan's early-war prediction of a "short, sharp, decisive" campaign against the rebels with the simple promise, "We intend to make it so. —1st Bat. Union Campaign Club."[13]

Like their Republican counterparts, the president's opponents formed similar urban veterans clubs. In New York City, veteran 3rd Corps brigadier J. H. Hobart Ward worked with Abram Duryea, an old Zouave from the 5th New York, to form the McClellan Legion for demobilized veterans supporting Little Mac. City newspapers reported the organization's ranks swelling to over six thousand, complete with a division in each ward led by junior officer veterans.[14] Politicians worked closely with the legion, Governor Horatio Seymour congratulating the organization on fighting "as faithfully and as patriotically" for the Constitution at home as its members had on the front lines.[15] Nor did McClellan himself shy away from endorsing the group. In a display of solidarity, the former Potomac commander prodded the legion in its work and asked members to disseminate campaign literature to comrades still in uniform, all while the pro-Lincoln Veteran Union Club, of course, worked to overpower the McClellan Legion in these efforts.[16] A former 2nd Corps regimental commander, Arthur F. Devereux, copied the legion's success by mobilizing Democratic soldiers in Boston under a similar pro-McClellan banner.[17]

Philadelphia veterans seemed even more energized than New Yorkers. A former Pennsylvania Reserve commander, Colonel William "Buck" McCandless, had earlier resigned in protest of emancipation policy. Offered a brigadier's star if he would return to the Army of the Potomac, McCandless replied publicly to Secretary of War Edwin Stanton that only upon the administration's return to "the original intention of prosecuting this war for the restoration of the Union" would he and other like-minded Democrats rejoin the war effort.[18] Until then, McCandless and others would form the McClellan Old Guard to endorse the Constitution as "the supreme law over President and people." Meeting at the Keystone Club, the Old Guard adopted resolutions denouncing Lincoln and Republican policy: "We did not enter the service for the purpose of attempting to make the negro our equal," the veterans proclaimed. McCandless was uncompromising, declaring that the employment of black troops debased the war effort and ruined any chance at reunification.[19]

Historians have correctly emphasized the importance of the soldier vote and its contribution to Lincoln's reelection. Yet they have too often overlooked the powerful role demobilized veterans played in the contest. The proliferation of wartime veteran campaign clubs reveals an inexorable militarization of the political process, a phenomenon that blurred the distinction between battlefield and home front just as it sharpened the partisan divide in both realms. Likewise, the episode demonstrates that discharged Army of the Potomac veterans had no intention of hanging up their uniforms and watching passively as a dramatic referendum on the war itself played out before them. Neither the president's nor McClellan's supporters could lay sole claim to the army's loyalty, but the appearance of pro-Republican political clubs among demobilized soldiers proves that many who had elected not to reenlist would nonetheless still cast themselves as the nation's political conscience.

AS DRAMATIC AS IT had been, the veteran activity of 1864 was merely a precursor to the political mobilization ignited in the wake of Appomattox and the Lincoln assassination. To be sure, paramilitary political activity dated to at least the Wide Awakes of 1860, but in the years after the war thousands of Union veterans worked to push partisan allegiances, sometimes to the brink of civil disorder. While scholars have emphasized the importance of groups such as the Grand Army of the Republic in replicating wartime bonds of service, especially as a means of coping with readjustment to civilian life, demobilized soldiers who watched the political events of Reconstruction remembered how central political activism had been to life in the Army of the Potomac. Not surprisingly, many veterans worked for years to carry the banner of political loyalty and defend their view of the war's meaning.

The most radical Republican veterans returning from the war organized their own group as early as September 1865. Led by 13th Massachusetts soldier Levi E. Dudley, the Soldiers' and Sailors' National Union League used much of the same language and appeal as wartime civilian union leagues. Initially pledging to resist heated political activity in the best antiparty tradition of the National Union movement, the Soldiers' League shifted after just a few short months to embracing open partisanship.[20] The league's first significant act was adopting and publishing resolutions endorsing the summary treason trial of Robert E. Lee. Insisting they represented the wishes of half a million "truly loyal" Union veterans, Dudley's comrades called for Lee to receive "the reward of the traitor" and to be shunned "as an object of execration, and as a warning to tyrants who would wrest from a people the natural rights of liberty."[21] Meetings in Washington, Philadelphia, and New York featured lectures on the evils of Confederate prisons, recalled the camaraderie with US Colored Troops (USCT), and praised the efforts of the Freedmen's Bureau.[22]

The radicalism of the Soldiers' League elicited a strong backlash from Democratic veterans, who resuscitated the old McClellan organizations with an eye toward broadening the base of support for President Andrew Johnson. Leading them in New York, as in 1864, was General Hobart Ward, who mustered the

United Service Society and organized speaking engagements at Delmonico's on Fifth Avenue.[23] Irish American veterans like Colonel James R. O'Beirne of the 37th New York proclaimed that they, the new president's supporters, were carrying out Lincoln's true wish for a soft peace. Dudley's comrades were little more than a "political machine" for the radicals, O'Beirne insisted. An obsession with freedmen's rights would only stoke the last embers of civil war, and anything that would imperil the wounded republic was tantamount to treason. One plucky Irishman, a member of the old Excelsior Brigade, admitted in a speech to these veterans that he had supported Lincoln as a War Democrat but affirmed that resorting to vengeance against the defeated South now struck him as nothing more than Cromwellian vindictiveness.[24]

The 1866 elections were the high-water mark of political engagement for Union veterans. After Iron Brigade veteran Lucius Fairchild and 9th Corps general Jacob D. Cox had already won the governorships of Wisconsin and Ohio the previous year, three more Army of the Potomac veterans—Ambrose Burnside in Rhode Island, Joshua Chamberlain in Maine, and John W. Geary in Pennsylvania—ran as Republicans in their respective states.[25] The congressional midterms at the same time produced an explosion of activity, bringing the nation to the brink of civil-military unrest and forcing the American republic to grapple with the political role of demobilized soldiers.

One of the great ironies of 1866 was that Republican veterans, men who had spent the better part of the war itself demanding loyalty to the sitting administration as an imperative in time of crisis, were leading the charge against President Johnson. Frustrated with the president's lukewarm Reconstruction policy, which included amnesty toward former foes and ambivalence toward freedmen, midwesterners in the Soldiers' League gravitated into the orbit of a new organization termed the Grand Army of the Republic (GAR). Illinois veterans in General John A. Logan's GAR worked to fight Democratic influence, while Governor Oliver P. Morton of Indiana hastened to mobilize his returning soldiers to "preserve unsullied," as one observer recalled, "the record of Indiana's soldiers from the taint of affiliation with the political party that had opposed the war."[26]

Among East Coast posts of the Soldiers' League, critics of the president regrouped into chapters of a new pro-Republican organization called the Boys in Blue. Recognizing how crucial their crusade against the copperheads had been during the war—whether in terms of voting at the front, publishing regimental resolutions, or writing opinion pieces for home front newspapers—members of the Boys in Blue used the same approach in 1866. In language previously reserved only for antiwar Democrats, the Philadelphia veterans assaulted the president in print as "recreant to the great principles of the loyal people of the country."[27] Five hundred of them gathered in Pittsburgh later that summer to represent the interests of twenty-five thousand statewide voting members of the Boys in Blue.[28] Led by Army of the Potomac figures such as Charles T. Collis, Joshua "Paddy" Owen, and Thomas L. Kane, the convention condemned Johnson and endorsed Republican candidate Geary for the governor's seat. "We demand that the leading traitors should be convicted and executed as an example to traitors for all time to come," the Boys in Blue declared.[29]

Absent Lincoln's leadership and with the Confederacy defeated on the battlefield the previous year, the promising "National Union" coalition splintered. A desperate President Johnson struggled to keep the movement alive, even as "War Democrats," orphaned by their own party, looked for a more permanent solution than their temporary wartime alliance with Republicans would allow. Just days before the president's infamous 1866 "Swing around the Circle" speaking tour, Johnson's core followers attempted a revival of the National Union Party to attract conservative Republicans and like-minded War Democrats. The movement spotlighted a cadre of Union officers to lend it credibility. At a Cleveland convention in August, the National Union platform to "sustain the administration" received support from Army of the Potomac officers Henry Slocum, Dan Sickles, Orlando Willcox, Alpheus Williams, William B. Franklin, George A. Custer, Solomon Meredith, Edward Bragg, and Henry Morrow. Despite its illustrious following, the party fizzled almost from the start.[30]

The more hard-line Democratic veterans focused their attacks on the Boys in Blue, seeking to portray their old comrades first and foremost as proponents of African American rights. This disagreement over the war's meaning cut to the quick. Eager to oppose former 12th Corps general John Geary's candidacy in Pennsylvania, supposedly sixteen hundred Democratic officers and men gathered in Harrisburg to declare publicly that "the war was for the Union and nothing else." Buck McCandless and fellow 5th Corps veteran General Jacob Sweitzer pledged their resistance to any legislation that would "make the negro the white man's equal."[31] Two thousand veterans likewise met in Lancaster to denounce the Geary candidacy and black civil rights as evidence radicals were willing to tear the nation apart again.[32]

Despite fierce National Union and Democratic activity that summer, Republican veterans almost everywhere eclipsed their rivals. In Boston, Detroit, Syracuse, and Cincinnati, chapters of the Boys in Blue and the GAR sponsored meetings that the Democratic press derided as one collective "Jacobin carnival."[33] Just prior to the election, fifteen thousand veterans rallied in Pittsburgh to endorse Johnson's opponents.[34] Levi Dudley, as always one of the key organizers, asserted that his Washington office was receiving a hundred letters daily from Union veterans urging Republicans to pursue an aggressive Reconstruction policy.[35] In Wisconsin, the one-armed Iron Brigade colonel and governor Lucius Fairchild urged his Republican veterans to prepare for a second civil war, this time between Congress and the president. Dudley's Soldiers' League and the Boys in Blue likewise warned their members to await a call to Washington in the hope of protecting all "loyal" officials.[36]

Spurred on by such a boisterous following, Dudley overplayed his hand when he asked Ulysses S. Grant for a few public words of motivation to the veterans. The general responded with a scolding message. Passions were too inflamed, the people too divided to make it proper for a vocal pronunciation of support, he stated, chiding the veterans that he would witness "with regret the action of any officer of the army taking a conspicuous part in the political dissensions of the day."[37] The implication was troubling: What place should legions of marching, threatening veterans hold in the fragile republic? Grant's attempt to disarm the activity arrived shortly before a landslide Republican victory, collectively forestalling any sort of collective march on Washington. But this burst of political activity in 1866, much of it predicated on the soldiers' hallowed place in the national dialogue concerning loyalty, offered an outlet for returning veterans. They organized, marched, and fought with each other to recover the passion of the conflict and lay claim to its meaning.

AIDED BY REPUBLICAN soldiers' organizations, the 1866 midterms went decisively to the Republicans. The next year, however, Democrats scored significant gains in statewide elections, offering a much-needed boon to the embattled president.[38] Johnson's impeachment proceedings in early 1868 made Republicans in the GAR and Boys in Blue even more outspoken, eliciting a strong backlash from opposing veterans and editors alike. Horace Greeley's *New York*

Tribune, which had long supported radical policy during the war itself, expressed fear about the prospect of militarized Republican veterans' circles— "soldiers of vengeance." Cautioning thousands of readers to beware political demagogues who would use veteran activity to their benefit, the editorial staff went on to identify "secret soldier associations" guilty of political "madness." "It will be a sad day for our party," Greeley's paper opined, "when soldiers find no better work than to prowl over the battle-fields of the past, and dig up the bodies of the slain."[39]

Conservative soldiers returning from war had organized the White Boys in Blue in 1866 to resist the notion that Republican groups spoke for all veterans. With the arrival of the presidential campaign, Democrats resuscitated the association in parts of the lower Midwest. The Muskingum County, Ohio, "Brigade" of three hundred White Boys pledged themselves to the defense of white supremacy on the grounds that radicals, represented by both those in Congress and various Republican veterans' organizations, threatened to plunge the nation into civil war again. The Democrats insisted on defeating the radical "anti-Union policy," including any belief in "Negro Suffrage and Equality, and also the parties and men who are in favor of degrading the white soldier to a level with the negro."[40]

Republicans lambasted the White Boys as a fraud. Newspapers highlighted how four Indiana members on trial for assaulting an African American, for example, reportedly confessed on cross-examination that they had never served in the Union army.[41] A Canton, Ohio, officer, humiliated by having received an invitation in the mail to a White Boys meeting, took to the pages of the *Hancock Jeffersonian* to express his disgust. Perhaps, he suggested, three like-minded societies—the White Boys in Blue, the Knights of the Golden Circle, and the Ku Klux Klan—should unite under one heinous banner and help rebels like Nathan Bedford Forrest, "the modern Herod who massacred the innocent at Fort Pillow, and whose name was cheered by Conservative Democratic soldiers."[42] Several Indiana members of the White Boys, disgusted with their organization's loose definition of "veteran," split off to form a "Fighting Boys in Blue" post.[43]

Grant was the obvious choice for the Republican nomination in 1868, and many veterans rejoiced at the prospect. Mobilized by Wisconsin governor Fairchild, radical veteran conventions in Washington and Chicago strongly endorsed the victor of Appomattox as their best hope for regaining the White

House, in the process insisting that the Republican Party was "the only political organization ... that is true to the principles of loyalty, liberty, and equality before the law."[44] In a subtle waving of the "bloody shirt" and nod toward the Republican view of loyalty, General John A. Logan, a prominent Army of the Tennessee veteran and one of the founders of the GAR, established Decoration Day that spring to commemorate the Union dead in all corners of the nation.[45]

Democrats, always nervous on the soldier vote, confronted a serious quandary in their own nomination battle two months later. McClellan failed in his bid for the soldier vote four years earlier, but some party officials believed the best way to reclaim veterans' loyalty was another Army of the Potomac general in 1868. Winfield Scott Hancock, famous for his command of the hard-hitting 2nd Corps, had been a no-nonsense Democrat who received mention in the 1864 nominating convention in Chicago. The idea of Hancock as a compromise candidate between Democratic factions relied on the fact that he had largely escaped the suspicions of disloyalty that ruined Charles Pomeroy Stone, Fitz John Porter, and McClellan himself. During the war, Hancock had complained to his wife that, as a McClellan admirer, "I do not belong to that class of generals whom the Republicans care to bolster up."[46] Later, appointed to command a military district comprising Texas and Louisiana in 1867, "Hancock the Superb" frustrated radicals by endorsing the return to southern civil administration, an action that caused his transfer from the post.[47] During the 1868 convention, Hancock was the odds-on favorite through several ballots, but the professional soldier, loath to embrace underhanded dealings, refused to campaign for himself. Instead, the party chose New York governor Horatio Seymour. Writing a friend in Rhode Island after the convention battle, Hancock confessed he would not have turned down the nomination but wished to work "to rebuke the spirit of revolution which ha[s] invaded every sacred precinct of liberty."[48]

Seymour's nomination over Hancock solidified veterans' enthusiasm for Grant, whose previous apathy toward politics rendered him moderate in the minds of most northerners. In Philadelphia, a Boys in Blue column five miles long marched downtown with banners snapping. "The Bucktails vote as they shot!" proclaimed the Tioga County veterans of the 149th Pennsylvania.[49] A 12th Corps veteran and chairman of the Boys in Blue post in Washington, DC, issued "orders" in northern newspapers for the nation's loyal veterans to "fall in" for Grant. "The shock of arms ceased with the surrender at Appomattox Court House," Henry A. Barnum wrote, "but the struggle of principle goes on." Appealing to the old soldiers' reverence for the wartime administration, he lamented, "Had Abraham Lincoln lived, doubtless our labors and toils, ere this, would have been over and past." As it was, only Grant could rescue the nation, restore the Union on honorable terms, and "[ground] the Republic at last upon the immutable basis of loyalty and justice, and equal rights for all. . . . Let us everywhere charge the enemy home."[50]

Even die-hard Democratic veterans admitted their former general could bring respectable authority to the White House. Jacob Sweitzer, a commander from the old 5th Corps, addressed the Boys in Blue convention at Pittsburgh in late September, stating that the current election was indeed a choice between "an honorable peace" and "confusion, anarchy, and war." Sweitzer had defended the Fugitive Slave Law as a lawyer, campaigned for Breckinridge in 1860, and voted for McClellan four years later, "Pendleton, peace platform, and all." But the alliance between midwestern Peace Democrats and former Confederates pushed Sweitzer into Grant's column. "I determined that no such flimsy barriers as party ties and party lines should keep me from doing what I believe to be my duty to myself and to my country," he proclaimed.[51]

The great commander triumphed on November 3, although the task of administering Reconstruction in the face of constant white southern violence taxed both Grant's administration and the northern public. Certain that their old general and new president would defend the cause, Union veterans entered the "quiescent years" of the 1870s convinced that 1868 signaled the last triumph of the Civil War; the fruits of their labor during the conflict were finally in safe hands. "Boys in Blue" and GAR members breathed a sigh of relief, hopeful of moving beyond constant fears of national upheaval.

While the mass of enlisted veterans settled into postwar society satisfied with their role in helping elect Grant, some high-ranking veterans' groups still debated Reconstruction politics. The Society of the Army of the Potomac, founded in February 1869, was one of several organizations for specific veterans of the war's major Union field armies. The society's constitution forbade "political or any other discussions foreign to the purposes" of maintaining camaraderie, but the meetings quickly descended into a postwar version of the same partisan haranguing that had paralyzed the high command during the conflict itself.[52]

All the great surviving generals were present at the society's inaugural meeting in New York City on Washington's birthday.[53] After a lengthy balloting process, Philip Sheridan emerged victorious as the society's president and worked with subordinates to inject subtle references to Republican loyalty in the organization's transactions. Veterans toasted the war's "loyal press," for instance, and Republican veteran John H. Martindale devoted an entire thirty-page address in 1870 to the questions of emancipation, civil rights, and racial equality. Organizing for the sake of simple camaraderie was well and good, Martindale allowed, but "we are citizens and patriots, having a deep and absorbing interest in the welfare of our whole country," and that welfare included assimilating "the emancipated African."[54] Immediately, Democratic members proposed a series of protest resolutions. They chastised Martindale for trying to make the society a "political machine" and reminded other members that some officers had fought for the maintenance of the Union "and for no other purposes whatsoever." The society's secretary noted that "these resolutions gave rise to considerable well-tempered debate."[55]

Martindale's address was out of step not only with conservatives in the society but also with members of the political class more widely who wished to move beyond the war's issues. Antiradical forces of every stripe, angry at the presence of widespread corruption in the administration and uniting under the banner of the Liberal Republican Party, feared that the Society of the Army of the Potomac would adopt the worst excesses of radicalism in the 1872 election. Grant's critics, including Buck McCandless and the Irish Brigade's St. Clair Mulholland, tried without success to mobilize Democratic veterans to defeat the incumbent president. Admitting defeat, they took a different tack in the weeks ahead of Election Day, arguing instead that the proper posture for civic-minded veterans was to abandon activism and recede back into the electorate. Reliable Republican veterans contributed handsomely to Grant's decisive re-election over journalist Horace Greeley, despite the fact that the absence of a serious Democratic challenger mitigated enthusiasm to mobilize, charge disloyalty, and wave the bloody shirt.[56]

After mounting corruption allegations and the onslaught of a worldwide financial depression, a sense of unease descended on Republicans within Grand Army posts and Boys in Blue chapters as the threat of Democratic redemption in 1876 loomed. Scandals and misdeeds shook veterans' confidence in Grant's administration.[57] Republican leaders worked overtime to motivate their posts. The commander of New Hampshire's Boys in Blue warned that civil war seemed imminent again: "The exigency of Gettysburg has returned upon us in a time of profound peace." Allowing the veterans of the Confederacy to assume power again in the South, he declared, would be to surrender all the war's gains along with fundamental "principles of human equality."[58] James A. Garfield, the ambitious commander in chief of the Boys in Blue, organized an Indianapolis rally in the "white heat of loyal enthusiasm" to mobilize support for Republican nominee Rutherford B. Hayes.[59] In Providence, Rhode Island, a parade of Union veterans carried banners supporting the Republicans and claiming Democratic candidate Samuel Tilden's idea of reform was "Hamburg Massacres," a reference to recent white supremacist attacks on African Americans in South Carolina.[60]

The resulting election provided no comfort for wary Republicans in blue. For weeks the outcome of the election remained uncertain. Democrats, including veterans mobilized by none other than Tilden confidant McClellan, feared the possibility of a veterans' march on Washington to install Hayes as president.[61] Republicans eagerly stoked the fire. Commanders of every "Boys in Blue" department pledged men and arms to the cause. A veteran of the 14th Connecticut promised to provide "four companies . . . thoroughly drilled and equipped."[62] Tensions slowly faded after a special commission voted to award Hayes the disputed electoral votes.[63] Veterans hoping for a stiff spine from Washington in the face of "redemption" violence proved harder to find, the wider northern public long since exhausted with protracted Republican efforts at reconstruction. To those veterans who had led the charge against compromise with disloyalty for over ten years, the events of early 1877 arrived as bitter anticlimax.

DESPITE WHAT PARTISAN papers and leaders alleged, Republican mobilization of veterans' groups in 1876 amounted only to a meager echo of the full-throated charge a decade earlier. Grant's tenure disillusioned many veterans, and the compromise ending military occupation left them exhausted from the task of defending the war's lingering ideal of loyalty in the public sphere for nearly fifteen years. The nation had moved on, and so had some of the former soldiers themselves. In October 1877, George Lemon, a veteran of the 125th New York, launched the *National Tribune* in part to rally graying veterans for pension reform, an issue that began to rival wartime loyalty as a dominant political consideration for some former soldiers. Also, in 1877, veterans in New Jersey, one of only three states won by McClellan in 1864, cheered Little Mac to the governor's mansion in November, horrifying die-hard Republican generals like Judson Kilpatrick and William S. Truex. In a speech to the state Republican convention, Kilpatrick blamed McClellan for having resisted emancipation and hard war: "What a party! False to liberty, disloyal in war, untrue to the best interests of the nation in peace."[64] Truex, former colonel of the 14th New Jersey, begged veterans to remember the example of Philip Kearny, the beloved 3rd Corps officer who insisted before his death in 1862 that McClellan was either an imbecile or a traitor.[65] Veterans heard these entreaties, but changing times and blossoming nostalgia began to heal old partisan wounds.

McClellan may have secured the statehouse in New Jersey, but by 1880 the Democratic Party was finally ready to try for the soldier vote again by pinning its White House hopes on Winfield Scott Hancock. Republicans, meanwhile, bucked Hayes for the former Army of the Cumberland general and Republican congressman James A. Garfield, a quintessential dark horse candidate. The presidential contest between Hancock and Garfield was the final proof of just how central Union soldiers had become to national politics.

Political clubs packed with veterans sprang to life for both candidates. The National Association of Hancock Veterans, meeting in New York that August, disparaged Republicans for keeping the war's partisanship alive with "blatant charges of disloyalty against the one-legged and one-armed soldiers who had dared to assert that in the war for the Union they had not fought for four years to strike the shackles from the slave and weld them into manacles for freemen."[66] McClellan joined the campaign team as honorary leader of the Hancock Veterans while former corps commander William F. "Baldy" Smith performed the rigorous work of mobilizing men and printing partisan literature, including four editions of the *Hancock Veteran* newspaper.

Republican Party leaders still expected the thread of wartime loyalty to be a powerful motivating force, but veterans' enthusiasm for the Republican cause in 1880 was not what it had been in 1866. The turmoil of partisan politics, corruption, and bargaining over Reconstruction left many men questioning their party loyalties. Some remained true to Grant and expressed disgust that the Republicans had nominated Garfield over the possibility of a third term for the war's victor. William McEntee, commander of Dahlgren Post 113 of the GAR in New York City, informed reporters in a heavily reprinted column that all his comrades were flocking to Hancock. "The nomination of Hancock following so closely on the defeat of Grant at Chicago," McEntee insisted, "acted like an electric shock on the military element."[67] The *Hancock Veteran* published scores of testimonials from Army of the Potomac men endorsing Hancock's leadership qualities. Even the famous Republican cartoonist Thomas Nast admired Hancock too much to attack his loyalty, insisting instead on discrediting the Democratic Party as a tool of southern interests. A particularly poignant cartoon showed Hancock reflecting on the victory at Gettysburg while grappling with the reality that the dead of Pickett's division—"the Silent (Democratic) Majority"—would have been his party's most vocal supporters.[68]

Undeterred, editors attempted to frame the 1880 election as a veterans' referendum on the question of Hancock's loyalty to the cause. A handful of veterans followed suit, but they were not nearly as overwhelming as the Garfield campaign hoped. Even where veterans attacked Hancock, it was usually in the vein of Nast, insisting the general was simply a dupe of the old disloyal Democratic Party. Andersonville survivor Amos A. Yeakel of the 145th Pennsylvania shook his head at his old commander for carrying the standard of treason. "Can I so far forget myself," he asked in Northern newspapers, "as to vote for the party which tried for four long years to dissolve our glorious union? No!"[69] Some veterans, such as former 9th Corps staff officer and USCT commander Giles Shurtleff, painted Hancock as an unfeeling martinet unworthy of veteran support. Shurtleff, by 1880 a professor at Oberlin College, ridiculed "the swearing of the brutal commander" at Fredericksburg. Other veterans circulated unsubstantiated rumors that Hancock had cursed the Irish Brigade in their attack on Marye's Heights (an attempt to hurt Irish Catholic turnout for Hancock, who was known for sympathies with the church).[70] The image of Hancock the martinet dovetailed with Republican mistrust for the detached, politically unreliable West Point circle, while Garfield enjoyed a reputation in his party as a trustworthy citizen-soldier.

Unsettled by shifting party dynamics in the wake of Reconstruction, untold numbers of nostalgic veterans laid aside their loyalty to the Republican Party and professed public loyalty to the one constant they had always shared with Democratic comrades—the memory of the Army of the Potomac itself. The political parties failed them, and they considered Hancock a man above partisanship. Second Corps veteran Charles A. Smith wrote to his old commander that he had cast his first ballot at Petersburg for Lincoln and "voted for every

Republican candidate from that day to this. . . . [But] as soon as you received the nomination I said, 'I shall never go back on my old commander.'"[71] Gilbert Chaddock of the 7th Michigan agreed, calling on all veterans of the 2nd Corps "keenly alive to the memories of the past . . . to sustain [Hancock]," while 5th Corps soldier and Republican L. E. McPherson assured Hancock, "You will receive the support and votes of thousands, who, like myself, could, under the circumstances, have followed no other leader; and you will be elected."[72]

By the eve of the election, serious doubts about Hancock's command of the complicated issues of the day had taken their toll, and his incoherent answers on key questions like the tariff gave informed readers across the country pause. Bad blood between Hancock and Grant returned with a vengeance when the former president attacked Hancock as a "weak, vain man" obsessed with securing the presidency ever since 1864. The episode conjured memories of Grant's "reassignment" of Hancock following his controversial Reconstruction order endorsing civilian rule in Louisiana and Texas. A serious gaffe from South Carolina "Redeemer" and Confederate veteran Wade Hampton fed the Republican narrative that Hancock would sell out any remaining fruits of Union success. Speaking to fellow southerners, Hampton declared that Hancock's victory would represent the final triumph of "the principle for which Lee and Johnson fought," unintentionally sending the campaign into frantic damage control.[73]

Little statistical record remains of exactly how Army of the Potomac veterans—or any Union veterans for that matter—voted in 1880. Hancock supporters insisted countless GAR and Boys in Blue veterans crossed party lines and voted Democratic, while Republicans claimed the mass of Union veterans resolved to "vote as they shot." Anecdotal evidence from Democratic and Republican newspapers alike shows a hesitancy among veterans to portray Hancock as personally disloyal, a remarkable change from the heady days when some Republican soldiers portrayed McClellan as Judas reincarnate. The final results gave Garfield a razor-thin victory.

HISTORIAN GERALD LINDERMAN's interpretation of Civil War veteranhood famously applied the term "hibernation" to the period of postwar inactivity between 1865 and the mid-1880s. Early attempts at veteran organization failed, Linderman notes, because of a conscious effort on the part of traumatized veterans to turn away from the war's demons.[74] More recently, scholars such as Brian Jordan have chosen to emphasize the remarkable extent to which Union veterans collectively sought solace and public benefits as proof of active engagement, not hibernation.[75] Recognizing the vociferous place Union veterans held in the nation's public partisanship through 1880 further revises the hibernation thesis. Thousands of Army of the Potomac veterans published, marched, argued, and threatened in a fashion remarkably similar to their wartime experiences. This fact should enhance our understanding of Union soldiers' readjustment to civilian life just as it reminds us of the war's positive, ideological meaning for its participants in blue.

So intense was the veterans' zeal concerning "loyalty" that only Hancock's nomination in 1880 heralded the final demise of a consistent Republican tendency to castigate all Democrats as copperheads. This denouement followed fifteen grueling years of heated argument in the public sphere, a phenomenon historians have largely neglected. Veterans never forgave the peace faction, but eventually the political nuances impossible in war returned as a result of shifting party dynamics, tensions between veterans and civilians, and the very passage of time itself. By the late 1880s, graying men in blue who dedicated monuments at Gettysburg and Antietam and met in GAR halls learned to embrace the demands of parenthood and pension reform over breathing new life into old partisanship, all while millions of northerners around them constructed a sanitized and romanticized image of the conflict in which the image of a contentious and radicalized soldiery no longer seemed to fit. Political passion receded as divisive issues passed from the stage. But the sacred principle so staunchly defended by Potomac soldiers remained as a watchword, inscribed as the final term on every GAR flag and in every member's heart: "Fraternity, Charity, and Loyalty."

NOTES

1. "The Traitor, Lee," *Lehigh (PA) Register,* March 20, 1866.

2. Examples include Drew Gilpin Faust, *This Republic of Suffering: Death and the American Civil War* (New York: Alfred A. Knopf, 2008); Michael C. C. Adams, *Living Hell: The Dark Side of the Civil War* (Baltimore: Johns Hopkins University Press, 2014); Brian Matthew Jordan, *Marching Home: Union Veterans and Their Unending Civil War* (New York: Liveright, 2014); Lesley J. Gordon, *A Bro-*

ken Regiment: *The 16th Connecticut's Civil War* (Baton Rouge: Louisiana State University Press, 2014); and Diane Miller Sommerville, *Aberration of Mind: Suicide and Suffering in the Civil War–Era South* (Chapel Hill: University of North Carolina Press, 2018).

3. This trend includes works such as James K. Hogue, *Uncivil War: Five New Orleans Street Battles and the Rise and Fall of Radical Reconstruction* (Baton Rouge: Louisiana State University Press, 2011); Mark Grimsley, "Wars for the American South: The First and Second Reconstructions Considered as Insurgencies," *Civil War History* 58, no. 1 (March 2012): 6–36; Douglas Egerton, *The Wars of Reconstruction: The Brief, Violent History of America's Most Progressive Era* (New York: Bloomsbury, 2014); Gregory P. Downs, *After Appomattox: Military Occupation and the Ends of War* (Cambridge, MA: Harvard University Press, 2015); Andrew Lang, *In the Wake of War: Military Occupation, Emancipation, and Civil War America* (Baton Rouge: Louisiana State University Press, 2017); Andrew Delbanco, *The War before the War: Fugitive Slaves and the Struggle for America's Soul from the Revolution to the Civil War* (New York: Penguin, 2018); and Joanne B. Freeman, *The Field of Blood: Violence in Congress and the Road to Civil War* (New York: Farrar, Straus and Giroux, 2018).

4. Mary Dearing, *Veterans in Politics: The Story of the G.A.R.* (Baton Rouge: Louisiana State University Press, 1952), focuses frequently on pensions and other entitlements but fortunately offers significant insights into wider issues important to the Republican camp. See also Larry M. Logue, "Union Veterans and Their Government: The Effects of Public Policies on Private Lives," *Journal of Interdisciplinary History* 22, no. 3 (Winter 1992): 411–34.

5. James Marten, *Sing Not War: The Lives of Union and Confederate Veterans in Gilded Age America* (Chapel Hill: University of North Carolina Press, 2011); Jordan, *Marching Home,* which builds on a broader trend of veterans' studies focusing on the difficulties of postwar reintegration. See also Bruno Cabanes, *La Victoire Endeuillée: La Sortie de Guerre des Soldats Français, 1918–1920* (Paris: Seuile, 2004).

6. For a fuller account of the political activity of Union soldiers during and immediately after the war, see the author's forthcoming volume from the University of North Carolina Press.

7. Authoritative interpretations of Republican policy and its progression can be found in Eric Foner, *Free Soil, Free Labor, Free Men: The Ideology of the Republican Party before the Civil War* (New York: Oxford University Press, 1995), and James Oakes, *Freedom National: The Destruction of Slavery in the United States, 1861–1865* (New York: W. W. Norton, 2012). On the party's general success among Union army voters and the importance of emancipation in soldier ideology, see James McPherson, *For Cause and Comrades: Why Men Fought in the Civil War* (New York: Oxford University Press, 1997), and Chandra Manning, *What This Cruel War Was Over: Soldiers, Slavery, and the Civil War* (New York: Alfred A. Knopf, 2007). Counterarguments that point to soldiers' reluctance concerning emancipation are found in Gary W. Gallagher, *The Union War* (Cambridge, MA: Harvard University Press, 2011); Jonathan W. White, *Emancipation, the Union Army, and the Reelection of Abraham Lincoln* (Baton Rouge: Louisiana State University Press, 2014); and Kristopher A. Teters, *Practical Liberators: Union Officers in the Western Theater during the Civil War* (Chapel Hill: University of North Carolina Press, 2018).

8. On Democratic political culture and ideology before and during the conflict, see Joel Silbey, *A Respectable Minority: The Democratic Party in the Civil War Era, 1860–1868* (New York: W. W. Norton, 1977); Jean H. Baker, *Affairs of Party: The Political Culture of Northern Democrats in the Mid-Nineteenth Century* (New York: Fordham University Press, 1984); Mark Neely, *Lincoln and the Democrats: The Politics of Opposition in the Civil War* (New York: Cambridge University Press, 2017); and

Adam I. P. Smith, *The Stormy Present: Conservatism and the Problem of Slavery in Northern Politics* (Chapel Hill: University of North Carolina Press, 2017). On the importance of republicanism as an animating force in early American politics, see Joyce Appleby, "Republicanism and Ideology," *American Quarterly* 37, no. 4 (Autumn 1985): 461–73.

9. "Army of the Potomac; Veterans Enlisting for a New Campaign against Traitors. Meeting of the Lincoln Veteran Soldiers Club. Seventh Ward. Grand Ratification Meeting. Hon. James R. Whiting, County Nominations. Democratic Assembly Nominations. Democratic Congressional Nominations," *New York Times,* October 14, 1864; "City Intelligence, the Veteran Union Club," *New York Evening Post,* September 19, 1864.

10. "Resolutions on the McClellan Testimonial Passed by the 119th Penna. Vols. 1863," Charles P. Herring Papers, Civil War Museum of Philadelphia, currently held by Heritage Center of the Union League of Philadelphia; "The McClellan Testimonial," *Philadelphia Press,* September 30, 1863.

11. "Headquarters First Battalion Union Campaign Club," *Philadelphia Press,* October 5, 1864.

12. "Meeting of Honorably Discharged Soldiers," *Daily Evening Bulletin* (Philadelphia), September 13, 1864; "Political, Military Union Club," *Philadelphia Press,* October 22, 1864; "The Torchlight Procession," *Philadelphia Press,* October 10, 1864.

13. "The Torchlight Procession."

14. "Gossip of the Political Campaign," *Irish American Weekly* (New York), October 15, 1864; "General McClellan Serenaded in New York—Immense Throng—Eight Thousand Torches in Line—Cheers for the Hero," *Centre Reporter* (Centre Hall, PA), October 9, 1864.

15. "Gossip of the Political Campaign," *Irish American Weekly* (New York), October 15, 1864.

16. George M. D. Bloss, *Life and Speeches of George H. Pendleton* (Cincinnati: Miami Printing and Publishing, 1868), 38–39; Stephen W. Sears, *George B. McClellan: The Young Napoleon* (New York: Ticknor and Fields, 1988), 380–81; "News from Washington; Movement of Rebels into Kentucky. Movements of Gen. Warren. The Steamer The Winslow Five Lives Lost. The Soldier's Vote. The Sanitary Commission. Veteran Soldiers for Lincoln and Johnson. Naval Accident," *New York Times,* October 9, 1864.

17. "Formation of a McClellan Legion," *Boston Post,* October 20, 1864.

18. "A Patriot Officer Declines Promotion," *Chilton (WI) Times,* September 17, 1864.

19. "Enthusiastic Meeting of the Old McClellan Guard," *Daily Age* (Philadelphia), September 28, 1864.

20. "Proceedings of the Meeting of the Soldiers' and Sailors' League on Saturday Night Last— The Preamble of the Constitution of the League," *Wheeling (WV) Daily Intelligencer,* March 20, 1866; see also *Constitution, By-Laws, and Rules of Order of the Soldiers' and Sailors' National Union League, Washington, D.C.* (Washington, DC: Gideon and Pearson, 1865).

21. "The Traitor, Lee," *Lehigh (PA) Register,* March 20, 1866; see also *An Address to All Honorably Discharged Soldiers and Sailors in the Loyal States, from the Soldiers' and Sailors' National Union League of Washington, D.C.* (Washington, DC: n.p., 1865), 1–2.

22. "The Soldiers and Sailors," *National Republican* (Washington, DC), April 3, 1866.

23. "United Service Society," *New York Evening Post,* August 3, 1865; "Serenade to General Ortega," *New York Post,* August 4, 1865; Dearing, *Veterans in Politics,* 68–69. See also "'The Boys in Blue,' Great Meeting of Soldiers and Sailors in New York, They Endorse the President and the Philadelphia Platform," *Daily Albany Argus,* September 5, 1866.

24. "Local News—Meeting of the Soldiers and Sailors," *Evening Star* (Washington, DC), August 24, 1866.

25. Sam Ross, *The Empty Sleeve: A Biography of Lucius Fairchild* (Madison: State Historical Society of Wisconsin, 1964), 66–94; Richard N. Current, "The Politics of Reconstruction in Wisconsin," *Wisconsin Magazine of History* 60, no. 2 (Winter 1976–1977): 83–108; Eugene D. Schmiel, *Citizen-General: Jacob Dolson Cox and the Civil War Era* (Athens: Ohio University Press, 2014), 176–97; William Marvel, *Burnside* (Chapel Hill: University of North Carolina Press, 1991), 419; Alice Rains Trulock, *In the Hands of Providence: Joshua L. Chamberlain and the American Civil War* (Chapel Hill: University of North Carolina Press, 1992), 334–37; Harry Marlin Tinkcom, *John White Geary: Soldier-Statesman, 1819–1873* (Philadelphia: University of Pennsylvania Press, 1940), 113–26; Erwin Stanley Bradley, *The Triumph of Militant Republicanism: A Study of Pennsylvania and Presidential Politics, 1860–1872* (Philadelphia: University of Pennsylvania Press, 1964), 252–87.

26. Dearing, *Veterans in Politics,* 85–98.

27. "Political—The Boys in Blue, Nominations for City Officers—An Address to the City of Philadelphia," *Daily Evening Bulletin* (Philadelphia), August 2, 1866.

28. "A True Soldiers' Convention," *Newark Daily Advertiser,* June 11, 1866.

29. "The Boys in Blue—Grand Soldiers' and Sailors' Convention at Pittsburgh—Eloquent and Patriotic Addresses and Resolutions—Geary Enthusiastically Endorsed," *Daily Evening Bulletin* (Philadelphia), June 6, 1866. Lucius Fairchild, a former Army of the Potomac officer and eventual governor of Wisconsin, publicly insisted that Davis should be hanged; see Ross, *The Empty Sleeve,* 79.

30. Mark Walgreen Summers, *The Ordeal of Reunion: A New History of Reconstruction* (Chapel Hill: University of North Carolina Press, 2014), 84–85; Robert D. Sawrey, *Dubious Victory: The Reconstruction Debate in Ohio* (Lexington: University Press of Kentucky, 1992), 71–73, 75–76; Brooks D. Simpson, *Let Us Have Peace: Ulysses S. Grant and the Politics of War and Reconstruction, 1861–1868* (Chapel Hill: University of North Carolina Press, 1991), 146–48; Silbey, *A Respectable Minority,* 183; "Johnsonism," *Daily Evening Bulletin* (Philadelphia), August 22, 1866.

31. "Pennsylvania—The Soldiers' Convention at Harrisburg—Magnificent Gathering of the Boys in Blue—Enthusiastic Endorsement of Johnson and Clymer," *Republican Compiler* (Gettysburg, PA), August 6, 1866; "Union Soldiers' Convention, They Endorse Heister Clymer and Repudiate Geary—A Grand Assemblage of the 'Boys in Blue,'" *Erie (PA) Observer,* August 9, 1866.

32. "The Soldiers Moving—But Not for Geary," *Lancaster (PA) Intelligencer,* May 30, 1866.

33. "Michigan—An Address to the Soldiers and Sailors—Their Duty Set Forth," *New York Tribune,* August 30, 1866; "Union Soldiers' and Sailors' Convention," *Albany Journal,* September 10, 1866; "The Jacobin Carnival Last Night," *Cincinnati Daily Enquirer,* September 9, 1866.

34. "Fifteen Thousand Honorably Discharged Union Soldiers . . . ," *Wellsboro (PA) Agitator,* October 3, 1866.

35. "Washington, September 4, 1866, The Soldiers and Sailors Truly Loyal," *Boston Journal,* September 5, 1866.

36. Dearing, *Veterans in Politics,* 105, 110; Ross, *The Empty Sleeve,* 92–93; Richard H. Zeitlin, "In Peace and War: Union Veterans and Cultural Symbols—The Flags of the Iron Brigade," in *Giants in Their Tall Black Hats: Essays on the Iron Brigade,* ed. Alan T. Nolan and Sharon Eggleston Vipond (Bloomington: Indiana University Press, 1998), 162–64.

37. Adam Badeau to Levi Edwin Dudley, September 18, 1866, quoted in John Y. Simon, *The Papers of Ulysses S. Grant* (Carbondale: Southern Illinois University Press, 1988), 16:547.

38. Silbey, *A Respectable Minority,* 195, 215.

39. "Soldiers of Vengeance," *New York Tribune,* July 2, 1867.

40. "Brigade of the White Boys in Blue," *Cleveland Plain Dealer,* September 19, 1867.

41. "The White Boys in Blue Who Never Wore the Blue," *Evening Telegraph* (Philadelphia), September 8, 1868, and "The 'White Boys in Blue' Claim to Have Been . . . ," *Juniata (PA) Sentinel,* September 23, 1868.

42. "Letter from General Manderson, He Executes the Duties of His Advisory Position—Healthy Advice for 'Conservative Soldiers,'" *Hancock Jeffersonian,* June 5, 1868.

43. "Cheering Signs of the Times," *Father Abraham* (Lancaster, PA), September 4, 1868.

44. Ross, *The Empty Sleeve,* 97–98.

45. Dearing, *Veterans in Politics,* 176–77.

46. Almira Hancock, *The Reminiscences of Winfield Scott Hancock* (New York: Charles L. Webster, 1887), 95.

47. James E. Sefton, *The United States Army and Reconstruction, 1865–1877* (Baton Rouge: Louisiana State University Press, 1967), 175–78; Downs, *After Appomattox,* 185.

48. Hancock, *Reminiscences of Winfield Scott Hancock,* 139.

49. "The Mass Meeting of the Boys in Blue . . . ," *Tioga County (NY) Agitator,* October 14, 1868.

50. "To the Boys in Blue," *Ebensburg (PA) Alleghenian,* September 3, 1868.

51. "Speech of General Sweitzer, He Wants to Vote as He Fought, and Therefore, Though a Democrat, Cannot Vote for Seymour and Frank Blair," *Ebensburg (PA) Alleghenian,* October 1, 1868.

52. "Constitution of the Society of the Army of the Potomac as Adopted at the Meeting of the Society, Held at Steinway Hall, New York, Monday July 5th and 6th 1869," in Society of the Army of the Potomac Minutes, Manuscript Division, Library of Congress (hereafter LOC).

53. "Proceedings of a Meeting of the Officers of the Army of the Potomac Held at the Armory of the 22nd Regiment New York State National Guard in the City of New York on the 22nd Day of February 1869," in Society of the Army of the Potomac Minutes, LOC.

54. "Proceedings of the First Annual Re-Union of the Society of the Army of the Potomac, Held in the City of New York, on the fifth and sixth days of July, one thousand eight hundred and sixty-nine," in Society of the Army of the Potomac Minutes, LOC; "Proceedings of the Second Annual Re-Union of the Society of the Army of the Potomac," in Society of the Army of the Potomac Minutes, LOC.

55. "Proceedings of the Second Annual Re-Union of the Society of the Army of the Potomac," in Society of the Army of the Potomac Minutes, LOC.

56. Dearing, *Veterans in Politics,* 200–218. For a discussion of the Liberal Republicans, see Eric Foner, *Reconstruction: America's Unfinished Revolution, 1863–1877* (New York: Harper and Row, 1988), 499–51; Heather Cox Richardson, *The Death of Reconstruction: Race, Labor, and Politics in the Post–Civil War North, 1865–1901* (Cambridge, MA: Harvard University Press, 2001), 102–4; and Andrew L. Slap, *The Doom of Reconstruction: The Liberal Republicans in the Civil War Era* (New York: Fordham University Press, 2006).

57. On debates within Republican veterans' organizations over whom to nominate, see "The

Grand Army in Politics," *Boston Traveler,* June 1, 1876. For Democratic veterans and misgivings about Tilden, see "New York, a Democrat on Democrats," *Cleveland Leader,* October 30, 1876. Recent scholarship has done much to reconsider Grant's presidency. For the most current reassessment see Charles W. Calhoun, *The Presidency of Ulysses S. Grant* (Lawrence: University Press of Kansas, 2017).

58. "Boys in Blue," *Lake Village Times* (Laconia, NH), September 16, 1876.

59. "Boys in Blue, Reunion at Indianapolis an Immense Affair," *Cincinnati Commercial Tribune,* September 21, 1876.

60. "Hayes and Wheeler, Grand Republican Demonstration, The City a Blaze of Glory," *Providence Evening Press,* November 4, 1876.

61. Republicans expressed similar fears about their opponents.

62. "The Boys in Blue, The Soldiers and Sailors of the Late War Organize Political Clubs," *Cincinnati Daily Gazette,* August 31, 1876.

63. On threats of violence as a recourse to election politics in the 1870s, see Gregory P. Downs, "The Mexicanization of American Politics: The United States' Transnational Path from Civil War to Stabilization," *American Historical Review* 117, no. 2 (April 2012): 387–409.

64. "The State Convention—A Large, Earnest and Dignified Assemblage of Jerseymen," *Trenton State Gazette,* September 26, 1877.

65. "A New Jersey Soldier on McClellan," *Trenton State Gazette,* October 22, 1877.

66. "The Hancock Veterans, An Address to Old Soldiers Adopted by Their National Executive Committee," *Ottawa (IL) Free Trader,* August 14, 1880.

67. "Gen. Hancock and the G.A.R.," *Spirit of Democracy,* August 24, 1880.

68. Fiona Deans Halloran, *Thomas Nast: The Father of American Political Cartoons* (Chapel Hill: University of North Carolina Press, 2013), 246–48.

69. "Political Topics," *Ogdensburg (NY) Journal,* August 6, 1880.

70. "The Charges against Hancock," *Belmont (OH) Chronicle,* September 9, 1880; "When the brave Irish brigade asked permission . . . ," *Jackson Standard,* October 7, 1880; Herbert J. Clancy, *The Presidential Election of 1880* (Chicago: Loyola University Press, 1958), 173.

71. "Will Never Go Back on His Old Commander," *Hancock Veteran,* September 9, 1880, in John B. Nicholson Collection, Henry E. Huntington Library.

72. "A True Man Is a True Citizen," *Hancock Veteran,* September 18, 1880, Nicholson Collection, Huntington Library; "Could Follow No Other Leader," *Hancock Veteran,* September 18, 1880, Nicholson Collection, Huntington Library.

73. Clancy, *The Presidential Election of 1880,* 199, 201–2, 210–11; Dearing, *Veterans in Politics,* 262–66.

74. Gerald Linderman, *Embattled Courage: The Experience of Combat in the American Civil War* (New York: Free Press, 1987), 266–75.

75. Jordan, *Marching Home,* 68–69.

"The Men Are Understood to Have Been Generally Americans, in the Employ of the Liberal Government"

Civil War Veterans and Mexico, 1865–1867

EVAN C. ROTHERA

O N JUNE 12, 1865, US consul Edward Conner of Guaymas complained to Secretary of State William H. Seward about US citizens crossing the US/Mexico border to fight with Benito Juárez and the Liberals against Emperor Ferdinand Maximilian's French and Imperial soldiers. Conner had good reason to complain. When Mexico suspended payments on its foreign debt in 1861, Great Britain, France, and Spain seized the Veracruz Customs House. However, France's Emperor Napoleon III, in order to create a French empire in the New World and surpass his more famous uncle, ordered his army to take Mexico City. Britain and Spain abandoned the venture, and General Ignacio Zaragoza's Liberal army defeated Napoleon's men at the Battle of Puebla on May 5, 1862.[1] Nevertheless, French soldiers soon chased the Liberals out of Mexico City and installed Maximilian, an Austrian aristocrat, on the Cactus Throne.[2] US soldiers who crossed the border to aid the Liberals irritated Conner. "We have scores of worthless fellows," he snarled, "deserters from Whalers, deserters from our Army and fugitives from California, who are noisy and boisterous in their declarations of friendship for the Mexicans and their opposition to the French." Many of these people "took service with the Mexicans some months since and were most prominent in their denunciations of the French." The "uncalled-for and senseless ajitation of the Monroe doctrine on the part of a few here, was rapidly creating prejudices and feelings of suspicion in the Minds of the French Officers." Conner deplored the fact that "the ajitation of the [Monroe] doctrine became a sort of pastime with some, and a passion with others" and threatened his good working relationship with the French commander.[3]

Consul Conner's complaints about US citizens agitating of the Monroe Doctrine resonated with Seward. The secretary of state, after all, wanted no part of a shooting war with France or Maximilian's Mexico, Napoleon III's client state.[4] However, while Conner's sentiments harmonized with the premier of Andrew Johnson's administration, they were profoundly out of sync with the general mood of the nation. Many of Conner's contemporaries favored US intervention in Mexico. Rather than returning to their homes, their fields, and their loved ones, some veterans preferred to fight in Mexico in another war. Many people throughout the Atlantic World saw the US Civil War and the French Intervention as interwoven conflicts or as battles in a larger war.

In a June 10, 1864, speech in Nashville, a year before Conner wrote to Seward, Andrew Johnson, then military governor of Tennessee and the Republican candidate for vice president, discussed slavery and emancipation and famously asserted that "treason must be made odious and traitors must be punished and impoverished."[5] Strikingly, Johnson did not confine himself to domestic issues. European nations, he growled, conspired to destroy the United States. While Johnson painted with overly broad strokes—not all Europeans, of course, wanted to see the United States ripped apart—he accurately captured Napoleon III's position.[6] Johnson deplored the French attempt to install Archduke Maximilian of Austria as Emperor Maximilian of Mexico. "The time is not far distant," he vowed, "when the rebellion will be put down, and then we will attend to this Mexican affair, and say to Louis Napoleon, 'You can set up no monarchy on this continent.'"[7] A US expedition into Mexico "would be a sort of recreation to the brave soldiers who are now fighting the battles of the Union, and the French concern would be quickly wiped out."[8] Johnson's assertion that the United States would clean up the mess in Mexico had more than a tinge of racial superiority. Nevertheless, his gaze, like that of many of his contemporaries, was hemispheric. He understood the need to vindicate the Monroe Doctrine and drive the French out of Mexico.[9]

Historian Kenneth Stampp famously labeled Andrew Johnson "the last Jacksonian."[10] Like Old Hickory, Johnson had little tolerance for European meddling in the New World. However, once a bullet elevated him to the presidential chair, he seemingly forgot about Mexico in favor of designing his lenient program of reconstruction.[11] Furthermore, Johnson allegedly deferred to Seward on foreign policy. "Willing to yield to Seward's pleas for a patient course of watchful waiting to force the French to withdraw—in the fall of 1865 he had even sent General John M. Schofield on a mission to Paris to diffuse the situation—Johnson drew upon himself the ire of more bellicose Republicans who wanted the French intruders expelled at once," Hans Trefousse writes.[12]

"Watchful waiting" is an ambiguous phrase. Seward never really defined what it meant, except that he wanted no part of a war with France.[13] Francis Preston Blair Sr., another old Jacksonian, huffed that Mexican affairs would not change while "France & her Puppet have a steadfast friend in the Secretary of State." The country, Blair growled, "may be pardoned for distrusting your disposition to maintain the inviolability of our continent from the invasion of European powers."[14]

The scholarly consensus is that Seward softened Johnson's bellicosity and Reconstruction took precedence over kicking the French out of Mexico, but the reality was hardly so cut and dried.[15] For one, Johnson did little to curtail the flow of US arms, munitions, and soldiers into Mexico. In addition, Seward was not the only man directing US foreign policy. Plenty of people—many of them veterans of the US Civil War—contested his policy of "watchful waiting." Seward faced challenges from the center and the periphery, from elite and nonelite actors, and from men as eminent as Ulysses S. Grant to the rank-and-file veterans who crossed the US/Mexico border to fight with the Liberals.[16] Involving a vast array of actors, the story of US foreign policy toward Mexico from 1865 to 1867 is a great deal more complicated than "watchful waiting."

Indeed, the rapprochement between the United States and Mexico, which began during the Secession Winter and continued throughout the US Civil War, became even more pronounced during this period.[17] Ulysses S. Grant, Matías Romero, Philip Sheridan, and Edward Lee Plumb, among others, re-invigorated an older way of understanding the two nations when they spoke of the United States and Mexico as "sister republics."[18] These men saw the US Civil War and the French Intervention as two battles in a much larger conflict and argued that each country should aid the other because the fate of one rested on the other. Proponents of assistance constantly emphasized the necessity of vindicating the Monroe Doctrine. While Civil War veterans were not the only actors, in many ways, they helped direct US policy in more belli-cose directions than Seward would have preferred. Furthermore, veterans did not enter a period of hibernation following the US Civil War, as some scholars have suggested.[19] In fact, veterans proved powerful political actors who used their authority to intervene in domestic and foreign affairs. In other words, rather than hibernating or withdrawing from politics for a generation, veterans understood the US Civil War and the French Intervention as profoundly interrelated conflicts, a point that historians have only recently come to consider. Veterans thought hemispherically and prodded an often reluctant secretary of state into responding to their initiatives.

THE STORY OF THE REBELS who fled the United States after the US Civil War to seek refuge in Mexico is reasonably well known. Virginian John Dooley, for instance, observed that several of his fellow rebels began to learn Spanish in a northern prison camp so they could "seek their fortunes in Mexico should the worst come to the worst."[20] William E. Ardrey noted that "the present state of the Country is very unsettled, + pregnant with Yankee tyranny, rife with rumors of the Mexican Question and very great apprehension of the U S + French Gov's being . . . in a war."[21] Mary Elizabeth Mitchell, Jefferson Davis's grandniece, wrote in her journal that her cousin, Jeff Bradford, "with my brother and several other of our relatives who are in his battalion of Scouts expect to cross the Mississippi when this Department is given up and join the Trans Mississippi department. If that also is surrendered, he will go into Mexico and offer his services to Maximilien." Mitchell hoped that "it will not be necessary for him to leave the Confederacy, for I feel sure this is not the end of the war."[22] Sterling Price, Jo Shelby, Edmund Kirby Smith, Matthew Fontaine Maury, John Bankhead Magruder, Isham Harris, and Henry Watkins Allen, to name only a few, fled to Mexico and sought shelter with Emperor Maximilian.[23] While some rebels received positions in the imperial government, others found their way into Maximilian's army, and many, through the Austrian's largesse, received land and settled in agricultural colonies.[24]

Some former Confederates claimed to sympathize with the Liberals, not Maximilian. In a letter to US general Gordon Granger, written several months after Robert E. Lee's surrender at Appomattox, Confederate general J. E. Harrison assured Granger that the disbanding of the Confederate forces in Texas was not "for the purpose of going into Mexico to join Maximilian." Discussions about leaving the United States for Mexico were a product, not a cause, of rebel disbandment. Some officers, he conceded, "believing they would be harshly dealt with by the US Government and that their only personal security was refuge in a foreign country, were disposed to go to Mexico and take commands of troops with them. But to my best knowledge and belief the subject never assumed any definite shape." In what seems a rather preposterous statement, especially given how many Confederates joined Maximilian, Harrison asserted, "Not only was there no general purpose to join Maximilian, but the more common feeling was in behalf of the Liberal cause." Harrison even noted that had the US authorities given it their blessing, "the movement might have been a serious one, and its entire direction given in favor of the Liberal party in Mexico." "No Texas organization," Harrison concluded, "has crossed or is expected to cross the Rio Grande; and so far as my information extends, the few adventurous individuals who do cross the river and had any previous connection with our army are likely to be found sympathizing with the Liberals" [25]

Harrison overlooked, either accidently or deliberately, the hundreds of former Confederates under Jo Shelby who crossed the Rio Grande to join Maximilian. [26] He overlooked, either accidentally or deliberately, high-profile fugitives like Isham Harris of Tennessee, Henry Watkins Allen of Louisiana, and Generals Edmund Kirby Smith, Jo Shelby, and John B. Magruder. More importantly, Harrison's denial that Confederate soldiers wanted anything to do with Maximilian flew in the face of what former rebels actually did when they arrived in Mexico. Harrison's analysis minimized the tendency among rebels to sympathize with and aid Conservatives and Imperialists. Thomas Alexander Hamilton demonstrated this tendency when he informed his friend Hamilton Yancey that the subject of an upcoming public debate was "will the occupation of Mexico by [Maximilian] be beneficial to the world or not[?]" In other words, continued Hamilton, "Will it be more beneficial to the human race to have a monarchical or republican form of government in Mexico[?]" Hamilton explained to Yancey that he intended to argue for monarchy. [27] Granted, Hamilton did not make plans to leave the United States for Mexico. Nor did his commitment to monarchy impel him to take up arms for the Austrian pretender. However, his sentiments rebuked Harrison's claim.

That said, it is problematic to contend rebels only went to Mexico to fight for monarchy. To be sure, some of them agreed with Hamilton. Others, however, might have thought along the same lines as Ulysses S. Grant, that the US Civil War would not end until the French left Mexico. If the wars were so intimately linked, fighting for Maximilian would prolong the US Civil War and hurt the Yankees. It might even mean, if Confederate assistance helped the Austrian pretender triumph, that they would have an ally who could help them fight the North. Joining with Maximilian, therefore, could destabilize both the Liberals and Yankees and, perhaps, secure victory against a weary North and roll back Reconstruction.[28] In this vision, rebels could ally with a European monarch and the borrowed soldiers of a French emperor and still fight for a certain vision of freedom.

One would be hard pressed to imagine a scenario in which Juárez would have welcomed a horde of ex-Confederate soldiers fighting under his banner, particularly given their racial prejudices. The idea, however, proved stubbornly persistent. Francis Preston Blair, an old Jacksonian, fretted about the French presence in Mexico. In a transcript of a conversation with Jefferson Davis, Blair argued Davis could drive Maximilian from the Cactus Throne and, by so doing, restore the position of the southern states in the Union. Transfer portions of your army to Texas, Blair advised, equip them, send them to Mexico, and Juárez and the Liberals will give you aid and assistance. Blair believed he and his son Montgomery could persuade Matías Romero, the Mexican minister to the United States, to "induce Juarez to devote all the power he can command on President Davis—a dictatorship if necessary—to restore the rights of Mexico & her people and provide for the stability of its government."[29]

In his mind, Blair's proposal to Jefferson Davis accomplished several ends. For one, it took care of the Confederacy. Davis and his fellow secessionists, by expelling the French and Imperialists, would vindicate the Monroe Doctrine. As an added bonus, they would have the sanction of the Liberals, so this would not be a repeat of the US war with Mexico. As icing on the cake, Davis could become not only the savior but also the dictator of Mexico. Having done that, he could make Mexico a haven for any southerners irritated about the living cheek to jowl with Yankees. Indeed, Mexico under Davis could become a safety valve to bleed off unhappy fire-eaters. Gather your armies in Texas, Blair whispered into Davis's ear, strike a blow deep into the vitals of the Austrian pretender, humiliate the French, and reap your reward. It is inconceivable to envision Juárez being receptive to this idea. That Blair entertained it demonstrates the often desperate schemes people contemplated about ways to end the war.[30] Blair clearly thought this was an excellent idea and wrote to Lincoln, "Davis I am convinced desires to make common cause with us for Republicanism on this continent."[31] Davis surely would have been surprised to hear that he concurred with Blair.

In sum, historians have paid a reasonably significant amount of attention to Confederate exiles in Mexico and have provided a general outline of their motivations. However, historians have spent considerably less time analyzing Union veterans who supported Mexico through words, deeds, or both.

WHILE WILLIAM H. SEWARD whispered into Johnson's ear that war with France should be avoided at all costs, U. S. Grant proclaimed exactly the opposite. Grant took exception to Seward's timidity. In a letter to Johnson, Grant groused that he regarded "the act of attempting to establish a monarchical government on this continent in Mexico, by foreign bayonets as an act of hostility against the Government of the United States."[32] In other words, the French violation of the Monroe Doctrine posed a threat to the Union. Furthermore, Grant did not need to remind Johnson that many rebels in the Trans-Mississippi theater had not surrendered.[33] Some of them were in the midst of crossing the border into Mexico. Napoleon's actions lengthened the odds against the North winning a successful peace.

Grant's language became sharper in a subsequent letter. "Looking upon the French occupation of Mexico as part and parcel of the late rebellion in the United States," he snarled, "and a necessary part of it to suppress before entire peace can be assured, I would respectfully recommend that a leave of absence be given to one of our General officers for the purpose of going to Mexico to give direction to such emigration as may go to that country." Grant also recommended selling arms to the Liberals, "the only Government we recognize on Mexican soil."[34] He insisted that peace in the United States was contingent upon peace in Mexico. Thus, in the space of a month Grant went from complaining about the French to advising Johnson of the propriety of sending a general to coordinate the movement of US citizens to Juárez's armies and selling weapons to the Liberals. Clearly, the general had no patience with "watchful waiting."

Grant's sentiments heartened Matías Romero, the Mexican minister to the United States.[35] An indefatigable proponent of US aid to Mexico, Romero conducted an impressive charm offensive during the period 1861–1867.[36] In addition to writing thousands of dispatches to the Mexican minister of foreign affairs, meeting frequently with Grant, Johnson, and high-level policy makers, Romero also set multiple plans into motion to help beleaguered Liberals and cultivated would-be allies.[37]

After recommending Johnson send a general to direct US citizens to Liberal armies, Grant, with assistance from Romero, began to work on General John Schofield. Grant praised Schofield's "aptitude, character, sound judgment, and military knowledge."[38] Schofield, a capable general, seemed willing to accept the assignment.[39] However, Seward disapproved of Schofield getting anywhere near Mexico at the head of an army. Instead, he crafted a plan to send Schofield to France on a diplomatic mission. Romero complained to the Mexican minister of foreign affairs that Seward "is indisputably the most influential man in this country" and "while he remains in the cabinet policy will not change."[40] Schofield assured Romero that Seward "had a well-matured plan that could not fail and ought to compel the French army to depart from Mexico."[41] Romero informed his bosses in early November 1865 that Schofield sailed to Paris on a confidential mission to talk to the US minister about whether the French were "disposed to retire from Mexico and, in the affirmative case, under what conditions."[42] Sensing a threat to his policy, Seward outfoxed Grant and Romero by sending Schofield to France. Seward was unquestionably a powerful voice when it came to foreign policy; however, he was not the only voice and, as this episode showed, he had to scramble to stymie Grant and Romero.[43]

Schofield was not the only general interested in crossing the border. In the midst of his conferences with Grant and Schofield, Romero received an agreement between US general Lew Wallace and Liberal general José María de Jesús Carvajal.[44] On April 26, 1865, Carvajal offered Wallace "a commission as Major General in the Mexican army."[45] Wallace would command "a corps or division of American troops, organized after the American system, not to exceed ten thousand (10,000) men in number," would not "be placed under command of any American or foreign officers, unless it be by special direction of the proper authority of my Government," and could select his own officers.[46] Wallace assured Carvajal he wanted to "instantly accept" the offer but worried acceptance would leave his family without provision. However, if Carvajal would "secure them [Wallace's family] beyond the ordinary chances of want or suffering during my absence or in the event of my death," he would accept the terms.[47] If Wallace gathered sufficient US soldiers to fight with the Liberals, Carvajal promised, the Mexican government would pay him $100,000.[48] Wallace accepted these generous conditions.[49]

This agreement displeased Romero. In addition to being skeptical about Carvajal's authority to recruit Wallace, Romero echoed Grant's dislike of Wallace.[50] Before Seward redirected Schofield to France, Romero planned to have Schofield take command of any men Wallace gathered once they crossed into Mexico.[51] Because Wallace did not sign up anywhere near ten thousand men, the issue of command never became a problem. However, plenty of people found their way to the Liberal forces without Wallace's aid. Generals and elites were not the only people scheming to aid Mexico.

Grant, Romero, Carvajal, Schofield, and Wallace placed a great deal of importance on getting the French out of Mexico, vindicating the Monroe Doctrine, and helping a sister republic.[52] Other people made similar arguments—both veterans and nonveterans. In a letter to Andrew Johnson, written shortly after Johnson's accession to the presidency, General Robert H. Milroy offered strident advice: "I hope you will teach the world that the Munroe [*sic*] Doctrine is a reality," Milroy snapped, "and that the great insult to our nation by a European power in forcing an emperor on our neighboring Republic in violation of that doctrine, while our hands were tied, will now be speedily avenged by at once giving Mexico all needed assistance in expelling the insolent intruder and tool of a foreign despot."[53] Grant and Romero would have agreed with Milroy's opinion.

Edward Lee Plumb, a friend of Romero, a proponent of US aid to Mexico, a railroad promoter, and a diplomatic officer, lobbied members of Congress to take action.[54] "Is it not now time," he badgered Senator Charles Sumner, that Congress should "by formal resolution let it be known to the world that the people of the United States have not abandoned the Monroe Doctrine, that they do not and cannot look with favor or with indiference [*sic*] on the attempt of a European Power to overthrow Republican institutions and to introduce an European form of Government into their neighbor and sister Republic."[55] Plumb also sent a letter to Sumner and Chairman Nathaniel P. Banks of the House Foreign Relations Committee decrying the "hollocaust of blood" produced by Maximilian's reign and suggesting the US had a moral duty to help a suffering sister republic.[56]

The language of "sister republics" proved popular. Participants in a dinner given in Romero's honor, from Romero himself to George Bancroft and David Dudley Field, utilized it frequently.[57] General John C. Frémont, the darling of Radical Republicans, derided the French desire "to plant an Austrian throne on the ruins of a sister republic" as "an attempt which shocks the public sentiment of this country, and which is eminently hostile to the stability of our institutions."[58] Upon being presented to President Benito Juárez, US minister to Mexico Thomas Corwin hoped "to be able to confirm our present friendly relations with Mexico by extending still further our commercial exchanges on principles mutually advantageous, thus binding together the sister Republics in bonds of interest, as well as those of sympathy, which grow out of the similarity of their respective political organization."[59] Career soldier Joseph C. Breckinridge told his father Robert C. Breckinridge that "this generation is pledged to interfere and place our finger in the hot fire of Mexico." Although some people "say we are unable to protect our Sister Republic from being ravished by this foreign bully while weak from the fever of the rebellion," he felt the United States should teach the Austrian pretender a sharp lesson.[60]

Furthermore, the language of "sister republics" was not confined to dinners, speeches, and correspondence. It appeared frequently in newspaper articles. At the beginning of the US Civil War, California newspapers commented, "Should the triumph of the Constitutional Government result in the restoration of peace to our sister Republic, it is hard to calculate the importance of the Mexican trade to this city."[61] The *New York Herald* opined that Lincoln's administration would lend "the influence and power of the United States, wherever it may be proper, for the security and welfare of our sister republics of the South."[62] The *Springfield Republican* growled, in the aftermath of the tripartite French, British, and Spanish intervention, that "the Monroe doctrine is not yet a dead letter." Furthermore, "There is no motive to induce any American to look with favor or toleration upon the designs of the old world dynasties against the liberties of a sister republic."[63]

Lincoln's political opponents quickly learned how to use this language as a cudgel against Republicans. The *World* lamented the "humiliating position" of the US government toward the French Intervention. "When a sister republic to whom we were bound by the ties of interest, neighborhood, and the standing pledge implied in the Monroe doctrine," the paper wailed, Seward did nothing.[64] The *Cleveland Daily Plain Dealer* charged the "shoddy party" with inviting "Louis Napoleon to destroy a sister Republic."[65] The *Plain Dealer's* argument was patently absurd, but the editor considered it an effective attack.[66] The *Sacramento Daily Union* moaned that "a servile European king planted upon the ruins of a sister republic is an ignominious conclusion to the Monroe doctrine proclaimed and maintained in the better days of American nationality."[67] After the conclusion of the US Civil War, many vowed the time had come to do something about the pestilential Austrian and vindicate the Monroe Doctrine.[68] "The people of this country," snapped the *Evening Post* "do not wish to sit still and do nothing."[69] Veterans, as well as nonveterans, through newspaper articles, toasts, speeches, and letters, made it very clear that they had no intention of letting what they believed to be an outrage against the United States and Mexico continue and, in so doing, put the French and Maximilian on notice.

Mexicans adeptly invoked this language as well. "The Mexican consul at Havana," noted the *Hartford Daily Courant,* "says that his government feels deeply that the United States should not only refuse to aid a sister republic struggling against a monarchy, but still more that it should aid her enemies."[70] The *Janesville Daily Gazette* printed a letter from Governor Diego Álvarez of Guerrero. Álvarez argued that the Imperialists and the French worked to exterminate democracy in Mexico. He hoped "the United States will hasten to co-operate in favor of a sister republic, for it is not alone Mexico which will be destroyed, but the very source of the democratic element."[71] Mexicans, according to the *Sacramento Daily Union,* wondered if "the United States fear the French and acquiesce in the occupation of a sister republic whose feelings and sympathies are with the Government of the United States."[72] Finally, the *Daily True Delta* printed the appeal of Francisco N. de Bordon, a "distinguished gentleman and patriot of our sister Republic, Mexico." Bordon offered a heartfelt plea to his "Republican brothers and sisters, supporters of the Monroe doctrine," asking if they could "behold this awful scene and bloodshed without a shudder?"[73]

When people deliberately and repeatedly linked the United States and Mexico as "sister republics," they reinvigorated an older way of conceptualizing the two nations. In the 1810s and 1820s, during the Spanish American revolutions, people in the United States displayed fervent enthusiasm about revolutions in the former Spanish colonies. Many considered the new countries sister republics.[74] However, this way of thinking had, for the most part, fallen out of use by the late 1820s.[75] By speaking about sister republics, proponents furthered US/Mexico rapprochement. If the United States and Mexico were sister republics, it would not be acceptable for the United States to do nothing, especially after the northern triumph. Furthermore, this language burned away some of the hostilities of the US war with Mexico and illustrated the profound way people in both countries began to reorder their visions of the world. Less than twenty years earlier, after all, the United States provoked a war with Mexico and took a considerable portion of Mexico's territory.[76] Now people saw themselves as partners in the republican experiment.

An important cabal of pro-Mexico men in Washington, such as Ulysses S. Grant and Matías Romero, played a critical role in articulating this argument. People cheered when Grant publicly rebuked French subjugation of Mexico.[77] Veterans numbered among the loudest voices calling for the United States to vindicate the Monroe Doctrine. That said, some of the schemes and speeches might seem rather limited. They were, after all, only words and aborted plans. However, moving from the center to the periphery suggests a different perspective. Plenty of people in the US/Mexico borderlands and throughout Mexico, from General Philip Sheridan to anonymous veterans, had their own impact on US/Mexico foreign policy.

"Little Phil" Sheridan, the commander of US forces in Texas, had no patience with Seward's policy and no use for watchful waiting. In fact, in a letter Sheridan sent to Grant, that Grant showed to Romero, Sheridan argued, "Seward was no friend of our cause."[78] One newspaper noted Sheridan "recently declared that 'the United States did not mean to rub elbows with an Austrian-French monarchy.'"[79] Plumb wrote to Sumner that after having "many very full and frank conversations" with Sheridan about political affairs, Plumb discovered that "our ideas harmonize so entirely both with reference to the Union cause and upon the subject of Mexican affairs, that doubtless greater frankness has been shown by him to me than would otherwise have been the case."[80]

Sheridan's opposition went beyond rhetoric. In a confidential letter to Andrew Johnson, J. E. P. Doyle, a reporter for the *New York Herald*, informed the president of a startling fact. "Last year while investigating certain matters at N. Orleans I discovered that that 'gallant little soldier' Phil. Sheridan, had authorized over his own signature, a filibustering expedition against France and Austria."[81] Sheridan, Doyle alleged, permitted Henry R. H. McIvor, a member of Liberal general Mariano Escobedo's staff to recruit men in the United States to fight with the Liberals. Sheridan's would have been a radically different type of filibuster than the antebellum filibustering expeditions led by men like William Walker and Narciso López.[82] For one, there was no proslavery taint, no concern he sought to win an empire for slavery. In addition, this filibusterer would have involved Mexicans and won the approval of President Juárez.

It is hard to verify if Sheridan permitted McIvor and Escobedo to recruit in the United States. If true, it was a flagrant violation of the Neutrality Act of 1818. However, given some of Sheridan's other actions, Doyle's charge was not out of the question. Little Phil often allowed his hatred of the French to lead him into gray areas of the law. Jerry Thompson noted that R. Clay Crawford and Arthur F. Reed secured commissions in the Liberal army and, "with tacit approval of the Federals, opened a recruiting office where they offered $50 a month in gold and all expenses for anyone who would join in an invasion of Mexico."[83] In addition, perhaps even more egregiously, when the US Army occupied Texas in 1865, Juan N. Cortina "was allowed to set up a recruiting office in Brownsville" and "the Federals were openly courting and sheltering Cortina and his guerrillas."[84] If Little Phil allowed McIvor and Escobedo to recruit, it was hardly his only violation of the Neutrality Act. Given Cortina's status as the bête noire of many Texans, it was not even his most egregious!

Sheridan not only permitted Mexican recruiting on the US side of the border but probably facilitated arms drops across the border. He had no interest in securing the border and curtailing the passage of people and arms from the United States into Mexico. Andrew Johnson knew full well Sheridan sympathized with Radical Republicans and opposed most of Johnson's policies. Johnson nevertheless appointed Sheridan commander of the Fifth Military District (Texas and Louisiana) created by the Military Reconstruction Acts of 1867. Johnson did not remove Sheridan until several months after Maximilian's execution. He clearly liked having Little Phil watching the French and Imperialists.[85]

Sheridan was the most famous pro-Liberal actor on the periphery but not the only one. Many veterans, nameless and known, crossed the border to fight in Mexico. Plenty of people wrote of their desire to fight. J. Frank Cumming, for instance, informed US senator John A. J. Creswell, "I am very anxious to get into the Service again & See the End of this rebellion & then be in a position to go against any foreign nation, (providing there should be a war between this Country & any foreign Country)."[86] Most of the people who fought with the

Liberals left minimal traces on the historical record. They might have left no trace at all save for their involvement in the French Intervention and the fact that US diplomats noticed them in their dispatches to the State Department or newspaper articles mentioned them. Their motivations are hard to discern. They might have been driven by ideology or the urge for adventure or may simply have been soldiers of fortune. Nevertheless, these men risked their lives alongside the Liberals.

From Tampico, US consul Franklin Chase reported a battle between several hundred French soldiers led by Colonel Dupin and a force of Liberals under Carvajal. The French took the field, but the Liberals fought like tigers. "The troops under the Mexican Genl Carbajal [*sic*] fought so bravely, wounded and killed so many of the French officers and soldiers, that they are declared to be nearly all Americans from our forces on the frontiers, or Texans enlisted under Carbajal in that section of the Country."[87] The French could not believe, despite their embarrassing loss at Puebla in 1862, and their mixed success dealing with roving Liberal armies, that Mexicans could fight. Carvajal's force, therefore, must have been composed of Texans. The French, as they shaded the truth to protect their own ego, unwittingly demonstrated that recruiting across the borders was a common phenomenon. While Carvajal did recruit in Texas and likely had some Texans in his ranks, Mexicans could, and did, fight just as well as men from the Lone Star State.[88]

From Matamoros, US vice commercial agent Lucius Avery informed the State Department that a Liberal force under the command of General Escobedo, "estimated at from 1800. to 3000. men," was poised to defeat the Imperialist defenders. Among Escobedo's force, noted Avery, "are said to be several companies of negroes, made up of deserters and discharged soldiers from the U.S. army."[89] R. Delevan Mussey, Andrew Johnson's private secretary and colonel of the 100th USCT, planned to persuade Secretary of War Edwin M. Stanton to send black troops to Arizona to quell Indian incursions. Once in Arizona, Mussey would "inform his superiors that all is quiet and there is nothing to fear from the Indians." The government would muster out the troops, who would then "follow their inclination to cross into Mexico and enter our [Liberal] service in Sonora." This plan, Romero noted somewhat wryly, was "obviously subject to many contingencies."[90] Nothing came of Mussey's plan, but black troops from the United States proved their manhood fighting against Imperialists as well as Confederates. Interestingly, when Matamoros fell to the

Liberals, Consul Chase commented that "both French and Mexicans who adhere to the cause of Imperiality" attributed "the late defeat of Mejia's forces on the northern frontiers to American Gold + American Rifles."[91]

Consul F. B. Elmer of La Paz sent fascinating descriptions of US citizen involvement with Liberals. On April 9, 1866, he reported that a ship was "boarded and captured by a small force of armed men under the command of one F. F. Dana." Dana carried orders from General Corona, the commander of the Liberal forces in Sinaloa. Dana's men, "with one exception, were natives of the United States, who had been sworn into the service of the Juarez Government."[92] Imperialists were so angry that they attempted to sever all communication between La Paz and the outside world.[93] Several months later, a squad of armed men seized a US sloop and took it to Cabo San Lucas. Shortly thereafter, the same squad of men "some ten or twelve in number who presented themselves as holding commissions under, and being in the employ of General Corona of the Liberal Army," boarded the steamer *Sierra Nevada*. No one knows, he observed, "whether the steamer passed under the control of these men or not." Elmer concluded by noting the general impression that "the men are understood to have been generally Americans, in the employ of the Liberal Government." Elmer's final comment, "The proceedings detailed above, partake more of the nature of piracy, than of legitimate warfare," is fascinating.[94] It is not a particularly vehement statement. Elmer sent information to the State Department but did little to attempt to stop this "piracy," if, indeed, he considered it a problem.

Numerous US citizens aided the Liberal cause. J. B. Hart "joined the Mexican troops at El Paso, and was present at the execution of that unfortunate prince [Maximilian]."[95] Samuel Brannan "loaned the struggling Republicans a large sum of money."[96] Dr. Eugene Wakefield "served as a surgeon in the Mexican Republican Army of Sonora during the French intervention; and was known by the name of 'Guarda campo.'"[97] H. W. Spencer traveled to Mexico on the pretext of visiting mines near Acapulco. US consul Lewis S. Ely gave him a pass, but when Spencer reached the Liberal camp, he joined Diego Álvarez's army. The French commander was exceedingly displeased about this turn of events.[98] Ben Ferris, a member of the 1st Colorado Volunteers helped repel Henry H. Sibley's invasion of New Mexico and later went to Mexico to fight with the Liberals.[99] Consuls did not overexert themselves to control the inflow of people. Sheridan and other military officers facilitated recruiting and arms shipments. To say that the US/Mexico border was porous would be an understatement.

ANDREW JOHNSON ALLOWED Sheridan and other borderlanders a great deal of latitude and said nothing about their near-routine violations of the Neutrality Act of 1818.[100] Trefousse correctly notes that Johnson faced two major international problems: the Mexican question and the Fenian issue. Fenians, or Irish nationalists, attempted, in the period after the US Civil War, to invade Canada. However, Johnson and Seward made "dutiful effort to suppress Fenian raids into Canada." The Fenians, Trefousse asserts, "could not understand that the neutrality laws as well as international comity obligated Johnson and Seward to try to stop them.[101]

The problem was not so much one of Fenian misunderstanding as Johnson's radically different responses to borders and the people who crossed them. After all, people violated the Neutrality Act of 1818 with relative impunity along the southern border: recruiting US citizens to fight in Mexico, shipping arms to the Liberals, sheltering Cortina, and crossing the US/Mexico border to fight with the Liberals. Johnson's choice not to prosecute neutrality violations and to turn a blind eye to Sheridan's actions, suggests that, even if he deferred to Seward on sending Schofield to France, the president maintained flexibility when it came to foreign policy.

The rapid demobilization of the US Army after Appomattox significantly reduced the size of the army. However, as historian Gregory P. Downs notes, the United States moved nearly fifty thousand soldiers to Texas to defend against both rebels and Maximilian's empire.[102] This army never invaded Mexico, much to Sheridan's disappointment. Nevertheless, Little Phil found many ways to aid the Liberals. Perhaps Johnson used Sheridan to warn the French, albeit indirectly, that if they thought things were bad with Seward's "watchful waiting," imagine how much worse they would become if he unleashed Little Phil. Veterans like Sheridan played an important role during this period. For one, acting in conjunction with some of their nonveteran counterparts, they put teeth into Seward's policy of watchful waiting. In addition, they helped further US/Mexico rapprochement by demonstrating that people in the United States were as invested in Liberal success as the Liberals had been in the success of the North during the US Civil War. Veterans, in other words, did not subside into somnolence during the years immediately following the US Civil War; theirs were often the loudest and most strident voices demanding that the United States do something to help Mexico, a sister republic.

Veteran actions meant the French received mixed messages. On the one hand, the United States professed to be neutral in its conflict with Mexico. On the other hand, Grant pressed the government to do something about the invaders and made his own foreign policy arrangements with Romero; the bellicose Sheridan crouched in Texas, waiting for a chance to carry the war into Mexico; and Johnson did not enforce the Neutrality Act of 1818, which, in any case, Sheridan and many nameless veterans rendered a dead letter on the southern border. Perhaps these actions allowed Seward to put teeth into his policy. While professing a belief in watchful waiting, he could, at the same time, give the French a taste of how ugly a war with the United States could become. In any case, one cannot escape the conclusion that the people at the periphery and the center discussed in this essay did much more to convince the French of the futility of their Mexican adventure than Seward's rather bland appeals. Veterans studies, a field that often focuses on domestic issues, would do well to think about veterans and international affairs and understand that veterans saw the hemispheric dimensions of their world and the US Civil War.

NOTES

The title of this chapter is from F. B. Elmer (hereafter FBE) to William H. Seward (hereafter WHS), October 29, 1866, roll 1, vol. 1, Despatches from U.S. Consuls in La Paz.

1. See David Hayes-Bautista, *El Cinco de Mayo: An American Tradition* (Berkeley: University of California Press, 2012).

2. See Alfred J. Hanna and Kathryn A. Hanna, *Napoleon III and Mexico: American Triumph over Monarchy* (Chapel Hill: University of North Carolina Press, 1971); Thomas D. Schoonover, *Dollars over Dominion: The Triumph of Liberalism in Mexican–United States Relations* (Baton Rouge: Louisiana State University Press, 1978); Robert E. May, ed., *The Union, the Confederacy, and the Atlantic Rim* (West Lafayette, IN: Purdue University Press, 1995); Patrick J. Kelly, "The North American Crisis of the 1860s," *Journal of the Civil War Era* 2 (September 2012): 337–68; Don H. Doyle, *The Cause of All Nations: An International History of the American Civil War* (New York: Basic Books, 2015); Don H. Doyle, ed., *American Civil Wars: The United States, Latin America, Europe, and the Crisis of the 1860s* (Chapel Hill: University of North Carolina Press, 2017); and Andrew E. Masich, *Civil War in the Southwest Borderlands, 1861–1867* (Norman: University of Oklahoma Press, 2017).

3. Edward Conner to WHS, June 12, 1865, reel 1, vol. 1, Despatches from US Consuls in Guaymas.

4. Seward's ideas about foreign policy evolved dramatically from 1861 to 1865. Case in point, in April 1861, he dropped a memo on Lincoln's desk advocating declaring war on France or Spain in order to spark nationalism in the US South and cause the Confederacy to come running home. See WHS to Abraham Lincoln (hereafter AL), April 1, 1861, Abraham Lincoln Papers, Library of Congress (hereafter AL Papers, LOC).

5. *Biographical Sketch of Andrew Johnson, of Tennessee, Together with His Speech at Nashville, June 10, 1864, and His Letter Accepting the Nomination as Vice President of the United States, Tendered Him by the National Union Convention* (Washington, DC: Union Congressional Committee, 1864), 8, 11. Radical Republicans believed Johnson sympathized with them. See George W. Julian, *Political Recollections: 1840 to 1872* (Chicago: James McClurg, 1884), 257.

6. Plenty of Europeans wanted to see the United States defeat the rebels. See Doyle, *The Cause of All Nations.*

7. *Biographical Sketch of Andrew Johnson,* 11.

8. Ibid., 11. The crowd responded to this line with "great applause." See also "A Voice from the South," *Sacramento Daily Union,* July 21, 1862.

9. For discussion of the Monroe Doctrine see Jay Sexton, *The Monroe Doctrine: Empire and Nation in Nineteenth-Century America* (New York: Hill and Wang, 2011).

10. Kenneth M. Stampp, *The Era of Reconstruction, 1865–1877* (New York: Alfred A. Knopf, 1965).

11. In recent years, historians have become more attentive to the international elements of Reconstruction. See Jay Sexton, "Toward a Synthesis of Foreign Relations in the Civil War Era, 1848–1877," *American Nineteenth Century History* 5 (Autumn 2004): 50–73; Mark M. Smith, "The Past as a Foreign Country: Reconstruction, Inside and Out," in *Reconstructions: New Perspectives on the Postbellum United States,* ed. Thomas J. Brown (New York: Oxford University Press, 2006), 117–40; Mark Wahlgren Summers, *The Ordeal of the Reunion: A New History of Reconstruction* (Chapel Hill: University of North Carolina Press, 2014), especially chapter 9; Andrew Zimmerman, "Reconstruction: Transnational History," in *Interpreting American History: Reconstruction,* ed. John David Smith (Kent, OH: Kent State University Press, 2016): 171–96; and David Prior, ed. *Reconstruction in a Globalizing World* (New York: Fordham University Press, 2018).

12. Hans L. Trefousse, *Andrew Johnson: A Biography* (New York: W. W. Norton, 1989), 261. Paul Bergeron, *Andrew Johnson's Civil War and Reconstruction* (Knoxville: University of Tennessee Press, 2011) spends little time discussing foreign policy. Annette Gordon-Reed argues, "Seward was firmly at the helm on matters of foreign policy." Gordon-Reed, *Andrew Johnson* (New York: Henry Holt, 2011), 107. This interpretation ignores the other actors who helped determine US foreign policy.

13. General William S. Rosecrans and Speaker of the House of Representatives Schuyler Colfax did not want war either. See "Visit of General Rosecrans to the Legislature," *Salem Register,* May 15, 1865, and "Speaker Colfax on 'The Next War,'" *Springfield Weekly Republican,* September 2, 1865.

14. Francis Preston Blair Sr. to Andrew Johnson, August 1, 1865, *Papers of Andrew Johnson,* vol. 8, *May–August 1865,* ed. Paul H. Bergeron (Knoxville: University of Tennessee Press, 1989), 8:523.

15. This interpretation neglects important comments from contemporaries. Horace Maynard, for instance, wrote, "Mr. Blair's late speech at Hagerstown has been published here [Cincinnati], & it is thought by some to be a reflex of your views on the Mexican Question." Horace Maynard to Andrew Johnson, July 18, 1865, *Papers of Andrew Johnson,* 8:430. The editors of the volume observe that Mont-

gomery Blair attacked "American spinelessness" and believed the United States should do more to aid Mexico (8:431n4). Far from being subservient to Seward's policy, many of Johnson's contemporaries thought his was diametrically opposed. See also Thomas D. Schoonover, ed., *Mexican Lobby: Matías Romero in Washington, 1861–1867* (Lexington: University Press of Kentucky, 2014), 98.

16. "I cannot get any other letter from Col. [Sprar?] now as he has gone to Mexico + will not be back for some months + very likely not at all." J. Frank Cumming to J. A. J. Creswell, August 23, 1865, John A. J. Creswell Papers, vol. 15, Manuscript Division, Library of Congress (hereafter JAJC Papers, LOC).

17. See Schoonover, *Dollars over Dominion,* and Evan C. Rothera, "Civil Wars and Reconstructions in America: The United States, Mexico, and Argentina, 1860–1880" (PhD diss., Pennsylvania State University, 2017).

18. "Nathan C. Brooks coined the term 'sister republics' following the Mexican-American War in an attempt to justify the US incursion into Mexico." Tatiana Seijas and Jake Frederick, *Spanish Dollars and Sister Republics: The Money That Made Mexico and the United States* (Lanham, MD: Rowman and Littlefield, 2017), 156. In fact, as Caitlin Fitz illustrates, this language sprang up decades earlier. See Caitlin Fitz, *Our Sister Republics: The United States in an Age of American Revolutions* (New York: W. W. Norton, 2016).

19. See Gerald E. Linderman, *Embattled Courage: The Experience of Combat in the American Civil War* (New York: Free Press, 1987), and David W. Blight, *Race and Reunion: The Civil War in American Memory* (Cambridge, MA: Harvard University Press, 2001). For challenges to the hibernation thesis see Brian Matthew Jordan, *Marching Home: Union Veterans and Their Unending Civil War* (New York: Liveright, 2014), and Brian Matthew Jordan, "The Hibernation That Wasn't: Rethinking Union Veterans Immediately after the Civil War," *Journal of the Civil War Era* 5, no. 4 (December 2015): 484–503.

20. Robert Emmett Curran, ed., *John Dooley's Civil War: An Irish American's Journey in the First Virginia Infantry Regiment* (Knoxville: University of Tennessee Press, 2012), 326.

21. Diary entry, November 23, 1865, William E. Ardrey Papers, 1861–1907, DC 001, Davidson College Archives and Special Collections, Davidson, NC.

22. Journal entry, May 6, 1865, Mary Elizabeth Mitchell Journal, #1917-z, Southern Historical Collection, Wilson Library, University of North Carolina at Chapel Hill.

23. See John N. Edwards, *Shelby's Expedition to Mexico: An Unwritten Leaf of the War* (Kansas City: Kansas City Times, 1872); Alexander Watkins Terrell, *From Texas to Mexico and the Court of Maximilian in 1865* (Dallas: Book Club of Texas, 1933); Vincent H. Cassidy and Amos E. Simpson, *Henry Watkins Allen of Louisiana* (Baton Rouge: Louisiana State University Press, 1964); Edwin Adams Davis, *Fallen Guidon: The Saga of Confederate General Jo Shelby's March to Mexico* (College Station: Texas A&M University Press, 1995); Daniel O'Flaherty, *General Jo Shelby: Undefeated Rebel* (Chapel Hill: University of North Carolina Press, 2000); Lewis L. Gould, *Alexander Watkins Terrell: Civil War Soldier, Texas Lawmaker, American Diplomat* (Austin: University of Texas Press, 2004); Deryl Sellmeyer, *Jo Shelby's Iron Brigade* (Gretna, LA: Pelican, 2007); and Anthony Arthur, *General Jo Shelby's March* (New York: Random House, 2010).

24. Andrew F. Rolle, *The Lost Cause: The Confederate Exodus to Mexico* (Norman: University of Oklahoma Press, 1965); Hanna and Hanna, *Napoleon III and Mexico;* Todd W. Wahlstrom, *The Southern Exodus to Mexico: Migration across the Borderlands after the American Civil War* (Lincoln: University of Nebraska Press, 2015).

25. J. E. Harrison to Gordon Granger, June 21, 1865, Carter-Harrison Family Papers, Accession #316, box 1, folder 21, Texas Collection, Baylor University.

26. To be fair, Anthony Arthur noted that Shelby wanted to fight for Juárez. His men, however, voted to seek shelter with Maximilian. See Arthur, *General Jo Shelby's March.*

27. Thomas Alexander Hamilton to Hamilton Yancey, March 10, 1866, in Benjamin C. Yancey Papers, #2594, Southern Historical Collection, Wilson Library, University of North Carolina at Chapel Hill.

28. George C. Rable, *Damn Yankees! Demonization and Defiance in the Confederate South* (Baton Rouge: Louisiana State University Press, 2015), analyzes the many ways white southerners demonized their opponents. Rable contends that this fierce hatred prolonged the war. Perhaps it also made some rebels unwilling to face life under their hated enemy and more likely to flee to foreign countries.

29. Francis Preston Blair Sr., Address to Jefferson Davis, January 12, 1865, AL Papers, LOC.

30. Romero cultivated the Blairs because of their connections. His goal, however, was a free Mexico, not one run by Jefferson Davis.

31. Francis Preston Blair Sr. to AL, February 8, 1865, AL Papers, LOC. William A. Blair considered Francis Preston Blair's a "dubious solution" that Lincoln "quickly shoved aside." William A. Blair, "Finding the End of America's Civil War," *American Historical Review* 120 (December 2015): 1758, 1759. Several weeks later Blair performed an amazing volte-face and suggested Garibaldi should go to Mexico and lead the Liberals. See Francis Preston Blair Sr., to AL, February 22, 1865, AL Papers, LOC.

32. Ulysses S. Grant to Andrew Johnson, June 19, 1865, in *Papers of Andrew Johnson,* 8:257.

33. As of the writing of this letter, General Stand Watie had not yet surrendered.

34. Ulysses S. Grant to Andrew Johnson, July 15, 1865, in *Papers of Andrew Johnson,* 8:410. Governor William G. Brownlow of Tennessee agreed with Grant. See "Gov Brownlow on the Negro," *Springfield (MA) Weekly Republican,* October 14, 1865.

35. The only full-length biography of Romero is Harry Bernstein, *Matías Romero, 1837–1898* (Mexico: Fondo de Cultura Económica, 1973). Romero needs a new full-length biography.

36. In 1865 alone, Romero lobbied Andrew Johnson, William H. Seward, Ulysses S. Grant, William T. Sherman, John Schofield, John Conness, Thaddeus Stevens, Elihu Washburne, Samuel S. Cox, Godlove Orth, Jacob Howard, Robert C. Schenck, Nathaniel Banks, Schuyler Colfax, Zachariah Chandler, Benjamin F. Wade, James McDougall, John Logan, James Beekman, Thurlow Weed, James Gordon Bennett, Montgomery Blair, William Dennison, James Speed, Philip H. Sheridan, and Francis Preston Blair Sr. See Schoonover, *Mexican Lobby,* 50–113.

37. Schoonover estimates Romero wrote five hundred to seven hundred dispatches each year totaling more than a million words! Schoonover, *Mexican Lobby,* x.

38. Schoonover, *Mexican Lobby,* 100.

39. Schofield believed when he composed his memoirs that "upon this subject there appeared to be no division of sentiment among the people of the United States. Certainly there was none among the responsible American statesmen of that time. It was their unanimous voice that the French intervention in Mexico must be speedily terminated; but there was naturally some division of opinion respecting the means by which this should be effected." John M. Schofield, *Forty-Six Years in the Army* (New York: Century, 1897), 378.

40. Schoonover, *Mexican Lobby,* 102.

41. Ibid., 103.

42. Ibid., 103.

43. See Schofield, *Forty-Six Years in the Army*, 378–93, and Donald B. Connelly, *John M. Schofield and the Politics of Generalship* (Chapel Hill: University of North Carolina Press, 2006), 182–86.

44. Joseph E. Chance, *José María de Jesús Carvajal: The Life and Times of a Mexican Revolutionary* (San Antonio: Trinity University Press, 2006), explores Carvajal and Wallace's attempts to purchase arms for Mexico. The information I present here expands the picture.

45. This commission entitled Wallace to "all the authorities, rights, privileges, and emoluments, incident to such a commission, according to the laws and Customs of the Mexican service." José M. J. Carvajal to Lew Wallace, April 26, 1865, box 1, folder 3, Oliver P. Morton Papers, 1855–1909, L113, Manuscript Section, Indiana Division, Indiana State Library (hereafter Morton Papers).

46. Ibid. Wallace sent copies of his correspondence with Carvajal to Senator Morton in 1868 when he sought compensation from Mexico.

47. Lew Wallace to General J. M. J. Carvajal, April 27, 1865, box 1, folder 3, Morton Papers.

48. José M. J. Carvajal to Lew Wallace, April 29, 1865, box 1, folder 3, Morton Papers.

49. Lew Wallace to General [Carvajal], April 30, 1865, box 1, folder 3, Morton Papers. Wallace's tenure in Mexico proved unpleasant. He did not command troops and was horrified by a pronunciamiento against Carvajal. Chance, *José María de Jesús Carvajal*. Wallace spent years dunning the Mexican government for compensation. See the letters between Romero and Carvajal, box 1, folder 3, Morton Papers.

50. Grant believed Wallace performed poorly at the battle of Shiloh. He told Romero "failure and discredit" marked Wallace's endeavors. Schoonover, *Mexican Lobby*, 100. Romero and Carvajal worked together to sell bonds. See "New Mexican Scheme," *World*, October 23, 1865.

51. This would have violated the terms of Wallace and Carvajal's agreement.

52. Admittedly, their motives varied. Wallace, for example, seemed more concerned about the money.

53. R. H. Milroy to Andrew Johnson, May 8, 1865, reel 14, Andrew Johnson Papers, LOC.

54. See Edward Lee Plumb (hereafter ELP) to My Dear Romero, May 10, 1865, vol. 6, Edward Lee Plumb Papers, 1825–1903, Manuscript Division, Library of Congress (hereafter Plumb Papers, LOC) for Plumb facilitating arms sales to Mexico.

55. ELP to Charles Sumner (hereafter CS), January 26, 1864, vol. 6, Plumb Papers, LOC.

56. ELP to N. P. Banks and CS, April 4, 1866, vol. 7, Plumb Papers, LOC. Banks, it is worth noting, was a veteran who served in both the eastern and western theaters of the US Civil War. His Red River expedition of 1864, which failed, was designed to, in part, show the flag to Maximilian.

57. *Dinner to Señor Matías Romero, Envoy Extraordinary and Minister Plenipotentiary from Mexico, on the 29th of March, 1864* (New York, 1866), 19. See also *Banquet to Señor Matias Romero, Envoy Extraordinary and Minister Plenipotentiary from Mexico to the United States, by the Citizens of New York. October 2, 1867* (New York: Hosford and Sons, 1867).

58. "The Reception of George Thompson," *Lowell (MA) Daily Citizen and News*, March 3, 1864. See also "Presentation of a Sword to General Hooker at the Union League Club," *Sacramento Daily Union*, June 28, 1865.

59. Juárez replied, "My government will take peculiar care to cultivate with diligent assiduity the cordial and frank relations which now happily bind the two Republics." "Further from Mexico," *Daily*

Picayune (New Orleans), June 13, 1861. Corwin's had been one of the loudest voices opposing the US war with Mexico.

60. Joseph C. Breckinridge to Robert J. Breckinridge, November 27, 1865, box 244, Breckinridge Family Papers, 1752–1965, Manuscript Division, Library of Congress.

61. See "A Steam Line of Guaymas," *Daily Evening Bulletin* (Philadelphia), April 10, 1861, and "Communication with Guaymas," *Sacramento Daily Union,* April 13, 1861. One of California's senators, James McDougall, detested the French presence in Mexico and worked with Romero. See Schoonover, *Mexican Lobby.*

62. "Dangers on the Isthmus of Panama," *New York Herald,* June 21, 1861.

63. "The Celebration of Washington's Day," *Springfield Republican,* March 1, 1862.

64. "Mr. Corwin's Return to the United States," *World,* May 27, 1864.

65. "A Desperate Hope," *Cleveland Daily Plain Dealer,* June 23, 1864. "Shoddy" referred to poorly manufactured supplies for the army and suggested all Republicans were corrupt war profiteers.

66. "The party, that acquiesced in French occupation of a sister Republic, and humbly, through Mr. Dayton in Paris, apologised to the Emperor, for the indignation, naturally, and mainly made by Democrats expressed to the floor of Congress, throws the blame upon those who have nothing to do with the control of the government." "The Boot on the Wrong Foot," *Wisconsin Daily Patriot,* October 22, 1864. For Republicans using Maximilian to attack copperheads see "Union Meeting in Sidney," *Cincinnati Daily Commercial,* August 1, 1863.

67. "The Arrival of Napoleon's Puppet," *Sacramento Daily Union,* July 11, 1864.

68. For various examples see "The Republic of Mexico," *Coos Republican,* November 21, 1865; "Pulpit Gems," *Daily Age,* December 9, 1865; and "The French-Mexican Question," *Savannah National Republican,* March 27, 1866.

69. "The United States and Mexico," *Evening Post,* July 27, 1865. See also "The Monroe Doctrine," *World,* July 13, 1865, and "The 'Signs,'" *Pittsfield Sun,* July 20, 1865, for anti-French speeches by Montgomery Blair and James Harlan.

70. "From Mexico," *Hartford Daily Courant,* January 7, 1863.

71. "Last Night's Report," *Janesville Daily Gazette,* July 28, 1863. See also "Important from Mexico," *Milwaukee Daily Sentinel,* July 29, 1863; "The Empire in Mexico," *New York Herald,* July 29, 1863; and "Important from Mexico," *Wisconsin Daily Patriot,* July 30, 1863.

72. "Interesting from Mexico," *Sacramento Daily Union,* August 8, 1863. See also "Later and Important News from Mexico," *Daily Evening Bulletin* (Philadelphia), August 7, 1863.

73. "The Monroe Doctrine," *Daily True Delta,* June 26, 1864. See also *Arguments in Favor of the Enforcement of the Monroe Doctrine, Contained in His Annual Message of 1823; And its application to our relations with our Sister Republic of Mexico, in 1864* (New Orleans: Era Book and Job Office, 1864), a series of essays on the Monroe Doctrine dedicated to Bordon.

74. "Mexico was underrepresented in the popular excitement in part because its rural and grassroots insurgency peaked in the early 1810s, when U.S. onlookers were distracted by their second war with Britain, and because when Mexico finally declared independence in the early 1820s, it did so as a monarchy." Fitz, *Our Sister Republics,* 15.

75. This language came back into vogue during the War of the Reform, but it really flourished during the post-1860 period.

76. See Paul Foos, *A Short, Offhand, Killing Affair: Soldiers and Social Conflict during the Mexican-*

American War (Chapel Hill: University of North Carolina Press, 2002); Amy S. Greenberg, *A Wicked War: Polk, Clay, Lincoln, and the 1846 U.S. Invasion of Mexico* (New York: Random House, 2012); and Peter Guardino, *The Dead March: A History of the Mexican-American War* (Cambridge, MA: Harvard University Press, 2017).

77. See "New York Items," *Providence Evening Press,* November 16, 1865, and "By Telegraph," *Argus,* November 17, 1865

78. Schoonover, *Mexican Lobby,* 100.

79. "Mexico," *Albany Evening Journal,* November 18, 1865. "Generals, as expressed emphatically by Sheridan, Logan, and others, all indicate that it should not be the policy of the U.S. to permit a monarchy supported by foreign arms to exist on the ruins of a sister Republic." "About Mexico," *New Mexico Press,* November 21, 1865.

80. ELP to CS, April 23, 1867, vol. 7, Plumb Papers, LOC.

81. J. E. P. Doyle to Andrew Johnson, October 12, 1867, reel 29, Andrew Johnson Papers, LOC.

82. See Robert E. May, *The Southern Dream of a Caribbean Empire* (Baton Rouge: Louisiana State University Press, 1973); Robert E. May, *Manifest Destiny's Underworld: Filibustering in Antebellum America* (Chapel Hill: University of North Carolina Press, 2002); and Tom Chaffin, *Fatal Glory: Narciso López and the First Clandestine U.S. War against Cuba* (1996; repr., Baton Rouge: Louisiana State University Press, 2003).

83. Jerry Thompson, *Cortina: Defending the Mexican Name in Texas* (College Station: Texas A&M University Press, 2007), 167. Thompson comments that recruits included "army deserters, outlaws, adventurers from Galveston, and border riffraff" (167).

84. Thompson, *Cortina,* 152. "It is said that several of those prisoners [from Cortina's band] are natives of the United States." Franklin Chase (hereafter FC) to WHS, May 8, 1866, reel 4, vol. 8, Despatches from U.S. Consuls in Tampico. See also Marquis de Lafayette Lane to WHS, November 2, 1865, reel 9, vol. 9, Despatches from U.S. Consuls in Veracruz, for a report that US deserters fought with Cortina.

85. See Robert Ryal Miller, *Arms across the Border: United States Aid to Juárez during the French Intervention in Mexico* (Philadelphia: American Philosophical Society, 1973).

86. J. Frank Cumming to John A. J. Creswell, February 7, 1864, vol. 5, JAJC Papers, LOC.

87. FC to WHS, April 27, 1864, reel 4, vol. 7, Despatches from U.S. Consuls in Tampico.

88. For rumors of Carvajal recruiting Texans see FC to Frederick W. Seward (hereafter FWS), April 18, 1865, reel 4, vol. 8, Despatches from U.S. Consuls in Tampico.

89. Lucius Avery to WHS, October 26, 1865, reel 3, vol. 8, Despatches from U.S. Consuls in Matamoros. For a different picture see William A. Dobak, *Freedom by the Sword: The U.S. Colored Troops, 1862–1867* (Washington, DC: Center for Military History, 2011), 451. See also "From the Rio Grande," *New-York Daily Tribune,* September 12, 1865.

90. Schoonover, *Mexican Lobby,* 97–98. Grant gave Mussey permission to leave the United States to serve in Mexico.

91. FC to FWS, July 2, 1866, reel 4, vol. 8, Despatches from U.S. Consuls in Tampico.

92. FBE to WHS, April 9, 1866, reel 1, vol. 1, Despatches from U.S. Consuls in La Paz.

93. FBE to WHS, May 1, 1866, and FBE to WHS, July 3, 1866, reel 1, vol. 1, Despatches from U.S. Consuls in La Paz.

94. FBE to WHS, October 29, 1866, reel 1, vol. 1, Despatches from U.S. Consuls in La Paz.

95. "An Old Timer," *Tombstone Prospector,* December 1, 1890.

96. "Samuel Brannan in Mexico," *Evening Bulletin,* August 23, 1880.

97. A. Willard to J. C. B. Davis, March 16, 1870, reel 2, vol. 2, Despatches from U.S. Consuls in Guaymas.

98. Lewis S. Ely to WHS, August 22, 1864, reel 3, vol. 5, Despatches from U.S. Consuls in Acapulco. Spencer served as US consul in Paris in the late 1850s. See *Executive Documents Printed by Order of the House of Representatives during the Second Session of the Thirty-Sixth Congress, 1860–'61* (Washington, DC: Government Printing Office, 1861), 9:42.

99. See Don E. Alberts, *The Battle of Glorieta: Union Victory in the West* (College Station: Texas A&M University Press, 1998), 169.

100. The United States prosecuted filibusterers under the Neutrality Act. "Thousands of additional Americans would have filibustered had it not been for developments beyond their control, including federal efforts to enforce the Neutrality Act." May, *Manifest Destiny's Underworld,* 52.

101. Trefousse, *Andrew Johnson,* 261.

102. Gregory P. Downs, *After Appomattox: Military Occupation and the Ends of War* (Cambridge, MA: Harvard University Press, 2015), 28.

Civil War Veteran Colonies
on the Western Frontier

KURT HACKEMER

ON SEPTEMBER 16, 1861, Albert Freeman Waugh left the comfortable civilian world of Sheboygan Falls, Wisconsin, behind and enlisted in Company H of the 1st Wisconsin Volunteer Infantry regiment. Private Waugh was shot through the knee at Perryville, spent six months recovering in a hospital, and returned to Sheboygan Falls in 1863 crippled for life. Even though he had been gone barely two years, he no longer felt at ease in his hometown. After several years of trying to reclaim his old life, he gave up. In 1872, he "took by force" his family and moved to Kansas, claiming that the "stumps and stones" in Wisconsin made farming impossible, an excuse that his son described decades later as "perfectly invalid at the time it was given."[1]

Over his wife's objections, Waugh relocated the family near the brand-new town of King City, also known as the Ashtabula Soldier's Colony. The colony was organized in Ashtabula, Ohio, in 1871 for Union army veterans and their families. The idea of "colonies" was not a new or novel concept. Dozens sprang up across Kansas in the 1870s organized around religion, geography, or country of origin, with the idea of providing mutual support in an uncertain environment. Similar colonies appeared in western Minnesota, the Dakotas, Colorado, and Nebraska, but soldier colonies catering to Union veterans were exceedingly rare, with less than ten dotted across the northern Great Plains. Soldier colonies, like other colonies, were an efficient and cost-effective mechanism for organizing and relocating veterans to the frontier after the US Civil War. But they were far more than that. A significant percentage who migrated west had been exposed to high-trauma combat during the war, and many used the anonymity and newness of the frontier to reintegrate into society on their own terms.[2]

Albert Waugh needed the solitude and lack of established social structure on the frontier to put his life back together. Although he served as a judge, county commissioner, and self-taught doctor, he did so quietly, always refusing "to make speeches or enter any public forum." Waugh's son later ascribed the move to a "joy of adventure" and "the desire to think one's own thoughts and determine one's own acts."[3] But the most important factor was the way the war annexed his life. As his son Frank recalled,

I know now that those days of grand excitement with the army, those wild forays into roadside groceries and farmyard smokehouses, those sleepless nights on the ground with eyes and heart open to the stars, those exhilarating marches through strange towns and over unfamiliar hills, and especially those hours of battle when all the desirable things of this world are relinquished and life itself staked against the ultimate gain of personal integrity—I know now that in these experiences all former things had passed away, and that there had arisen in their place an imperious demand for a new life—a life of new objectives and new sanctions. Such a life could not be projected upon the old background. It tore itself free from the old environment and began again upon the virgin sheet of the untouched Kansas prairie.[4]

The war changed Albert Waugh, causing "the breaking up of life to its very depths," and moving to Kansas became a crucial piece of his rehabilitation. Frank Waugh very deliberately contrasted "the explosives which wrecked the past for my father" with "the quiet activities in which he rebuilt his new life in Kansas," declaring the latter to be far more significant than the former. In the story Frank told about "one typical man—a typical soldier of the civil war," he found "a type endlessly reproduced" not only in the Civil War but also in the veterans he knew from the First World War. It was the First World War that led Frank to better understand Albert's journey: "how in the holocaust of war the past was utterly consumed and its ashes abandoned," and then "how in a new land a new life was framed."[5] That same story occurred repeatedly in the veteran colonies.

The war was disruptive, taking soldiers away from family and social networks for extended periods of time. When they returned home, they often found that two parallel changes had occurred, both of which made reintegration into civilian life difficult. First, they learned that life at home had progressed without them. The economic, social, and political events that defined people and their relationships with each other had continued unabated, and no amount of letter writing nor the occasional furlough could prevent the persistent feeling of disconnection. The new veterans lamented lost economic opportunities, unfulfilled relationships, missed community celebrations, lack of engagement with local politics, and aging children and parents. Somehow, they would have to find their way in this familiar but changed world.[6]

Second, veterans learned that the war altered the social norms that had defined them as civilians. As soldiers, they ranged over vast distances, interacting with individuals and cultures quite different than what they had known. They engaged in sanctioned theft and destruction of property as foragers, grew used to a more rough-and-tumble existence in their all-male world, and might engage in the organized killing of fellow human beings. Returning home to a civilian population that welcomed them back but expected minimal disruption could be an overwhelming challenge. Many succeeded in that reintegration, but many did not. Those who did not often entered a period described by historian Gerald Linderman as "hibernation" because they found the gulf between civilian and veteran comprehension of the war irreconcilable. It was only in the 1880s, when veterans accepted a less realistic public version of their wartime experiences, that a shared national dialog about the war emerged.[7]

Combat veterans struggled to reconcile the adrenaline associated with battle with the carnage and destruction they witnessed, and many found themselves dealing with postwar trauma. The concept had not yet been described medically, making it all but impossible for historians to assign the "trauma" label to specific veterans using contemporary records. At the same time, the scale and ferocity of Civil War combat makes it impossible to deny that soldiers experienced it. While symptoms of trauma cannot be assigned to specific veterans, markers can be identified that indicate the likelihood that specific groups of soldiers had wartime experiences that might induce trauma.[8]

One such marker stands out for its prevalence in the context of westward migration in general and with veteran colonies in particular: William Fox's Three Hundred Fighting Regiments that experienced the war's most brutal fighting. Fox collected casualty statistics for every Union regiment, a process that took him decades. Implicit in Fox's identification of the Three Hundred Fighting Regiments was a connection between casualties and trauma. "In the long run," he suggested, "active service brings its many scars; where the musketry was the hottest, the dead lay thickest; and there is no better way to find the fighting regiments than to follow up the bloody trail which marked their brave advance."[9] Context for the Three Hundred Fighting Regiments is provided by Frederick H. Dyer, who spent the postwar years cataloging all 3,559 Union army units of approximately regimental size. Combining the information collected by Fox and Dyer suggests that the Three Hundred Fighting Regiments made up approximately 8.4 percent of all Union army units, providing a useful benchmark against which to compare the extent to which veterans who migrated to the frontier and especially veterans who settled in soldier colonies had been exposed to wartime trauma.[10]

As veterans returned home, many successfully reintegrated back into civilian life, but many could not. Some withdrew within themselves and lived distant lives even as they remained with their families. Others turned to the bottle seeking release, and the stereotype of the alcoholic veteran became familiar across the North. Many could not figure out how to live with their families and found refuge in newly established soldiers' homes or became homeless. Still others began acting irrationally and erratically, and desperate relatives committed them to asylums. Tensions between veterans and civilians mounted, and the homecoming celebrations from the early summer of 1865 were soon replaced with concerns that veterans might represent a public menace.[11]

Many veterans craved a new start where they could rebuild their lives on their own terms. Like Albert Waugh, they wanted "to think one's own thoughts and determine one's own acts." A substantial number headed to the frontier, where a recent analysis of almost six thousand veterans who migrated to the Dakota Territory reveals a much higher likelihood of exposure to wartime trauma. Although the Three Hundred Fighting Regiments comprised approximately 8.4 percent of the Union army, members of those regiments made up 21.4 percent of the veterans in the southern half of the Dakota Territory. The number of wounded veterans in the Dakota Territory confirms that these men were more likely to have encountered wartime trauma. Veterans of the Three Hundred Fighting Regiments were twice as likely to have been wounded as veterans from other units who settled in the Dakota Territory. Strikingly, veterans from all units in the Dakota Territory were twice as likely to have been wounded as Union army veterans in general. This suggests a strong correlation between soldiers who experienced trauma and veterans who migrated to the frontier.[12]

Moving west seemed relatively straightforward. The Homestead Act of 1862 theoretically opened a billion acres of government land to settlement. Interested parties found a quarter section of available land, paid a nominal filing fee to establish a temporary claim, and had to establish residency. After six months, the homesteader could either buy the claim or live on the claim for five years and improve it with a dwelling and cultivation. At that point, the homesteader would own the land. However, it was rarely that simple. It took a fair amount of capital to set up a viable farm, and new settlers hoped for favorable conditions so they could make it to the second year. As Gilbert Fite notes, "There were thousands whose dreams were shattered by the awful realities which successful farmers and the optimistic promoters failed to mention." Still, it seemed worth the risk, for settlers migrating to the Great Plains in the 1860s and 1870s accumulated wealth at rates that exceeded other agricultural areas in the rest of the northern United States.[13]

Veterans had some advantages over the general population when moving west. In 1871, Congress modified the Homestead Act to allow Union veterans to count each year of Civil War service toward the law's five-year residency requirement. Military service could be beneficial in other ways, especially for those who had been wounded or disabled during the war and received federal pensions. In the case of the Dakota Territory, 24 percent of all veterans were on the pension rolls in 1885, significantly higher than the 6.5 percent of all veterans who received a pension. Those monthly payments provided guaranteed income during a transition that might otherwise be fraught with economic uncertainty. As the executive secretary of the United States Sanitary Commission opined in 1865, the federal government should provide suitably large pensions so that veterans be "suffered to go where they please."[14]

The advantages of reduced filing times under the modified Homestead Act and access to pension funds were still not enough to entice many veterans. The northern plains could be a harsh and unforgiving place, devoid of the social contact and institutions that had defined their lives up to that point. The answer for some was to move west with like-minded souls and collectively settle in a colony, a mechanism widely used by other settlers sharing some common interest, religious affiliation, or ethnic background.[15]

During the 1870s and 1880s, colonies sprang up across the northern plains. The Dakota Territory, Kansas, and Nebraska vigorously advertised for settlers using immigration boards that often cooperated with the railroads. Boosters like George Batchelder assured potential settlers that "the man of small means can purchase excellent lands cheap, and by a judicious investment of a small capital, he will become rich in a few years." Others more explicitly suggested the plains as the perfect location for colonies, noting, "It will be found on examination that a very large proportion of new towns and new settlements, perhaps the vast majority of those in the new States, have been started" by cooperative associations. These efforts worked. Ellis County, Kansas, for example, became home to twenty-four colonies of various types during the 1870s; a 1906 examination of settlement patterns in the state observed, "Foreigners have peopled Kansas by groups and colonies rather than as individuals acting independently." Migrants arrived in ever-increasing numbers, facilitated in large part by the railroads, which offered package deals of land and transportation to colonies. This was no small thing at a time when railway tickets alone for a family of five heading west could cost the equivalent of six months' wages.[16]

The advertising, promotion, and boosterism that appealed to so many religious organizations and ethnic groups found a similarly receptive audience among veterans. A recent study suggests they had higher geographic mobility than nonveterans and were already more likely than the rest of the population to move west, attributing their wanderlust to the fact that the war had already taught them to leave home. Whether a result of wanderlust or the fact that so many veterans had difficulty readjusting to their home communities after the war, the frontier called. In early 1870, a group of disabled veterans from Dayton, Ohio, proposed "to form an agricultural colony in the west" consisting of twenty-five otherwise able-bodied men who had each lost either an arm or a leg. An important component of their plan was that each veteran would be drawing a fifteen-dollar monthly pension, which would provide the capital necessary for their venture. This colony, a newspaper writer suggested, would be better than "living an aimless life in an asylum."[17]

Although a wholly insufficient inducement for many blue-coated ex-soldiers, the 1871 amendment made to the Homestead Act nonetheless encouraged other cohorts of Union veterans to create four of the first viable soldier colonies on the Plains. Observers speculated that "under its provisions colonies of soldiers will be formed to go out and settle in the Territories and new States," and the Grand Army of the Republic (GAR) advised its various posts that "preparations to take advantage of the act should be commenced immediately." It wanted colonies to be coordinated through the GAR "in order to secure unity of action and mutual aid and support," with an optimistic goal "to organize in the Territories a soldiers' state." Whether or not they were affiliated with the GAR, veterans across the North began meeting, which led to an initial wave of colonies in Minnesota, Nebraska, and Kansas.[18]

In Sidney, Ohio, for example, organizers elected officers and announced that "soldiers from all parts of Ohio will be invited to become members." They began planning for a colony of at least one thousand veterans that would go west sometime the following summer and proposed "to carry the project out on a gigantic scale."[19] Similarly ambitious meetings took place in Massachusetts and Pennsylvania. Veterans in places like Warren, Ohio, watched communities create organizing committees, identify potential settlers, and collect dues that would fund exploratory parties looking for colony sites, and decided that they, too, were "desirous that initiatory steps be taken toward the formation of a society of this kind, and thus avail themselves of the benefits of this act."[20]

Several such efforts failed to gain momentum. Barely one week after an initial meeting held in Upper Sandusky, Ohio, organizers suggested that representatives be sent to the nearby town of Tiffin to discuss merging their efforts. In Tiffin, twenty families expressed strong interest in setting up a colony, "and many more have expressed their intention to unite," which must have been encouraging to the organizers in Upper Sandusky. Indeed, by early June, the *Tiffin Tribune* reported that a locating committee had been sent to Kansas to identify potential colony sites and that they would make a report to potential colonists. Alas, it was not to be. The effort stalled, with "the object in view having failed of accomplishment." Those who had paid dues were advised that the organization had disbanded and to stop at the Wyandot County Bank to get a refund.[21]

Other efforts were more successful, most notably in Ashtabula, Ohio. Organizers there did not exclude nonveterans from joining the venture, a strategy also adopted by other successful veteran colonies. "Any person ... whether citizen, or Soldier" could pay two dollars to join the association, entitling them to collective benefits like negotiated rail rates or land selection. The first meeting of the Ashtabula County Soldiers' Free Homestead Colony drew over three hundred interested people. One of its selling points was an organizational structure and approval process designed to prevent land speculation, ensuring fair land prices for all involved. This approach resonated well with potential colonists, and the colony soon had membership requests from Ohio and neighboring states, which led to the colony directors changing the name to the

Soldiers' and Citizens Mutual Benefit Free Homestead Colony. They reasoned that "by thus uniting [we] will have good society and soon secure to ourselves all the advantages of older countries of schools, churches, &c, [and] also avoid the trials and privations of frontier life alone." This combination of veterans and nonveterans created a critical mass that led to a successful colonization effort in Kansas.[22]

The connection between potential colonies and railroads was evident from the beginning. The Ashtabula colonists, for example, planned that "each member, and family shall be entitled to first class passage over all Railroads from which the Directors may secure special rates." Similarly, the New England Military and Naval Bureau of Migration worked closely with the Northern Pacific Railroad to facilitate migration. Colonies that proposed to either seek homesteads on public land or purchase land directly from the railroads received special rates.[23] The railroads did their part and vigorously advertised in eastern newspapers about opportunities available to veterans. The Northern Pacific Railroad, for example, let readers know that its commissioner of immigration was working closely with New England Bureau of Migration to create veteran colonies. The Union Pacific Railroad touted "Cheap Farms! Free Homes!" in the "best farming and mineral land in America" through its land commissioner, with a specific appeal to veterans. Those purchasing land directly from the railroad received free passes from the East. The ads ran widely in 1872 but tailed off in 1873, perhaps in response to the nationwide depression that began that year.[24]

The Ashtabula colony went out of its way to assure participants the organizers did not materially benefit from the colony, but this was not the case elsewhere. For example, Colonel Henry Wilson, one of the organizers of the Ohio Soldiers' and Citizens' Colony that settled in Colony, Kansas, signed a contract that resulted in a series of kickbacks from the Leavenworth, Lawrence & Galveston Railroad. In return for guaranteeing sales of at least fifty quarter sections of land, Wilson received a 3 percent commission on all land sold. In addition, although the railroad sold land to colonists at a discount, buyers only received 5 percent of the reduction, while Wilson received the rest. Colonists received free or reduced transportation and land that made migration west feasible, but others profited even more.[25]

Furnished with free or reduced transportation, and with access to affordable land, veterans began heading west. In 1871 and 1872, four veteran colonies successfully took root in Gibbon, Nebraska; King City, Kansas; Detroit Lakes,

Minnesota; and Colony, Kansas. Members of the Soldiers' Free Homestead Colony who arrived in Gibbon in April 1871 probably had the most abrupt introduction to the northern plains. Colonists collected in Chicago and made their way to Omaha, where they boarded the train that took them to the colony site. The train left Omaha on April 6 at 6:00 p.m., which caused a rumor to circulate "that we were being taken on a night train because, if we saw the country in the day time we would desert before reaching the destination." When they arrived in Gibbon the following afternoon, they found nothing but a railroad section house and a siding on which the Union Pacific left some passenger cars and box cars to serve as temporary shelter. Just a week before, "a prairie fire had swept over the entire country leaving it black, bleak, desolate and uninviting." One colonist turned around and left, but the rest, about sixty-five families, stayed. An April blizzard roared in three days later and tested their resolve by piling snow "as high as the tops of the cars in which the colonists were staying." Nevertheless, no colonists left, and by April 18, sixty-one homestead claims had been filed with the nearest land office. This was done communally, with lots drawn to see who would have first choice of the surrounding land. By July 1872, almost 150 families, including both veterans and nonveterans, had found their way to the colony.[26]

The migrations to King City, Detroit Lakes, and Colony occurred in similar fashion, albeit with slightly less drama. The Ashtabula colonists arrived in King City in June 1871. Within one year of founding, King City contained twenty-five houses and several businesses, including two general stores, a brickyard, a lumberyard, two hotels, a blacksmith shop, and a farm machinery dealer. A post office and doctor's office quickly followed. However, in 1873, King City failed to become the county seat in a local election. The recently arrived colonists relocated both themselves and many of their buildings to the new county seat in McPherson, which was also home to a significant number of Civil War veterans who migrated to the area individually.[27]

The New England Military and Naval Bureau of Migration sent a delegation west in the spring of 1871 to look for a suitable colony site along the line of the Northern Pacific Railroad. The site they found, Detroit Lakes, was in western Minnesota close to the Dakota Territory border where "the soil, water, timber and scenery seemed everything that could be desired." The first families began arriving in the summer and fall of 1871, but the railroad was still forty miles away from the colony site, although it would reach Detroit Lakes by the end of the year. The bulk of the colonists arrived the following spring, with more following in 1873, until almost three hundred had made the journey. As in King City, homesteads and businesses were quickly established, and the local newspaper reported in the fall of 1872 that "to get a good claim . . . a soldier, or 'any other man,' will now have to go four or five miles from Detroit." Many of the original colonists had moved on by the 1880s, but the core of a successful community had been established.[28]

The Ohio Soldiers' Colony that settled in Colony in the spring of 1872 moved "in the midst of thickly settled communities" in eastern Kansas rather than the open frontier, but its experiences were roughly the same. The initial colony consisted of about one hundred people who quickly established homesteads, businesses, schools, and churches on all of the available railroad land. They were joined by a community of Dunkards, which likely increased their negotiating power with the Leavenworth, Lawrence & Galveston Railroad. Four years later, eighty-five inhabitants remained, described as "a class of good, energetic citizens."[29]

Between 1872 and 1878, enthusiasm for creating veteran colonies dwindled, likely as a result of the Panic of 1873 and its aftermath. Railroads certainly became less interested in potential colonies and stopped advertising in newspapers by 1878. However, the following decade saw the formation of six more veteran colonies in Kansas, Nebraska, Minnesota, and the Dakota Territory, at least three of which survive as permanent communities. Despite the lack of promotion, settlers still used the railroads to move west, sometimes with discounted fares, and either homesteaded or purchased land from other sellers.

This second wave of veteran colonies began with a January 1878 gathering in Chicago to organize a soldiers and sailors colony "to locate on government lands" in Trego County, Kansas. Like the earlier colonies, promoters welcomed both civilians and veterans, collected a modest membership fee, and sent a locating committee west to find suitable land. They identified their spot in western Kansas along the line of the Union Pacific Railroad and founded the town of Collyer. Members of the advance party erected "Colony House" next to the railroad to serve as temporary shelter for arriving settlers and provided a team and wagon to get them to their claims. An unclear title to the land forced the Chicago Colony, as it became known, to relocate a half mile away from the railroad, but a steady stream of colonists arrived in 1878, 1879, and 1880. Their staggered arrival occurred because of special congressional legislation "providing members of the Chicago soldiers' and citizens' colony, who make selections of homesteads in specified townships, shall be allowed two years after filing a declaratory statement within which to make entries," as long as "each person locating a homestead and filing his declaratory statement shall improve not less than five acres the second year from location." Potential colonists received encouragement from local boosters who nonetheless admitted, "Inconveniences, of course, are experienced, but with a hearty appetite and plenty of hope, we live in anticipation of happy days in a land of plenty." Those "inconveniences" caused the population to fluctuate when crops failed in the 1880s, with the population of original settlers falling to thirty-seven men, women, and children by 1888, but Collyer survived.[30]

As new counties in the Dakota Territory formed and opened for settlement in the 1880s, two more veteran colonies took root in the newly created towns of Gettysburg and Loyalton. Railroads played an important role by offering discounted passenger and freight rates. Unlike at most veteran colonies, the rail lines were still relatively distant from these town sites, but boosters were optimistic that the railroads would arrive soon. The Gettysburg colony, which advertised itself as "The Soldiers Home," first organized in Chicago in the spring of 1883. Approximately one hundred colonists made the initial trip west that spring. Confusion about property titles and competing claims resulted in the town site moving to adjoining land the following spring, but seven hundred settlers quickly occupied the surrounding countryside by fall. Organizers invited "all classes of business men" to join the veterans and successfully lobbied the Chicago and North Western Railroad to extend its line through the new community, and by 1887 the town alone boasted four hundred residents.[31] As Gettysburg established itself, a group of veterans near Royalton, Vermont, organized a colony of their own. The Vermont Colony met with various railroad representatives in early 1885 to identify a location "offering the best railroad facilities, best soil and other natural advantages" and negotiate bulk passenger and freight rates. They settled on a site in Edmunds County, which they christened Loyalton, and the first settlers arrived that same spring. A Vermont newspaper suggested this was a good thing, noting that "once settled in a brawling region, even this small colony of sturdy soldier-farmers could but spread abroad a law-abiding influence, and aid in subduing cowboyism and the soil together." By the end of May, 119 soldiers' claims had been filed, representing 350 immigrants. A much-coveted railroad line was operating by 1887 but was placed a mile from Loyalton. As a result, some residents moved to nearby towns or even returned to Vermont, but the majority stayed.[32]

There are three colonies in this time period about which little is known, two in Nebraska and one in Kansas. The Henderson Soldiers' Colony settled along the line of the Burlington and Missouri River Railroad in the spring of 1880 in Furnas County in southwestern Nebraska, where it founded the town of Garfield. One year later, forty-five families called the colony home, although the town had not developed much since settlement. A local store was set to open, and plans were made for a post office. No public building or school had yet been built, but the colonists were confident that "a few prosperous seasons will see us with both." The colony seems to have disappeared shortly thereafter, marked only by a cemetery.[33] The second Nebraska colony appeared three years later as a regional creation. Veterans who settled in Lincoln decided to jointly "take homesteads in the Niobrara country" in northwestern Nebraska, where they founded the town of Logan. The railroads were involved with the creation of Logan, but only to the extent that they provided discounted passenger and freight fares to the general area. Nearly three hundred migrants, primarily veterans, took up land and timber claims in what became a prosperous town.[34] The third colony was formed in 1886 in Colokan, Kansas, located in Greeley County on the Colorado-Kansas border on the line of the Denver, Memphis and Atlantic Railroad. Numbers appear to have been small relative to other veteran colonies, with only twenty charter members available when a GAR post was organized in 1888. The colony merged with a nearby United Presbyterian colony in 1887, but Colokan died out soon after when it failed to get a coveted rail depot. The town site was formally vacated by the Kansas legislature in 1897.[35]

The economic benefits of collective action clearly influenced veterans' decisions to migrate west, but another less obvious reason explains the appeal of colonies: processing wartime trauma. Modern studies of posttraumatic growth suggest some correlation between the severity of wartime trauma and the ability to recover from that trauma. One longitudinal study of modern veterans found that those "with heavy combat experience reported higher levels of emotional and behavior problems, but that over time, they became more resilient and less helpless than their light-combat and no-combat veteran peers." Indeed, a recent model of posttraumatic growth suggests that the sociocultural context in which veterans process trauma is critical to recovery, as are the reactions of those with whom they discuss traumatic events. Whether veterans consciously recognized it or not, these specialized colonies provided the context, comradeship, and common understanding they needed to process trauma.[36]

A study of 5,390 veterans in the Dakota Territory demonstrates that veterans who moved to the frontier were far more likely than veterans in general to have experienced wartime trauma, defined by their service in the Three Hundred Fighting Regiments (see Table 1). A sample of 359 veterans from seven of the veteran colonies reveals that exposure to trauma was even higher in these communities than on the frontier in general. In the Dakota Territory study, 21.4 percent of veterans linked to a specific unit served in the Three Hundred Fighting Regiments. In the seven veteran colonies, that percentage climbed to 30.6 percent, almost four times higher than the 8.4 percent of veterans identified nationally as having served in these units.[37]

As was the case with Albert Waugh, there are clues suggesting that some of these veterans had wartime trauma that needed to be processed. In Gibbon, Nebraska, most colonists "were veterans of the Civil War who found in this new life an answer to their restlessness." Those restless veterans included men like Adam Zimmerman, who had been wounded in the head at Petersburg. When he was found "on the battlefield, he had maggots in his head and they could see the pulsation in his brain. They had to put a steel plate in his head." Newspapers in Colony, Kansas, reported gatherings of veterans where "the boys were called upon to tell Army yarns," or where a "baker's dozen of old veterans" met on the anniversary of the Battle of Shiloh to reminisce with each other. Within just a few months of its founding, Gettysburg, Dakota Territory, saw the establishment of a local GAR post. At its first meeting "old battle scenes, hard marches, and old jokes were rehearsed and talked over, and general good feeling prevailed" as veterans interacted with those who would best understand them.[38]

Veterans in more established parts of the United States regularly used their status to engage collectively in political activity, often under the auspices of the GAR. Some of this activity revolved around national issues like pension legislation, but scholars have repeatedly noted veterans' engagement with state and regional political affairs, most often as agents of the Republican Party. Stuart McConnell, for example, has argued that one way veterans dealt with the alienation they felt from the civilian population was through "soldier candidacies and self help." He hypothesizes that assuming a leadership role in a local post was "a marker of ascendancy in the local Republican party." The GAR played

TABLE 1. Veterans in High-Trauma Units

Location	No. in 300 Fighting Regiments	No. not in 300 Fighting Regiments	Total	% in 300 Fighting Regiments
Collyer, KS	5	27	32	15.6
Colony, KS	5	9	14	35.7
Detroit Lakes, MN	12	24	36	33.3
Gettysburg, DT	24	65	89	27.0
Gibbon, NE	22	45	67	32.8
King City, KS	12	18	30	40.0
Loyalton, DT	30	61	91	33.0
	110	249	359	30.6

Sources: Collyer Descriptive Book, Grand Army of the Republic Post Records (Bound), ca. 1880–1943, box 12, Kansas State Historical Society; "Chicago Soldiers' and Sailors' Colony," *Western Kansas World*, March 24, 1888; Dennis Northcott, *Iowa, Kansas and Nebraska Civil War Veterans: Compilation of the Death Rolls of the Departments of Iowa, Kansas and Nebraska, Grand Army of the Republic, 1883–1948* (St. Louis: Dennis Northcott, 2007); W. A. Johnson, *The History of Anderson County, Kansas, from Its First Settlement to the Fourth of July, 1876* (Garnett, KS: Kauffman and Iler, 1877); US Congress, Senate, "List of Pensioners on the Roll, January 1, 1883," Senate Ex. Doc. 84, parts 1–5, 47th Cong., 2nd Sess., Serial Set 2078–2082; George W. Kingsbury, *History of Dakota Territory* (Chicago: S. J. Clarke, 1915); Mabel Vohland and Avnelle Pool Lauer, *The Golden Record*, vol. 1 (Gibbon, NE: n.p., 1976); *Biographical Souvenir of the Counties of Buffalo, Kearney and Phelps, Nebraska. Containing Portraits and Biographies of all of the Presidents of the United States, and of the Governors of the State. Also of Many of the Prominent and Representative Citizens and Sketches of Many of the Early Settled Families of These Counties* (Chicago: F. A. Battey, 1890); Samuel Clay Bassett, *Buffalo County Nebraska and Its People. A Record of Settlement, Organization, Progress and Achievement*, 2 vols. (Chicago, S. J. Clarke, 1916); *History of the State of Kansas, Containing a Full Account of Its Growth from an Uninhabited Territory to a Wealthy and Important State* (Chicago: A. T. Andreas, 1883), 811–12; "Men of Area Who Served as Soldiers in Civil War," in *Historical Articles Written by Anton Peterson* (McPherson, KS: n.p., n.d.); J. A. Piper, *Roster of Soldiers, Sailors, and Marines of the War of 1812, the Mexican War, and the War of the Rebellion Residing in Nebraska, June 1, 1895* (York, NE: Nebraska Newspaper Union, 1895); Nebraska Civil War Veterans Database, http://www.nebraskahistory.org/databases/necivilwarveterans.shtml; Alvin H. Wilcox, *A Pioneer History of Becker County Minnesota* (St. Paul, MN: Pioneer, 1907), 325–27; *The Soldiers of Becker County: In Commemoration of the 150th Anniversary of the Start of the Civil War* (Detroit Lakes, MN: Becker County Historical Society, n.d.); GAR File, Becker County Historical Society, Detroit Lakes, MN; Civil War Veterans File, Becker County Historical Society, Detroit Lakes, MN; National Park Service, Soldiers and Sailors Database, https://www.nps.gov/civilwar /soldiers-and-sailors-database.htm; Civil War Veteran's 1885 Census, South Dakota State Historical Society, Pierre, SD, https://history.sd.gov/Archives/Data/civilwar/.

an important role in state politics in places like Illinois, Indiana, and Ohio despite the fact that it had nonpartisanship regulations in place.[39]

Those who came to the veteran colonies were not as politically active as their national counterparts. The GAR was certainly there, with posts created in the first few months of settlement in Detroit Lakes, Minnesota, and Gettysburg, Dakota Territory. These two colonies are notable because local newspapers from the moment of their founding are still extant. Although not perfect indicators of political activity, the limited amount of such activity in the pages of the *Detroit Lakes Weekly Record* and the *Gettysburg Herald* stands out. Indeed, the *Weekly Record* commented, "Politics have not begun to rage, as yet, in this vicinity" just a few months after the colonists' arrival. Veterans figured prominently in a local Detroit Lakes election a few months later, when five of six elected supervisors were veterans, as were both candidates for assessor. Even so, both candidates for town clerk and both candidates for town treasurer were not veterans. Political engagement in Gettysburg also tended to be local, although the *Gettysburg Herald* noted, "It would give us great pleasure to advocate the election of certain Gettysburg men at a proper time" for county offices. In both communities, newspapers stayed remarkably silent when it came to engagement with state and national political questions. Political participation was reasonably circumscribed, reinforcing the notion that the colonies existed for the collective well-being of those who made the journey west.[40]

What the newspapers reveal instead is active membership in the GAR that focused on social events, Memorial Day, and Fourth of July celebrations. In Detroit Lakes, for example, the local GAR post developed a reputation for theatrical productions whose profits benefited its charity fund. Some productions required "an unseemly amount of prompting," but it is notable that newspaper coverage of the local GAR post focused more on the local talent pool than any pressing political issues. In Gettysburg, local veterans' highest priority was a building for their GAR post that would add "to our already fast-growing town and aid the veterans to get a home." The hall was built and served as the center of local GAR activities. In the first six years of the *Gettysburg Herald*, only one item appears commenting on a national issue. A letter from "One Who Wore the Blue" that originally appeared in another county newspaper castigated that editor for opposing veteran pensions. The writer concluded, "Newspapers that use such language against the soldier, unless they retract it are not worthy of the patronage of free Dakota." With the exception of that single letter, territorial and national political issues affecting veterans received no coverage. It is also interesting to note that, with one exception, not a single advertisement appeared in either the *Weekly Record* or the *Gettysburg Herald* that either appealed to veterans or touted the veteran status of the advertiser. The exception was an advertisement that ran repeatedly in the *Gettysburg Herald*'s early years encouraging potential colonists to come west.[41]

The only consistent mention of veterans in either newspaper came from stories associated with Memorial Day or the Fourth of July. They noted organizational meetings and event programs, celebrated remembrance and patriotism, and encouraged their local communities to turn out. These holidays invariably featured ceremonies organized by the local GAR post, with the *Gettysburg Herald* noting that the 1888 Fourth of July celebration "was marred by no serious accident, no brawls, no drunkenness. It was sensibly and gloriously celebrated." In both communities, that was the full extent to which veteran status was celebrated. Otherwise, veterans went quietly about their lives.[42]

And that, perhaps, is exactly what those veterans wanted and needed. They were more likely than veterans in general to have experienced trauma during the war, which in turn made it that much more difficult to reintegrate into civilian life after the war. When they moved to the frontier, they deliberately chose to do so in the company of fellow veterans with whom they shared a common bond. Veteran colonies offered the chance to rebuild lives in an environment without the established social structures that seemed so limiting back home. On the frontier, veterans could define new relationships and even entirely new existences on their own terms. As Frank Waugh remembered of his father, in creating a new community "he was building solidly a new life and a new character in place of those so passionately renounced." Unlike their counterparts in the states they left behind, the residents of veteran colonies rarely sought social and political prominence, especially beyond their communities. Given the prevalence of trauma, perhaps that makes sense. All they wanted to do was reclaim their lives. The veteran colonies provided a mechanism for doing just that.[43]

NOTES

1. Wisconsin Adjutant General's Office, *Roster of Wisconsin Volunteers, War of the Rebellion, 1861–1865*, 2 vols. (Madison: Democrat Printing, 1886), 1:337; Frank Albert Waugh, "Pioneering in Kansas:

Albert Freeman Waugh and His Neighbors on the Kansas Prairies in the 70's and 80's," McPherson County History Collection, Kansas State Historical Society, 147–48.

2. Waugh, "Pioneering in Kansas," 10, 149; Edna Nyquist, *Pioneer Life and Lore of McPherson County, Kansas* (McPherson, KS: Democrat-Opinion Press, 1932), 51, 57; Craig Miner, *West of Wichita: Settling the High Plains of Kansas, 1865–1890* (Lawrence: University Press of Kansas, 1986), 67–68.

3. Waugh, "Pioneering in Kansas," 17–19, 25.

4. Ibid., 148.

5. Ibid., 152–55.

6. Brian Matthew Jordan, *Marching Home: Union Veterans and Their Unending Civil War* (New York: Liveright, 2014), 50–52; Reid Mitchell, *The Vacant Chair: The Northern Soldier Leaves Home* (New York: Oxford University Press, 1993), 135–37; Dixon Wecter, "The Veteran Wins Through," in *The Civil War Veteran: A Historical Reader,* ed. Larry M. Logue and Michael Barton (New York: New York University Press, 2007), 83–85; Paul Cimbala, *Veterans North and South: The Transition from Soldier to Civilian after the American Civil War* (Santa Barbara, CA: Praeger, 2015), 21–22, 38–39, 47–51.

7. David W. Blight, *Race and Reunion: The Civil War in American Memory* (Cambridge, MA: Harvard University Press, 2001), 140–45; Stuart McConnell, *Glorious Contentment: The Grand Army of the Republic, 1865–1900* (Chapel Hill: University of North Carolina Press, 1992), 20–24; James Marten, *Sing Not War: The Lives of Union and Confederate Veterans in Gilded Age America* (Chapel Hill: University of North Carolina Press, 2011), 256–59; Gerald F. Linderman, *Embattled Courage: The Experience of Combat in the American Civil War* (New York: Free Press, 1989), 266–72.

8. Reid Mitchell, *Civil War Soldiers* (New York: Viking, 1988), 206–9; In his "A Note on Posttraumatic Stress Disorder and Civil War Veterans," Paul Cimbala cautions historians against assigning the post-traumatic stress disorder (PTSD) label to all forms of trauma, and that advice has been followed here. PTSD is a very specific trauma diagnosis, far too specific to be assigned to groups of Civil War veterans. It may work for individuals, but only in situations where precise symptoms have somehow been recorded. See Cimbala, *Veterans North and South,* xv–xviii.

9. William F. Fox, *Regimental Losses in the American Civil War, 1861–1865. A Treatise on the Extent and Nature of the Mortuary Losses in the Union Regiments, With Full and Exhaustive Statistics Compiled from the Official Records on File in the State Military Bureaus and at Washington* (Albany, NY: Albany Publishing, 1889), 122.

10. Frederick H. Dyer, *A Compendium of the War of the Rebellion,* 3 vols. (Des Moines: Dyer, 1908; repr., New York: T. Yoseloff, 1959), 1:39.

11. Lesley Gordon, "The 16th Connecticut in War, Captivity, and Memory," in *Union Soldiers and the Northern Home Front: Wartime Experiences, Postwar Adjustments,* ed. Paul Cimbala and Randall M. Miller (New York: Fordham University Press, 2002), 352–53; Linderman, *Embattled Courage,* 272–97; Eric T. Dean Jr., *Shook over Hell: Post-Traumatic Stress, Vietnam, and the Civil War* (Cambridge, MA: Harvard University Press, 1997), 100–14; Marten, *Sing Not War,* 100–114; Mitchell, *Civil War Soldiers,* 206–9; Caroline E. Janney, *Remembering the Civil War: Reunion and the Limits of Reconciliation* (Chapel Hill: University of North Carolina Press, 2013), 104–5; Jordan, *Marching Home,* 52–60, 69–71; Cimbala, *Veterans North and South,* 87–93.

12. Waugh, "Pioneering in Kansas," 25; Marten, *Sing Not War,* 270–71; Kurt Hackemer, "Wartime Trauma and the Lure of the Frontier: Civil War Veterans in Dakota Territory," *Journal of Military History* 81 (January 2017): 83.

13. Greg Bradsher, "How the West Was Settled: The 150-Year-Old Homestead Act Lured Americans Looking for a New Life and New Opportunities," *Prologue* 44 (Winter 2012), 27–28; Patricia Nelson Limerick, *The Legacy of Conquest: The Unbroken Past of the American West* (New York: W. W. Norton, 1987), 125–26; Richard White, *"It's Your Misfortune and None of My Own": A History of the American West* (Norman: University of Oklahoma Press, 1991), 143–44; Robert V. Hine and John Mack Faragher, *The American West: A New Interpretive History* (New Haven, CT: Yale University Press, 333–34); Gilbert Fite, "Daydreams and Nightmares: The Late Nineteenth-Century Agricultural Frontiers," *Agricultural History* 40 (October 1966): 288; James I. Stewart, "Essays on the Economic History of the American Frontier," *Journal of Economic History* 65 (June 2005): 524–25; Heather Cox Richardson, *The Greatest Nation of the Earth: Republican Economic Policies during the Civil War* (Cambridge, MA: Harvard University Press, 1997).

14. Bradsher, "How the West Was Settled," 27–28; Jordan, *Marching Home,* 181–82; Cimbala, *Veterans North and South,* 76; Hackemer, "Wartime Trauma and the Lure of the Frontier," 81; William H. Glasson, *Federal Military Pensions in the United States* (New York: Oxford University Press, 1918), 134; Theda Skocpol, "America's First Social Security System: The Expansion of Benefits for Civil War Veterans," *Political Science Quarterly* 108 (Spring 1993): 95, 115–16; Edward T. Devine, *Disabled Soldiers and Sailors Pensions and Training* (New York: Oxford University Press, 1919), 45.

15. Hine and Faragher, *The American West,* 362; James M. Jasper, *Restless Nation: Starting Over in America* (Chicago: University of Chicago Press, 2000), 84–89; Bill G. Reid, "The Concept of Soldier Settlement in American History," *North Dakota Quarterly* 36 (1968): 50; Miner, *West of Wichita,* 68.

16. George Alexander Batchelder, *A Sketch of the History and Resources of Dakota Territory* (Yankton, Dakota Territory: Press Steam Power Printing, 1870), 240; Edwin A. Curley, *Nebraska, Its Advantages, Resources, and Drawbacks* (London: Sampson Low, Marston, Low and Searle, 1875), 396; Miner, *West of Wichita,* 67; Wallace Eden Miller, *The Peopling of Kansas* (Columbus, OH: Fred J. Heer, 1906), 67; Everett Dick, *The Sod House Frontier, 1854–1890: A Social History of the Northern Plains from the Creation of Kansas & Nebraska to the Admission of the Dakotas* (Lincoln, NE: Johnsen, 1954), 185–201; Robert P. Sutton, *Communal Utopias and the American Experience: Religious Communities, 1732–2000* (Westport, CT: Praeger, 2003), 105–7; Hine and Faragher, *The American West,* 336; "Colonies Kansas Has Harbored. Tragic History of Most of Them," *Wichita Eagle,* August 12, 1908.

17. Chulhee Lee, "Military Service and Economic Mobility: Evidence from the American Civil War," *Explorations in Economic History* 49 (July 2012): 367–79; "A Colony of Soldiers," *Western Reserve Chronicle,* February 9, 1870.

18. "Provisions of the New Soldier's Homestead Bill," *Delaware Gazette,* January 20, 1871; "Land Grant to Soldiers," *Catoctin Clarion,* March 11, 1871.

19. "A Soldier's Colony," *Delaware Gazette,* January 27, 1871.

20. "Soldier's Free Homestead Colony," *Ashtabula Weekly Telegraph,* March 11, 1871; "Attention Soldiers," *Belmont Chronicle,* March 16, 1871; "Soldier's Colony of Northern Ohio Proceedings," *Tiffin Tribune,* March 23, 1871; *Wyandot County Republican,* March 23, 1871; *Green Mountain Freeman,* April 5, 1871; *Emporia News,* April 14, 1871; *New Orleans Republican,* April 16, 1871; "Soldier's Colony," *Western Reserve Chronicle,* March 1, 1871.

21. *Wyandot County Republican,* April 13, 1871; "Colony," *Tiffin Tribune,* April 20, 1871; "Colony," *Tiffin Tribune,* June 1, 1871; *Wyandot County Republican,* June 1, 1871; "Wyandot County," *Tiffin Tribune,* June 8, 1871.

22. "Soldier's Free Homestead Colony of Ashtabula County," *Ashtabula Weekly Telegraph,* March 11, 1871; "Ashtabula Co. Soldier's Free Homestead Colony," *Ashtabula Weekly Telegraph,* March 18, 1871; "Colony Proceedings," *Ashtabula Weekly Telegraph,* March 25, 1871.

23. "Soldier's Free Homestead Colony of Ashtabula County," *Ashtabula Weekly Telegraph,* March 11, 1871; *Green Mountain Freeman,* February 7, 1872; "Soldier's Homesteads," *Elk County Advocate,* May 30, 1872.

24. "Homesteads for Ex-Soldiers," *Middlebury Register,* March 19, 1872; *Bloomfield Times,* March 26, 1872.

25. "Col. Wilson," *Eaton Democrat,* September 9, 1878.

26. Samuel Clay Bassett, *Buffalo County Nebraska and Its People: A Record of Settlement, Organization, Progress and Achievement* (Chicago: S. J. Clarke, 1916), 80–85; Leroy A. Walker, "The Settlement of Gibbon," *Buffalo Tales* 2 (September 1979): 1–5; Mabel Vohland, *Trail Dust to Star Dust* (Kearney, NE: Zimmerman, 1971), 24–25.

27. "The Ashtabula Colony That Came to McPherson County," unknown newspaper from March 19, 1934, in Papers of James A. Cassler, Linn Peterson Collection, McPherson Public Library, McPherson, Kansas; "A 40 Year Ago Item from Files of Republican Reveals an Interesting History of King City," *McPherson Daily Republican,* April 23, 1940; *History of the State of Kansas, Containing a Full Account of Its Growth from an Uninhabited Territory to a Wealthy and Important State* (Chicago: A. T. Andreas, 1883), 811–12; "The Town of King City," in Papers of James A. Cassler; "Men of Area Who Served as Soldiers in Civil War," in *Historical Articles Written by Anton Peterson* (McPherson, KS: n.p., n.d.), Linn Peterson Collection, McPherson Public Library, McPherson, Kansas.

28. "The New England Military Colony at Detroit Lake Minnesota," *Minnesotian-Herald,* December 2, 1871; Alvin H. Wilcox, *A Pioneer History of Becker County Minnesota* (St. Paul, MN: Pioneer, 1907), 322–27; *Weekly Record,* September 7, 1872.

29. "Ohio Soldiers' Colony," *Belmont Chronicle,* December 7, 1871; W. A. Johnson, *The History of Anderson County, Kansas, from Its First Settlement to the Fourth of July, 1876* (Garnett, KS: Kauffman and Iler, 1877), 283–85; unknown Anderson County newspaper, February 1, 1872, in Dorothy Kipper Lickteig, *Anderson County Early Gleanings,* vol. 1, *1867–1900* (n.p., 1993), 31; unknown Anderson County newspaper, April 4, 1872, in Lickteig, *Anderson County Early Gleanings,* 1:33.

30. *Nebraska Advertiser,* January 31, 1878; Ethel M. Harvey, comp., *History of Collyer, Kansas* (Collyer, KS: n.p., 1976), 1–3; "Proclamation of Gov. St. John in 1878 Brought About the Organization of Trego County," *Hays Daily News,* November 30, 1932, in Trego County Clippings, 1878–1997, vol. 1, Kansas State Historical Society; Mrs. Ray Purinton, "History of Collyer, Kansas," *Local History as Presented to the Trego County Historical Society* (Collyer, KS: n.p., 1973), 1–2; "Miscellaneous," *Daily Globe,* June 13, 1878; "Collyer Cawings," *World,* December 27, 1879, in Trego County Clippings, 1878–1997, vol. 1; "Chicago Soldiers' and Sailors' Colony," *Western Kansas World,* March 24, 1888.

31. *Daily Press & Dakotian,* April 9, 1883; *Gettysburg Herald,* July 31, 1883; *Potter County News,* June 8, 1933; "Southern Dakota," *Daily Press & Dakotian,* September 24, 1883; Ross Richardson, "Railroads," in *Through 75 Years, 1883–1958* comp. Cece Stilgebouer and Ruth Stilgebouer (Pierre, SD: State Publishing, 1958), 19.

32. "Royalton," *Burlington Weekly Free Press,* February 20, 1885; "The Vermont Colony," *Daily Globe,* May 23, 1885; *Loyalton Journal,* October 23, 1885, in *History of Loyalton South Dakota from Its*

Proposal to Its End by Loyalton Patrons (n.p., 1983), 4–6; *Devil's Lake Inter-Ocean,* March 21, 1885; Stella Bailey Stevenson, "Vermont City," in *History of Loyalton South Dakota,* 9–10.

33. "Pioneer Privations. The Henderson Soldiers' Colony Battles Bravely against Adversity," *Omaha Daily Bee,* March 26, 1881. Garfield, Nebraska, does not appear on a county-level map published in 1883. See "New Rail Road and County Map of Nebraska," in George F. Cram, *Illustrated Family Atlas of the World* (Chicago: George F. Cram, 1883).

34. *Columbus Journal,* July 18, 1883; *Columbus Journal,* August 8, 1883; *Omaha Daily Bee,* October 8, 1883; *Omaha Daily Bee,* October 16, 1883; *McCook Weekly Tribune,* April 10, 1884; Logan County Extension Council Historical Committee, *Logan County Nebraska* (Logan, NE: Logan County Extension Council Historical Committee, 1962), 3; and "Logan County. By an Early Settler," in *Compendium of History Reminiscence and Biography of Western Nebraska* (Chicago: Alden, 1909), 158–59.

35. Amy Bickel, "Dead Towns of Kansas," May 24, 2013, http://kansasghosttowns.blogspot.com/2013/05/go-west-young-man-greeley-county-ghost.html, accessed July 26, 2016; "Department News," *National Tribune,* October 11, 1888; "To Lop Off Additions. Bill Affecting 68 Towns Reported Favorably," *Topeka State Journal,* February 15, 1897.

36. Richard G. Tedeschi and Richard J. McNally, "Can We Facilitate Posttraumatic Growth in Combat Veterans?," *American Psychologist* 66 (January 2011): 21; Brad Larner and Adrian Blow, "A Model of Meaning-Making Coping and Growth in Combat Veterans," *Review of General Psychology* 15 (2011): 194; L. G. Calhoun, A. Cann, and R. G. Tedesci, "The Posttraumatic Growth Model: Sociocultural Considerations," in *Posttraumatic Growth and Culturally Competent Practice: Lessons Learned from around the Globe,* ed. T. Weiss and R. Berger (New York: Wiley, 2010), 1–14.

37. Hackemer, "Wartime Trauma and the Lure of the Frontier," 83.

38. Leroy A. Walker, "The Settlement of Gibbon," *Buffalo Tales* 8 (September 1979), 3–4; *Baylee Family Remembrances,* Gibbon Heritage Center, Gibbon, Nebraska, 3; "Interview with Otto Lowell," in *Historical Stories and Remembrances as Compiled by Members of the Soldiers Free Homestead Association,* Buffalo County Historical Society, Kearney, Nebraska; "Civil War Veteran," in *Historical Stories and Remembrances;* Dorothy Kipper Lickteig, *Colony Kansas Newspaper Clips,* vol. 1, *1882–1907* (n.p., 2012), 69–70; "The G.A.R.," *Gettysburg Herald,* September 11, 1883.

39. Cimbala, *Veterans North and South,* 111–17; McConnell, *Glorious Contentment,* 97, 113; Mary R. Dearing, *Veterans in Politics: The Story of the G.A.R.* (Baton Rouge: Louisiana State University Press, 1952), 192–94, 221–39, 290.

40. "Installation and Camp Fire by John S. Loomis Post, No. 30, G.A.R.," *Weekly Record,* January 18, 1873; "The Town Election," *Weekly Record,* March 15, 1873; "The G.A.R.," *Gettysburg Herald,* September 11, 1883; *Weekly Record,* June 15, 1872; "Candidates for County Offices," *Gettysburg Herald,* June 19, 1884.

41. "G.A.R. Entertainment," *Weekly Record,* February 21, 1874; "Toodles," *Weekly Record,* April 4, 1874; *Gettysburg Herald,* July 3, 1884; "An Old Soldier Speaks," *Gettysburg Herald,* June 2, 1886.

42. "Attention Soldiers!," *Gettysburg Herald,* May 8, 1884; "Preparations for Memorial Day," *Gettysburg Herald,* May 15, 1884; "The Fourth at Gettysburg," *Gettysburg Herald,* July 10, 1884; "We Celebrated," *Gettysburg Herald,* July 4, 1888; "Celebration of Memorial Day," *Weekly Record,* May 23, 1874; "Last Call. Grand Time on the Fourth," *Weekly Record,* June 27, 1874.

43. Waugh, "Pioneering in Kansas," 155.

The Trials of Frank James

Guerrilla Veteranhood and the Double Edge of Wartime Notoriety

MATTHEW CHRISTOPHER HULBERT

O N JULY 26, 1865, sixteen men shuffled into line at Samuel's Depot, a provincial general store located forty miles south of Louisville, Kentucky. They did not whoop the rebel yell. They did not sport gray uniforms or Enfield rifle-muskets or any other hallmark of Johnny Reb—save war-weariness. Despite their haggard appearance, they had spilled much blood on behalf of the Confederate cause. They were guerrillas out of western Missouri, the last remnant of William Clarke Quantrill's once-formidable band of bushwhackers. These were men known the country over for massacres at Lawrence (1863), Baxter Springs (1863), and Centralia (1864), renowned, as it were, for perfecting a style of warfare that thrived on the home front, disconnected from the War Departments and Treasuries of the Union or the Confederacy. Among the assembled that morning stood Alexander F. James—better known, both then and now, as Frank.[1]

A turbulent sequence of events brought James and company to Samuel's Depot. On May 10, they made a desperate retreat from the barn of the nearby Wakefield Farm. As rain fell and pro-Union guerrilla hunters thundered down on their camp, the Missourians scattered. They had dispersed in this fashion countless times before; most reached their mounts and found safety beyond the tree line. Only on this occasion, Quantrill came up short. He fell, paralyzed from the armpit down, with a bullet in his back. The architect of the Lawrence Massacre died in Union custody on June 6.[2]

Stranded hundreds of miles from home and reeling from the loss of their chieftain, the bushwhackers held a contentious council of war in the living room of Alexander Sayers, a prominent local landowner and southern sympathizer. Sayers's young daughter, Ora, recalled a group of bearded men yelling and cursing at one another as they struggled to make a decision—the only time she could remember her father allowing anyone to use profanity in his home. Eventually, they determined to surrender if, and only if, the government of Kentucky would deal with them as legitimate combatants. T. W. Samuels—the sheriff of Nelson County and in all likelihood at distant relative of Frank James's stepfather, Dr. Reuben Samuel—helped convince the Quantrill men to surrender while Wilson T. Samuels, Sayers's brother-in-law, brokered the July 26 meeting with Union officials.[3]

When Captain Robert Young of the 54th Kentucky Mounted Infantry arrived at Samuel's Depot, he found the men lined up on the store's front porch, ready to submit. He also found a sizable contingent of women and children watching his every move. The bushwhackers refused to take chances. Fearing perfidy—and really, no one knew more about trickery and ambuscade than they did—Quantrill's men believed a double cross less likely with so many witnesses in attendance. Young was true to his word; each of the sixteen men was paroled as promised. He also provided them with all of the necessary paperwork to take back to Missouri. James's parole form even included a handwritten addendum, which stated that he would be allowed to keep his horse, arms, and equipment by direct order of Major General John M. Palmer, commander of all federal forces in Kentucky. This personal favor probably stemmed from James's connection to the influential Samuels family—which also included William T. Samuels, Kentucky's auditor of public accounts in 1865.[4]

Unbeknownst to the newly designated "civilians," the groundwork had already been laid in Missouri to sidestep their deal with Young. Weeks earlier, around the time Quantrill had been shot, Major General Grenville M. Dodge, federal commander of the Department of Missouri, declared to his subordinates that bushwhackers "will be allowed to surrender by giving up all the horses, arms, and equipments, and will not be molested by the military authorities so long as they obey the laws where they reside." However, in a postscript marked "Private," Dodge let the rest of the plan, and his true intentions, slip: "In any surrender [of bushwhackers], be careful that no quarter is given against any civil action that may be brought against them for any crimes committed. Nothing need be said about this. We deal with them only from the military point of view." In other words, disarm dangerous bushwhackers with paroles and then let the civil courts retroactively punish them for atrocities committed as non-state-sanctioned combatants during the war. The Missouri officers who operated under this pretense and allowed guerrillas to surrender in good faith effectively did so with their fingers crossed.[5]

For most defeated rebels in 1865, formal surrender to the Union meant the end of soldiering, a somber trek to whatever remained of home, and the beginning of veteranhood. Frank James was not like most Confederates. Owing to the legal immunities he believed his formal surrender in Kentucky entitled him to and the volatile situation that awaited him in Missouri, his war did not give way to veteran status just yet. It could not—because it was not actually over.[6]

IN THE LAST TWO DECADES, historians have made a concerted effort to understand the veteranhood experiences of men from the war's regular theaters. From Stuart McConnell's *Glorious Contentment: The Grand Army of the Republic, 1865–1900* to Brian Matthew Jordan's *Marching Home: Union Veterans and Their Unending Civil War,* scholars have uncovered how veterans dealt with physical disabilities, how they settled (or failed to settle) back into the social and economic rhythms of civilian life, how they made sense of their wartime experiences and played primary roles in commemorating the causes for which they sacrificed, and how families and communities coped with a generation of men inexorably changed by unprecedented levels of destruction and death. Additionally, historians such as Diane Miller Sommerville, Wayne Wei-Siang Hsieh, Peter Carmichael, and Dillon J. Carroll have started to reassess the personal consequences of war—mental illness, suicide, chronic brain trauma, posttraumatic stress disorder—and to connect the dots between veterans of the US Civil War and contemporary conflicts. Despite these strides in the study of veteranhood, however, the subject remains deeply problematic when it comes to men who eschewed regular channels of military service.[7]

At first glance, this void in scholarship is surprising. Within just the past ten years, historians have shed tremendous new light on Civil War irregulars, particularly on the conflict in the Missouri-Kansas borderlands and the people who waged it. Daniel Sutherland's *A Savage Conflict* proves once and for all that guerrilla activity directly influenced the outcome of the broader war. Joseph Beilein's *Bushwhackers* pulls back the curtain on guerrilla logistics; he chronicles how the female kin of irregulars functioned as domestic quartermasters and literally made guerrilla warfare possible from the household. In a series of groundbreaking essays, Andrew Fialka harnesses the power of geographic information system (GIS) mapping technologies to reveal fundamental patterns triggering outbreaks of seemingly random irregular violence. And much of my own work has focused on understanding how and why irregular violence was whitewashed from mainstream Civil War memory narratives and commemorative movements. Yet despite this veritable renaissance in the subfield of guerrilla studies, we have largely avoided the task of conceptualizing "guerrilla veteranhood" to any meaningful degree.[8]

Much of the difficulty is rooted in the fact that bushwhackers—which are here distinguished from partisan rangers and cavalry raiders—did not keep official rosters or records of their day-to-day activities. Along these same lines, the fluid nature of irregular command and the geographically condensed nature of guerrilla campaigning meant men generally came and went as they pleased. Thus, for example, it is impossible to know precisely how many men partook in the Centralia Massacre of 1864. Extant records do not allow us to identify who many of the local men involved were, where exactly they came from, how long they fought as guerrillas (if they fought at all), or how long they remained guerrillas. This arrangement makes piecing together how many men actually fought as guerrillas based on anecdotal evidence and government accounts an extremely difficult task for historians. As a result, it is equally difficult to draw collective conclusions about the veteranhood experiences of former guerrillas, because to identify a wide swath of veterans, we must first be able to identify a wide swath of guerrillas.[9]

To be sure, we know a great deal about a select few ex-irregulars—figures like William Quantrill, William "Bloody Bill" Anderson, George Todd, Jim Jackson, Upton Hayes, Archie Clement, Coleman Younger, and Frank James. We recall them because they achieved a level of notoriety—in the true, pejorative sense of the word—during the war itself; they distinguished themselves as leaders or die-hard members of irregular units that wrought havoc of national note. In turn, they were targets especially prized by regular military forces during the war. Of course, by definition, their notoriety meant they were not representative of the whole. Such a disconnect would initially seem to negate their value to any elongated study of postwar veteranhood. But just as a biographer can fill in the space around a subject to give it shape, so too can we explore the postbellum lives of those myriad nameless bushwhackers who essentially hid in plain sight as veterans of the irregular war. The remainder of this essay will do just that: chronicle the process through which Frank James transitioned from pro-Confederate guerrilla to Civil War veteran—and will use his experience as an exceptional, nonrepresentative figure to put forth a set of general observations concerning guerrilla veteranhood.

IN THE GUERRILLA WAR that raged throughout the Missouri-Kansas borderlands from 1861 to 1865, the traditional line that distinguished battlefront from home front effectively disappeared. Bands of armed men—be they bushwhackers, jayhawkers, Red Legs, raiders, or home guards—prowled lonely backroads, muddy fields, meadows, barns, stables, corncribs, general stores, houses, and even churches. Easy to reload and fire on horseback, the revolver was the guerrillas' weapon of choice. More often than not, they rode under moonlit skies, utilizing mobility, local knowledge, visual deception, and ambush to strike death blows against their enemies. No domestic space was too personal, no ground too sacred to inoculate it from violation. The conflict's domestic setting and the absence of boundaries created widespread paranoia. Over time, paranoia blossomed into full-fledged terror—and terror itself became a weapon for guerrillas, nearly as powerful as the revolver.[10]

Like the broader war, it was a politically inflected struggle—that is, Union versus Confederate—but one that left virtually no room for neutrality and that created its own unique varieties of trauma. Men and women of all ages, races, and ethnicities, and their children too, became victims. Just as often, they became guerrillas themselves: as spies, quartermasters, messengers, triage nurses, diplomats, and combatants. Under these circumstances, households doubled as fortresses and supply depots; interior lines, Jominian precepts, and Napoleonic stratagems gave way to arson, torture, rape, plunder, assassination, and even massacre. In short, it was a hyperlocal, hyperpersonal conflict, fought within but also apart from the regular war. Most important to recognize, though, is that for many residents of the guerrilla theater, this mode of irregular warfare was the status quo. It was their regular wartime experience.[11]

When secessionist fire-eaters fired on Fort Sumter in April 1861, Frank James was eighteen years old, living with his mother, Zerelda James, and stepfather, Dr. Reuben Samuel, on a farm in Kearney, Clay County, Missouri. In September of that year, Frank fought briefly in the Battle of Lexington as part of the pro-Confederate Missouri State Guard—and might never have become a bushwhacker had he not taken sick, become separated from his unit, and been forced to surrender to Union authorities. His captors granted a parole and sent Frank James home to Kearney, where he was harassed by Unionist militiamen and eventually driven into the bush. There he fell in with the guerrilla command of William Clarke Quantrill. By most accounts, James was a uniquely intelligent but ferocious fighter; he quickly rose to a place of prominence among the band, occasionally taking charge of a small detachment of men. (Eventually, his younger brother, Jesse James, also joined the guerrilla war—but Jesse gravitated toward the leadership of William "Bloody Bill" Anderson, Quantrill's more reckless rival.)[12]

As one of Quantrill's regulars, Frank James participated in the three most infamous massacres carried out by guerrillas not just in the Missouri-Kansas conflict but in the entire Civil War. On August 21, 1863, a mass of three hundred to four hundred bushwhackers executed a surprise attack on Lawrence, Kansas. The raiders struck the town just after daybreak. After first eliminating a small group of unarmed Union recruits encamped in town, Quantrill's men peeled off into smaller squadrons. They canvassed the town, block by block, killing, looting, drinking, and burning as they went. When all was said and done, the butcher's bill totaled nearly two hundred men and boys, some gunned down in the street, others at their front doors. Still more were burned alive or drowned while trying in vain to hide from the guerrillas. When Quantrill and company bolted from Lawrence, they left a hellscape in rearview: newly orphaned children in shock, their mothers sobbing over corpses; soot-covered survivors combing through rubble for the dead, all while the smoke produced by 182 torched buildings billowed around them.[13]

In the aftermath of the Lawrence Massacre, Union authorities back east could no longer turn a blind eye to the borderland's "guerrilla problem." As a result, Quantrill and his men achieved national notoriety—status that made wintering outside of Missouri a necessity for survival. In October 1863, while en route to winter quarters in Texas, the band pulled off another slaughter. After unsuccessfully besieging Fort Baxter, Kansas, the bushwhackers stumbled across Union major general and commander of the District of the Frontier James G. Blunt's headquarters as it relocated from Kansas to Arkansas. Wearing Union uniforms, Quantrill, James, and the rest of the men initially deceived Blunt's caravan and approached within a few hundred yards. When Blunt finally realized what was happening, he hastily ordered his hopelessly outnumbered escort into line of battle. When the guerrillas charged, the federals fled—more than eighty were run down and slaughtered. With two massacres now under their belts, the guerrillas went to Texas. By the time they returned to Missouri in 1864, Quantrill had lost overall command of the group due to internal disagreements. Many longtime followers—including Frank James—remained loyal to him, but Bill Anderson seized power over the main force.[14]

Under Anderson's direction, the Missourians pulled off one last great ambush, known today as the Centralia Massacre. In reality, it was a pair of massacres. On September 27, 1864, the bushwhackers hijacked a train in Centralia, Missouri. They forced a group of unarmed Union soldiers—men on furlough from Sherman's campaigning in Georgia—to disembark and line up alongside the track. One man, Sergeant Thomas M. Goodman, was pulled from the line and kept as a hostage; the rest of his comrades, twenty-two in sum, were executed on the spot. Major A. V. E. Johnston and the 39th Missouri Mounted Infantry responded to the attack. They tracked some of the guerrillas to an open field not far from the rail depot. The field was surrounded by thick foliage on three sides and its perimeter was lined by deep channel cuts. Johnston learned this second fact the hard way: as his men dismounted and formed a line of battle, hundreds of mounted guerrillas who had been concealed in the channels rose up and lurched out of the woods. They swarmed Johnston's men, catching the 39th in a deadly, close-quarters crossfire. More than 120 of the troopers, including their commander, were slain. The bushwhackers celebrated the rout by taking scalps, mutilating corpses, and grotesquely posing the dead bodies in ways they found amusing.[15]

The Union's policy response to the Lawrence Massacre had been General Order No. 11. The controversial edict, issued by General Thomas Ewing Jr., forcibly removed residents of Jackson, Cass, Bates, and Vernon Counties; if the Union army could not catch up with guerrillas in the field, it would make the households and female kin of Quantrill's men pay the price. Following the Centralia Massacre, Union brass began training and dispatching special units to track down and eliminate specific, high-profile guerrilla targets. These factors, combined with the Confederacy's rapidly fading prospects for achieving independence or preserving slavery, are what prompted Quantrill to take his last loyal followers to Kentucky. There, he believed, they could escape the effects of General Order No. 11 and the antiguerrilla operators; moreover, he dreamed that once in the Bluegrass State, they could team up with Kentucky bushwhackers like Henry Magruder, Bill Marion, Jerome M. Clarke, and Samuel "One Armed" Berry to relive the glories of 1863.[16]

Quantrill and his men did some minor raiding in Kentucky. Even though he no longer led the borderland's most notorious guerrilla band, his presence in the state put Union authorities on high alert. They greatly feared the possibility that Quantrill could pull off a Lawrence-like raid in Kentucky, which might, in turn, trigger the creation of countless new bushwhackers. Accordingly, Unionist leaders sent Edwin Terrell, a highly proficient guerrilla hunter (read: a ruthless killer who was essentially a guerrilla himself), to assassinate Quantrill and his men. Terrell's unit sprang the ambush at the Wakefield Farm, ultimately ending Quantrill's life and leaving Frank James at the mercy of Palmer and Young.[17]

When Frank James and his comrades returned to Missouri, their Kentucky-issued paroles did little to make life easier. The hostilities roused between kin and neighbors by years of guerrilla war did not simply dissipate because Confederate commanders capitulated on faraway battlefields. The problem James and other former members of Quantrill's and Anderson's bands faced was the double edge of wartime notoriety. As bushwhackers, their grisly résumés—capped off by the massacres at Lawrence, Baxter Springs, and Centralia, but including dozens of other raids and killings—were unparalleled. They were household names, feared men, men who could wipe out entire towns and columns of Union soldiers, let alone pay unwanted visits to individual citizens or families on isolated farms after the sun went down. In what became a vicious cycle, they harnessed the terror produced by their irregular tactics and used it to bolster the effectiveness of those tactics.

When the Confederate experiment collapsed and the guerrilla war ground to a halt, the opposite blade swung back against James and company. Because they crossed a notoriety threshold during the war, traumatized Unionists sought to get even with them during Reconstruction. This scenario was exacerbated by the unavoidable fact that many of the highest-profile guerrillas had either not survived the war or died very soon after its conclusion. Quantrill was dead. Anderson was dead. George Todd, another of Quantrill's rivals who seized power for himself in Texas, was dead. Richard Yeager, Fernando Scott, Clark Hockensmith, Andy Blunt, and Upton Hayes were all belowground. In June 1865, Jim Jackson, a peer of and frequent collaborator with Quantrill, was hunted down and killed by a posse of revenge-seeking Unionists after he had surrendered and taken the oath of allegiance. In December 1866, Archie Clements—the diminutive killer who took over Anderson's band following the latter's death—was gunned down by Union soldiers. He died face down in the street, riddled with bullets, attempting to cock a revolver with his teeth.[18]

The vacuum created by these deaths, especially those of Quantrill and Anderson, left middle-tier, but still quite well-known, ex-guerrillas like Frank James to take the proverbial heat in their places. He found himself in this position along with his brother, Jesse, Archie Clements (albeit very briefly before his violent demise late in 1866), Cole and John Younger, John Jarrett, George and Oliver Shepherd, Jim Cummins, and Clell Miller. As T. J. Stiles contends in *Jesse James: Last Rebel of the Civil War*, Jesse James fell into his criminal career as an extension of his wartime guerrilla activities. He functioned, as Stiles shows convincingly, as a pro-Confederate terrorist, pushing back against Union occupation of the South, the end of slavery, and what he deemed unfair Reconstruction policies. The basic tenets of this argument can—and in this case, should—be extended to include Frank James and the other bushwhackers turned members of the James-Younger Gang. They shared a common political ideology and viewed Union victory as anathema to their social and economic interests as southerners. That said, a major influence on Frank James as he turned to banditry was undoubtedly his belief that Union authorities would not allow him to live peacefully as a regular citizen of postbellum Missouri. Put differently, because the elder James brother did not believe he could enter veteranhood on the same schedule as his counterparts from the regular war, he simply kept on fighting as a guerrilla until he believed it was possible. From there, an endless loop developed: Frank James stole and occasionally killed because he believed he was hunted, and he was hunted because he committed those crimes.[19]

Whether or not Frank James was correct in thinking he could not return home to a normal life in western Missouri—and observers have debated this potential justification for his criminal career for decades—the important factor here is that James genuinely believed it and acted accordingly. He took part in several robberies spanning from 1866 to 1881, but four merit attention. The first, of the Clay County Savings Association at Liberty, Missouri, in February 1866, was the ex-guerrillas' initial foray into banditry. (Ironically, while Jesse James would later become the gang's figurehead, he was not present at this first hijacking.) Archie Clements led James and several other former subordinates of Quantrill and Anderson; they made off with $60,000 and left one bystander, a student at William Jewell College, dead in the street.[20]

The second important robbery came a decade later. In 1876, the James-Younger gang attempted to raid the bank at Northfield, Minnesota. The job was botched from the start; it left multiple members of the gang, including Clell Miller, dead—and all three of the Younger brothers imprisoned. Northfield was the last time the James brothers would ride with a band of former guerrillas. It also marked the beginning of a new phase in Frank James's life. After escaping from Minnesota, he relocated to Tennessee with his wife, Ann. Living in disguise, they had a son and started attending church services. He took to field and plow with genuine gusto. This was the life Frank James had hoped would be possible when he surrendered to Captain Young at Samuel's Depot—a family, honest labor, an easing of the paranoia that follows men who live and die by the gun.[21]

In 1881, Jesse James pressured Frank into resuming his criminal career. They held up a train in Winston, Missouri, and managed to kill the conductor and a passenger in the process. One of their accomplices was captured after bragging about the heist; he implicated the James brothers to law enforcement. This lack of loyalty was the difference between working with other former guerrillas and random ne'er-do-wells who had not made their bones during the war. In 1882, a payroll was robbed in Muscle Shoals, Alabama, and the stickup was attributed to Frank and Jesse James. (As T. J. Stiles and other historians have shown, Frank James was almost certainly innocent of the robbery committed in Alabama.) Later in 1882, Robert and Charlie Ford, two of Jesse James's more recent sidekicks, struck a bargain with T. T. Crittenden, a former Union officer and current governor of Missouri: they would assassinate Jesse James and end Crittenden's bandit problem in exchange for immunity. On April 3, the Ford brothers shot James to death in his St. Joseph, Missouri, living room.[22]

Following the state-sponsored assassination of his brother, Frank James feared a similar fate. With the help of newspaper pundit John Newman Edwards, James negotiated the terms of his own surrender with Crittenden. This time, however, he knew exactly where he stood with state officials in Missouri; this time, he would not be allowed to retain his gun or to ride off for home. Instead, he would be forced to stand trial for the train robbery in Winston and remain in jail until it was decided one way or the other. The silver lining was that the state of Missouri would not allow him to be extradited to Minnesota to answer for his role in the debacle at Northfield. On October 5, 1882, he arrived in Jefferson City, Missouri, met with Governor Crittenden at the McCarthy House Hotel, and handed over his guns. He reportedly said to Crittenden, "I surrender my arms to you ... they have not been out of my possession since 1864,"—a reminder of just how long Frank James believed he had been at war.[23]

The legal proceedings began on July 21, 1883. The case of the lead prosecutor, William Wallace, hinged almost entirely on the testimony of Richard "Dick" Liddil, a former criminal associate of the James brothers, but not an ex-guerrilla. Liddil, an admitted thief and murderer, testified that James had not only participated in the Winston robbery but had killed Frank McMillan, the passenger shot during the heist. James's attorneys, including former lieutenant governor Charles P. Johnson and Judge Charles F. Phillips, dismantled Liddil's credibility on cross-examination. Former Confederate general Joseph Orville Shelby testified on behalf of the defense. Despite arriving in court intoxicated, his unassailable reputation as a local Confederate war hero generated support for James. Governor Crittenden also testified on James's behalf. As a chief executive who needed to appear tough on crime but also a Democrat, the governor understood the benefit of playing both sides of the public relations fence. Most interesting, though, were the closing remarks made by John F. Phillips and William Wallace and how both men attempted to manipulate memories of the guerrilla war to the advantage of their respective cases.[24]

While addressing the court on James's behalf, Phillips stated:

In that fierce, internecine strife, which swept the land like a tornado, dividing families, arraying father against son and brother against brother, in deadliest contention, Frank James and I stood in mortal antagonism. It was my fortune to see his flag go down in desperate defeat, while mine went up in permanent triumph. I was the victor, he was the vanquished. ... And when I recall all the local bitterness of that day, with its crimination and recrimination, and its reprisals and outrages, peculiar to neither side in Missouri, with the bad blood it engendered, and to day behold the magnificent picture of a civilized state, reposing in peace, exulting in plenty, and marching on to higher achievements in the arts of peace and social order, my heart swells with pride and gratitude to the God of our deliverance. ... Gentlemen of the jury, the best test for understanding the conduct of others is, often, to put yourself in their places. Surround yourself by the same circumstances which environed Frank James—a man hunted and outlawed—whose name the public press of the country had for years associated with that of Jesse James, Cummings, Ryan, and Liddil, to whom was attributed every daring robbery and outrage from the north of Kentucky to the valley of the Arkansas river.[25]

Speaking to the jury on behalf of the state, Wallace countered:

I can only say, that on the border of our state, where the red lightning of murder played the fiercest along the western sky and the dogs of war were turned loose on defenseless women and children, I saw it all; when torch, and fire, and sword and rapine, and pillage, and plunder, and robbery, and murder, and assassination were abroad in the land, when sabred horsemen shot across the prairies and devouring flames leaped from farm to farm and house to house, until both earth and sky seemed blaze with living horrors . . . and I sincerely trust, gentlemen, that wherever you may have been in that dark hour, or whatever may have been your experience, your regard for your oaths will now be such that all attempts to kindle in your hearts the hates of other days, will be hurled back by you as insults to your honor, your intelligence, and your conscience. . . . Again, it is adroitly urged that the defendant ought not to be held strictly accountable for this crime, because, if done by him, it was done in just revenge. Possibly, some juror says, "there is something in that, too," we will see. Gov. Johnson, you remember, said "possibly the defendant could not live here and lead a quiet life after the war" . . . Oh, no, gentlemen, this is all a pretext. Money, not revenge, is the demon that has wrought his woe.[26]

In spite of Wallace's pleading, the jury speedily acquitted Frank James. Even then, he could not enter a peaceful phase of guerrilla veteranhood. The defeated prosecutors made a deal with authorities in Alabama: if James was not convicted in Missouri, he would be extradited to Huntsville to stand trial for the Muscle Shoals robbery. Much to the dismay of the prosecutor and of Unionists in both states, the Alabama jury—made up of many former Confederates—also acquitted Frank James. For a moment, however, it seemed as if this second triumph would be as short-lived as the first. Rumors swirled that Wallace and other officials in Missouri, who still technically retained legal jurisdiction over James, would either haul him back to Missouri in irons to stand trial for a different robbery or possibly extradite him to Minnesota. The latter was James's worst nightmare. In Northfield, jurors would not view him as a favorite son or a fellow ex-Confederate. In the end, neither option came to fruition. Governor Crittenden canceled any further prosecution of James, and he was allowed to live as a free and private citizen. The election of former Confederate general John S. Marmaduke as governor in 1885 only ensured James's freedom.[27]

Nearly two decades after the end of the Civil War, Frank James finally settled into veteranhood. He tried a number of different jobs, including farm work, and attended multiple reunions of the Quantrill Men Survivor's Association in the 1900s. He died in 1915, survived by his son, Robert James, and his wife, Anne Ralston James. His odyssey toward veteran status was admittedly an unusual one: it involved robberies, murders, assassinations, multiple trials, and multiple surrenders. His first acquittal revealed that locally, Missourians were ready to allow the most notorious ex-bushwhackers to move on from the war. Even as Wallace begged them not to consider James's postwar criminal career as part of his extended wartime résumé, they did. The second acquittal, in Alabama, illustrated that other former Confederates agreed with that assessment—or at least that they were willing to stick it to Union authorities by freeing an anti-Reconstruction terrorist. In any case, the uniqueness of James's postwar narrative helps prove basic rules concerning the majority of former guerrillas in the Missouri-Kansas borderlands and their own veteranhood experiences.[28]

Unlike Frank James, who trekked to Kentucky with Quantrill, most bushwhackers never really left home during the war—so they had no experience in surrendering to another state's government or military officials. Nor was it possible, as a result, for them to have felt double-crossed by Missouri's policies for surrendering guerrillas. Perhaps more importantly, most bushwhackers had not needed to escape from western Missouri in the first place, because they had never crossed the threshold of wartime notoriety and become primary targets of the state. The diehards of Quantrill's and Anderson's bands, by virtue of the many massacres they executed, had crossed that threshold. Expressed another way, unlike Frank James, the vast majority of ex-guerrillas had been known only at the most local of levels during the war. When the war ended, the state had no real interest prolonging hostilities by punishing them in civil courts— these men and their communities were the civil courts.

Unlike Frank James, who could not return home to Kearney once his criminal career began—and who held that his criminal career began because he could not return home to Kearney safely in the first place—most former bushwhackers found support and protection from the same sources they had known during the war: the household and their extended kinship networks. Thus, in exponentially more cases than not, ex-bushwhackers did not become bandits or politically motivated terrorists. They did not turn to crime because they did not believe it was necessary for their postbellum survival. If they had, there would be many accounts similar to that of Frank James. In this instance, the utter lack of social evidence pertaining to former guerrillas constitutes a silence in the archive, but not a hindrance to our understanding. Instead, it is a critical piece of evidence unto itself. It tells us that as a general rule, despite the attention paid to men like James, guerrilla veterans did precisely what regular veterans did: they returned to their families, they dealt with lingering physical and emotional trauma, they came to terms (sometimes violently) with a social hierarchy irrevocably altered by emancipation, and they resumed farming.[29]

This conclusion might strike some readers as odd given the nature of guerrilla warfare in the borderlands. It was brutal, personal, and perpetrated by men within and against their own local communities. Homes and churches went up in smoke. Men died in their own fields and barns and parlors, gunned down, often by unseen assailants. Women, left alone because their fathers and husbands and brothers had taken to the bush, found themselves at the mercy of their enemies—rape was not uncommon. Children were abused, traumatized, and cast out into the cold. The elderly were not spared the full range of irregular horrors on account of their venerability. But to the people who lived in the Missouri-Kansas guerrilla theater, this return to home and to the soil after four years of social chaos and domestic bloodletting would not have been unusual. They had not waited for news from faraway battlefields—they had lived in, on, and among the primary sites of irregular strife. To them, guerrilla war was regular war. And because their concept of what had been "normal" during the war revolved around guerrillas having been their version of regular combatants, there was no reason for them not to accept defeated bushwhackers home as veterans just as easterners accepted regular soldiers.[30]

In this light, a jury of Missourians acquitting Frank James made perfect sense. Doing so was simply the logical extension of a prolonged war in the guerrilla theater—just as Judge Phillips seemed to know the jurors would understand in his closing address. In asking Missourians to clear memories of the war from their minds and to consider James solely as a postwar criminal, Wallace might have had the letter of the law on his side, but he erred grievously in assessing the human component of the trial. He essentially asked jurors to rethink their fundamental understandings of the Civil War. They could not—and would not—detach Frank James's activities as a bushwhacker under Quantrill from his banditry later in the 1860s, 1870s, and 1880s because in the context of the guerrilla theater, no clear line separated the two phases. Both periods involved the same tactics in the same domestic space against the same perceived enemy oppressor. Whether Wallace liked it or not, to many pro-Confederate Missourians, Frank James's war had not ended until he surrendered himself to Crittenden in 1882.

Of course, this is by no means the end of the story on guerrilla veteranhood. In fact, it is just the tip of the iceberg. Many fundamental questions still remain: Did guerrilla veterans have a more difficult time coping emotionally with trauma because, unlike regular soldiers, they came home to live on the sites of their past battles? Furthermore, in the guerrilla theater, to what extent did demographics generally considered civilians in the regular theater—women, children, the elderly—suffer from the same trauma-borne ailments as male bushwhackers? Did the exceptions—the Frank Jameses of our story—suffer from similar trauma-based ailments on a delayed timeframe because they continued to operate in a wartime mode long after Appomattox? Finally, how did the untold, nameless bushwhackers feel about trends in collective memory that gradually wrote them out of mainstream Civil War narratives and, in doing so, devalued their veteran status? We know how many of the Quantrill men— again, the exceptions—marshaled their notoriety to deal with the evolutions of social memory, but as of yet, we cannot account for men who left no written record of their irregular service.

These questions require answers, too, but the exceptionality of Frank James and his trials can only yield so much. If we are to accurately blueprint the postwar experiences of irregular combatants in the western borderlands (and in other locales in which guerrilla war was endemic), future onus will not be on the narrative of a guerrilla turned bandit turned veteran. Instead, it will be on historians to abandon familiar methods in favor of developing new, interdisciplinary approaches for analyzing all aspects of US veteranhood—including comparisons across wars and centuries. In simplest terms, whether we are trying to understand veterans from the regular theater or their peers from the guerrilla theater, the burden will be on us to adopt the scholarly equivalent of irregular tactics.

NOTES

I would like to thank Kylie Hulbert, Joseph Beilein, and Patrick Lewis for graciously commenting on drafts of this essay.

1. On the surrender at Samuel's Depot see William E. Connelley, *Quantrill and the Border Wars* (Cedar Rapids, IA: Torch, 1909), 478–79; Richard S. Brownlee, *Gray Ghosts of the Confederacy: Guerrilla Warfare in the West, 1861–1865* (Baton Rouge: Louisiana State University Press, 1958), 240; Albert Castel, *William Clarke Quantrill* (New York: F. Fell, 1962), 220.

2. Castel, *William Clarke Quantrill*, 471–79; Albert Castel, "Quantrill's Missouri Bushwhackers in Kentucky: The End of the Trail," in *A Kentucky Sampler: Essays from the Filson Club Quarterly, 1926–1976*, ed. Lowell Hayes Harrison and Nelson L. Dawson (Lexington: University Press of Kentucky, 1977), 215–17.

3. Ora Samuels's account of the meeting held in her father's living room was relayed to me by her grandnephew, Bill Samuels Jr. Ora was six years old when the 1865 meeting took place and, in the late 1940s, served as a babysitter for Bill Samuels Jr., at which time she told him the story on more than one occasion. Ora Sayers also kept one of the pistols Frank James carried at the surrender; the gun is now in the possession of Bill Samuels Jr. at the main office of the Maker's Mark Distillery. The connection between the Samuels family and Quantrill's men ran very deep. Two of Ora's cousins, Sarah and Mary Rachel Samuels, went on to marry Donnie and Bud Pence, respectively. The Pence brothers were among the Quantrill men who surrendered at Samuel's Depot. As previously mentioned, Alexander Sayers was the brother-in-law of Wilson Samuels (father of Sarah and Mary), while Wilson and T. W. Samuels were first cousins. Frank James considered himself kin to T. W. and Wilson because both sides believed Dr. Reuben Samuel had descended from the same line of Samuelses but had at some point dropped the "s" from his surname. Correspondence penned well after the war shows that Frank James maintained his relationships with the Samuels branch of the family. Even the Wakefields, owners of the farm on which Quantrill was fatally shot, were related to the Samuels clan by marriage. See "Frank James to Sarah 'Bell' Samuels Pence, 18 Jan 1909," Maker's Mark Distillery Archive, Loretto, KY.

4. Frank James Parole Papers, July 26, 1865, Maker's Mark Distillery Archive, Loretto, KY; Palmer took a much harder stance against guerrillas hailing from Kentucky, which included funding (but never discarding plausible deniability) the guerrilla hunter program that eliminated Hercules Walker and Bill Marion and allowing the farcical trial and speedy execution of Jerome M. Clark, alias Sue Mundy. In addition to pressure mounted by the Samuels family, Palmer acted leniently with the Missourians because they helped avenge the outrage of a local woman by renegade regular soldiers—an operation that involved Frank James killing a man. On the guerrilla hunter program, see "Edwin Terrill to Governor Thomas E. Bramlette, 17 June 1865," *Civil War Governors of Kentucky Digital Doc-*

umentary Edition, KYR-0001-004-1942. On the rapists executed by James and company, see John M. Palmer, *The Personal Recollections of John M. Palmer: The Story of an Earnest Life* (Cincinnati: R. Clark, 1901), 268–72.

5. *Official Records of the War of the Rebellion* (hereafter *OR*), series 1, vol. 48, part II, 512–13.

6. For discussions of treason prosecutions see Noel C. Fisher, *War at Every Door: Partisan Politics and Guerrilla Violence in East Tennessee, 1860–1869* (Chapel Hill: University of North Carolina Press, 1997), and William A. Blair, *With Malice Toward Some: Treason and Loyalty in the Civil War Era* (Chapel Hill: University of North Carolina Press, 2014).

7. On veterans from the regular theater see Stuart McConnell, *Glorious Contentment: The Grand Army of the Republic, 1865–1900* (Chapel Hill: University of North Carolina Press, 1992); Barbara Gannon, *The Won Cause: Black and White Comradeship in the Grand Army of the Republic* (Chapel Hill: University of North Carolina Press, 2011); James Marten, *Sing Not War: The Lives of Union and Confederate Veterans in Gilded Age America* (Chapel Hill: University of North Carolina Press, 2011); Paul Cimbala, *Veterans North and South: The Transition from Soldier to Civilian after the American Civil War* (Santa Barbara, CA: Praeger, 2015); Donald R. Shaffer, *After the Glory: The Struggles of Black Civil War Veterans* (Lawrence: University Press of Kansas, 2004); and Brian Matthew Jordan, *Marching Home: Union Veterans and Their Unending Civil War* (New York: Liveright, 2014). On trauma and emotional/psychological issues see Diane M. Sommerville, *Aberration of Mind: Suicide and Suffering in the Civil War–Era South* (Chapel Hill: University of North Carolina Press, 2018); Peter Carmichael, "The Trophies of Victory and the Relics of Defeat: Returning Home in the Spring of 1865," in *War Matters: Material Culture in the Civil War Era,* ed. Joan E. Cashin (Chapel Hill: University of North Carolina Press, 2018), 198–221; Dillon J. Carroll, "'The God Who Shielded Me Before . . . yet Watches over Us All': Confederate Soldiers, Mental Illness, and Religion," *Civil War History* 61, no. 3 (September 2015): 252–80; and Dillon Carroll, "The Scourge of War: Injury and Suffering in the American Civil War" (PhD diss., University of Georgia, 2016); and Wayne Wei-Siang Hsieh, "'Go to Your Gawd Like a Soldier': Transnational Reflections on Veteranhood," *Journal of the Civil War Era* 5, no. 4 (December 2015): 551–77.

8. For cutting-edge work on Civil War guerrillas see Andrew Fialka, "Controlled Chaos: Spatiotemporal Patterns within Missouri's Irregular Civil War," in *The Civil War Guerrilla: Unfolding the Black Flag in History, Memory, and Myth,* ed. Joseph M. Beilein Jr. and Matthew C. Hulbert (Lexington: University Press of Kentucky, 2015), 43–70; and "A Spatial Approach to Civil War Missouri's Domestic Supply Line," in *The Guerrilla Hunters: Irregular Conflict During the Civil War,* ed. Brian D. McKnight and Barton A. Myers (Baton Rouge: Louisiana State University Press, 2017), 282–304; Joseph M. Beilein Jr., *Bushwhackers: Guerrilla Warfare, Manhood, and the Household in Civil War Missouri* (Kent, OH: Kent State University Press, 2016); Matthew C. Hulbert, *The Ghosts of Guerrilla Memory: How Civil War Bushwhackers Became Gunslingers in the American West* (Athens: University of Georgia Press, 2016); and Daniel E. Sutherland, *A Savage Conflict: The Decisive Role of Guerrillas in the American Civil War* (Chapel Hill: University of North Carolina Press, 2009).

9. On attempting to recover the wartime activities of bushwhackers through "social-network analysis," see Aaron Astor's excellent essay, "Who Is 'Tinker Dave' Beaty? Hunting Guerrilla Social Networks," in *The Guerrilla Hunters,* ed. McKnight and Myers, 101–22. This essay intentionally differentiates between cavalry raiders (regular cavalry used occasionally to perform irregular tasks such as cutting telegraph lines, raiding supply depots, or disrupting rail traffic), partisan rangers (units

granted permission by the Confederacy to serve as professional guerrillas—that is, to perform guerrilla tasks under the legal umbrella of the regular War Department), and bushwhackers (men who lacked official connections to either War Department and waged irregular war on their own terms, generally at the local level, and who were not afforded any legal protections by the Lieber Code). The distinction is critical because only the lowest tier of guerrilla—the bushwhacker—lacked the legal standing that made a quick transition to veteranhood possible for regular soldiers.

10. As Fialka has demonstrated with GIS mapping, the guerrilla war (in hindsight) was not a totally random affair, but participants often perceived it that way. This perceived chaos heightened the ability of guerrillas to wield terror.

11. On the nature of irregular war, see Philip S. Paludan, *Victims: A True Story of the Civil War* (Knoxville: University of Tennessee Press, 1981); Matthew C. Hulbert, "How to Remember 'This Damnable Guerrilla Warfare': Four Vignettes from Civil War Missouri," *Civil War History* 59, no. 2 (June 2013): 142–67; Joseph M. Beilein Jr., "The Guerrilla Shirt: A Labor of Love and the Style of Rebellion in Civil War Missouri," *Civil War History* 58, no. 2 (June 2012): 151–79; Michael Fellman, *Inside War: The Guerrilla Conflict in Missouri during the American Civil War* (New York: Oxford University Press, 1989); and Fisher, *War at Every Door*.

12. R. M. Lankford, *The Encyclopedia of Quantrill's Guerrillas* (Evening Shade, AR: R. M. Lankford, 1999), 119–22, 122–24; Frank Triplett, *The Life and Times of Jesse James* (Old Saybrook, CT: Konecky and Konecky, 2016), 2–3; T. J. Stiles, *Jesse James: Last Rebel of the Civil War* (New York: Alfred A. Knopf, 2002), 18, 89–90.

13. On the Lawrence Massacre, see Connelley, *Quantrill and the Border Wars*, 284–395; Matthew C. Hulbert, "Larkin Skaggs and the Massacre(s) at Lawrence," in *The Guerrilla Hunters*, ed. McKnight and Myers, 260–81; Richard Cordley, *A History of Lawrence, Kansas: From the First Settlement to the Close of the Rebellion* (Lawrence, KS: E. F. Caldwell, 1895), chapter 5; *OR*, series 1, vol. 24, part III, 467–68, 470; *OR*, series 1, vol. 24, part II, 579–85; L. D. Bailey, *Quantrill's Raid on Lawrence* (Kansas State Historical Society, 1899); and Andrew Walker, *Recollections of Quantrill's Guerrillas* (Weatherford, TX, 1910), ed. Joanne Chiles Eakin (Independence, MO: Two Trails, 1996), 56–63.

14. Connelley, *Quantrill and the Border Wars*, 421–27; Nicole Etcheson, "Massacre at Baxter Spring," *New York Times* Disunion Blog, October 7, 2013; Kip Lindberg and Matt Matthews, "'It Haunts Me Night and Day': The Baxter Springs Massacre," *North & South* 4, no. 5 (June 2001), 42–52; "The Lawrence Massacre—An Appeal," *New York Times*, August 27, 1863; "The Lawrence Massacre," *New York Times*, August 26, 1863; "The Massacres at Lawrence," *Chicago Tribune*, September 1, 1863; Castel, *William Clarke Quantrill*, 150–52, 157–58, 165–66, 169–72.

15. Brownlee, *Gray Ghosts*, 216–20; Thomas D. Thiessen, Douglas D. Scott, Steve J. Dasovich, eds., "'This Work of Fiends': Historical and Archaeological Perspectives on the Confederate Guerrilla Actions at Centralia, Missouri, September 27, 1864," Friends of the Centralia Battlefield and Missouri Civil War Heritage Foundation, 2008; Albert Castel and Tom Goodrich, *Bloody Bill Anderson: The Short, Savage Life of a Civil War Guerrilla* (Mechanicsburg, PA: Stackpole, 1998), 79–86, 88–92; Thomas M. Goodman, *A Thrilling Record* (Des Moines: Mills's, 1868).

16. *OR*, series 1, vol. 24, part III, 471–74 (includes the correspondence discussing Ewing's plan to issue the order and the text of the order itself). A specially trained guerrilla hunter unit caught up with and killed Bloody Bill Anderson in October 1864. See Matthew C. Hulbert, "Killing Bloody

Bill," *New York Times* Disunion Blog, October 29, 2014, and Castel, "Quantrill's Missouri Bushwhackers in Kentucky," 214–15.

17. OR, series 1, vol. 48, part I, 1077; OR, series 1, vol. 48, part II, 325; Palmer, *The Personal Recollections*, 268. For the full account of Terrell and Quantrill, see Matthew C. Hulbert, "The Rise and Fall of Edwin Terrell, Guerrilla Hunter, U.S.A.," *Ohio Valley History* 18, no. 3 (Fall 2018): 42–61.

18. Brownlee, *Gray Ghosts*, 253, 254, 256, 259, 260, 261; Jim Cummins, *The Guerilla* (1908; repr., Kansas City, MO: Promise Land, 2004), 39–41; Joanne Chiles Eakin and Donald Hale, eds., *Branded as Rebels: A List of Bushwhackers, Guerrillas, Partisan Rangers, Confederates and Southern Sympathizers from Missouri during the War Years* (Lee's Summit, MO: J. C. Eakin and D. R. Hale, 1993), 198; Lankford, *Encyclopedia*, 118.

19. In *Jesse James: Last Rebel of the Civil War,* Stiles breaks sharply from the conclusions found in Michael Fellman's *Inside War.* Rather than bloodlust, crime, nihilism, and sociopathy, as Fellman suggests, Stiles pieces together the legitimate political ideologies that motivated guerrillas to fight during the war and in some cases—as in those of the James and Younger brothers—afterward. The propagandizing of John Newman Edwards in *Noted Guerrillas* (1877) only exacerbated the situation; the book heightened the legend of the surviving bushwhackers turned bandits, making them bigger targets in the process.

20. Castel, *William Clarke Quantrill,* 222–23; Stiles, *Jesse James,* 170–73.

21. Castel, *William Clarke Quantrill,* 225–29; Stiles, *Jesse James,* 351–52.

22. Castel, *William Clarke Quantrill,* 230; Triplett, *Life and Times,* 194–99; Stiles, *Jesse James,* 364–65.

23. "John Newman Edwards to Frank James, 17 July 1882" (C1973), John Newman Edwards Letters, State Historical Society of Missouri, Columbia, Missouri (hereafter SHSM-C); "John Newman Edwards to Frank James, 18 August 1882" (C1973), John Newman Edwards Letters, SHSM-C; Stiles, *Jesse James,* 378–79; and Hulbert, *The Ghosts of Guerrilla Memory,* 182, 187. Jesse James was not the first ex-guerrilla to be targeted by the state. Jim Anderson, brother of Bloody Bill, effectively had a bounty put on his head by Missouri governor Thomas Fletcher in 1866: "If they [Anderson] can be captured or killed it would be the best thing for the state I know of." See "1866 Letter from Governor Thomas C. Fletcher to Unnamed Union Colonel" (K0220), State Historical Society of Missouri–Kansas City Research Center.

24. "Frank James to Ann Ralston James, 30 September 1883," image in possession of author; "Frank James to Ann Ralston James, 11 March 1884," image in possession of author; "John Newman Edwards to Frank James, 27 March 1884," image in possession of author; "John Newman Edwards to Frank James, 11 April 1884," image in possession of author; "John Newman Edwards to Frank James, 24 February 1885," image in possession of author. Frank James, Dick Liddil, and Clarence B. Hite, *The Trial of Frank James for Murder: With the Confessions of Dick Liddil and Clarence Hite and History of the "James Gang"* (Kansas City, MO: George Miller, Jr., 1898; repr. Yale Library, Making of Modern Law Collection, n.d.) For overviews of Frank James's trials in Missouri and Alabama see Gerard S. Petrone, *Judgement at Gallatin: The Trial of Frank James* (Lubbock: Texas Tech University Press, 1998), and James P. Muehlberger, *The Lost Cause: The Trials of Frank and Jesse James* (Yardley: Westholme, 2013).

25. James, Liddil, and Hite, *The Trial of Frank James,* 152–55, 157–58.

26. Ibid., *The Trial of Frank James,* 194–96, 198, 273–76, 278.

27. "Capias—Warrant, Frank James, Daviess County, Grand Larceny, February 1884," Missouri State Archives, Jefferson City, MO; Petrone, *Judgement at Gallatin*, 191–96; Stiles, *Jesse James*, 380.

28. A useful comparison is that of high-profile Confederates who survived the war such as Davis, Lee, Longstreet, or Beauregard. They were the most famous men associated with their cause in the regular theater still living, just as high-profile bushwhackers were among the most famous—or in this case, notorious—men to survive the war in the guerrilla theater. Neither high-profile group's transition to veteranhood mirrored that of the nameless rank-and-file from their respective theaters of war, partly because men from both groups were held more responsible for wartime death and destruction.

29. On silences in the archive as evidence of broader data trends see Ann Stoler, *Along the Archival Grain: Epistemic Anxieties and Colonial Common Sense* (Princeton, NJ: Princeton University Press, 2008), and Luisa Passerini, "Memories Between Silence and Oblivion," in *Memory, History, Nation: Contested Pasts,* ed. Katharine Hodgkin and Susannah Radstone (Piscataway, NJ: Transaction, 2003), 238–54.

30. The notion that irregular wartime experiences necessarily created irregular postwar memories is detailed in Hulbert, *The Ghosts of Guerrilla Memory*. Here I contend similarly that the transition to guerrilla veteranhood from guerrilla warfare was directly influenced by the nature of the latter and its role as regular wartime experience for many borderland residents.

Speaking for Themselves

Disabled Veterans and Civil War Medical Photography

SARAH HANDLEY-COUSINS

I N FEBRUARY 1887, Rowland Ward, a farmer from upstate New York, wrote a letter to President Grover Cleveland, asking him for an increase in his pension. Ward served with the 4th New York Heavy Artillery until August 1864, when a shell fragment struck him in the face at the Battle of Ream's Station, tearing off his lower jaw. Though the wound had been closed by the army surgeon J. C. McKee, it left him only a small mouth opening and no ability to chew. He never ate solid food again. By the time he wrote to Cleveland, he had already applied for and received several small pension increases, ensuring that his rate remained commensurate with a rating of total disability, which Ward believed he met. After reaching out to others—including Surgeon General John Hamilton and Pension Commissioner John Black—Ward took his case to the president himself: "I have the Heart decease and deaf I am 69 years old in march if you can do anything for me I should take it as a great faver for I cannot whork. . . . I have to have everything that I eat prepared for me in A liquid form and I cannot masticate any thing."[1] His pleas must have worked, because Cleveland eventually approved a special act of Congress in 1889 raising Ward's pension to fifty dollars a month.

What distinguishes Rowland Ward's pension file from thousands of others is that his profoundly altered face was well-known to the Surgeon General's Office and to the clerks of the Pension Bureau. Indeed, a copy of his photograph, trimmed into a small oval, was glued to his disability discharge form in his pension file. After he was wounded, Ward was packed off to Lincoln Hospital in Washington, DC, where J. C. McKee performed cheiloplastic surgery and had Ward photographed several times. Thus the details of his condition, and its minute changes over time as he slowly healed, were carefully recorded.

Together, the visual and textual record of his ordeal was displayed in the Army Medical Museum and published in the *Medical and Surgical History of the War of the Rebellion*. At some point, a clerk in the Pension Bureau received a copy of one of the photographs, cropped it down, and affixed it to Ward's disability paperwork, ensuring that anyone who opened the file would see exactly what Ward and his doctors described in his many applications and medical examinations. There could be no question what the war did to Rowland Ward.

Ward's photograph composed part of the much larger project undertaken by the Office of the Surgeon General to document the medical history of the Civil War. In 1862, when the Army Medical Museum was created, Surgeon General William Hammond required that physicians treating soldiers send case files, physical remains, sketches, and photographs to stock the museum, supplemented by images created under the direction of the museum itself. Later, this same material would serve as the basis for the case studies, data, and illustrations published in the official medical history of the war, the *Medical and Surgical History of the War of the Rebellion*.[2] As Shauna Devine demonstrates, medical photography was a critical step in the professionalization of US medicine. At the same time, according to scholars J. T. H. Connor and Michael Rhode, both the photographers and their subjects believed the photographs represented more than scientific documentation of medical conditions. Rather, they created a "visual culture of medicine" that captured the ethos of the war. Others have interpreted the photographs as the most truthful visual representations of the conflict: the photographic version of "writing degree zero," or realistic writing without artifice.[3] In general, scholars have concluded that the photographs served two purposes: to document the medical reality of the war and to function as part of the larger process of memory creation.[4] Yet many suggest the photographs also served a practical purpose, documenting disabilities for use in pension applications, suggesting that both medical professionals and patients benefited from this arrangement.[5]

While Civil War medical photography has been aptly interpreted in several modes, it has yet to be viewed through the frame of disability history. This essay will place Civil War medical photography within the larger context of visual representations of disabled people and complicate the interpretation that the photographs were part of a project that was beneficial to both physicians and patients. Although medical photographs were sometimes used in pension files, my research suggests that this supplies evidence of Union veterans' own self-advocacy, as opposed to an effort by the Army Medical Department to assist grievously wounded ex-soldiers. Veterans might have gleaned fringe benefits from the project to document the war's bodily toll, but only through their own determination. Fleshing out the stories behind those few pension file pictures reveals just how much work there is yet to do to understand Civil War disability.

WHILE THE ARMY MEDICAL MUSEUM collected many medical curiosities and specimens, the visual holdings of the museum's collection, consisting of photographs, sketches, lithographs, and paintings, have long garnered scholarly and public interest. The images are striking and continue to demand the attention of viewers more than a century after they were taken. Since 2011, an exhibition curated by the National Library of Medicine, called "Life and Limb: The Toll of the American Civil War," has been traveling across the United States, prominently displaying several of these images.[6] Literary scholar Kathy Newman writes that the images "assaulted my senses as no CNN footage ever had," including the live coverage of the Persian Gulf War.[7] While the suffering inflicted by the Civil War can seem distant and abstract with the passage of time, there is something particularly powerful about these images that forces the viewer to confront the painful reality of the wages of war.

Indeed, according to J. T. H. Connor and Michael Rhode, "photographers and their subjects 'knew' that they were participating in more than a simple, objective visual recording of a biomedical condition or injury."[8] This is an appealing thought: it is a powerful idea that the doctors, photographers, and patients worked together to create a record of the bodily aftermath of the war, permanently inscribing in the history books what the war had wrought on the human body. However, very little exists about what the curators, photographers, and subjects thought about while the images were taken. Did soldiers resent sitting for portraits or think of them as an extension of their patriotic duty? Did photographers see it as another day on the job or a sacred honor? Whether all involved believed they were doing more than simply collecting medical data is not entirely clear.

Soldiers' bodies held tremendous potential to create meaning out of the war. Authors and artists deployed them in image, poetry, and prose to shape a memory of the war that emphasized the righteousness of the Union cause.

Bodies of disabled soldiers proved particularly useful because wounds fostered both pity and political capital. Postwar popular magazines and newspapers, for example, contained many sentimental stories and poems featuring pathetic old soldiers who reassured readers that their wounds had contributed to the Union victory. One poem, written by E. Jay Allen, a veteran of the 155th Pennsylvania in 1886, describes an aging veteran "in whose gleaming eyes / the glory of the past doth shine" and assures him that his sacrifices were critical to the outcome of the war: "They noble deeds, who 'gainst the wrong / The flag of freedom first unfurled / And suffering, made the nation strong."[9] The Civil War generation yearned to find meaning in the bodies of disabled veterans; thus they were often linked to Union victory. E. Jay Allen's poem also indicates that veterans themselves eagerly contributed to crafting the narrative of the war. Brian Matthew Jordan writes about a veteran who referred to himself as a "living monument of that late cruel and bloody Rebellion," fashioning his own body into a kind of witness to future generations.[10]

Megan Kate Nelson demonstrates that images of disabled veterans played a critical role in the postwar public's attempt to understand the wounds of war.[11] Disabled soldiers appeared on the pages of the most widely read periodicals in engravings that showed them in a generally sympathetic light. Thomas Waterman Wood's painting *The Veteran* depicts a black Union veteran saluting while leaning on his crutches, having lost a leg, his gun and bayonet hanging on the wall behind him. The soldier is still couched in militaria—Union uniform, weapons within reach, encircled by knapsack, flag, and tent—linking him to the trappings of patriotic masculinity. While many images were created to bolster the victorious memory of the war, Nelson argues, others suggested more discomfort at disability. Winslow Homer's illustration for an 1865 *Harper's Weekly* story entitled *Our Watering Places, The Empty Sleeve at Newport* is one such example. This particular image depicts a veteran sitting passively as his female companion leans forward aggressively to drive their carriage. The veteran's face looks drawn and resigned, and the veil of the woman's hat blows onto his own, giving the impression that he is wearing a feminine headpiece. Homer's engraving suggests that perhaps veterans would be unable to reclaim their previous roles, both within their interpersonal relationships and within society at large.

Veterans sometimes used images of their disabled bodies for their own benefit. A significant postwar problem for many disabled veterans—particularly those who had physical differences that barred them from returning to their prewar trades—was earning an income. As disabled people had for centuries, veterans sometimes used their wounds to solicit charity. Some had themselves photographed for begging cards, small cartes de visite they distributed to passersby when asking for alms. In begging cards, veterans controlled the ways they revealed or posed their bodies, setting the terms on which able-bodied viewers viewed and understood their bodily differences. One such card, reproduced in Robert Bogdan's *Picturing Disability*, features two Union veterans, each apparently missing his left arm. One man wears a medal on his lapel, and each holds a symbol of the conflict: a rifle and a US flag. The men crafted the image in such a way that unmistakably linked their disability to the war, cause, and country but also reaffirmed their masculinity, as indicated by the foregrounded rifle. In a society that believed disability and pauperism went hand in hand, visually linking their wounds to the war with overtly patriotic and masculine symbols separated themselves from other disabled people and made them worthy of charitable giving rather than indolent paupers taking advantage of the public's generosity.[12]

One veteran who became well known for using his image on begging cards was Benjamin Franklin Work. (He eventually dropped his last name to capitalize on the name recognition that came with sharing a name with a founding father.) Franklin enlisted in 1862 and served with the 12th Iowa Infantry. The unit saw some of the most intense fighting at Shiloh, and, not long after, Franklin was discharged for a disability. A few months later he enlisted again, this time in the 2nd Minnesota Cavalry.[13] He served with the cavalry for the remainder of the war and remained in the service after the war ended, as the cavalry units turned their attention to the intensifying conflicts with western Native tribes. In December 1865, Franklin received a furlough. On his way to Fort Ridgley, he was caught in a blizzard and was snowbound for eight days without shelter. By the time he was rescued, he suffered severe frostbite, and the physicians at Fort Ridgley had no choice but to amputate all four of his limbs. After his discharge from the army, Franklin struggled to make ends meet. Though he was a soldier when he lost his limbs, securing a pension was not straightforward because Franklin's wounds were not technically a result of the war but rather of a freak snowstorm during a furlough. Nonetheless, he eventually received support through a special act of Congress.[14]

To supplement his pension, Franklin had himself photographed and turned the images into begging cards. One, most likely taken in 1873, showed him wearing civilian garb and standing on the stumps of his legs. Franklin appeared to be using adaptive technologies of his own devising. Rather than prosthetics, he had contraptions that looked like shoes fitted to his legs, no doubt to help stabilize him and cushion the ends of his legs from the impact of walking. His crutches were also uniquely suited to his needs. They were short, fitting under his arms, but with the addition of loops of leather that fit around his wrists, which made it possible for him to control their movement. Franklin's story appeared on the back of the begging card. It appealed to public sympathy by calling him "the UNFORTUNATE SOLDIER," suggested he was the only veteran in the United States without hands and feet, and assured those who might purchase his card that he was "trying to sell his Photographs for the benefit of his family."[15] Franklin was particularly skilled in selling his cards. Unsatisfied to stand on street corners and ask for charity, he traveled to Washington, DC, in 1889 to sell his photographs at President Harrison's inauguration. Franklin had himself photographed numerous times and in numerous poses. Most resemble the 1873 image: standing on his adaptive shoes using crutches or seated with the crutches nearby, as if testifying to his reliance on their assistance. A later photograph was more revealing, showing an older, shirtless Franklin reclining on a chair, holding his stumps aloft to display the scars on the ends of his limbs.[16]

Franklin's case is useful here because it demonstrates the complexity of begging cards. The cards offered Franklin the opportunity to capitalize on his disability by appealing to people's charitableness, particularly toward disabled soldiers. On his early begging cards, which feature the story of the blizzard on the reverse, Franklin worked to establish his worth. People in the nineteenth-century United States were suspicious of those who asked for alms and separated the poor into two categories: the worthy and unworthy. The worthy were in need because of events outside of their control, while the unworthy, or paupers, were simply lazy and manipulative moochers.[17] The begging cards, complete with an explanation for why he asked for alms, attempted to situate Franklin within the category of the worthy. Robert Bogdan adds that begging cards also attempted to place disabled charity seekers within "ideas of rugged individualism and American capitalism."[18] They were not simply a plea for alms but an attempt to make the best of their situation by leveraging their disability to earn an income.

On the other hand, Franklin was trapped in the same position experienced by many disabled people in the public eye. While he may have been entrepreneurial, he had to emphasize and exploit his bodily difference to catch the attention of potential patrons. Franklin's images fall somewhere between two of the visual rhetorics Rosemarie Garland-Thompson describes in her study of disability photography: the sentimental and the exotic. His earlier photographs appealed more strongly to the pity of the viewer, while the later one—by far the most graphic—strayed into the territory of the freak show, emphasizing Franklin's bodily difference "for the viewers' amusement and amazement" to maximize profit.[19] After all, Franklin's pictures emerged as the freak show was at its height; they would certainly have been read and collected within that context.[20] The ultimate result was mixed: Franklin capitalized on his disability by selling his images, but it is overly simplistic to interpret this as purely empowering. Rather, the pictures reflect the experience of physical difference in an ableist society and tell the story of a man who had few options but to put his body on display for a living.

Benjamin Franklin's images, however, were not medical photography—his photographs were taken by civilian photographers for his own purposes. The images taken by the Army Medical Department (AMD) during and after the Civil War present a different story of disability photography. These pictures functioned as one part of a larger effort to record the medical history of the war. In 1862, Surgeon General William Hammond issued a series of circulars and orders that authorized the creation of the Army Medical Museum to serve as a repository for medical specimens and an institution for learning. He directed army surgeons to "diligently collect and forward to the office of the Surgeon General all specimens of morbid anatomy, surgical or medical, which may be regarded as valuable; together with projectiles and foreign bodies removed; and such other matter as may prove of interest in the study of military medicine and surgery."[21] In addition to this preserved matter, AMD surgeons worked to record injuries visually using photography, paintings, and sketches. Implicitly, Circular No. 2 gave the AMD the right to the bodies of sick and injured soldiers. The document made it clear that soldiers had signed their bodies, as well as their lives, over to the service of the US government. In an age well before consent laws, this was all the authorization physicians needed to seize amputated body parts and disinter corpses from graves and display these items to the public through medical museums and exhibitions.[22] As civilians used the idea and image of disabled Civil War veterans as a political tool or scapegoat, the AMD used them as materia medica in the advancement of the US medical profession.

In an 1871 article for *Lippincott's Magazine,* Assistant Surgeon General J. J. Woodward attempted to explain the purpose of the museum to a nonmedical audience and situated the museum and its many specimens as part of the advance of medical knowledge. "The science of Medicine is essentially progressive; with increasing knowledge comes more subtle skill, and the advances already made warrant hopefulness as to the future."[23] Times of "pestilence and war" served to inspire "the genius of those who have devoted themselves to medical pursuits," he argued, leading to "new discoveries, and to accumulate stores of knowledge which serve to increase their usefulness in ordinary times."[24] The museum and its specimens were vital to the future of medical education but also to cementing the centrality of anatomical expertise to the medical profession, which helped assure "regular" physicians would have a professional edge over the anatomically naïve, like homeopaths, midwives, and quacks.[25] The war presented the Army Medical Department with massive numbers of sick and wounded soldiers. Preserving what they could of those patients ensured that training benefits would accrue long after the cessation of hostilities.

The medical photography collected by the Army Medical Museum was just one part of the larger project of documenting the Civil War's medical history. Photography and artistic renderings could show how wounds healed over time, document the stages of erysipelas or gangrene, and capture the overall effects of a missing limb or bullet wound in ways that preserving small pieces of necrosed bone could not. Photography ensured that the history of the work physicians performed during the war was not lost but also that nonmilitary medical professionals, both contemporary and future, learned from the wounded.[26] In this way, Woodward argued, the museum could make a major impact on doctors, medicals schools, and libraries around the world. During the war, the museum began to circulate printed images, with accompanying case histories, for surgeons to use in their field practice. "Since the war," he added, "a large number of photographs of this class, with many others of medical and microscopical specimens, have been given away, not merely to medical officers of the army, but also to the medical societies, libraries and medical colleges, as well as to foreign museums and other institutions."[27] Photographs, in other words, did what specimens could not: transport the knowledge gathered by the museum beyond its own walls.

What soldiers and veterans felt about being photographed, however, is largely a mystery. If there are records of soldiers talking to doctors about being photographed, or asking not to be photographed, they are waiting to be discovered. Some surgeons believed they shared a similar perspective about the photographs with their patients. John Shaw Billings, who served the Army Medical Library between 1883 and 1893, argued as much in an address to a gathering of physicians: "The old pensioner likes to keep the battered ball which crippled him, and so these relics have an interest beyond that which is purely professional."[28] Billings was certainly not wrong; Joshua Lawrence Chamberlain, as just one example, kept the ball that wounded him in his home. Billings also noted, "That the nation is not crippled by its loss takes nothing from their interest, and the fact we are physicians does not imply that we look upon them from a medical or scientific standpoint only." What exactly he meant by this is unclear, because he also emphasizes that sentiment had no place in the museum: "For scientific and professional purposes, we of course, want a history of the specimen, which will as far as possible, give the data connected with its peculiarities, and among these may be race, occupation, and even name, though the emotional element does not enter into it at all."[29] Whatever additional contemplations the physicians of the Army Medical Museum may have had, Billings clearly believed that photographs and specimens were primarily valuable not as talismans of the war but because of their medical significance. If they also inspired a deeper feeling, that was only secondary.

Though it is difficult to ascertain the perspective of soldiers and veterans, pension files offer some clues as to how soldiers thought about and used images of their own bodies. Rowland Ward, the former private of the 4th New York Heavy Artillery who lost his jaw, often referred to his photographs in his communications with the Pension Bureau. Ward wrote to the surgeon general in 1869 to ask that copies of the photographs and his case history be sent to the Pension Bureau. The *Medical and Surgical History of the War of the Rebellion* indicates that "the letter, with photographs and a history of his case, was forwarded to the Pension Office."[30] It seems likely, then, that the small oval photograph glued to Ward's Certificate of Disability Discharge was supplied by the Army Medical Museum. In a deposition conducted in 1888, recorded by a notary public, Ward referred again to his connection to the Army Medical Museum: "His case was attended by U.S. Army Surgeons and all the particulars in regard thereto are fully reported, and Photographs nos. 168, 169, 170, & 186 in the Army Medical Museum show the appearance of the wound in various phases. And deponent begs leave to refer to the report of the Medical officer of the government and to such photographs as a part of his case."[31] Several letters in his pension file suggest that Ward did not have copies of these photographs, instead relying on the Surgeon General's Office to forward the image to the Pension Bureau, or asking pension clerks to consult with the Army Medical Museum. Ward did, however, have copies of his history from the *Medical and Surgical History of the War of the Rebellion*, and he sent several to the Pension Bureau over the years. In 1886, Ward sent the Pension Bureau a history of his case with a letter asking about the possibility of a pension increase or arrears. A copy remains attached to the letter.[32] In 1897, Ward wrote yet again to the Pension Bureau in a fairly cryptic letter intended to report what he believed was a case of pension fraud. Ward intentionally did not sign the letter ("i shall not sine my name on this") but added a postscript that again brought up his case history from the *Medical and Surgical History*, which he enclosed: "Plese examine the loose sheet it will tell you all about me."[33] Several decades after Ward's death, his widow was still sending copies of his history—in 1932, she wrote that she had just had additional copies printed up.

Ward's letters to the Pension Bureau demonstrate that he believed his photographs and case history were important tools he could use to support his claim for a pension; however, these tools did not free him from the bureaucratic nightmare of the Pension Bureau. Ward's disability—though clearly apparent in the photographs of his face—did not fit into the categories created by the Pension Bureau to designate payouts. The bureau calculated pensions based on a veteran's ability to perform manual labor and focused on the functionality of fingers, hands, arms, feet, and legs. Other disabilities were calculated by judging how they compared to those deemed most incompatible to manual labor. For example, in 1872, "The statutory rates covered the loss of both hands, both feet, the sight in both eyes, the sight in one eye, and one hand, foot, arm, or leg; total disability in hands, feet, arms, or legs; a disability equivalent to the loss of hand or foot; requirements of regular aid and attendance; and total deafness." From there, disabilities were further broken down into grades: first grade was a "permanent disability requiring the regular aid and attendance of another person," a second grade made a veteran incapable of manual labor, and a third grade was anything "equivalent to the loss of a hand or foot."[34] Beyond that, disabilities could be further broken down into portions of a third-grade rate in degrees of eighteen.

It was hard to situate Ward's disability within these guidelines. Though Ward's facial wounds significantly impacted his daily life, they did not interfere with his ability to perform manual labor. The official documentation of his disability helped convey its severity, even though it did not exactly fit specifications. In 1888, he took his case to the US House of Representatives. His case history from the *Medical and Surgical History* was entered into the record, with the added note, "His condition is surely deplorable, and in fact worse than that of persons who have lost both hands or both feet, for which disabilities a higher rate of pension that that asked for in the bill is provided."[35] By the time of his death, Ward received fifty dollars a month.

Brigadier General Henry A. Barnum had a similar experience. In 1862, at the Battle of Malvern Hill, a rebel bullet sliced through his abdomen, leaving him with a wound that never healed. In order to stave off infection, Barnum had to keep the wound open and draining; he did so by using a soft rope ring made of oakum that he turned by degrees throughout the day. Barnum also sat—or, more accurately, stood—for the photographers of the Army Medical Museum, and his case also appears in the *Medical and Surgical History of the War of the Rebellion.* Yet Barnum also had difficulty obtaining a pension he considered commensurate with his level of disability. Though found "totally" disabled for the purposes of manual labor, he was pensioned at a fairly low monthly rate when first approved in 1866. In 1888, Barnum wrote to attorney George M. Lockwood, asking for assistance in getting his pension rate raised. "My sufferings in the past year have been much greater than formerly," Barnum wrote, "on account of frequent & *severe* abscesses caused by exfoliated dead bone."[36] To support his claim, he did something Ward could not do: he enclosed a photograph, taken around 1881. While Ward had copies of his case history, he needed to ask the Surgeon General's Office to supply the Pension Bureau with his photograph. Barnum, on the other hand, seemed to have several photographs in his own possession. "I will send with this a photo of the wound, which may aid my case—No, on reflection I think at Comr. Dudley's request I gave him one to file with the papers in my case—If you do not find such an one with my papers, let me know & I will send one for inspection &

return as I have no other."[37] This letter indicates that Barnum had, at least at one point, several copies of photographs he could use to strengthen his pension application. His persistence apparently paid off. That same year, his photograph, along with testimony from his physician, convinced the Pension Bureau to double his payout for "total helplessness requiring the regular aid and attendance of another person."[38]

The pension file of Eben Smith—an amputee who was the subject of three paintings and one photograph commissioned by the museum—indicates that images were not used as evidence in a pension case unless the veteran himself entered them. A painting of Smith, made by Hermann Faber, hung prominently in the Army Medical Museum. Indeed, Michael Rhode and J. T. H. Connor quote journalist Louis Bagger's powerful description of the experience of viewing the painting: "There is on the wall, in the northwest corner of the room, a small gallery of watercolor paintings. . . . Among these is one, the picture of a young man, a mere boy of eighteen or nineteen, resting on a couch. . . . It is a beautiful face, almost perfect in its contour, with hazel eyes and long, wavy, brown hair; but there is such an expression in the eyes and features as tells—oh, what a tale!—of suffering, long and patiently borne."[39] The painting is powerful: Smith is propped up by a large pillow, facing away from the painter, naked from the waist down to reveal the healing stump of his hip.[40]

If Smith knew that journalists wrote about viewing his body as it appeared in the paintings at the museum, he gave no indication in his pension files. In fact, Smith never made mention of the existence of any of the images in his pension documents, nor do any of those who wrote on his behalf, including his wife and members of his Grand Army of the Republic (GAR) post. It is not as though Smith did not need the support: letters submitted on his behalf describe the old soldier suffering from chronic pain at the surgical site and in constant fear that the fragile artery at the base of his stump would burst. This made it impossible for him to wear a prosthetic leg. In the 1880s, in need of more constant care, Smith moved from Maine to Wisconsin to live with his brother and sister-in-law. He was largely unable to leave the house. During the winter, he could not use his crutches in the snow, and in the summer, his sister-in-law testified, "He is unable to walk but a short distance and is always accompanied by some member of the family to assist him in case of accident with which he is very liable to meet when walking."[41] He was unable to work. Though Smith and his supporters testified more than once that he required constant care, he was classified second grade (unfit for manual labor but not requiring care) and only given minimal increases, until a lengthy testimonial written and signed by numerous comrades from his GAR post helped convince Congress to pass a private pension bill raising his pension to sixty dollars.[42]

The medical photography arranged and collected by the surgeon general and Army Medical Museum could be powerful evidence in pension claims, as demonstrated by both Henry Barnum's and Rowland Ward's case files. That does not, however, indicate that the photographs were part of a quid pro quo relationship between patient and physician. Neither Barnum's nor Ward's pension file includes an indication of support from a representative of the museum or the Surgeon General's Office. Instead, it was veterans and their advocates who deployed the *Medical and Surgical History of the War of the Rebellion* case histories or photographs. Ward wrote to the surgeon general in 1869 asking for help with his pension application, hoping that the photographs and case history could strengthen his case. In subsequent years, he repeatedly pointed out the existence of his photographs in correspondence with the Pension Bureau. Likewise, Barnum referred his photographs in letters to his attorney, and went so far as to send along a copy of the photograph to ensure it was included as evidence. Eben Smith, on the other hand, whose image was recorded four times in the Army Medical Museum, did not have any images included in pension files, although the strength of their testimony could have helped Smith earn a much-needed pension increase. Smith never mentioned the images, and there is no evidence that he requested that the Army Medical Museum forward them to the Pension Bureau. The pension files, then, are examples of self-advocacy, evidence that disabled veterans used what they could to ensure they were fairly supported by the state for their suffering. This was something that veterans did for themselves.

HISTORIANS CONTINUOUSLY rediscover, reinvent, and reinterpret the Civil War through modern eyes. In recent years, the medical photography produced by and for the Army Medical Museum during the war has become a symbol of the suffering and horror of the war. Perhaps news coverage of soldier amputees, home from war zones in Iraq and Afghanistan and using cutting-edge prosthetics, sparked new interest in the photographs. Freshly attuned to the destruction war can visit on the body, perhaps we see an equivalence between photographs taken then and now. Since Vietnam, images of disabled veterans, like flag-draped coffins, have come to indicate truth. Even when military or political authorities obscure the motivations for a conflict, we believe the body does not lie. This idea appears in interpretations of Civil War medical photography. Mick Gidley suggests that "Civil War medical photographs could be 'photography degree zero'" because they offer the most honest, truthful, and accurate depictions of suffering.[43] Suffering is clear in these images; it is difficult to look at the photographs of Rowland Ward's gaping neck, devoid of bottom jaw, and fail to comprehend the pain the war wrought. Yet in some ways images of disabled veterans have become voyeuristic shortcuts that allow us to get at the war's destruction without engaging in messy stories with confounding characters and unclear legacies. In her analysis of photography and disability, Rosemarie Garland-Thompson argues, "The history of disabled people in the western world is in part the history of being on display, of being visually conspicuous while being politically and socially erased."[44] The veterans who were painted and photographed by the artists of the Army Medical Museum embodied this paradox: images of their bodies were displayed and examined, used for ends other than their own, yet when it came to individual compensation, they were left to advocate for themselves. If these images truly spoke for themselves, why did disabled veterans have to work so hard to be heard?

Rather than being the most revealing or honest artifacts of the war, I would argue that these images actually conceal a great deal. What appears self-evident in an image is in reality only the opening to more mysteries. Did Rowland Ward yearn to share in family meals? Did Eben Smith feel trapped in his sister-in-law's Wisconsin home, when snowdrifts meant he could not get out for fresh air? Were disabled soldiers comforted by a knowledge that their losses helped bring victory or medical progress, or did it make little difference when they were in pain or immobile? Even if historians may never be able to answer these questions, it must be said that our narratives of the war sometimes leave little room in which to ask them. Our words, Wayne Wei-siang Hsieh writes, too often impose "on war a narrative or causal coherence it does not possess."[45] Until we embrace disabled veterans as the subjects of their own stories—not symbols to be deployed in the service of our own narratives—the history of Civil War disability will remain incomplete.

NOTES

1. Rowland Ward to Grover Cleveland, February 7, 1887, Rowland Ward Pension Case File, Certificate Number 47,031, National Archives and Records Administration, Washington, DC (hereafter NARA).

2. Joseph K. Barnes, *The Medical and Surgical History of the War of the Rebellion (1861–65)*, 2 vols. (Washington, DC: Government Printing Office, 1870).

3. Shauna M. Devine, *Learning from the Wounded: The Civil War and the Rise of American Medical Science* (Chapel Hill: University of North Carolina Press, 2014); J. T. H. Connor and Michael Rhode, "Shooting Soldiers: Civil War Medical Images, Memory, and Identity in America," *InVisible Culture* 5 (2003); Mick Gidley, "Painful Looks: Reading Civil War Photographs," in *Life and Limb: Perspectives on the American Civil War*, ed. David Seed, Stephen C. Kenny, and Chris Williams (Liverpool: Liverpool University Press, 2015), 100.

4. See Alan Trachtenberg, *Reading American Photographs: Images as History, Mathew Brady to Walker Evans* (New York: Hill and Wang, 1989); Lisa A. Long, *Rehabilitating Bodies: Health, History, and the American Civil War* (Philadelphia: University of Pennsylvania Press, 2004); and Franny Nudelman, *John Brown's Body: Slavery, Violence, & the Culture of Civil War* (Chapel Hill: University of North Carolina Press, 2004).

5. See, e.g., Connor and Rhode, "Shooting Soldiers."

6. "Life and Limb: The Toll of the American Civil War," National Library of Medicine, National Institutes of Health, https://www.nlm.nih.gov/exhibition/lifeandlimb/index.html.

7. Kathy M. Newman, "Wounds and Wounding in the American Civil War: A (Visual) History," *Yale Journal of Criticism* 6 (1993): 63.

8. Connor and Rhode, "Shooting Soldiers."

9. E. Jay Allen, "The Veteran," *Salt Lake Tribune*, July 7, 1887. For more on how disabled Civil War soldiers and veterans were used in the media see Frances Clarke, *War Stories: Suffering and Sacrifice in the Civil War North* (Chicago: University of Chicago Press, 2011), and John A. Casey Jr., *New Men: Reconstructing the Image of the Veteran in Late-Nineteenth Century American Literature and Culture* (New York: Fordham University Press, 2015).

10. Brian Matthew Jordan, "'Living Monuments': Union Veteran Amputees and the Embodied Memory of the Civil War," *Civil War History* 57 (2011): 121.

11. Megan Kate Nelson, *Ruin Nation: Destruction in the American Civil War* (Athens: University of Georgia Press, 2012), 186.

12. See Robert Bogdan, *Picturing Disability: Beggar, Freak, Citizen, and Other Photographic Rhetoric* (Syracuse, NY: Syracuse University Press, 2012), 31. Bogdan notes that it is not always clear in these cards whether or not the individual presenting themselves as disabled truly was disabled. The men in the image could be nondisabled men passing themselves off as veteran amputees. As Bogdan writes, "Whether beggars were truly disabled or not does not change the way they appeared on their cards" (24). The legitimacy of their disability was less a factor in the photograph's interpretation than the subjects' framing and use of disability. Another carte de visite begging card is described by Connor and Rhode, "Shooting Soldiers."

13. "Report," May 24, 1866, *Reports of Committees of the Senate of the United States, 39th Congress* (Washington, DC: Government Printing Office, 1866).

14. Ibid.

15. Bailey & Magraw Photography, *Benjamin Franklin,* 1873, Archives and Special Collections, University Libraries, University of South Dakota. This claim was not true, according to writer Marlin Peterson, but was further evidence of Franklin's skill for marketing his image. "Author Speaks on the Curious Life of Ben Franklin Work," *New Ulm Journal,* New Ulm, Minnesota, n.d. Franklin was not the main source of support for his wife and stepchildren. His wife, Georgianna Way, considered a Minnesota pioneer, maintained a boarding house in Blue Earth, Minnesota, until 1910. Undoubtedly, this business provided the majority of the family's income.

16. A. B. Russ, "Mrs. Georgianna Franklin-Way," Faribault County Historical Society, http://www.fchistorical.org/index.php/archives/mrs-georgianna-franklin-way; "Author Speaks on the Curious Life of Ben Franklin Work," *New Ulm Journal,* New Ulm, Minnesota, n.d.; Martin County Historical Society, "Benjamin Franklin, The Unfortunate Soldier"; "Pvt. Benjamin Franklin," National Museum of Health and Medicine, https://www.flickr.com/photos/medicalmuseum/3299288889/in/photolist-62xHDc. Marlin Peterson testified that Franklin's begging cards traveled long distances; one even turned up in Australia.

17. See Michael B. Katz, *In The Shadow of the Poorhouse: A Social History of Welfare in America* (New York: Basic Books, 1986, 1996), and Nancy Fraser and Linda Gordon, "A Genealogy of Dependency: Tracing a Keyword of the U. S. Welfare State," *Signs* 19 (1994): 309–36.

18. Bogdan, *Picturing Disability,* 40–41.

19. Rosemarie Garland-Thomson, "Seeing the Disabled: Visual Rhetorics of Disability in Popular Photography," in *The New Disability History: American Perspectives,* ed. Paul K. Longmore and Lauri Umansky (New York: New York University, 2001), 344.

20. Robert Bogdan, "The Social Construction of Freaks," in *Freakery: Cultural Spectacles of the Extraordinary Body,* ed. Rosemarie Garland-Thomson (New York: New York University Press, 1992), 23.

21. William Grace, *The Army Surgeon's Manual, for the Use of Medical Officers, Cadets, Chaplains and Hospital Stewards* (New York: Bailliere Brothers, 1864), 101. Many thanks to Michael Rhode, who helped me make sense of the implications of Circular no. 2.

22. See Sarah Handley-Cousins, *Bodies in Blue: Disability in the Civil War North* (Athens: University of Georgia Press, 2019); Devine, *Learning from the Wounded.*

23. J. J. Woodward, "The Army Medical Museum at Washington," *Lippincott's Magazine of Popular Literature and Science* 7, no. 15 (March 1871): 233..

24. Ibid.

25. For the professionalization of US medicine, see Devine, *Learning from the Wounded;* Paul Starr, *The Social Transformation of American Medicine* (New York: Basic Books, 1982); Ira Rutkow, *Seeking the Cure: The History of American Medicine* (New York: Simon and Schuster, 2010); Charles Rosenberg, *The Care of Strangers: The Rise of America's Hospital System* (New York: Basic Books, 1987); and Margaret Humphries, *Marrow of Tragedy: The Health Crisis of the American Civil War* (Baltimore: Johns Hopkins University Press, 2013).

26. Devine, *Learning from the Wounded.*

27. Woodward, "The Army Medical Museum at Washington," 242.

28. J. S. Billings, *Medical Museums, with Special Reference to the Army Medical Museum at Washington* (Medical News, 1888), 35.

29. Ibid., 26.

30. Barnes, *Medical and Surgical History of the War of the Rebellion,* vol. 2, part I, 373–74.

31. Deposition of Rowland Ward, September 27, 1888, Rowland Ward Pension Case File, Certificate Number 47,031, NARA.

32. Rowland Ward to Commissioner Black, n.d. (ca. 1886), Rowland Ward Pension Case File, Certification Number 47,031, NARA.

33. Rowland Ward to "Commissioner Pension," June 27, 1895, Rowland Ward Pension Case File, Certificate Number 47,031, NARA. In 1895, Ward was seventy-seven years old and likely experiencing some dementia. A newspaper article from 1898 reports that he was examined before a jury to determine his competency—his wife and children were concerned that he was "acting strangely," and they were not sure "what he does with his pension money which comes in a draft of $150 every quarter." Not long after, Ward was declared incompetent and placed under guardianship. Aa few months after that, he passed away. "The Case of Rowland Ward," *Nunda News,* May 28, 1898; *Corning Journal,* August 21, 1884; "He Lived 36 Years Without a Jawbone," *New York World,* July 3, 1898; "Funeral of Rowland Ward Largely Attended at Hunt, Last Sunday," *Nunda News,* June 18, 1898.

34. Dora Costa, *The Evolution of Retirement: An American Economic History, 1880–1990* (Chicago: University of Chicago Press, 1998), 199.

35. Report to accompany bill HR 11578, December 14, 1888, *The Reports of Committees of the House of Representatives for the Second Session of the Fiftieth Congress, 1888–1889* (Washington, DC: Government Printing Office, 1889).

36. H. A. Barnum to George M. Lockwood, January 6, 1888, Henry A. Barnum Pension Case File, Certificate Number 78,753, NARA. Emphasis in original.

37. Ibid. It is not clear whether this photograph was the one that Barnum previously sent to Commissioner Dudley or one that he sent at a later time.

38. Unknown to "Mr. Commissioner," October 16, 1890, Henry A. Barnum Pension Case File, Certificate Number 78,753, NARA. I have located three images of Barnum's wounds, two taken by the AMD and one that appears to have been taken under different circumstances.

39. Connor and Rhode, "Shooting Soldiers," n.p.

40. Ibid. Another painting shows Smith, looking even younger, wearing a Union army jacket and smoking a cigar. A third shows Smith looking emaciated in black and white. The photograph of Smith, taken in 1867 by physician B. B. Breed, depicts the handsome nineteen-year-old, now a veteran, wearing civilian clothing.

41. Deposition of Mary Smith, January 17, 1888, Eben E. Smith Pension Case File, Certificate Number 46,943, NARA.

42. Members of the John M. Read GAR Post no. 155 to "The Senate and House of Representatives of the United States in Congress assembled," Eben E. Smith Pension Case File, Certificate 46,943, NARA.

43. Gidley, "Painful Looks: Reading Civil War Photographs," 100.

44. Garland-Thompson, "Seeing the Disabled," 348. See also David Serlin, introduction to *Phallacies: Historical Intersections of Masculinity and Disability,* ed. Kathleen Brian and James W. Trent Jr. (New York: Oxford University Press, 2017).

45. Wayne Wei-siang Hsieh, review of Earl J. Hess, *The Battle of Ezra Church and the Struggle for Atlanta* (Chapel Hill: University of North Carolina Press, 2015), in *Civil War Monitor,* November 18, 2015, n.p.

II

NARRATING
THE PAST

Remembering "That Dark Episode"

Union and Confederate Ex-Prisoners of War
and Their Captivity Narratives

ANGELA M. RIOTTO

URING THE US Civil War, 410,000 soldiers were held as prisoners of war. Of those, fifty-six thousand—or nearly 7 percent of all soldiers who perished in the conflict—died in prison.[1] To the end of their lives, survivors of Civil War military prisons sought to inform nonprisoners about what really happened to them in captivity. In a quest to make their experiences part of the larger narrative and memory of the war, both Union and Confederate ex-prisoners wrote memoirs, published prison diaries, appeared before congressional committees, addressed veterans' conventions, and sponsored monuments. They urged their fellow citizens to "kindly remember the old soldiers, and especially the surviving prisoners of the late war."[2]

The impending mortality of the Civil War generation prompted many Union and Confederate veterans to share their memories of the war. The US public, who longed to be a part of the war's legacy, welcomed the resulting surge in war-related writings. A cursory review of turn-of-the-century literature reveals the public's fascination with romanticized, albeit gruesome, war stories.[3] By publishing their accounts, veterans contributed to an emerging public memory of the war that emphasized sacrifice and heroism. Furthermore, at memorial events across the country, people commemorated Civil War veterans—living manifestations of the characters in their favorite war stories. Battle-hardened veterans embodied this invented history, but prisoners of war did not. Not accustomed to silencing their views and just as eager to share their stories of the war, Union and Confederate ex-prisoners added their voices to the growing chorus.

Incarceration in Civil War military prisons denied thousands of men the opportunity to prove themselves as soldiers on the battlefield. As such, they found their place in society less clearly defined. Many former prisoners who shared their stories believed they occupied a liminal place in society, in which they simultaneously identified as veterans, victims, resisters, and survivors. Viewed singly, any one of their narratives might seem merely a fascinating tale of personal suffering (and often resilience). Yet considered as a body of literature, these narratives reveal the development of a collective prisoner-of-war memory that was distinct from, yet in conversation with, public memory of the conflict. An analysis of former prisoners' narratives from their first appearance in 1862 to 1930 reveals that Union and Confederate ex-prisoners rejected the dominant public memory of the war and promulgated their own collective memory and veteran identity.[4]

Ex-prisoners presumed, and rightly so, that the American public preferred stories of brave soldiers over those of starving prisoners of war.[5] More specifically, they feared that people would rather hear about the "imagined" war than the "real" war. Popular, veteran-focused literature created a new "reality" of war that did not always exist for men in the field or in prison.[6] While numerous wartime accounts spoke to camaraderie among enemies, valiant battlefield charges, and courage under fire, ex-prisoners contended that far darker experiences also formed part of the "real" war and merited inclusion into the war's history. Even though they believed nonprisoners could never truly understand what it was like to watch friends "die with nothing around but filth; to be consumed by a slow fever or starve for days," ex-prisoners insisted on sharing their memories because they feared the loss of their history.[7] One survivor of Andersonville lamented, "The country has heard much of the heroism and sacrifices of these loyal youths who fell on the field of battle, but it has heard little of the still greater number who died in the prison pen."[8] In response to the nation's increasing indifference, survivors of Civil War prisons endeavored to commemorate their fallen comrades—and to find both meaning and honor in their suffering. It occurred to one Union ex-prisoner that it was his and his fellow survivors' responsibility to "each leave a pen picture of at least the mildest part of our prison life," so that their fellow citizens would not forget them once the "last survivors' tongues are hushed."[9]

Ex-prisoners also faced questions about what it meant to be a man in the post–Civil War United States. In particular, the social and economic turbulence that characterized the postbellum period—industrialization, urbanization, and the presence of thousands of disabled veterans—brought questions of gender, specifically about masculinity, to the fore.[10] Ex-prisoners' writings reveal this turmoil. Considering themselves to be a distinct group of veterans, ex-prisoners repeatedly asserted their manhood and stressed their military service. They understood their wartime sacrifices as noble and wanted to make sure that their fellow citizens also understood that even though they had surrendered and suffered indescribable hardships, they remained honorable men worthy of remembrance.[11]

Narratives of imprisonment appeared as early as 1862. As thousands of soldiers languished in Union and Confederate military prisons, those who escaped or were released shared their stories with family, friends, and the public.[12] Union and Confederate ex-prisoners published their narratives for a variety of reasons. Many asserted that their comrades pleaded for them to broadcast the realities of imprisonment in hopes that the suffering of "sixteen hundred officers of our army, and from thirty to forty thousand privates, good men and true" would end.[13] Others published for profit.[14] Some nonprisoners published the accounts of men who died before they could impart their experiences to a wider audience. The resulting literature was a mix of propaganda—pro-exchange, antislavery, pro-Union or pro-Confederate—and celebrations of the authors' bravery, perseverance, and masculinity. By publishing their accounts, ex-prisoners attempted to promote themselves as determined, honorable men who bravely performed their duty to their nation no matter the consequences. They especially felt it their duty to share their experiences in an effort to influence exchange policy, motivate the men still fighting, and possibly save the lives of their comrades still confined.

During the war, authors additionally sought to prove to themselves and to the public that they were not cowards.[15] To substantiate their claims of bravery and manliness, ex-prisoners often recounted exciting tales of escape and resistance.[16] Benjamin Calef and A. O. Abbott both shared an uplifting story of resistance in which Union officers imprisoned in Macon, Georgia, celebrated the Fourth of July. They told of how the men allegedly gathered around to sing "The Star-Spangled Banner," when one prisoner revealed a tiny US flag he had secreted into prison. All the men greeted this flag with cheers, but the prison commander ordered them to disperse. Fearing punishment another prisoner tried to hide the flag, but the others refused and proudly waved it in spite of the prison commander's presence.[17] This short anecdote conveyed the prisoners' unwavering patriotism—just as they would lay their lives down on the battle-field, they would also do so in prison to save their dear flag.[18] By portraying themselves as patriots who dutifully resisted their captors, ex-prisoners not only glorified their own masculinity, courage, and honor but also reminded readers of their duty to help their nation's soldiers. Furthermore, by sharing tales of escape and resistance, prisoners developed a distinct wartime identity as honorable soldiers fighting for a cause even though imprisoned.[19]

With the end of the war, charges of abuse and mistreatment, which ap-peared intermittently in wartime accounts, became staples of postwar prison narratives.[20] As part of this second surge in narratives, ex-prisoners, especially survivors of southern military prisons, shed their singular identity as resolute heroes and began to define themselves and their comrades as victims of enemy cruelty. During the trial of Captain Henry Wirz in summer 1865, nearly 160 Andersonville survivors, civilians, and ex-Confederates testified to Wirz's bru-tal punishments, the "deadline"—the perimeter around the stockade beyond which prisoners were liable to be shot—and the horrible conditions within the stockade.[21] Along with testifying at Wirz's trial, Union ex-prisoners, including those who were not confined in Andersonville, published their memories of captivity. From 1862 to 1866, former Union prisoners published fifty-four books and articles, twenty-eight of which appeared in 1865–1866.[22]

Three tropes dominate the narratives from the immediate postwar period, though they were not mutually exclusive. The first offered a hybrid of sensa-tionalized adventures and accusations. In these, ex-prisoners highlighted dar-ing escapes and resistance as well as allegations of cruelty. Themes of torture, starvation, and barbarity appeared with, and often overshadowed, wartime con-cerns and adventure.[23] In the second trope, ex-prisoners portrayed themselves and their comrades as virtuous, innocent victims abused by the Confederate government.[24] Resistance narratives comprised the third trope, in which ex-prisoners depicted themselves as active resisters who defied the enemy and remained loyal to the cause regardless of their suffering. By sharing these over-lapping, and sometimes conflicting, memories, survivors of Confederate pris-ons attempted to gain recognition for their misery, commemorate their dead comrades, and exact vengeance on those they blamed for their suffering.[25]

A third cluster of prisoners' accounts appeared in the late 1870s and 1880s. As Union veterans petitioned for pensions, ex-prisoners' continued to describe their many sufferings and blamed them on Confederate leaders. Not surprisingly, these Reconstruction-era writings bear a marked resemblance to the testimonies provided at the Wirz trial in 1865. Indeed, many of these stories mirror each other because Union soldiers held in southern prison camps, regardless of location, experienced similar problems of sanitation, poor rations, and disease.

Although accounts of captivity in the North are far less numerous, due to lack of resources and fear of federal retribution during Reconstruction, rebel ex-prisoners also published their stories. The end of federal Reconstruction brought both opportunities and challenges in their attempts to gain recognition for their suffering and enshrine themselves into public memory of the war, or, more precisely, into the Lost Cause version of the war. With the removal of federal troops and the establishment of the Southern Historical Society, ex-Confederates gained new venues to share their interpretations of the war and commemorate the cause of southern independence, as it was rooted in white supremacy and racial oppression.[26] As part of this literary surge, survivors of northern prisons depicted themselves as worthy subjects of remembrance.[27] Similar to Union ex-prisoners, former Confederates identified themselves as victims of a brutal enemy who also deserved to be recognized for their wartime sacrifices.[28]

In accounts published predominantly between 1877 and 1890, rebel ex-prisoners claimed that they experienced priviation in northern prisons. Former Confederate vice president Alexander Stephens also shared his thoughts on Civil War prisons and asserted that southerners held in northern prisons faced treatment "as bad as any now described in exaggerated statements going the rounds about barbarities at Andersonville, Salisbury, Belle Isle, and Libby."[29] Interpretations like Stephens's, along with the *Southern Historical Society Papers,* not only celebrated the alleged righteousness of the Confederate cause but stressed the lethality of northern prisons.[30] The theme of victimhood and need for recognition is an overarching theme through both Union and Confederate ex-prisoners' memories during this time period, but ex-Confederates' emphasis on honor, the purported righteousness of the southern cause, and white supremacy distinguishes Confederate captivity narratives from those written by Union veterans.

The fourth wave of narratives began in the late 1880s and continued until around 1930 as the last prisoners of war passed away. Concerned that drums and bugles would drown out their voices, or that future generations would forget them completely, ex-prisoners, both Union and Confederate, increasingly shared their reminiscences with a wider reading public. Ezra Hoyt Ripple of Pennsylvania warned his fellow survivors, "We would all sooner listen to a description of a grand battle where all the bravery and dash of trained soldiers in assault and defense is portrayed in the most vivid and glowing colors than to a tale of which has little in it but that which is revolting, sickening, and sorrowful."[31] Ripple feared that great battles and officers would earn a place in the history books, but common participants and individual struggles would be lost.[32] John Wyeth, a survivor of a northern military prison, echoed Ripple's concern and urged former Confederates to come forward with their stories. Wyeth, who waited decades to publish his memoir, ultimately did so because "the southern side of prison life has not yet been fully written."[33] Several answered the call, including those who had already published their accounts.[34] For former prisoners, like Ripple and Wyeth, memories of "heroic sacrifice, and unselfishness, and undying loyalty" existed alongside memories of "starvation and suffering and death."[35]

The editors of *Century Magazine* helped contribute to this final wave of prisoners' recollections when they invited and published several prisoner-of-war narratives, including those written by former rebels. Indeed, by the late nineteenth century, white southerners had succeeded in deflecting much of the enduring northern criticism from the war.[36] These later accounts, published in the 1890s and beyond, were not merely tales of adventure and bravery; they were also stories of reconciliation in which both Union and Confederates served honorably. Victory in the Spanish-American War and the impending mortality of Civil War generation also helped to nurture reconciliationist attitudes among US citizens.[37]

Although some former prisoners tried to exchange their animosity for feelings of mutual respect, tales of diseased, starving men still did not easily fit into the public memory of the war. Many former Confederates, for instance, seem to have had much difficulty coming to terms with their wartime experiences. Ex-prisoners, in particular, had difficulty forgiving confiscation of their possessions following capture. They blamed the seizures on enemy cruelty rather than necessity. According to some authors, Union guards "amused themselves" by confiscating their baggage, and once they arrived at their final destinations, Union authorities systematically robbed them.[38] Sounding remarkably similar to Union ex-prisoners' descriptions of Wirz, Miles Sherrill informed his readers, "Major Beal [of Elmira] greeted us with the most bitter oaths....He swore that he was going to send us out and have us shot."[39] By invoking rhetoric used by Andersonville survivors, Sherrill and other former rebels asked readers to imagine a Wirz-like villain abusing innocent men and stealing their possessions. By appropriating language and images similar to well-circulated Union narratives, rebel ex-prisoners likened their suffering to that of Union prisoners without saying it outright. These analogies prompted readers to sympathize with ex-rebels and acknowledge their suffering and survival alongside that of Union ex-prisoners.

As support for reconciliation swelled in the late 1880s, more and more ex-prisoners published stories that emphasized shared heroics, sacrifice, and perseverance. The more than sixty narratives that appeared following the Spanish-American War highlighted patriotism, courage, and honor and concealed feelings of hatred and accusations of cruelty. One former prisoner explained his change in feeling: "The Blue and Gray have since worn the Blue in the war with Spain—an evidence of reconciliation between the Confederate and Union soldiers of 1861–'65."[40] With the Civil War and the Spanish-American War, the United States had become "a great, powerful, and prosperous country," and former prisoners, along with their fellow citizens, hoped they could forgive and celebrate each other's sacrifices in the name of patriotism.[41]

As part of the growing culture of reconciliation, some former prisoners revised previous assessments of prison life and republished their memoirs. Thomas Mann, who initially published his hate-filled memoir in 1867, republished it in *Century Magazine*. Censoring his bitterness and omitting "nearly all of the explosive adjectives," Mann wanted his "Yankee in Andersonville" to inspire others to share their experiences. He contended that only half had been told of Andersonville, Charleston, and Florence, and he urged others to share their stories.[42] Henry Davidson, Warren Goss, Anthony Keiley, and several others published revised versions of their memoirs.[43] These men initially published shortly after the war when the public yearned to read about the horrors of military prisons. Their earlier pieces were sensational tales with well-defined villains and heroes. While people still enjoyed these novel-like works, former prisoners writing around the turn of the century now wanted to record what they believed to be the true history of their imprisonment. This is not to say that former prisoners admitted to lying in their earlier narratives. Rather, they recognized that their previous accounts might have been too vindictive toward their former captors, and now they sought to offer more balanced assessments.

Some former prisoners did indeed grow to appreciate the sacrifices of their comrades and their enemies. Prisoners turned authors often told of their comrades' struggles against the enemy before capture, often describing them as "gallant," "determined," and "faithful."[44] The public wanted to hear stories of courageous and unwavering stands against overwhelming odds, and former prisoners gave readers what they wanted. This theme of gallant volunteers who faced the enemy continued, and intensified, in the twentieth century as the United States faced new enemies abroad.[45] Survivors frequently told of faithful soldiers who stared death in the face and remained resolute even when far behind the "enemy's lines and under a hostile flag."[46] Stories such as these not only allowed the author to grieve for and commemorate his lost comrades but also asked the audience to acknowledge prisoners' sacrifice for their country when many preferred to read about grand battlefield actions.

Still, many more former prisoners remained resentful. Appalled that his fellow survivors could "smother the sight of those wrongs with charity and forgiveness," William Clifton continued to engage in "bloody shirt" politics and pledged to bring all of the horrors of southern prisons into current memory.[47] The editor of *Sparks from the Camp Fire* also offered bitter commentary toward Confederate officials, which echoed sentiments shared during the Wirz trial and Reconstruction.[48] Henry Milton Roach, late of the 78th Ohio, proved unable to separate himself from the indignant rhetoric. Roach, who spent the final year of the war in Andersonville, initially published his narrative in 1865. He later handwrote a twenty-three-page memoir in 1892. Roach did not revise his earlier piece, and his later work included just as much hatred as the previous.[49] Abram Price likewise remained bitter. In his description of his capture at Chickamauga, he recounted that devious Confederates wearing blue clothes and carrying a captured Ohio flag apprehended him. His capture was made almost unbearable by the fact that the rebels taunted their captives. He also lobbed insults at southerners who allegedly "spat on the prisoners" during transport to prison.[50] His memoir, although published in the early twentieth century, possessed the same tone and tropes as accounts from the immediate postwar period. Price could not and would not reconcile with his former enemies, because as another ex-prisoner explained, the enemy was as "cruel as cruel could be, under this nineteenth century civilization." The sites of Civil War prisons, he wrote, were forever "those places of terrible memory."[51]

Stories of Andersonville, the infamous southern military prison, continued to fascinate readers into the twentieth century.[52] Even though "Andersonville had been freely discussed," survivors contended that the "truth has not been half told," because only someone who experienced it could truly understand the horrors.[53] Northerners continued to search for whom or what was to blame for the unprecedented suffering within that stockade. Wirz continued to play the role of villain in later-published narratives. Ex-prisoners depicted him on horseback with his infamous revolver or at the head of his snarling bloodhounds, cursing innocent men. Writing in 1887, Bjorn Aslakson of the 9th Minnesota Volunteers juxtaposed Wirz's "ruthlessness and needless inhumanity" to "heroic and gallant" soldiers.[54] Authors of later published narratives depicted Wirz in the same manner as immediate postwar publications, often emphasizing his penchant for profanity and abuse. Henry Roach stated, "Major Henry Wirz made his appearance and greeted us with all the abusive epithets he could command."[55] While a few Andersonville survivors tempered their hatred toward Wirz—and even penned apologies—others did not forgive the man they believed responsible for their suffering. By specifying manifold sufferings, survivors attempted to convey the full extent of their misery and urged readers to acknowledge their veteranhood as distinct.

Regardless of ex-prisoners' place of imprisonment or growing reconciliationist feelings, those who published their stories continued to include fanciful stories of escape. Both Union and Confederate ex-prisoners found additional meaning in having lived through a personal adventure and often included tales of daring and ingenious escapes, even if fabricated. Common tropes of fooling the guards, tunneling with case knives, and jumping from trains continued to appear in published narratives. These stories elevated some prisoners' experiences above the others and demonstrated their ingenuity, determination, and perseverance. Tales of escape and resistance conveyed to readers that although prisoners were mistreated and deliberately starved, they were not helpless, passive victims.

Writing in 1886, one survivor of Andersonville concluded his memoir by confiding, "Perhaps no description can convey to those who did not share them an adequate idea of such horrors, for like other deep experiences, these also could only be known experimentally." Nevertheless, he like other survivors of Civil War military prisons felt "called upon to live for the honor of the fair land for which so many died."[56] By publishing their accounts of captivity, survivors of Civil War prisons simultaneously sought to commemorate their dead comrades, find some meaning in their suffering, and promote their distinct veteran identity. They wanted to be remembered for their heroism and sacrifice and they hoped that their stories would eventually become enshrined in America's public memory of the war, so that their sufferings would never be forgotten.

NOTES

1. J. David Hacker, "A Census-Based Count of the Civil War Dead," *Civil War History* 57, no. 4 (Dec. 2011): 207–48.

2. Chester D. Berry, *Loss of the Sultana and Reminiscences or Survivors: History of a Disaster Where Over One Thousand Five Hundred Human Beings Were Lost, Most of Them Being Exchanged Prisoners of War on Their Way Home after Privation and Suffering from One to Twenty-Three Months in Cahaba and Andersonville Prisons* (Lansing, MI: Darius D. Thorp, 1892), 7; "Samuel H. Raudebauch Testimony," in Berry, *Loss of the Sultana*, 296.

3. Joan Waugh, "Ulysses S. Grant, Historian," in *The Memory of the Civil War in American Culture*, ed. Alice Fahs and Joan Waugh (Chapel Hill: University of North Carolina Press, 2004), 9, 23; James M. McPherson, "Long-Legged Yankee Lies: The Southern Textbook Crusade," in *The Memory of the Civil War in American Culture*, ed. Fahs and Waugh, 64.

4. For discussions of social and collective memory see John Bodnar, *Remaking America: Public Memory, Commemoration, and Patriotism in the Twentieth Century* (Princeton, NJ: Princeton University Press, 1992); Jay Winter, *Sites of Memory, Sites of Mourning: The Great War in European Cultural History* (Cambridge: Cambridge University Press, 1995); Eric Leed, "Fateful Memories: Industrialized War and Traumatic Neuroses," *Journal of Contemporary History* 35 (January 2000): 85–100; David W. Blight, *Race and Reunion: The Civil War in American Memory* (Cambridge, MA: Harvard University Press, 2001); Jay Winter, *Remembering War: The Great War between Memory and History in the Twentieth Century* (New Haven, CT: Yale University Press, 2006); and Laura E. Matthew, *Memories of Conquest: Becoming Mexicano in Colonial Guatemala* (Chapel Hill: University of North Carolina Press, 2012).

5. Melvin Grigsby, *The Smoked Yank* (Sioux Falls, SD: Dakota Bell, 1888); George S. Burkhardt, *Confederate Rage, and Yankee Wrath: No Quarter in the Civil War* (Carbondale: Southern Illinois University Press, 2007), 7.

6. Alice Fahs, *The Imagined Civil War: Popular Literature of the North and South, 1861–1865* (Chapel Hill: University of North Carolina Press, 2001), 95.

7. H. M. Richards, "In Rebel Prisons a Tribute to Samuel B. Trafford," *Lebanon County Historical Society* 8, no. 8 (September 1922): 276; A. Noel Blakeman, *Personal Recollections of the War of the Rebellion: Addresses Delivered before the Commandery of the State of New York, Military Order of the*

Loyal Legion of the United States, second series (New York: G. P. Putnam's Sons, 1912); James B. Pumphrey, "A Story of Eighteen Months in a Military Prison, the Escape, Reminiscences Etc.," MIC 17, Civil War Collection, 1804–1895, Ohio History Center, Columbus, OH (hereafter OHC), 4; William B. Clifton, *Libby and Andersonville Prisons: A True Sketch* (Indianapolis: privately printed, 1910), 8; Frank E. Moran, *Bastiles of the Confederacy: A Reply to Jefferson Davis* (Baltimore: printed for the family of the author, 1890), 200; Robert Drummond, "Memoirs," Robert Loudon Drummond Recollections, ca. 1914, #1051-z, Southern Historical Collection, University of North Carolina at Chapel Hill (hereafter SHC), 30; Robert C. Doyle, *Voices from Captivity: Interpreting the American POW Narrative* (Lawrence: University Press of Kansas, 1994), 287.

8. John McElroy, *Andersonville: A Story of Rebel Military Prisons, Fifteen Months a Guest of the So-Called Southern Confederacy, A Private Soldier's Experience, Richmond, Andersonville, Savannah, Millen, Blackshear, and Florence* (Toledo: D. R. Locke, 1879), xv; see also Hiram H. Hardesty, "The Confederate Prison Pens," in *The Military History of Ohio: Its Border Annals, Its Part in the Indian Wars, in the War of 1812, in the Mexican War, and in the War of the Rebellion, with a Prefix, Giving a Compendium of the History of the United States . . . Special Local Department in Editions by Counties, Giving a Roster of Ohio's Rank and File from the County in the War of the Rebellion, Regimental Histories, with Histories of Its G.A.R. and Ladies' Auxiliary Posts, and Camps of Sons of Veterans* (Toledo: H. H. Hardesty, 1886), 297.

9. Samuel Boggs, *Eighteen Months under the Rebel Flag, a Condensed Pen-Picture of Belle Isle, Danville, Andersonville, Charleston, Florence, and Libby Prisons* (Lovington, IL: privately printed, 1887), 4.

10. Brian Craig Miller, *Empty Sleeves: Amputation in the Civil War South* (Athens: University of Georgia Press, 2015), 5.

11. Gail Bederman, *Manliness and Civilization: A Cultural History of Gender and Race in the United States, 1880–1917* (Chicago: University of Chicago Press, 1995); Kristin L. Hoganson, *Fighting for American Manhood: How Gender Politics Provoked the Spanish-American and Philippine-American Wars* (New Haven, CT: Yale University Press, 1998).

12. Federico Fernandez Cavada, *Libby Life: Experiences of a Prisoner of War in Richmond, Va., 1863–1864* (Philadelphia: King and Baird, 1864), 10.

13. Frederic Denison, "Letter 1," in *Prison Life among the Rebels: Recollections of a Union Chaplain*, ed. Edward D. Jervey (Kent, OH: Kent State University Press, 1990); see also H. M. Davidson, *Fourteen Months in Southern Prisons; Being a Narrative of the Treatment of Federal Prisoners of War in the Rebel Military Prisons of Richmond, Danville, Andersonville, Savannah, and Millen; Describing the Author's Escape with Two Comrades, from Andersonville and the Blood Hounds; His Adventures during a Fourteen Nights' March in the Swamps of Western Georgia, and His Subsequent Re-capture; to Which Is Added a Large List of Those Who Died in Various Prisons in the Confederacy* (Milwaukee: Daily Wisconsin, 1865), viii; Gilbert E. Sabre, *Nineteen Months a Prisoner of War: Narrative of Lieutenant G. E. Sabre, Second Rhode Island Cavalry, of His Experience in the War Prisons and Stockades of Morton, Mobile, Atlanta, Libby, Belle Island, Andersonville, Macon, Charleston, and Columbia and His Escape to the Union Lines; to Which Is Appended a List of Officers Confined at Columbia, during the Winter of 1864 and 1865* (New York: American News, 1865), 174; Michael Corcoran, *The Captivity of General Corcoran, the Only Authentic and Reliable Narrative of the Trials and Sufferings Endured, during his Twelve Months' Imprisonment in Richmond and Other Southern Cities* (Philadelphia: Barclay, 1862), 21, 89; F. F. Kinner,

One Year's Soldiering: Embracing the Battles of Fort Donelson and Shiloh, and the Capture of Two Hundred Officers and Me of the Fourteenth Iowa Infantry, and Their Confinement Six Months and a Half in Rebel Prisons (Lancaster: E. H. Thomas, 1863), 1.

14. Benjamin Cloyd, *Haunted by Atrocity: Civil War Prisons in American Memory* (Baton Rouge: Louisiana State University Press, 2010), 41, 54.

15. William Howard Merrell, *Five Months in Rebeldom; or Notes from the Diary of a Bull Run Prisoner, at Richmond* (Rochester: Adams and Dabney, 1862), 41. See Mark E. Neely Jr., *The Civil War and the Limits of Destruction* (Cambridge, MA: Harvard University Press, 2007), 170–97 for an excellent discussion of the use of photographs of Andersonville survivors as an argument for retaliation.

16. Isaac N. Johnston, *Four Months in Libby, and the Campaign against Atlanta* (Cincinnati: R. P. Thompson, Methodist Book Concern, 1864), 3, 44; Kinner, *One Year's Soldiering*, 2, 4; Corcoran, *The Captivity*, 85; Doyle, *Voices from Captivity*, 171; Robert Scott Davis, "Escape from Andersonville: A Study in Isolation and Imprisonment," *Journal of Military History* 67 (October 2003): 1069.

17. B. S. Calef, "Prison Life in the Confederacy," *Harper's Monthly*, July 1865, 142; Allen O. Abbott, *Prison Life in the South: At Richmond, Macon, Savannah, Charleston, Columbia, Charlotte, Raleigh, Goldsborough and Andersonville, during the Years of 1864 and 1865* (New York: Harper and Brothers, 1865), 78–79.

18. In the obituary of Andrew Roy, the author assured the newspaper's readers that Roy was a patriot who served his country well, even though captured. The obituary clarified that Roy discarded his pick and shovel to join the 10th Pennsylvania when the war began and he was captured only after being wounded at Gaines Mills. "Obituary of Andrew Roy," Andrew Roy Papers, VFM 3489, OHC.

19. Kinner, *One Year's Soldiering*, 3–4, 60; Sabre, *Nineteen Months a Prisoner of War*, 106; Johnston, *Four Months*, 44; and Merrell, *Five Months*, 8.

20. George Rable, *Damned Yankees! Demonization and Defiance in the Confederate South* (Baton Rouge: Louisiana State University Press, 2015), 6.

21. Elliot G. Storke, *A Complete History of the Great American Rebellion* (Auburn Publishing, 1863), 1:76, 566, 708.

22. William Hesseltine, *Civil War Prisons: A Study in War Psychology* (Columbus: Ohio State University Press, 1930); Ann Fabian, *The Unvarnished Truth: Personal Narratives of Nineteenth-Century America* (Berkeley: University of California Press, 2000).

23. William Burson, *A Race for Liberty; My Capture, Imprisonment, and Escape* (Wellsville: W. G. Foster, 1867).

24. James Young, *Writing and Rewriting the Holocaust: Narrative and Consequences of Interpretation* (Bloomington: Indiana University Press, 1988), 21; Joseph E. Davis, "Victim Narratives and Victim Selves: False Memory Syndrome and the Power of Accounts," *Social Problems* 52, no. 4 (November 2005): 529–48; Antony Rowland, "The Oasis Poets: Perpetrators, Victims, and Soldier Testimony," *Comparative Literature* 63, no. 4 (Fall 2011): 366–82.

25. Abner R. Small, *The Road to Richmond: The Civil War Memoirs of Major Abner R. Small of the Sixteenth Maine Volunteers. Together with the Diary Which He Kept When He Was a Prisoner of War* (New York: Fordham University Press, 2000); Ambrose Spencer, *A Narrative of Andersonville, Drawn from the Evidence Elicited on the Trial of Henry Wirz, the Jailer* (New York: Harper and Brothers, 1866), 134; Lesley J. Gordon, "Storms of Indignation: The Art of Andersonville as Postwar Propaganda," *Georgia Historical Quarterly* 75, no. 3 (Fall 1991): 587–600; Samuel Hawkins Marshall

Byers, *What I Saw in Dixie: Or, Sixteen Months in Rebel Prisons* (Dansville: Robbins and Poore, 1868), 36.

26. John William Jones, "Editorial Department: Our First Paper," *Southern Historical Society Papers* (hereafter *SHSP*) 1, no. 1 (1876): 41; Sarah E. Gardner, *Blood and Irony: Southern White Women's Narratives of the Civil War, 1861–1937* (Chapel Hill: University of North Carolina Press, 2004), 60; John William Jones, *Confederate View of the Treatment of Prisoners* (Richmond: Southern Historical Society, 1876); William A. Blair, *Cities of the Dead: Contesting the Memory of the Civil War in the South, 1865–1914* (Chapel Hill: University of North Carolina Press, 2004), 6; Yael A. Sternhell, "The After-lives of a Confederate Archive: Civil War Documents and the Making of Sectional Reconciliation," *Journal of American History* 102, no. 4 (Mar. 2016): 1025–50; Gaines M. Foster, *Ghosts of the Confederacy: Defeat, the Lost Cause, and the Emergence of the New South, 1865–1913* (New York: Oxford University Press, 1987), 47–62; Richard D. Starnes, "Forever Faithful: The Southern Historical Society and Confederate Historical Memory," *Southern Cultures* 2 (Winter 1996): 177–94.

27. During the war, 12 percent of Confederate prisoners died, compared to 15.5 percent of Union prisoners. Michael P. Gray, *The Business of Captivity: Elmira and Its Civil War Prison* (Kent, OH: Kent State University Press, 2001), 104, 153–54; Benton McAdams, *Rebels at Rock Island: The Story of a Civil War Prison* (DeKalb: Northern Illinois University, 2000), xi–xiii; James M. Gillespie, *Andersonvilles of the North: The Myths and Realities of Northern Treatment of Civil War Confederate Prisoners* (Denton: University of North Texas Press, 2008), 113; Paul J. Springer and Glenn Robins, *Transforming Civil War Prisons: Lincoln, Lieber, and the Politics of Captivity* (New York: Routledge, 2014), 82.

28. Walter Addison, "Recollections of a Confederate Soldier of the Prison-Pens of Point Lookout, Md. and Elmira, New York," Thomas Jefferson Green Papers, SHC, 1, 8; A. M. Keiley, *In Vinculis; or, The Prisoner of War* (New York: Blelock, 1866); Joe Barbiere, *Scraps from the Prison Table at Camp Chase and Johnson's Island* (Doylestown, PA: W. W. H. Davis, 1868), 291, 305, 330–31; Edward Wellington Boate, "The True Story of Andersonville Told by a Federal Prisoner," *SHSP* 10, no. 1 (January–December 1882): 25–32; R. Randolph Stevenson, *The Southern Side; or, Andersonville Prison* (Baltimore: Turnbull Brothers, 1876); Jones, *Confederate View of the Treatment of Prisoners*, 115; Isaiah White, "Andersonville Prison: Testimony of Dr. Isaiah W. White," *SHSP* 17 (January–December 1889): 383–88; Alexander H. Stephens, *Recollections of Alexander H. Stephens: His Diary Kept When a Prisoner at Fort Warren, Boston Harbour, 1865; Giving Incidents and Reflections of His Prison Life and Some Letters and Reminiscences*, ed. Myrta Avary (New York: Doubleday, Page, 1910).

29. Stephens, *Recollections*, 235.

30. Blight, *Race and Reunion;* Drew Gilpin Faust, "Battle over Bodies: Burying and Reburying the Civil War Dead, 1865–1871," in *Wars within a War: Controversy and Conflict over the American Civil War,* ed., Joan Waugh and Gary Gallagher (Chapel Hill: University of North Carolina Press, 2009), 184.

31. Ezra Hoyt Ripple, *Dancing along the Deadline: The Andersonville Memoir of a Prisoner of the Confederacy,* ed. Mark Snell (Novato: Presidio, 1996), 6.

32. *Constitution and By-Laws of the Ohio Association of Union Ex-Prisoners of War, Together with the Register of Members and Proceedings at the Reunion Held at Marietta, June 10 and 11, 1891* (Cincinnati: Comrade Thomas Macon, 1892), 5; Samuel Miller Quincy, *History of the Second Massachusetts Regiment of Infantry: A Prisoner's Diary. A Paper Read at the Officers' Reunion in Boston, May 11, 1877* (Boston: George H. Ellis, 1882) 3, 19; R. M. Collins, *Chapters from the Unwritten History of the War*

between the States (St. Louis: Nixon-Jones, 1893), 7; Ripple, *Dancing along the Deadline,* 7; James Hutson, "Memoir," James Hutson Papers, ARCH COLL, bay 5, row 157, face C, shelf 5, box 1, US Army Heritage and Education Center, Carlisle, PA (hereafter USAHEC), 1, 3.

33. John A. Wyeth, "Cold Cheer at Camp Morton," *Century Magazine* (hereafter *Century*), April 1891, 852.

34. A. M. Keiley, "Prison-Pens North," *SHSP* 18 (January–December 1891): 333–40.

35. "Charles Frederick Crisp, Late of the 10th VA Infantry, Co. K, Prisoner of War at Ft. Delaware, Elected to Speak," *Weekly Miners' Journal* (Pottsville, PA), December 11, 1891; Alexander Swanger, "Back to the Old Prison," Alexander J. Swanger Papers, 1894–1897, VFM 1911, OHC, 16–17; John H. King, *Three Hundred Days in a Yankee Prison: Reminiscences of War Life Captivity, Imprisonment at Camp Chase, Ohio* (Atlanta: Jas. P. Daves, 1904), 77; Henry B. Furness, "A General Account of Prison Life and Prisons in the South during the War of the Rebellion Including Statistical Information Pertaining to Prisoners of War," in *Prisoners of War and Military Prisons,* ed. Asa B. Isham, Henry M. Davidson, and Henry B. Furness (Cincinnati: Lyman and Cushing, 1890), 403.

36. Cloyd, *Haunted by Atrocity,* 180.

37. Blight, *Race and Reunion,* 243; Foster, *Ghosts of the Confederacy,* 184.

38. Charles T. Loehr, "Point Lookout: Address before Pickett Camp Confederate Veterans, Oct. 10, 1890," (originally published in *Richmond Times,* October 11, 1890), *SHSP* 18 (January–December 1891): 116; James Marion Howard, "Short Sketch of My Early Life," file 500-315, Chemung County Historical Society, Elmira, NY, 12.

39. Miles O. Sherrill, *A Soldier's Story: Prison Life and Other Incidents* (Raleigh: privately printed, 1904), 8–9.

40. Ibid., 18–19.

41. Robert Kellogg, "Memorandum of Proposed Remarks at Dedication of the Connecticut Monument in the National Cemetery at Andersonville, Ga., October 1907 by Robert H. Kellogg, Delaware, Ohio, Sergeant Major 16th Conn. Volunteers," VFM 2634, Robert H. Kellogg Papers, OHC, 5; Furness, "A General Account," 402; William B. Smith, *On Wheels and How I Came There; A Real Story for Real Boys and Girls, Giving the Personal Experiences and Observations of a Fifteen-Year-Old Yankee Boy as Soldier and Prisoner in the American Civil War* (New York: Hunt and Eaton, 1892), 8.

42. T. H. Mann, "A Yankee in Andersonville," *Century* 40 (July 1890): 447–60; Thomas H. Mann, *Fighting with the Eighteenth Massachusetts: The Civil War Memoir of Thomas H. Mann,* ed. John J. Hennessey and Henry L. Mann (Baton Rouge: Louisiana State University Press, 2000), xv.

43. Henry Davidson, "Experience in Rebel Prisons for United States Soldiers at Richmond, Danville, Andersonville, Savannah, and Millen," in *Prisoners of War and Military Prisons,* ed. Isham, Davidson, and Furness, 149–398; Warren Lee Goss, *The Soldier's Story of His Captivity at Andersonville, Belle Isle, and other Rebel Prisons* (Boston: Lee and Shepard, 1867); Goss, "The Responsibility for Andersonville," *North American Review* 150, no. 402 (May 1890): 660–62; Keiley, *In Vinculis;* Keiley, "Prison-Pens North"; and A. W. Wash, "Camp, Field, and Prison Life," in *Prisoners of War and Military Prisons,* ed. Isham, Davidson, and Furness, 135.

44. Kellogg, "Memorandum," 1; Alonzo Cooper, *In and Out of Rebel Prisons* (Oswego, NY: R. J. Oliphant, 1888), dedication; Ole Steensland, "Address by Ole Steensland of Perry, Wis.: At the Reunion of the Fifteenth Wisconsin Infantry, at Scandia Hall, Chicago, August 29th, 1900," Wisconsin

in the Civil War Pamphlets, Wisconsin Historical Society, Madison, WI, 12; and John R. King, *My Experience in the Confederate Army and in Northern Prisons Written from Memory* (Clarksburg, WV: United Daughters of the Confederacy, 1917), 24.

45. Foster, *Ghosts of the Confederacy,* 145, 149; Blight, *Race and Reunion,* 351; Nina Silber, *The Romance of Reunion: Northerners and the South, 1865–1900* (Chapel Hill: University of North Carolina Press, 1993), 180; Caroline E. Janney, *Remembering the Civil War: Reunion and the Limits of Reconciliation* (Chapel Hill: University of North Carolina Press, 2013), 230; John Oldfield, "Remembering the *Maine:* The United States and Sectional Reconciliation," in *The Crisis of 1898: Colonial Redistribution and Nationalist Mobilization,* ed. Angel Smith and Emma Davila-Cox (New York: St. Martin's, 1999), 45; Hoganson, *Fighting for American Manhood,* 124; W. Scott Poole, *Never Surrender: Confederate Memory and Conservatism in the South Carolina Upcountry* (Athens: University of Georgia Press, 2004), 190; Carol Reardon, "Billy Yank and Johnny Reb Take on the World: Civil War Veterans' Views of War, Liberty, and Empire," in *America, War and Power: Defining the State, 1775–2005,* ed. Lawrence Sondhaus and A. James Fuller (New York: Routledge, 2007), 64.

46. Kellogg, "Memorandum," 4; Daniels, "War Reminiscences—No. 14," *Morris Chronicle,* July 20, 1904; Charles Chesterman, "Life in a Rebel Prison," ANDE 1005, Andersonville National Historic Site, Andersonville, GA (hereafter ANHS), 4.

47. Clifton, *Libby and Andersonville Prisons,* 2, 8; see also Patrick J. Kelly "The Election of 1896 and the Restructuring of Civil War Memory," in *The Memory of the Civil War in American Culture,* ed. Fahs and Waugh, 45, 182.

48. "Prison Pens of Dixie," in *Sparks from the Camp Fire,* ed. Joseph Morton Jr. (Philadelphia: Keystone, 1890), 177–83; Charles Currie, "Incidents Related by a Surviving Ex-Prisoner," in *Sparks from the Camp Fire,* ed. Morton, 196.

49. Henry Milton Roach, "Account of My Stay in Andersonville Prison from September 1864 to June 1865, as related by Henry Milton Roach, 78th Ohio Volunteer Infantry," Research Library, ANHS, 2, 3.

50. Abram J. Price, "A Narrative of Prison Life and Escape," Abram J. Price Manuscript, VFM 4493, OHC, 4–5, 6; Price, "A Southern Odyssey: The Narrative of Abram Price," ed. James K. Richard, *Timeline* 6, no. 4 (August–September 1989): 24–33.

51. Price, "A Narrative of Prison Life"; Clay MaCauley, "From Chancellorsville to Libby Prison," in *Glimpses of the Nation's Struggle* (St. Paul, MN: St. Paul Book and Stationary, 1887), 179–201.

52. Livingston Saylor, "My Experience While a Prisoner of War, September 30, 1908," *Publications of the Historical Society of Schuylkill County* (Pottsville, PA: Daily Republican Press, 1910), 2:388; Kellogg, "Memorandum," 2; Rossiter Johnson, "Adds to Recollections of Andersonville Prison," *Times Union,* January 5, 1920, Robert H. Kellogg Papers, OHC; Daniels, "War Reminiscences—No. 1 and 4," *Morris Chronicle,* April 13, 1904, May 4, 1904; Joseph W. O'Neall, "Andersonville Prison as Experienced and Written by Joseph W. O'Neall," *Western Star,* February 11, 1912; John Chester White, "Libby Prison Report, (1908)," ARCH COLL bay 5, row 177, face O, shelf 7, box 1, folder 2, USA-HEC, 1.

53. Roach, "Account of My Stay," 6; Cooper, *In and Out of Rebel Prisons,* v, 41; Steensland, "Address," 2; Richard Williams, "Seven Months in Andersonville Prison Georgia," in *Biographical and Genealogical History of Wayne, Fayette, Union and Franklin Counties, Indiana* (Chicago: Lewis, 1899), Research Library, ANHS, 2:1.

54. Bjorn Aslakson, "Ten Months in Andersonville, Savannah, Millen, Blackshire, and Thomasville Confederacy Prisons," ARCH COLL bay 4, row 135, face T, shelf 3, box 3, USAHEC, 1.

55. Roach, "Account of My Stay in Andersonville Prison," 3.

56. George G. Russell, *Reminiscences of Andersonville Prison: A Paper Read by Comrade Geo. G. Russell Before Post 34, G.A.R., Tuesday, June 22* (Salem, MA: Observer, 1886), 8.

"Exposing False History"

The Voice of the Union Veteran in the Pages of the National Tribune

STEVEN E. SODERGREN

U NHERALDED, without previous announcement of any sort, a new candidate for public favor introduces itself into the journalistic world." Thus began the editorial page of the first issue of the *National Tribune* in October 1877, a Washington, DC,–based monthly newspaper that served "the interests of Soldiers and Sailors of the late war, and all pensioners of the United States." The first edition explained that the goal of the paper was to advocate for pension reform in Congress, with the entire front page devoted to news on the struggle for proper pensions and bounty payments.[1] The coming years would transform the mission of the paper into a wider forum for veterans of the US Civil War to express their feelings on national and personal issues. By 1881, the paper expanded to weekly publication and continued to offer news of national interest but broadened its mission to ensure "that those who have served the country faithfully, either in the Army or the Navy, shall not be forgotten."[2] As part of this new focus, the paper began to include more soldier narratives in a section entitled "Fighting Them Over: What Our Veterans Have to Say about Their Old Campaigns." This section, coupled with the paper's editorials and letters to the editor, increasingly became concerned with major issues in Civil War remembrance, including the local and national activities of the Grand Army of the Republic. The paper soon became the single largest periodical devoted to the Union war veteran. Given the paper's influence, it clearly conveyed the issues northern veterans dwelt upon at the end of the nineteenth century as well as their opinions of how they wanted to be viewed by history and how the country should memorialize the war.

George Lemon, the founding editor of the *Tribune*, originally had more in mind than a mere veteran's newsletter. As stated in the paper's first edition, there was "a necessity for its existence"; namely, advocacy for the expansion and refinement of the federal pension laws for the veterans and families of all of America's major conflicts.[3] Such advocacy was no surprise coming from Lemon, a wounded veteran of the 125th New York Volunteer Infantry, who also happened to be one of the most powerful pension attorneys in the country. Lemon's firm was at the heart of the growing pension movement and handled some 135,000 claims by 1885.[4] This clear self-interest in the expansion of the pension system has led one historian to note that Lemon's advocacy efforts meant that "he and other pension agents stood to benefit hugely despite doing little actual work."[5] Yet, while Lemon was the formative influence on the *Tribune* as it rapidly became the national mouthpiece in favor of expanded pension offerings for veterans, the paper endured long after he completed his tenure as editor. In 1884, Illinois veteran John McElroy took over as managing editor, a position he held until his death in 1929. McElroy, who made a name for himself through the published account of his time at Andersonville and subsequent leadership of the National Association of Ex-Prisoners of War, brought renewed emphasis on historical narrative to the paper. This led to diminishing attention to pension agitation and more room for wartime accounts and serialization of books like William Tecumseh Sherman's *Memoirs*.[6]

The Union veteran community certainly responded to this national publication devoted to their story and welfare, and circulation of the *Tribune* peaked at over 300,000.[7] The rise of this new periodical corresponded with, and perhaps contributed to, the rise of the most potent US veteran organization of the nineteenth century, the Grand Army of the Republic (GAR). Most historians of the GAR have identified the link the *Tribune* had with its rise in the 1880s. Stuart McConnell, who offers perhaps the most detailed treatment of the subject, notes that after a promising start immediately following the war the GAR was "virtually moribund" by 1872.[8] The late 1870s brought an upswing of interest, however, and "the revival of the Grand Army owed much to George Lemon" and his efforts via the *National Tribune*.[9] The paper made its support for the GAR quite clear; by the 1880s there was a "G.A.R. Watch" section of the *Tribune* that kept readers up to date on GAR activities. One such section in 1885 included a piece entitled "Why All Should Join," which stated that the GAR "unites men together solely for their own good and for that of the country. That community is best of which has the largest and most flourishing G.A.R. post."[10] The *National Tribune* offered a literary outlet for

Union veterans while simultaneously reinforcing the need for veterans to band together in organizations like the GAR.

With such immense circulation, it is perhaps surprising that the *National Tribune* remains a little-studied window into the Union veterans' voice following the war. Many authors have acknowledged that the *Tribune* left its mark on the veteran community—one author refers to it as "the most prominent paper for ex-soldiers"—but few have looked beyond the paper's commentary on various hot-button issues of the postwar world.[11] The paper offers a rich vein of source material for those seeking information on the pension advocacy movement, the political thinking of veterans on a variety of national issues at the turn of the century, and northern feelings regarding reconciliation with their former enemies. Several historians have tackled these topics to various degrees using the *National Tribune* as a resource, but none have focused on the paper for its own merits. For example, recent authors such as Stuart Mc-Connell and Caroline Janney explore the private and public activities of the Grand Army of the Republic and other veteran organizations, illuminating some long-overlooked stories in the process, but they utilize the *National Tribune* sporadically without offering any extended discussion of its purpose or content for the Union veteran community.[12] One must probe deeper than its advocacy for the Grand Army of the Republic or the partisan agenda behind the paper and look at how veterans used the *Tribune* as a means to communicate and compose a proper historical narrative of the war. In reviewing the articles of the *National Tribune,* one discovers the concerns of the paper's editors, contributors, and readers as to how the past should be retold for both the present and the future.

While the most prominent of the postwar veteran papers, the *National Tribune* was part of a larger wave of publications seeking to harness and direct the interests of the ex-soldier community. As Brian Matthew Jordan has pointed out, "Newspapers like the *Tribune* became important hubs of information about fraternal societies organized by and for Union veterans," and there were numerous others in the field even before Lemon started publishing in 1877.[13] One of the first to emerge following the end of the war was the *Soldier's Friend,* a New York–based periodical that provided continuity for veterans seeking to adjust to the postwar world. The paper provided news on the early days of the GAR and had a section devoted to information on the regular army and navy for men who wished to keep in touch with comrades who stayed in the military.[14] While the *Friend* ended its publication run by the 1870s, the *Tribune's* start in 1877 heralded a new era of periodicals for the discriminating veteran. Regional papers emerged throughout the North, with Jordan noting, "Within a decade of Appomattox, nearly every major northern city boasted a veterans' newspaper."[15] Each of these tapped into a growing desire for connection within the veteran community that the GAR exploited. While the *National Tribune* became the most popular of such periodicals, smaller papers like the *Grand Army Record* and the *Grand Army Review* challenged the *Tribune's* market share and called Lemon out for his blatant self-interest in the pension movement.[16] Beyond the veteran community, the *Tribune* and its periodical peers reflected the larger movement of Gilded Age consumerism emerging at the end of the nineteenth century.[17]

This movement spread to the South, as the smaller market of the former Confederacy contained a healthy series of publications geared toward southern soldiers. Foremost among them was the *Confederate Veteran*, the "official organ" of the United Confederate Veterans (UCV). Founded in 1893, the *Confederate Veteran* reached peak circulation of roughly twenty-two thousand and became a valuable tool for advancing the Lost Cause.[18] As David Blight notes, the *Confederate Veteran* "became the voice of the UCV, the clearinghouse for Lost Cause thought, and the vehicle by which ex-Confederates built a powerful memory community that lasted into the 1930s."[19] The contents of the *Veteran* certainly conformed to the "Lost Cause" mythos that was erected following the war, but much like the *National Tribune* was for the North, the *Confederate Veteran* soon became a forum for the war's survivors to correspond with one another and discuss their memories of the conflict. Contributors to the southern paper praised this and other elements of the publication, with one going so far as to proclaim that "in the annals of historical literature the Veteran is the most unique in design and the most satisfying in the elements of truth."[20]

As increasingly documented by historians, Union soldiers in the postwar period developed a concern with the presentation of the past to the public, particularly schoolchildren. Southern veterans who contributed to the *Confederate Veteran* shared this concern.[21] In that paper, contributors grew wary in the 1880s of the "renegade pseudo-educator" and "prostitute historians" in the North sending messages to their children through school textbooks that the South had been wrong in its struggle for independence and called for local school boards to ban such texts wherever possible.[22] In the *National Tribune*, Union veterans paralleled such rhetoric with claims that "degenerate school histories" were spreading "Confederate misinformation" about the war.[23] This became particularly important to northern contributors beginning in the 1890s, around the same time that it caught the attention of Confederate veterans. One *Tribune* article challenged the "unsavory nature" of school histories in Louisiana, while another called for "a purgation of whatever is prejudicious to the truth of history."[24] In a lengthy treatment on the perspective of history emerging from the South, an 1896 article claimed southerners only endorsed books that provided "a flagrantly distorted view of the rebel side, and are grossly unfair to the Unionists." The article concluded with a strong denunciation of "Southern History," identifying "a widely-organized, most determined effort to pervert history, to shut out knowledge from the youth of one-third of the country, and to poison their minds with the most dangerous teachings."[25]

While decrying northern publishers and Confederate veterans for catering to the desire of southern readers seeking the familiar comfort of the "Lost Cause" from their school histories, contributors to the *Tribune* made clear that the public could only properly read about the past from a plainly patriotic standpoint. Such patriotism would naturally include an acknowledgment of the righteousness of the Union cause. The real problem, according to an 1897 report from the GAR's auxiliary Women's Relief Corps, was that school histories "lack the true patriotic ring, and do not present a right view of things." In this report, published in a later edition of the *Tribune,* the Women's Relief Corps pledged to help the GAR bring about "a satisfactory revision of our school histories."[26] That same year, the *Tribune* published a report from the GAR's National Committee on School Histories, which stipulated that children should be "taught that this is a Nation with the best Government in the world." Another report from the New York department of the GAR identified their exact specifications from a proper published history: "We have had in mind . . . that a school history must be brief, and should contain facts, not conclusions; that it should be truthful and impartial and not offensive to the Senator or the peasant, the New Yorker or the South Carolinian; yet we cannot avoid the convictions that treason can and should be made odious, and that loyalty to the flag and honor to the honorable dead should be cherished, next to Godliness, even in school histories." As the New York report concluded, "Past history teaches us that no man can be a man without patriotism."[27]

Ultimately, the key to sustaining a patriotic presentation of the war among the public was recognition of the sacrifices made by the Union veteran. Increasingly, the *National Tribune* identified the growing movement behind recognition of a national Decoration Day (soon to be Memorial Day) as the way to obtain such proper acknowledgment of the Union veteran. Beginning as early as 1881, the *Tribune* made a tradition of documenting Decoration Day observances around the country while actively campaigning for readers to contribute Decoration Day stories and articles.[28] Reprinted speeches and impassioned articles typically filled the paper in the summer months in order to display the honors that were bestowed upon the fallen veteran each Decoration Day. These contributions made clear the importance of the occasion, with "inspiration" being one of the more common terms cited by authors. "It is the recitation of the deeds of their fallen comrades that will have the deepest inspiration for those who celebrate the day," noted one article in 1882, "and the orator may be sure that no panegyric will so quickly touch their hearts as one which simply recounts their triumphs."[29] Decoration Day observances were an important ceremonial reminder of the war for the public, and one *Tribune* contributor emphasized that the occasion "is not intended as one for mirth and festivities, but rather for the cultivation of grateful feelings and patriotic thoughts."[30]

Union veterans made clear that they had tremendous concern about the presentation and remembrance of their wartime deeds to the public, but the question remained as to who should write the history of war and how it should be constructed. Perhaps not surprisingly, the pages of the *Tribune* are filled with comments about the value of the newspaper in providing a proper recollection of the war for modern audiences. Foremost among those who praised the value of the paper were the editors. "Every line in the paper is well worth reading," noted an 1897 column summarizing the merits of the paper and calling for more subscribers.[31] While the column made clear that the paper was intent on publishing news on current events and major issues facing the lives of Union veterans, a solicitation for written contributions a few years earlier makes clear another attraction for readers:

> The Editor would be glad to receive articles of from 3,000 to 6,000 words, or serial papers of greater length, for publication on the first page of, and written exclusively for, *The National Tribune*. The subjects submitted should be of interest to the veterans in general, and should be treated with especial

regard to historical accuracy of statement. Articles on the behavior of some particular regiment or brigade on some field whereon it distinguished itself, in some campaign in which it took a prominent part, in some siege wherein it acted defensively or offensively; reminiscences of prison life, the march or the camp; personal adventures, all such are solicited, will receive due consideration, and if available will have early insertion.[32]

This call for wartime memories was placed in the "Fighting Them Over" section of the paper, a section that had already become one of the most compelling for those veterans wishing to share and debate their recollections of the war.

"Fighting Them Over" was an obvious attraction for those seeking to sort through the memories of their wartime experiences. The section worked its way from page 7 of the *Tribune* up to page 3 by the 1890s before the "Recitals and Reminiscences" section replaced it after 1900. Acclaim came quick and often for the newspaper and its segment devoted to veterans' recollections, with one W. A. Simmons writing to the *Tribune* in 1883 to commend the efforts of such a "soldier's paper." He urged the editors to publish as many letters as possible in "Fighting Them Over": "Let the seventh page—which is the best of all—spread out all you can."[33] In another piece from 1883, one contributor compared the *National Tribune* to a "monster Camp-fire around which fifty thousand veterans gather every week to compare experiences."[34] More than a decade later, a writer noted that "everywhere the issues of The National Tribune Library are recognized as the most reliable statements of history published. They are written in the immediate neighborhood of the best possible data, and no pains are spared to make every statement and every figure as absolutely correct as it is possible to be."[35] The *National Tribune* was apparently the way to sort out the past, but to what end?

The answer lay in the "truth of history." This exact phrase recurs throughout the more than fifty-year run of the paper, as veterans made clear their preference for the identification and development of a single objective history for future generations. In a speech published in the *Tribune*, General Harry White, commander of the National Association of Union Ex-Prisoners of War, stated that his organization worked "to preserve and record the truth of history on the treatment and exchange of prisoners of war in the great rebellion."[36] On a more individual level, in 1881 the *Tribune* published General William Rosecrans's response to critics of his handling of the Battle of Chickamauga, wherein he claimed that he would "respect the truth of history and send to the press a correction."[37] Beyond the normally published content, "truth" was the primary motivator for those who offered their contributions to the "Fighting Them Over" section of the paper. B. H. Tripp of the 7th Wisconsin wrote his account of the Iron Brigade's action at Gettysburg "in the interest of true history," while another Gettysburg veteran, Isaac Hall of the 97th New York, offered his contribution "for the vindication of historic truth."[38] The single truth of history was the goal to be obtained through the contribution and review of soldier accounts in the paper, or as James Beale of the 12th Massachusetts noted, "The truth hurts no one; it is equivocation that is damaging."[39]

The *Tribune* appeared to be a key element of the "truth" process; as one article put it in 1897, "Let us have the paper read in every family in the neighborhood, that it may tell the truth, and mold public opinion in favor of the veterans."[40] However, to reach the "simple, unvarnished truth" of the war would entail a detailed and repeated review of accounts of the conflict, both north and south.[41] This review process often involved condemnation of the growing "Lost Cause" advocates to the south and the efforts to vindicate their role in the conflict. In a letter published in the *Tribune* in 1896, Ohio veteran John Wilkin noted how in the South "there seems to be a concerted effort there to swell the number of men on the Union side and lessen the number on the Southern side." Wilkin called upon the *Tribune* to challenge such "crooked history" before concluding, "I write this to show you that we appreciate your services to the country in exposing false history—willfully false."[42] Contributors and readers of the *Tribune* were convinced that there was an active effort to subvert the construction of the "truth"; therefore, they must offer their own contributions to the historical narrative in order to avoid the establishment of a "false history." One contributor would quote an unidentified source in a 1901 article who stated, "Truth is a Krupp gun, before which Falsehood's armor, however thick, cannot stand. One shot may accomplish nothing, or two, or three, but keep firing, it will be pierced at last, and its builders and defenders will be covered with confusion."[43]

The need for establishing the "truth" was a clear and present concern for those contributors and readers of the *National Tribune*, but their fears for the portrayal of history extended to the future as well. As C. W. McKay noted in his 1908 letter to the paper, "It is the duty of those who helped to make the history to correct the false statements while they are still alive and can do it, so that coming generations shall have a correct history."[44] In offering his comments on a recent account of the Battle of Franklin, Ohio veteran W. W. Gist appeared to concur with McKay when he stated, "I only desire to have the exact facts preserved for future historians."[45] As participants in the conflict, veterans recognized the value in their accounts of the war, and they hoped to have the record put straight before their generation was no longer capable of doing so. Other articles suggested more personal motivations behind straightening out the past for the future. In a speech from Abner Doubleday reprinted in the *Tribune,* the general suggested that all veterans should write their own history of the war "for the benefit of [their] children and for the use of the historian of the future."[46] Major General R. G. Minty went one step beyond Doubleday, claiming that every veteran should "use his best efforts to have a truthful history of that gigantic struggle handed down to our children and children's children."[47] Proper acknowledgement of one's wartime contributions by the historical community was welcome, but acknowledgement by one's descendants held a special allure for the Union veteran.

What is particularly revealing about how this almost heroic quest for "truth" appeared in the *National Tribune* is the divide it exposed within the veteran community of the North. Many contributors made clear that the *Tribune* should focus on publishing the story of the war's enlisted men, since it was the officer corps that primarily benefited from the praise of historians. An article entitled "Mission of the National Tribune" declared that the newspaper would tell the "truth" of the common soldier despite most other papers and histories that were devoted to "ignoring the subordinates of every grade, whose brains and courage, and enthusiasm in the cause were the stones which built up the monument to the fortunate General's fame."[48] A contributor from Wisconsin agreed, stating, "While we have in the various histories prepared by professional military writers a trustworthy record of the campaigns of the civil war, regarded from the officer's standpoint, the story of the struggle as the private soldier saw it, is now being given to the public for the first time through the columns of *The Tribune.*"[49] The common veteran was the only proper source for the "truth" of the war, though once the official records and maps of the war began to be published by the US War Department in the 1880s, many contributors called for both amateur and professional historians to rely upon them as a starting point for any thorough study of the conflict.[50]

While some targeted the historical community for inflating the importance of officers at the expense of the enlisted man's story, others hinted that the officers themselves hoarded the credit of history. In an 1894 article written by one E. R. P. Shurly of Chicago, the author went to great lengths to explain why General Crawford should not receive credit for the creation of a ferry across the Shenandoah River in 1862; the 26th New York and 22nd Maine regiments actually did the work. "The Lord forbid that I should reflect upon so good an officer, but history demands truth," Shurly proclaimed in an effort to temper his criticisms of Crawford, before concluding that "there were many things that Generals were brevetted for that were accomplished by men in subordinate positions."[51] Others were more direct in targeting the deliberate efforts of some officers to place their names in history. As First Sergeant H. Allspaugh, an Iowa veteran, noted toward the end of his account of the Battle of Chickamauga, "Had those valiant Generals *with a literary tendency* fought as hard to earn a reputation as they have for the last 20 years to sustain their claims to an imperishable name, they would be known by a grateful country and occupy their desired position."[52] For these veterans, the war's true glory belonged to the simple soldiers who modestly did their duty without seeking public acclaim.

Ultimately, it would be the enlisted man's job, through the pages of the *National Tribune*, to tell the "truth of history." Yet the exact "truth" could be a contentious issue, and the *Tribune* contained disputes, most friendly but some decidedly less so, over what really happened. While Union veterans routinely targeted "false" southern histories, they just as often challenged each other in the effort to construct the historical "truth." The friendlier discussions involved filling in the "omissions" of the past—stories that should be told but for some reason had failed to make the history books. One contributor felt the action at Orchard Knob had not received proper attention for its role in ending the siege of Chattanooga in 1863. This needed correction: "Justice to the brave and patriotic men who wrought this great deed of arms demands that a due presentation should be made of their important services on that memorable occasion."[53] Sometimes articles called for the proper treatment of particular commanders who had been ignored by the history books. One piece in 1910 identified the "scant praise" directed toward General George Meade and suggested that "to the student of history, loving justice, adequate recognition of his great abilities has never been given him."[54] Finally, Sergeant Major W. F. Bacon of the 13th Illinois Cavalry wrote to the *Tribune* to plead for the "meek and innocent mule-whacker" of the Union army to have "justice be done him by our historians."[55]

Calls for recognition of particular units that escaped historical notice appeared more frequently. C. W. McKay, a New York veteran, complimented the paper in 1908 for its recent pieces on Chancellorsville and Gettysburg before proclaiming, "I am at a loss to understand why you so utterly ignore the part taken by Bushbeck's Brigade of the Eleventh Corps." After providing a lengthy explanation of the role played by this unit, McKay concluded by almost apologizing: "I have not written the above in a spirit of criticism, but that the truth may be known and the credit placed where it belongs."[56] George Harrington of the 40th New York called out his fellow veterans for failing to compose a proper history of the 3rd Corps, expressing concern that no "first-class scribes" had stepped forward to do the work. Such work was necessary, since "all the survivors claim is their legitimate portion of the credit and to be placed on par with other organizations who participated in that conflict."[57] Given the increasing calls for seemingly obscure units to be recognized by history, many readers of the *National Tribune* probably agreed with the veteran who wrote to the paper in 1885 suggesting that the veterans of every single regiment that served in the war should see to it that their unit had a proper history written.[58]

Nearly all could agree that each unit deserved its moment in the sun, but more quarrelsome issues involved the correction of errors from published accounts of the war or from other contributions to the *Tribune*. In such exchanges, some men questioned the honor and reputation of those involved. As previously mentioned, General Rosecrans felt the need to provide the "truth of history" in response to the "unmitigated calumnies" that were "undermining my good name among my fellow country-men."[59] A few years later, veteran James Beale responded to General Oliver Otis Howard's account of Gettysburg in the *Tribune* by identifying what he considered erroneous comments about the actions of Generals Meade and Hancock. Beale concluded his corrections with the backhanded comment towards Howard, "It is to be regretted that a brave soldier, who lost an arm in the service, should be so conspicuously unfair in his utterances."[60] Two editions later, A. R. Barlow defended Howard from Beale's "terrific attack." Barlow accused Beale of "falsifying the record," and took his fellow veteran to task by claiming, "Beale is actuated by a mean spirit in his hashed up article."[61] Such attacks and counterattacks were legion, with comments ranging from one veteran defending General Sherman from the "colossal lying" about him having burned Marietta, Georgia, to the contributor who identified the errors in an account from a wartime chaplain and concluded with some exaggeration, "No greater misrepresentation was ever penned by man."[62]

When it came to correcting the historical record, Union veterans demonstrated particular sensitivity to claims made against beloved former commanders. Contributors often jumped to defend the reputation of a particular commander, even if it put them at odds with their fellow veterans. Citing efforts to "falsify" the historical record, Captain Henry Castle of the 73rd Illinois wrote in 1900 to praise the legacy of General Philip Sheridan. After a lengthy piece citing Sheridan's accomplishments, Castle closed by stating that his efforts were actually unnecessary: "The luster of his great renown permits no brightening at my hands; he needs no defense; his immortality is secure."[63] Several years later, an officer wrote in to defend General Joseph Hooker from claims that the men of the Army of the Potomac lost confidence in him following the Battle of Chancellorsville. Such a claim was "as far from the truth as darkness is from light," noted William LeDue. "Ask the soldiers who served in that campaign, many of whom are yet living, if they then, or ever, lost confidence in Hooker."[64] Sometimes efforts to protect the reputation of favorite officers meant calling into question the accounts of other, possibly more famous, Union commanders. In a speech reprinted in the *Tribune*, General Alvin Hovey challenged claims made in William Sherman's *Memoirs* regarding the Battle of Shiloh. In particular, he called out Sherman for making "false statements" about General Lew Wallace's division getting lost on its way to the battle, arguing that it was "unjust" of Sherman to call into question the bravery and competence of Wallace and his men.[65]

Gettysburg often proved the central focus of this give-and-take behind the efforts to correct perceived "errors" in the historical narrative. Several contributors weighed in on the discussion of who deserved proper credit for critical moments of the battle. It was hardly surprising to see Union veterans, much like their Confederate counterparts, wrangle over their role in the most pivotal battle of the war.[66] The dispute over which unit began the battle on the first day occupied many of the *Tribune*'s columns in 1892, one of the first being B. H. Tripp's account claiming that it was the Iron Brigade of the 1st Corps that was first on the field.[67] Less than a month later, H. H. Lyman wrote to point out that Tripp's piece "is so full of gross error that I am surprised by its publication." Lyman made clear that it was Cutler's brigade that had been first on the field and that veterans seeking to write their own accounts of the war must check the official records whenever possible "lest you find yourself in a hole along with Comrade Tripp."[68] Years earlier, E. S. Coan, color guard for the 20th Maine, wrote to the paper in response to a letter from one Joseph Fisher that claimed the 20th Maine had not been responsible for the legendary capture of Little Round Top. Coan could barely contain his emotions as he wrote in response, "It seems to me that if my pen does not endeavor to refute the statements that it [Fisher's letter] contains the very rocks of Round Top will cry out with indignation, and that our comrades in the National Cemetery at Gettysburg that fell under the colors of the 20th Me. will rise from their graves and affirm the truth."[69] As such comments indicate, some of the most passionate discussion in the *Tribune* occurred among those seeking to clarify and correct the historical record.

Whether filling omissions or rendering corrections, contributors to the *Tribune* made clear that they spoke up out of a sense of historical "justice." Errors in the historical record could not be allowed to stand. In his advocacy for recognition of Bushbeck's brigade, C. W. McKay made clear that his goal was that "truth and justice shall prevail," while B. H. Tripp concluded his piece on the Iron Brigade's role in Gettysburg by explaining it as "a question of justice."[70] In his piece highlighting the exploits of Philip Sheridan, Captain Castle explained his motivation for doing so as "justice to my comrades who served with him in the Army of the Cumberland, and to whom each episode of that service is a precious treasure, has impelled me to gather and briefly record the proofs with which the statements I have just made can be impregnably buttressed."[71] One officer wrote in a similar vein that he was obligated to praise the men under him who took Selma, Alabama, in 1865, since "it is the sacred duty of every man who was placed in a position of command to see that history does justice to *the noble men* who served their country under him."[72] This feeling of obligation to the "justice" of history empowered these veterans to speak out and offer their own contributions to the "truth of history" being debated within the *National Tribune.*

One particularly moving contribution to the paper came in 1901 and demonstrated the passion and level of detail often contained in the search for "truth" and "justice." In an unusually long letter to the editor of the *Tribune,* Frank Bruner, a veteran of the 70th US Colored Troops, targeted the

"Perversion of History" within a recent biography of Nathan Bedford Forrest. Referring specifically to the effort in the biography to downplay the massacre of Union soldiers at Fort Pillow, Bruner's article was peppered with words like "malicious" and "outrage." Bruner systematically utilized wartime correspondence, including the *Official Records* published by the War Department, to make clear that "our men were shot down and bayoneted like dogs, without regard to color," while Forrest and his men were guilty of "doctoring their reports and intimidation of prisoners who were captured at the fort." In conclusion, Bruner sought to explain his desire for such a lengthy correction: "This little article is not to stir up strife anew or rekindle the flames of war passion, but to compel would-be historians not to pervert the truth at this late day to extol the name and fame of any soldier, either blue or gray. It is more the province to do justice to the colored soldiers, especially those that fought so valiantly and gallantly as those at Fort Pillow."[73] For Union veterans like Bruner, some portrayals of the war could not stand without a response.

This desire for correction was at the heart of most contributions from the northern veterans who read the *National Tribune*, and it reveals a reactive pattern among them when it came to discussing the history of the war. While identifying historical omissions displayed some assertiveness on behalf of the veteran community in taking hold of the construction of the historical narrative, the increased emphasis on corrections demonstrates that soldiers were more content to read autobiographical accounts and histories of the war by other authors (often serialized or advertised in the pages of the *Tribune*) and offer critiques of their content. This made sense as the veterans aged into a community of working professionals, most of whom lacked the time and resources to sit down and write a proper history of the war. Instead, they took advantage of the snippets of history that they consumed from the *Tribune*, contributing if and when the moment struck them as appropriate, such as when the commonly held exploits of their own unit or commander were called into question. The fact that many disputes over corrections entailed the reputation of prominent generals or units ensured that any disparaging comments would not be taken lightly. The level of effort and detail committed to such disputes might look to some as "quibbling" over the past rather than facing the larger issues of the war, such as the legacy of slavery and emancipation. While this is true to a certain extent, one should not overlook the genuine concern these men felt for the presentation of the past and the passion that they exerted in preserving their version of it.

AMID THE VARIOUS struggles over the presentation of the Civil War in the *National Tribune*, veterans displayed a remarkable self-awareness that their perspectives and memories were inherently limited. Despite the calls for an objective "truth" of the war, many veterans recognized that their own participation in the conflict was an inherently subjective experience and time made memories more fragmentary. John Dineen claimed as much when he waded into a 1909 debate between various contributors as to the role Carroll's brigade played on Cemetery Hill at Gettysburg. In defending the actions of his own 33rd Massachusetts in repelling an attack by Louisiana troops, Dineen noted that most veterans were "old, gray and grizzly-looking, only waiting until the lights go out and taps sounded." Thus he was forced to confess near the end of his contribution, "Of course, I am not infallible; neither do I wish to be understood so."[74] Perhaps the most remarkable display of self-awareness came from Brigadier General Peter Michie, a postwar instructor at West Point who gave a speech in 1893 about his experiences during the war. In that speech, reprinted in its entirety in the *Tribune*, Michie began with a meditation on memory, stating:

> It is, however, a most remarkable fact that our memory retains only our own story, and soon forgets those related by our comrades; so that history continually repeats itself and yet is ever fresh and new. But what is the result upon the storyteller? Are we not all the creations of our own imaginations? Do we not unconsciously enlarge on the striking points and incidents of our past experience and at every repetition unwittingly tone down those that lessen our importance? It has been well said that "no man is a hero to his valet." With how much more truth can it be said that "every hero is only a vainglorious fellow to himself." It is, therefore, with a good deal of misgiving that I now undertake to relate anything of my personal experience in the events that happened nearly 30 years ago; but I hope I shall disarm your criticism by announcing at the outset that I distrust my own story, because of my imperfect memory, my undisciplined enthusiasm.[75]

Michie clearly understood that memory was a funny thing, and he was not inclined to trust in his alone.

In another speech reprinted in the *National Tribune* in 1881, general and former president Ulysses S. Grant noted, "It makes little difference what may be written about the battles of the rebellion; the country has been saved by the patriotism and valor of the Union soldiery, and we are enjoying the full blessings of a united people."[76] While the readers of the *Tribune* no doubt warmly received the praise of their former commander, the comments of many contributors to that paper indicate that they clearly disagreed that there was little value to working out the details of the war's battles. Within their repeated and sometimes heated discussions over the minutiae of battlefield placements and the proper distribution of the war's glory lies the true feelings of Union veterans regarding more abstract concepts like truth and history. While some modern authors have delved into the paper's many editions looking for help piecing together the events and details of the war, few have sought to look at the paper as a window into the postwar perceptions of the Union veteran. These men were intensely concerned with establishing the "truth" of the past and securing their legacy for future generations, though they could not all always agree precisely how to do so. Their struggle over the history of the war in the *National Tribune* is a revealing look at what these soldiers wanted from the past and how they chose to present it for the future.

NOTES

1. "Introductory" and masthead, *National Tribune,* October 1, 1877.

2. "Our Platform," *National Tribune,* August 20, 1881.

3. "Introductory," *National Tribune,* October 1, 1877.

4. Wallace Evan Davies, *Patriotism on Parade: The Story of Veterans' and Hereditary Organizations in America, 1783–1900* (Cambridge, MA: Harvard University Press, 1955), 164. For more on Lemon's work in the pension movement, see Mary R. Dearing, *Veterans in Politics: The Story of the G.A.R.* (Baton Rouge: Louisiana State University Press, 1952), and Stuart McConnell, *Glorious Contentment: The Grand Army of the Republic, 1865–1900* (Chapel Hill: University of North Carolina Press, 1992).

5. McConnell, *Glorious Contentment,* 114. Wallace Davies also identifies a level of opportunism behind Lemon's founding of the *Tribune,* referring to him as "the most notorious pension claims agent in Washington." Davies, *Patriotism on Parade,* 106.

6. Davies, *Patriotism on Parade,* 107. McElroy's book, *Andersonville: A Story of Rebel Prisons,* was a best seller and frequently advertised in the *National Tribune* once he took over as editor. See *National Tribune,* September 30, 1897, for one example.

7. Richard A. Sauers, *"To Care for Him Who Has Borne the Battle": Research Guide to Civil War Material in the National Tribune* (Jackson, KY: History Shop, 1995), xi.

8. McConnell, *Glorious Contentment*, xiv.

9. Ibid., 147. Several other historians have connected the rise of the *National Tribune* with that of the Grand Army of the Republic. David Blight describes the *Tribune* as "the principal GAR newspaper" at its founding. Blight, *Race and Reunion: The Civil War in American Memory* (Cambridge, MA: Harvard University Press, 2001), 181. See also Davies, *Patriotism on Parade*, 36–38, and Dearing, *Veterans in Politics*, 268–75.

10. "Why All Should Join," *National Tribune*, February 19, 1885.

11. Davies, *Patriotism on Parade*, 28.

12. See McConnell, *Glorious Contentment*, and Caroline E. Janney, *Remembering the Civil War: Reunion and the Limits of Reconciliation* (Chapel Hill: University of North Carolina Press, 2013). Other authors have utilized the *National Tribune* as a source in their discussions of the political activity of Civil War veterans. See Davies, *Patriotism on Parade*, and Dearing, *Veterans in Politics*. More recently, the *Tribune* has been a source for those looking at the construction of historical memory following the Civil War. See Blight, *Race and Reunion;* James Marten, *Sing Not War: The Lives of Union and Confederate Veterans in Gilded Age America* (Chapel Hill: University of North Carolina Press, 2011); and Brian Matthew Jordan, *Marching Home: Union Veterans and Their Unending Civil War* (New York: Liveright, 2014).

13. Jordan, *Marching Home*, 79.

14. *Soldier's Friend*, June 1868.

15. Jordan, *Marching Home*, 76.

16. Davies, *Patriotism on Parade*, 108–10.

17. Marten, *Sing Not War*, 147–48.

18. John A. Simpson, *S. A. Cunningham and the Confederate Heritage* (Athens: University of Georgia Press, 1994), 95–97.

19. Blight, *Race and Reunion*, 277.

20. Letter from John Witherspoon DuBose, *Confederate Veteran*, February 1916. For more on the *Confederate Veteran*, see Steven E. Sodergren, "'The Great Weight of Responsibility': The Struggle over History and Memory in *Confederate Veteran Magazine*," *Southern Cultures* 19 (Fall 2013): 26–45.

21. For more discussion on the concern expressed by northern veterans over the presentation of history in schools, see Blight, *Race and Reunion;* McConnell, *Glorious Contentment*, 224–32; and Janney, *Remembering the Civil War*, 183–86.

22. "Propaganda Perverting History," *Confederate Veteran*, May 1921, and "Our History in High Places," *Confederate Veteran*, July 1930. For more on the campaign against northern textbooks by former Confederates, see James McPherson, "Long-Legged Yankee Lies: The Southern Textbook Crusade," in *The Memory of the Civil War in American Culture*, ed. Alice Fahs and Joan Waugh (Chapel Hill: University of North Carolina Press, 2004), 64–78.

23. "Vicious School Histories," *National Tribune*, April 4, 1901.

24. "School Histories: What They Use in the State of Louisiana," *National Tribune*, March 12, 1891; "Vicious School Histories," *National Tribune*, March 7, 1901.

25. "Southern History," *National Tribune*, July 9, 1896.

26. "The Relief Corps: News and Gossip of the Great Auxiliary," *National Tribune*, July 15, 1897.

27. "The Report on School Histories," *National Tribune*, March 25, 1897; "Facts Gone Astray: Patriotism Discounted in New York School Histories," *National Tribune*, May 13, 1897.

28. "Decoration Day All Over the Land," *National Tribune*, June 1, 1881. See also "Honors to the Dead," *National Tribune*, June 10, 1882.

29. "Decoration Day Oratory," *National Tribune*, May 13, 1882.

30. "Decoration Day," *National Tribune*, June 1879. For extensive discussion of the growth of the Decoration Day phenomenon, see Blight, *Race and Reunion*, 64–97, and Janney, *Remembering the Civil War*.

31. "Brief Prospectus of the National Tribune for 1897–1898," *National Tribune*, September 30, 1897.

32. *National Tribune*, October 25, 1894.

33. "The Vicksburg Canal—Some Sensible Observations," *National Tribune*, June 28, 1883.

34. "Our Weekly Camp-Fire," *National Tribune*, May 17, 1883.

35. "The National Tribune Library," *National Tribune*, October 8, 1896.

36. "Address of Gen. Harry White," *National Tribune*, January 27, 1910.

37. "Gen. Sherman's Letter: What General Rosecrans Says of It," *National Tribune*, October 8, 1881.

38. "At Gettysburg: Substantiating the Claim that the Iron Brigade Opened the Battle," *National Tribune*, September 22, 1892; "Iverson's Brigade, and the Part the 97th New York Played in its Capture," *National Tribune*, June 26, 1884.

39. "Gettysburg: A Review of Gen. Howard's Account of the Battle," *National Tribune*, January 1, 1885.

40. *National Tribune*, January 14, 1897.

41. "Chickamauga: The Struggle of Sunday as Seen by an Enlisted Man on Horse Shoe Ridge," *National Tribune*, October 7, 1886.

42. "The Rebel Army—A Union Veteran Does Some Thinking and Figuring," *National Tribune*, January 16, 1896.

43. "Pickett or Pettigrew: It Was Pettigrew's North Carolinians Rather Than Pickett's Virginians Who Bore the Brunt of the Charge at Gettysburg," *National Tribune*, October 10, 1901.

44. "Bushbeck's Brigade Has Never Received Proper Credit for Its Good Work at Chancellorsville and Gettysburg," *National Tribune*, October 8, 1908.

45. "Battle of Franklin: The Loss of the Brigades Was Mainly in the Last Line of Battle," *National Tribune*, March 28, 1907.

46. "Corps Meetings," *National Tribune*, May 14, 1885.

47. "Capture of Selma: Wilson's Rough Riders Go over the Rebel Works," *National Tribune*, October 1, 1891.

48. "Mission of the National Tribune," *National Tribune*, April 30, 1885.

49. "Our Weekly Camp-Fire," *National Tribune*, May 17, 1883.

50. See "At Gettysburg: Cutler's Brigade Opened the Battle—Claim of Iron Brigade Refuted," *National Tribune*, September 22, 1892, and "The Capture of Fort Pillow," *National Tribune*, April 18, 1901.

51. "Built a Ferry: How a Captain's Plan Saved Two Organizations from Capture," *National Tribune*, October 25, 1894.

52. "Chickamauga: The Struggle of Sunday as Seen by an Enlisted Man on Horse Shoe Ridge," *National Tribune,* October 7, 1886. Emphasis in original.

53. "Orchard Knob: Raising the Long Siege of Chattanooga," *National Tribune,* April 5, 1888.

54. "People," *National Tribune,* December 29, 1910.

55. "The Mule-Whacker," *National Tribune,* May 20, 1886.

56. "Bushbeck's Brigade Has Never Received the Proper Credit for Its Good Work at Chancellorsville and Gettysburg," *National Tribune,* October 8, 1908.

57. "The Third Army Corps to the Front," *National Tribune,* October 2, 1884.

58. "He Thinks Each Regiment Should Have a History Written," *National Tribune,* October 29, 1885.

59. "Gen. Sherman's Letter: What General Rosecrans Says of It," *National Tribune,* October 8, 1881.

60. "Gettysburg: A Review of Gen. Howard's Account of the Battle," *National Tribune,* January 1, 1885.

61. "A Defense of the Eleventh Corps," *National Tribune,* January 15, 1885.

62. "Truth of History: Gross Perversion of Facts by a Northern Newspaper," *National Tribune,* December 21, 1882; "Mobile: Col. Brown Corrects Chaplain Howard," *National Tribune,* May 20, 1886.

63. "Sheridan with the Army of the Cumberland: History of the Masterly Services of Little Phil from Perryville to Missionary Ridge," *National Tribune,* October 25, 1900.

64. "Hooker and His Army: Gen. Le Due Indignantly Denies that Hooker Had Lost the Confidence of His Men," *National Tribune,* July 9, 1908.

65. "Pittsburg Landing. Are the Charges of Surprise True or False? Facts Reviewed," *National Tribune,* February 1, 1883.

66. For the fullest treatment on the veterans' debate over the legacy of Gettysburg and their role in it, see Carol Reardon, *Pickett's Charge in History and Memory* (Chapel Hill: University of North Carolina Press, 1997).

67. "At Gettysburg: Substantiating the Claim That the Iron Brigade Opened the Battle," *National Tribune,* September 22, 1892.

68. "At Gettysburg: Cutler's Brigade Opened the Battle—Claim of Iron Brigade Refuted," *National Tribune,* October 12, 1892.

69. "Round Top: A Shot from the 20th Maine, Aimed at Comrade Fisher," *National Tribune,* June 4, 1885.

70. "Bushbeck's Brigade Has Never Received the Proper Credit for Its Good Work at Chancellorsville and Gettysburg," *National Tribune,* October 8, 1908; "At Gettysburg: Substantiating the Claim that the Iron Brigade Opened the Battle," *National Tribune,* September 22, 1892.

71. "Sheridan with the Army of the Cumberland: History of the Masterly Services of Little Phil from Perryville to Missionary Ridge," *National Tribune,* October 25, 1900.

72. "Capture of Selma: Wilson's Rough Riders Go over the Rebel Works," *National Tribune,* October 1, 1891. Emphasis in original.

73. "The Capture of Fort Pillow: A Criticism of the Biography of Gen. N. B. Forrest by Dr. John A. Wyeth—A Protest against the Perversion of History—A Defense of Colored Troops," *National Tribune,* April 18, 1901. This was not a rare moment of African American troops being praised

in the *National Tribune*. See Andre Fleche, "'Shoulder to Shoulder as Comrades Tried': Black and White Union Veterans and Civil War Memory," *Civil War History* 51 (2005): 175–201. Fleche utilizes the *Tribune* extensively as a source, noting, "In the pages of the *National Tribune*, the white commemoration of black service received the fullest treatment" (185).

74. "On East Cemetery Hill," *National Tribune*, June 10, 1909.

75. "A Regular at Fort Wagner," *National Tribune*, August 24, 1893.

76. "General Grant," *National Tribune*, September 17, 1881.

"It Is Natural That Each Comrade Should Think His Corps the Best"

Sheridan's Veterans Refight the 1864 Shenandoah Valley Campaign

JONATHAN A. NOYALAS

I N 1886, the Boston-based Deland and Barta published George N. Carpenter's *History of the Eighth Vermont Volunteers.* Carpenter, a veteran of the regiment, wrote a colorful account of his regiment's service from its mobilization in February 1862 through its arrival home in the summer of 1865.[1] While the regiment endured much throughout the conflict, Carpenter believed the 8th Vermont's defining moment came in the autumn of 1864, during Major General Philip Henry Sheridan's 1864 Shenandoah Valley Campaign. Carpenter contended that the 8th Vermont's path to "martial glory" did not truly begin until the Vermonters arrived in the Shenandoah Valley in the summer of 1864.[2] "The jaded soldiers who rallied round his standard, from the plodding campaigns of Louisiana or the vanquished battle-fields of the Atlantic slope," Carpenter observed, "found in this new theatre of action the romance of war. . . . The greatest generalship on both sides was there to contend for mastery, and victory, if achieved, would crown the conquerors with laurels of glory."[3]

For the veterans of the Army of the Shenandoah, the 1864 Shenandoah Valley Campaign resulted in more than battlefield success at Winchester, Fisher's Hill, Tom's Brook, and Cedar Creek. Gaining control of this region—which, until Sheridan's victories, functioned as an avenue of invasion into the North, a point from which to threaten Washington, DC, and a source of provender for Confederate forces operating in the Old Dominion—proved a crucial step on the road to ultimate Union victory. Additionally, as many historians have noted, the timing of Union victories in the Shenandoah Valley significantly aided President Abraham Lincoln's bid for reelection.

The campaign's overall significance, then, made everyone who fought in it realize the importance of recording its history. Fifteen years after the campaign, Sheridan contended: "No army will have prouder recollections to advert to, or to commemorate."[4] Little Phil's veterans agreed. Among them was R. L. Nye, who fought in General George Crook's 8th Corps (Army of West Virginia). During a gathering of veterans in Marietta, Ohio, in 1879, Nye urged the comrades who fought alongside him in the Shenandoah Valley to begin the process of "preserving your war memories, and . . . collect and record the facts of your history."[5]

By the time Nye made this appeal, seventeen regiments that fought with the Army of the Shenandoah had already published regimental histories.[6] Only two of those regimental histories told the story of units in Crook's command.[7] The first, A. H. Windsor's *History of the Ninety-First Regiment, O.V.I.*, published several months after Appomattox, offered a "short sketch" of the regiment's service.[8] Nine years later First Lieutenant Charles M. Keyes released *The Military History of the 123rd Regiment Ohio Volunteer Infantry*. Keyes, who believed his book would have no "interest to the general reader," devoted one of the book's thirteen chapters to the regiment's time with Sheridan in the Shenandoah Valley. Keyes related human-interest stories, succinctly recorded the ebb and flow of battles, and praised the entire Army of the Shenandoah's conduct during the campaign, giving credit to other commands in the army and criticizing no part of Sheridan's command.[9]

Although Windsor's and Keyes's regimental histories preserved part of the 8th Corps's role in Sheridan's campaign, Nye felt uneasy about how Crook's veterans lagged in the campaign to record its history. Nye implored his comrades: "Other corps have given considerable attention to such things, and have collected and put in durable form records which it would be impossible for those not witnesses of the occurrences to make. . . . Through Cedar Creek—the record of this army [Crook's Army of West Virginia] was one of modest but gallant devotion to hard and perilous duty. . . . It is due to you and to your children, as well as to the country, that this record be preserved."[10]

While Nye urged Crook's veterans to "perform" their "duty" in writing regimental histories, he reminded his comrades not to disparage the reputation of the other corps in the Army of the Shenandoah. If veterans sought to write a history of their regiment, Nye believed regimental historians should always treat the other units of the Army of the Shenandoah—General Horatio Wright's 6th Corps, General William Emory's 19th Corps, and General Alfred T. A. Torbert's cavalry—with respect. Nye explained: "In the achievements of these corps we have a just pride. Their victories are our victories; their defeats are our defeats. In their successes we rejoice; in our failures they have no cause for shame."[11]

For Nye, histories preserved not only a legacy for the living but, more significantly, served as a tribute to "those who stood—and those who fell—by our side" for "the great principles upon which the war was fought, and of its grand results."[12] Although not explicitly stated during the gathering in Marietta, Ohio, the various reproachful comments made in articles and regimental histories by veterans of the 6th Corps heavily criticizing Crook's command for its performance at the Battle of Cedar Creek likely irritated Nye. Veterans of Crook's command had their fighting prowess called into question and reputations shattered at Cedar Creek. The two divisions of Crook's command, led by Colonel Joseph Thoburn and Colonel Rutherford B. Hayes, were the first units assaulted by General Jubal A. Early's rebel army during the early hours of October 19, 1864. By most accounts Crook's men, surprised by the attack, broke in confusion within thirty minutes.[13]

One of the first public attacks against Crook's command—troops that helped win the day at the Third Battle of Winchester on September 19 and proved the most crucial element of Sheridan's victory at the Battle of Fisher's Hill three days later—came in the form of a poem titled "Battle of Cedar Creek, October 19, 1864," published in 1865 by G. P. Hardwick. One of the poem's lines stated that Crook's "Eighth Corps ran away" and that after the men fled the field, they retreated "so far behind" the Union position because they believed the Union army "lost the day." The anonymously penned poem, presumably written by a veteran of the 6th Corps, praised the 6th Corps as the day's savior. The poem's author depicted Crook's command as cowards. "Eighth, come up with me, I say," the poem's author wrote, "Come up upon this crest of hill / you'll see a glorious sight / You won't get hurt, you need not fire / But see that Sixth Corps fight!"[14]

Some of the proud "wearers of the Greek cross" who penned regimental histories and articles in the war's aftermath carried the theme of that poem into their published accounts. Some 6th Corps veterans even suggested that had they been positioned on the army's extreme eastern flank to confront Jubal Early's assault (ahead of Crook's divisions), the Confederate attack would have failed. Crook's veterans took exception to this and defended their conduct, largely in the widely circulated *National Tribune*. J. H. Prather, a veteran of the 91st Ohio who served with Crook in the Shenandoah Valley, condemned the 6th Corps's veterans thirty years after the battle for perpetuating the idea that the 6th Corps would have performed differently. Prather explained: "If the Sixth Corps had occupied the position of the Army of West Virginia on that fateful morning at Cedar Creek, it would have done one of three things: surrendered unconditionally, suffered a swift and awful massacre, or skipped out at the rate of 18 miles an hour."[15]

Some of the 6th Corps's veterans viewed Crook's "mountain creepers" as inferior soldiers and frequently made "mean, slurring remarks" against them; however, the desire of some of General Wright's veterans to tarnish the 8th Corps's legacy stemmed from the need of the 6th Corps's veterans to differentiate its service from the rest of the Army of the Shenandoah at Cedar Creek.[16] In the battle's aftermath, newspaper coverage did little to distinguish the efforts of various units. Indeed, newspaper accounts published after the battle initially suggested that no element of the Army of the Shenandoah put up a fight and slowed Early's morning onslaught. Six days after the fight the *New York Tribune* reported: "Dislodged from its works, the army fell back in disorder, and all efforts to rally it, or restore order failed." Less than two weeks later *Harper's Weekly* stated, "Early approached under cover of a heavy fog, and flanking the extreme right of the Federal line . . . and attacking in the centre, had thrown the entire line into confusion, and driven it several miles."[17]

Gross generalizations about the morning attack that first appeared in newspapers eventually spilled into early histories of the conflict. For instance, Dr. James Moore, a retired US Army surgeon, published *A Complete History of the Great Rebellion* in 1866. Moore informed readers that Early's assault "completely routed" the Army of the Shenandoah and intimated that no portion of the Army of the Shenandoah attempted to blunt Early's onslaught. The entire Union command quickly became a mess of "fugitives, who swarmed around, hotly pursued by the yelling foe, amid the crash of musketry, and the booming of artillery."[18]

This interpretation of what occurred during the morning phase of the battle troubled veterans of General George W. Getty's division of the 6th Corps, who made a determined stand atop Cemetery Hill northwest of Middletown. George T. Stevens, the surgeon of the 77th New York Infantry and the author of *Three Years in the Sixth Corps,* wanted to clarify the record as to what occurred on the morning of October 19. Stevens berated authors who minimized 6th Corps's bravery at Cedar Creek. "Certain erudite historians, now have sent broadcast over our land, compilations of newspaper paragraphs under the sounding titles of historians of the rebellion, powerful gentleman," Stevens explained, "who, from their comfortable quarters in northern homes, watched our battles from afar . . . have gravely misinformed their readers that our whole army, including the Sixth corps, was driven pell-mell six miles to the rear."[19] Stevens asserted, emphatically, "The Sixth Corps was not driven back."[20] Indeed, Stevens not only avowed that Early's men did not drive the 6th Corps back but claimed that the thirty-five regiments under Wright's command single-handedly turned a disaster into a Union victory. With complete disregard for the tenacious fighting of the 19th Corps, which stood its ground for nearly an hour, or Sheridan's dramatic arrival, Stevens boldly asserted, "The grand old Sixth corps, directed by our own loved General Getty, had turned the fortunes of the day."[21]

Veterans who did not serve in the 6th Corps had difficulty accepting Stevens's statements. Francis Henry Buffum, a veteran of the 14th New Hampshire Infantry, fumed with indignation. Buffum, like many veterans of Crook's and Emory's commands, did not deny that the 6th Corps fought well at Cedar Creek. Still, Buffum refused to subscribe to the notion that the 6th Corps single-handedly saved the day. What was more, he questioned those veterans' ability to narrate the past. "After it got to do anything: it always fought splendidly," he declared, "yet few of its members can be trusted to write history."[22] From Buffum's perspective, the only reason the 6th Corps offered any significant resistance to Early's attack was because it was the last infantry corps to confront Early and had significant time to prepare. Buffum accused the 6th Corps of turning "over in their blankets once too many times" on the morning of October 19 while the rest of the army tried to slow Early's onslaught. While his regiment and the 19th Corps fought "for an hour a stern, hopeless battle," Buffum wondered what happened to the 6th Corps.[23]

Emory's veterans echoed this sentiment. For instance, the 29th Maine's John Mead Gould commented, "All accounts agree that the 6th corps did well, and they ought to have done well. There is nothing better in battle to go in last."[24] S. D. Harrold took "exception" to the claim by Getty's veterans that they "alone" turned the tide. "I claim," Harrold fumed in the *National Tri-*

bune: "There were other troops that faced the enemy from first to last as well as Gen. Getty and his little division, and that the Nineteenth Corps had men killed before any part of Gen. Getty's little division saw a rebel to shoot at."[25] While many of Emory's veterans vented their frustrations in the *National Tribune,* C. A. Savage of the 8th Indiana used poetry to remind the 6th Corps that any success they enjoyed at Cedar Creek rested on the sacrifices of Crook's and Emory's troops. "Now when the Eight Corps all had run," Savage penned, "Old Early thought it jovial fun / But General Grover (bless his name) / Said he would help them play the game . . . / He formed a line the pike along / To check old Early and his throng / And here he held the Rebs at bay / Till he was flanked from every way / This gave the Sixth Corps time to form."[26]

While veterans of the 19th Corps took affront to the manner in which the Sixth Corps's veterans heaped praise on themselves for their actions at Cedar Creek, nothing infuriated the veterans of Emory's command more than the manner in which some of Wright's veterans attempted to place all of the blame on the shoulders of Emory's regiments for two potentially costly blunders that occurred during the Third Battle of Winchester.

The first gaffe for which Wright's veterans placed all of the fault on Emory's corps was the delayed advance of the Army of the Shenandoah. Sheridan hoped his 6th and 19th Corps would march hastily to Winchester and strike the lone Confederate division commanded by General Stephen D. Ramseur in the early morning hours of September 19—before Early could concentrate his other divisions, which were spread throughout Frederick and Berkeley Counties. However, the Union army did not advance until 11:40 a.m.[27] The delayed Union advance permitted Early time to concentrate his forces and made the Army of the Shenandoah's task of winning the battle more difficult.

In the battle's immediate aftermath, various newspapers reported the sole reason for the army's delay was the "non-arrival of the 19th Corps, who through misconception of orders, had failed to come up at the proper time."[28] A correspondent for *Harper's Weekly* observed, "Sheridan . . . after having got the Sixth Corps across the Opequon, was compelled to wait full two hours for the arrival of the Nineteenth, and as a consequence of this to form an entirely new plan of battle in the face of an enemy already prepared and in line."[29]

Newspaper coverage in the battle's aftermath enraged Emory's veterans. They knew that the army's delayed advance was not due to any ineptitude but to Emory's obeying Wright's order to halt on the east side of Opequon Creek "to let the Sixth Corps" lead the advance with "Wright's entire wagon train in the rear of his corps."[30] Wright's insistence on having the corps's wagon train follow caused the delay, but Emory's troops endured the criticism. While Emory wanted every newspaper reporter to "eat his lie" about the 19th Corps at Winchester, he fumed even more when authors relied on those newspaper accounts for early histories of the conflict. When *New York Times* war correspondent William Swinton penned his *Campaigns of the Army of the Potomac*, he sent the manuscript to Emory for critique. It did not take "Old Brick Top" long to discover that newspapers served as Swinton's main source for his discussion of the Third Battle of Winchester. Swinton copied nearly verbatim wartime explanations that the delay "was caused by the non-arrival of the Nineteenth Corps under General Emory, who had moved his column to the rear of the baggage-train of the Sixth Corps, instead of keeping his command closed up in the rear of the infantry of the Sixth."[31]

Although Emory offered Swinton evidence, including a note from Sheridan and Wright, denouncing the "newspaper version as a lie and slander," Swinton did not correct his manuscript prior to publication.[32] After the book's release Emory warned that if Swinton "had not corrected it in a footnote, or in the second edition, his book should be burned wherever found, as containing a libel, known by the author to be such."[33]

Swinton never corrected the account, and numerous veterans of Wright's corps reiterated it in regimental histories in the ensuing decades. Three years after publication of *Campaigns of the Army of the Potomac*, a veteran of Wright's command, Aldace Walker, echoed in his *The Vermont Brigade in the Shenandoah Valley* that the 6th Corps got into position early that morning poised to attack Early's scattered command but could not because of the 19th Corps's failure to get on the field quickly. "Our corps was alone confronting the enemy. There were two or three anxious hours, but Early was engaged in hurrying up his detachment from Bunker Hill." Walker continued in condemnation: "The Nineteenth Corps being ordered to follow the Sixth" did not keep "closed up on our column. It is certain with this loss of time . . . we lost the opportunity of attacking the enemy in detail, and gave him time to prepare for our reception."[34]

Nineteenth Corps regimental historians fired back. While veterans such as D. H. Hanaburgh of the 128th New York freely admitted the 19th Corps did arrive on the field several hours later than anticipated, he asserted that the delay resulted from Wright's insistence on having the 6th Corps's wagons immediately follow his command instead of Emory's troops. Three decades after the Third Battle of Winchester, Hanaburgh attempted to correct the record: "Wright, with the authority of his rank ... ordered Emory to halt his column, and allow the sixth to pass. This, with an extra large wagon-train of Wright's causing a long delay, somewhat frustrating Sheridan's plans."[35]

After the war Wright's veterans not only blamed the 19th Corps for the delayed Union advance but also held it culpable for a second blunder during the Third Battle of Winchester—a gap that opened in the Union line between the 6th and 19th Corps during the initial advance. Although soldiers from General David A. Russell's division plugged the breach initially exploited by rebels from General Robert E. Rodes's division, Wright's veterans refused to assume blame for a moment that could have proven disastrous for Sheridan's army.

Colonel Joseph Warren Keifer, a brigade commander in the 6th Corps, believed responsibility for the potentially cataclysmic gap rested solely on the Emory's soldiers. Keifer, in his two-volume memoir published in 1900, observed that the "Nineteenth Corps was ordered to form on the right of the Sixth and to connect with it. . . . The Nineteenth did not make a close connection on the right of the Sixth."[36]

Again, Emory's veterans took exception to this criticism. Francis Buffum smarted at Aldace Walker's assertion that once the 19th Corps arrived on the field it advanced "impetuously and with little order." Buffum believed "false criticism" was another attempt to remove responsibility for a potentially egregious blunder from the 6th Corps. Infuriated over how Walker—someone Buffum referred to as "the eulogist of the Vermont Brigade"—derided the 19th Corps's legacy, he angrily wrote that the 6th Corps "did not lack in appreciation of its own services, nor, sometimes, in disparagement of other organizations."[37]

Being widely blamed for the delay and the creation of a gap in the Union line at Winchester angered Emory's veterans because it made them appear inept and because the accusatory rhetoric dishonored the memory of the 314 men of the 19th Corps who perished at Winchester.[38] D. C. Anderson of the 11th Indiana Infantry, part of General Cuvier Grover's division of Emory's corps, penned a scathing article in the *National Tribune*. Anderson condemned veterans of the 6th Corps for selfishly presenting a false and incomplete history. Such a history not only elided the crucial role Emory's regiments played in the

1864 Shenandoah Valley Campaign but dishonored the memory of comrades slain in battle in a shallow effort to establish faultless glory. Anderson noted, "Our association with the Sixth Corps never was that of comradeship." He asserted, "Survivors of the Nineteenth Corps need no apologists for their action in the Shenandoah Valley, and it is not for that purpose that I have written, but to preserve an honorable memory of those brave comrades who fell.... We know the jealous dispositions of the Sixth Corps; but the families and friends of our comrades who 'crossed the dark river' in ... battle do not know whether the diatribe of these comrades is true or not, and for this reason I have answered them."[39]

While veterans from Sheridan's three infantry corps wrangled for decades in regimental histories and articles about which units should shoulder blame for certain blunders during the campaign, or which units should be laureled with praise for the campaign's ultimate success, they neglected a significant element of the Army of the Shenandoah—Sheridan's cavalry.

Sheridan's mounted troopers performed important work throughout the campaign. They played perhaps the most critical role at the Third Battle of Winchester with an attack on Early's left flank. Furthermore, they performed important work in carrying out the burning of the town. They won a victory in the all-cavalry fight at Tom's Brook. Finally, they delivered crushing blows against Early's flanks during the Union counterattack at Cedar Creek.

As veterans of Sheridan's cavalry read articles in the *National Tribune* or perused the pages of regimental histories, they noticed the conspicuous absence of discussions of their role in the campaign. S. E. Armstrong, a sergeant in the 22nd New York Cavalry, gave Sheridan's infantry veterans "A Blast from a Cavalryman's Bugle" in the *National Tribune* for failing to recognize the role Sheridan's troopers played at Cedar Creek. From his home in Barker, New York, Armstrong fumed with indignation at the perspective of "most of the writers, [that] the infantry did all the fighting at Cedar Creek."[40] Armstrong, who served with General George Armstrong Custer's division at Cedar Creek, lambasted infantry regimental historians who neglected to mention the important part cavalry played in Sheridan's success. "If my memory serves me right, the cavalry, especially Custer's Division," Armstrong wrote, "had a little something to say about it." Armstrong was correct. Custer's division, which anchored the Army of the Shenandoah's western flank during the Union counterassault on the afternoon of October 19, played a crucial role by working in concert with Emory's infantry to crush Early's left flank. In addition, they also captured forty-five artillery pieces, several hundred rebel prisoners, seventeen wagons, six ambulances, and other rebel stores in Cedar Creek's final phase.[41]

Armstrong saw little difference in the efforts of any of Sheridan's infantry regiments at Cedar Creek. While some infantry corps might have held their position longer than others, all three infantry corps retreated north through Middletown by late morning. In so far as Armstrong was concerned, "There was not much difference in the infantry. We found stragglers from all the corps—Eighth, Nineteenth and Sixth." Although initially venomous in his remarks, Armstrong concluded in a conciliatory manner. He hoped his "comrades" would "remember that there was such a branch of service as cavalry" when writing in the future.[42]

Cavalry veterans resented infantry veterans ignoring the important role they played in the Shenandoah Valley because it did disservice to the memory of General Alfred T. A. Torbert, the commander of the Army of the Shenandoah's cavalry corps. Cavalry veteran John Danby believed, with some justice, that the writings of infantry veterans who lionized their regiments, their corps, and their commanding generals overshadowed Torbert and his men. Danby hoped to set the record straight, particularly regarding the important role Torbert played at Cedar Creek. "I always thought that General Torbert deserved much more credit than he got for the success of the battle. He had skillfully got his cavalry and artillery out of the tangle and had the army in good shape for fighting. He had sent to stop the infantry stragglers who were breaking to the rear."[43]

After decades of articles, Walter Kempster, a cavalry veteran from New York, hoped to clarify the role the cavalry played in the Shenandoah Valley. Kempster disliked a paper delivered by 6th Corps veteran Charles Anson about Cedar Creek in 1912, because it "resembles nearly every paper written about this remarkable battle, by making little reference to the action of the cavalry."[44] From Kempster's perspective, Torbert's cavalry, not the stalwart defense of Getty's division atop Cemetery Hill, saved the Army of the Shenandoah from complete ruin. Kempster argued that Sheridan's cavalry, although they "fought at times under most discouraging circumstances" during Cedar Creek, "never faltered, never lost their organization, and, but for their superb fighting, the battle of Cedar Creek would have had a very different termination." Kempster, like other cavalrymen, appeared to have no desire to disparage the role Sheridan's infantry regiments played during the campaign. However, he wanted to make certain that histories of the campaign presented a complete account of the important roles of all elements of the Army of the Shenandoah. Excluding Sheridan's cavalry from written accounts of the campaign "is like giving the play of Hamlet, with the character of Hamlet left out."[45]

The efforts of cavalry veterans to make sure their role in the campaign appeared in articles, essays, and books angered some infantry veterans, particularly from Wright's corps. For example, an article by R. Hannaford of the 2nd Ohio Cavalry attempting to set the record straight on the cavalry's role during "the most wonderful battle of the whole war, Cedar Creek," made some veterans of Wright's infantry seethe. Hannaford, who proclaimed that Sheridan's cavalry were the most "free from bias" as historians, wrote that when his regiment viewed the battlefield around 8:30 a.m., it seemed that no organized element of the Union army stood in Early's path. "Heavy battle lines of rebs steadily and resistlessly moving straight towards us. Opposing them was nothing," Hannaford wrote.[46]

Hannaford implied that none of the infantry corps did anything to slow Early's onslaught. No evidence exists that Crook's or Emory's veterans took issue with this observation, but some 6th Corps veterans balked at Hannaford's statements. S. A. Bendon believed Hannaford's article was nothing more than an attempt to capture all of the credit for Union success at Cedar Creek for the 2nd Ohio Cavalry. From his home in Portsmouth, Iowa, Bendon furiously penned a note to the editors of the *National Tribune* complaining that Hannaford "has too poor an opinion of his infantry friends, and seems to think that if it had not been for the 2nd Ohio Cav. Early and his rebels would have gone down the pike and 'scooped' all the foot-men in the Union army."[47]

While veterans from various corps attempted to refine their legacies, and at times berated the reputations of other elements of the Army of the Shenandoah, some veterans viewed postwar bickering as pointless. Nineteenth Corps veteran I. H. Stanley numbered among those who grew tired of the war of words. Incensed over the constant animosity and venomous pens of some 6th Corps veterans, Stanley wrote an article for the *National Tribune* that declared "that all . . . corps were necessary" to the Army of the Shenandoah's success. Stanley believed the time had come for veterans from Wright's command to come to grips with the reality that the effort of an army, not a particular part of the army, achieved success. In his discussion of Cedar Creek, Stanley stated unequivocally that if any element of the Army of the Shenandoah "had been absent, Jube would have followed us back to Harper's Ferry."[48]

Several months later, W. E. Webster, a veteran of the 1st New York Light Artillery Battery, echoed Stanley's remarks. Although attached to the 6th Corps, he believed every single soldier in the Army of the Shenandoah, from private soldiers to Sheridan himself, played an important role in doing what no other Union army had done in the Confederacy's breadbasket—achieving ultimate military success. While Webster understood that "it is natural that each comrade should think his corps the best," he did not believe exhibiting corps pride should come at the cost of the army's other units. In 1894, he published an article in the *National Tribune*. "I am proud to say I was a member of the Sixth Corps," Webster explained, "and we did some work while in the Valley, and I am free to say the Eighth and Nineteenth Corps did good fighting before and after Cedar Creek."[49]

While some of Sheridan's veterans attempted to convince their fellow comrades that all played an important role in Union victory, perhaps no one more vociferously urged the Army of the Shenandoah's veterans to stop the postwar wrangling over credit and blame than Rutherford B. Hayes. During a meeting of the Military Order of the Loyal Legion of the United States' Ohio Commandery on March 6, 1889, Hayes condemned his comrades for criticizing other units. As a brigade and division commander in Crook's corps, Hayes reminded veterans that criticisms should not be levied against another regiment as "the wisest and brave of men can not see all that occurs in a battle, and this had led me to very often regret to see the accounts that we sometimes see in print."[50] As was the case with most publications that criticized various elements of the Army of the Shenandoah, "We hear that such an organization behaved badly, from a person who perhaps knows nothing of the situation of that organization." Since the soldiers all served in the same army and either succeeded or failed together, Hayes encouraged veterans "to be careful to be very charitable toward their neighbors. It is so difficult to put ourselves in their places." During his remarks, Hayes singled out veterans of the 6th Corps who criticized Crook's command in postwar publications for putting up no significant resistance during the initial Confederate assault at Cedar Creek. Hayes urged Wright's veterans to put themselves into the shoes of Colonel Joseph Thoburn's division—the first to feel the weight of Early's onslaught in the early hours of October 19, 1864—and to imagine how they would have responded to a surprise attack by an overwhelmingly numerically superior force. "Suppose you had been with that division where Colonel Thoburn was killed," Hayes posited to veterans of the 6th Corps, "which was surprised in the morning— would you have done better?"[51]

The former president of the United States offered advice to future veterans who intended to write about the campaign. "The practical lesson that I would draw from all this loose talk that I have been giving to you is, that battles can not be known in their entirety, from beginning to end, from one end of a long line to another by one man. No one is authorized to say that in some distant part of the field there was bad behavior, or inexcusable behavior." As had been the case so many times, especially with Cedar Creek and the conduct of Crook's regiments, "There may have been disaster, but if I had been there with my favorite troops the same disaster would perhaps have occurred."[52]

Hayes, who informed a contingent of veterans in Portsmouth, Ohio, in 1885, that soldiers should never seek "popularity," understood veteran impulses to embellish wartime service. Wittily, Hayes informed the veterans, "If you were to take what you hear as the history of the great war, it would seem that that regiment which attends [a reunion] . . . had done all the fighting of the war."[53] Embellishment of fact was one thing, but calling into question the bravery of men who served as part of a victorious army was unconscionable. In Hayes's estimation at least "three-fourths" of the items published about the campaign created too many "unpleasant controversies . . . between soldiers."[54]

Hayes's earnest appeal notwithstanding, postwar rancor among Sheridan's veterans continued as the twentieth century dawned. From the perspective of Edward Armstrong, a veteran of the 139th Pennsylvania, veterans fought their campaigns over again not to point out the "blunder[s] of the officers and men" from other corps, but because they were so eager to ensure that no one would ever forget what they had contributed to a war "for civilization, for freedom, for manhood and for progress."[55]

NOTES

1. For a brief synopsis of the 8th Vermont Infantry's service see *The Union Army: A History of the Military Affairs in the Loyal States 1861–1865—Records of the Regiments in the Union Army—Cyclopedia of Battles—Memoirs of Commanders and Soldiers* (Madison, WI: Federal Publishing, 1908), 1:112–14.

2. George N. Carpenter, *History of the Eighth Vermont Volunteers, 1861–1865* (Boston: Deland and Barta, 1886), 164.

3. Ibid.

4. General P. H. Sheridan to General B. D. Fearing, August 21, 1879, quoted in *Report on the Proceedings of the Society of the Army of West Virginia at Its First Three Meetings* (Cincinnati: Peter G. Thomson, 1880), 24.

5. Address of Colonel R. L. Nye, Marietta, Ohio, September 19, 1879, quoted in ibid., 36.

6. By the time of the meeting in Marietta, Ohio, in 1879, five regiments from the 6th Corps published histories: E. M. Haynes, *A History of the Tenth Regiment, Vermont Volunteers: With Biographical Sketches of the Officers Who Fell in Battle and a Complete Roster* (n.p.: Tenth Vermont Regimental Association, 1870); Osceola Lewis, *History of the One Hundred and Thirty-Eighth Regiment, Pennsylvania Volunteer Infantry* (Norristown, PA: Wills, Iredell and Jenkins, 1866); George T. Stevens, *Three Years in the Sixth Corps: A Concise Narrative of Events in the Army of the Potomac, from 1861 to the Close of the Rebellion, April 1865* (Albany, NY: S. R. Gray, 1866); Theodore F. Vaill, *History of the Second Connecticut Volunteer Heavy Artillery, Originally the Nineteenth Connecticut Volunteers* (Winsted, CT: Winsted, 1868); Aldace Walker, *The Vermont Brigade in the Shenandoah Valley: 1864* (Burlington: Free Press Association, 1869). A total of six regimental histories appeared before 1879 by veterans of General William H. Emory's 19th Corps: Harris H. Beecher, *Record of the 114th Regiment, N.Y.S.V.: Where It Went, What It Saw, and What It Did* (Norwich, CT: J. F. Hubbard Jr., 1866); Orton S. Clark, *The One Hundred and Sixteenth Regiment of New York State Volunteers* (Buffalo: Matthews and Warren, 1868); John Mead Gould, *History of the First-Tenth-Twenty-Ninth Maine Regiment* (Portland, ME: Stephen Berry, 1871); Elias Porter Pellett, *History of the 114th Regiment, New York State Volunteers: Containing a Perfect Record of Its Service, Embracing All Its Marches, Campaigns, Battles, Sieges, and Sea Voyages, with a Biographical Sketch of Each Officer, and a Complete Roster of the Regiment* (Norwich, CT: Telegraph and Chronicle, 1866); George W. Powers, *The Story of the Thirty Eighth Regiment of Massachusetts Volunteers* (Cambridge, MA: Dakin and Metcalf, 1866); Homer Sprague, *History of the 13th Regiment of Connecticut Volunteers during the Great Rebellion* (Hartford, CT: Case, Lockwood, 1867). Three cavalry regiments that served with the Army of the Shenandoah also published histories by 1879: Frederic Denison, *Sabres and Spurs: The First Regiment Rhode Island Cavalry in the Civil War* (n.p.: First Rhode Island Cavalry Association, 1876); Theo. F. Rodenbough, *From Everglade to Canon with the Second Dragoons, 1836–1875* (New York: Van Nostrand, 1875); James H. Stevenson, *Boots and Saddles—A History of the First Volunteer Cavalry of the War Known as the First New York (Lincoln) Cavalry* (Harrisburg, PA: Patriot, 1879).

7. The first regimental history published by a veteran of Crook's command was A. H. Windsor, *History of the Ninety-First Regiment, O.V.I.* (Cincinnati: Gazette, 1865). The next regimental history penned by a veteran of Crook's corps did not appear until nine years later: Charles M. Keyes, *The Military History of the 123rd Regiment Ohio Volunteer Infantry* (Sandusky, OH: Register, 1874). A third regimental history appeared in 1879: William S. Lincoln, *Life with the 34th Massachusetts Infantry in the War of the Rebellion* (Worcester, MA: Noyes, Snow, 1879).

8. Windsor, *History of the Ninety-First Regiment*, 5.

9. Keyes, *The Military History of the 123rd Regiment Ohio Volunteer Infantry*, 84–102.

10. Address of Colonel R. L. Nye, Marietta, Ohio, September 19, 1879, quoted in *Report on the Proceedings of the Society of the Army of West Virginia*, 36–37.

11. Ibid.

12. Ibid., 37.

13. For additional information about Early's surprise assault on the morning of October 19, 1864 and the speed with which the Confederate offensive swept through Crook's two divisions see Jonathan A. Noyalas, *The Battle of Cedar Creek: Victory from the Jaws of Defeat* (Charleston, SC: History, 2009), 34–40.

14. "Battle of Cedar Creek, October 19, 1864," George J. Howard Civil War Letters, 1862–1865, Vermont Historical Society Library, Barre, VT.

15. *National Tribune*, March 22, 1894.

16. Russell Hastings, "Russell Hastings Memoir," Russell Hastings Papers, Rutherford B. Hayes Presidential Center, Fremont, OH (hereafter RBHPC); Stevens, *Three Years in the Sixth Corps*, 418.

17. *New York Tribune*, October 25, 1864; *Harper's Weekly*, November 5, 1864.

18. James Moore, *A Complete History of the Great Rebellion: Or the Civil War in the United States, 1861–1865* (New York: Hurst, 1866), 465–66.

19. Stevens, *Three Years in the Sixth Corps*, 421.

20. Ibid.

21. Ibid., 422.

22. Francis Henry Buffum, *A Memorial of the Great Rebellion: Being a History of the Fourteenth Regiment New Hampshire Volunteers, Covering Its Three Years of Service, with Original Sketches of Army Life, 1862–1865* (Boston: Franklin, 1882), 204.

23. Buffum, *A Memorial of the Great Rebellion*, 281–82.

24. Gould, *First-Tenth-Twenty-Ninth Maine*, 550.

25. *National Tribune*, October 8, 1896.

26. C. A. Savage, "Battle of Cedar Creek, October 19, 1864," quoted in James K. Ewer, *The Third Massachusetts Cavalry in the War for the Union* (Maplewood: Historical Committee of the Regimental Association, 1903), 231.

27. For further discussion of the issues surrounding the delay see Brandon H. Beck and Roger U. Delauter, *The Third Battle of Winchester* (Lynchburg: H. E. Howard, 1997), 29–31, and Scott C. Patchan, *The Last Battle of Winchester: Phil Sheridan, Jubal Early, and the Shenandoah Valley Campaign, August 7–September 9, 1864* (El Dorado Hills, CA: Savas Beatie, 2013), 230–31.

28. *New York Tribune*, September 21, 1864.

29. *Harper's Weekly*, October 8, 1864.

30. Richard B. Irwin, *History of the Nineteenth Army Corps* (New York: G. P. Putnam's Sons, 1892), 379–80.

31. William Swinton, *Campaigns of the Army of the Potomac: A Critical History of Operations in Virginia Maryland and Pennsylvania from the Commencement to the Close of the War 1861–5* (New York: Charles B. Richardson, 1866), 557.

32. Gould, *First-Tenth-Twenty-Ninth Maine*, 504.

33. Ibid.

34. Walker, *The Vermont Brigade*, 93.

35. D. H. Hanaburgh, *History of the One Hundred and Twenty-Eighth Regiment, New York Volunteers (U.S. Infantry) in the Late Civil War* (Poughkeepsie, NY: Enterprise, 1894), 145.

36. Joseph Warren Keifer, *Slavery and Four Years of War: A Political History of Slavery in the*

United States, Together with a Narrative of the Campaigns and Battles of the Civil War in Which the Author Took Part: 1861–1865 (New York: G. P. Putnam's Sons, 1900), 2:110–11.

37. Buffum, *A Memorial of the Great Rebellion,* 207.

38. Patchan, *The Last Battle of Winchester,* 492.

39. *National Tribune,* November 24, 1887.

40. *National Tribune,* July 28, 1887.

41. Ibid. See also Gregory J. W. Urwin, *Custer Victorious: The Civil War Battles of General George Armstrong Custer* (East Brunswick, NJ: Associated University Presses, 1983), 215.

42. *National Tribune,* July 28, 1887.

43. W. C. King and W. P. Derby, comps., *Camp-Fire Sketches and Battlefield Echoes of the Rebellion* (Springfield, MA: W.C. King, 1887), 367.

44. Walter Kempster, "The Cavalry at Cedar Creek: Remarks on Companion Anson's Papers, Written by the Unanimous Request of the Commandery," in *War Papers Read before the Commandery of the State of Wisconsin, Military Order of the Loyal Legion of the United States* (Milwaukee: Burdick and Allen), 4:369. See Charles H. Anson, "Battle of Cedar Creek, October 19th, 1864," in ibid., 355–67.

45. Kempster, "The Cavalry at Cedar Creek," 375.

46. *National Tribune,* March 1, 1894.

47. *National Tribune,* April 5, 1894.

48. *National Tribune,* November 8, 1894.

49. *National Tribune,* February 1, 1894.

50. Rutherford B. Hayes, "Incidents at the Battle of Cedar Creek," in *Sketches of War History 1861–1865: Papers Prepared for the Ohio Commandery of the Military Order of the Loyal Legion of the United States,* ed. W. H. Chamberlin (Cincinnati: Robert Clarke, 1896), 244.

51. Ibid., 244–45.

52. Ibid.

53. Speech of Rutherford B. Hayes, September 16, 1885, 9th Reunion of the Society of the Army of West Virginia, Portsmouth, Ohio, Rutherford B. Hayes Papers, RBHPC.

54. Hayes, "Incidents at the Battle of Cedar Creek," 245.

55. *National Tribune,* March 25, 1897; Speech of Rutherford B. Hayes, September 10, 1886, 10th Reunion of the Society of the Army of West Virginia, Portsmouth, Ohio, Rutherford B. Hayes Papers, RBHPC.

A Building Very Useful

The Grand Army Memorial Hall in US Civic Life, 1880–1920

JONATHAN D. NEU

OR YEARS AFTER Appomattox, the citizens of Rockville, Connecticut, considered erecting a commemorative marker to honor their town's Civil War heroes. During Memorial Day ceremonies in 1884, community leaders reminded the audience of its obligations to the Union's defenders and recommended that the town appropriate sufficient funds to erect a soldiers' monument. However, Rockville patriarch Dwight Loomis, who served the district in Congress during the war, demurred. Instead of a mere monument, Loomis suggested constructing "a large and handsome building" that would "not only be a fitting memorial for the soldiers, but at the same time be of use and benefit to the town."[1] Veterans and nonveterans agreed, ultimately directing some $90,000 in public funds toward the construction of a memorial building. Upon its completion in 1890, the three-story Romanesque structure was a spectacular example of multifunctional design, encompassing a one-thousand-seat auditorium, municipal offices, courtrooms, a law library, and police headquarters. Additionally, the building housed the meeting hall and anterooms of Rockville's local chapter of the Grand Army of the Republic (GAR), the Thomas F. Burpee Post No. 71.

Organized in 1884 by twenty-three area Union veterans, Burpee Post was named in memory of the locally born colonel of the 21st Connecticut Volunteer Infantry, who fell at the Battle of Cold Harbor twenty years earlier.[2] The post steadily grew in membership over the years and soon sought permanent headquarters to conduct its fraternal meetings. The town's memorial building was the obvious choice, and much of its second floor was turned over for Burpee Post's use. Opening their September 1890 business meeting in their new quarters, the post's veterans acknowledged the community's generosity in recognizing their wartime sacrifices and reserving space for their fraternal activities. In a set of resolutions, the members praised the townspeople for "erect[ing] a magnificent edifice as a lasting *Memorial*" to Rockville's defenders and promised to be "doubly mindful of our duties as citizens and freemen and [to] always strive to merit the confidence reposed in us as loyal citizens."[3] In subsequent years, the comrades built up an impressive library and relic collection in their GAR hall and frequently threw open their doors to all comers for lectures, musical programs, and other public events. Together, Rockville soldiers and civilians created a dynamic community center—a place at once commemorative of the war dead, practical for the town's day-to-day business, and essential for the town's GAR veterans to meet and communicate their memory of the Civil War.

The construction of the Rockville Memorial Building is just one example underscoring an overlooked relationship between Grand Army veterans and northern nonveterans. In the postwar decades, both sides cooperatively mobilized to create freestanding memorial structures that not only assumed fraternal utility as meeting places for GAR members but also provided civic utility for citizens at large. In communities of all sizes, GAR veterans and their civilian allies collaborated in support of these memorial halls that honored the soldier dead and veteran living in a more impressive (and, typically, more expensive) commemorative expression than the more familiar soldiers' monuments that cropped up after the Civil War.[4] At the same time, these expansive structures had ample space to serve the needs of nonveterans too, becoming many towns' newest civic centers. Meanwhile, aging Union veterans proved remarkably successful in promoting these ventures, not only leveraging GAR post influence to propose the structures but also negotiating with town and state officials, architects, urban planners, voters, and other key groups whose support was necessary to raise them. Veterans were thus enmeshed in the social and political networks of their communities in previously unnoticed ways.

Analysis of post–Civil War memorial halls refines two key points in GAR scholarship. First, the typical interpretation of late nineteenth- and early twentieth-century fraternities—private, guarded, privileged—should not be extended wholesale to the spaces in which GAR veterans met. Because historians have often emphasized these fraternities as organizations of retreat, protected as they were by secret ritual and safeguarded by members' maleness, it is tempting to view the GAR memorial hall as disconnected from the world around it.

Dubbing the fraternal lodge, as many scholars have, an "asylum," a "refuge," or an "oasis" from the era's disconcerting social changes presumes an insularity for this space, separate from the web of community interactions going on around it.[5] Indeed, the exclusive nature of GAR membership—requiring honorable military service on behalf of the Union—suggests even stronger barriers to entrée into the order's fraternal space.[6] Certainly some veterans articulated a desire for detachment from their fellow citizens. One GAR officer, for instance, noting the ascent of the nation's younger generations, suggested to his comrades that "we might as well begin to learn to stand aside, and that it is happy for us that we may, in the safe retreat of the Post-room, turn our backs upon the new fields, and keep fresh in the mind the memories of that yesterday the full import of whose events we only know."[7] This characterization must not be taken too far, however, as numerous GAR posts would come to meet in memorial halls whose interconnections with community rhythms are unmistakable.

Second, the construction of memorial halls should be differentiated from the many soldiers' monuments—statues, pillars, obelisks, and other "silent" commemorative markers—that Union veterans dedicated. When examined at all, the memorial hall is treated as a private and hallowed space reserved for revered Grand Army veterans, useful only to them while alive and left dormant and sacrosanct after their deaths.[8] Overlooking GAR members' many memorial hall initiatives across the country obscures the fact that these were rarely isolated and single-purpose buildings used exclusively by veterans. Further, these structures should not be classified alongside the many Masonic temples and other fraternal buildings erected during this era.[9] Although a chief function was to serve as a meeting place for the local GAR post, memorial halls were also lively community institutions that served public needs in many other ways. Moreover, these commemorative structures brought to their neighborhoods an aesthetic and architectural appeal during an age when community improvement enthusiasm swept the country. In short, memorial halls were proposed and designed with more than Union veterans' interests in mind. They were deeply intertwined with not only Civil War commemoration but also civic reform impulses that Grand Army veterans and their nonveteran allies were remarkably successful in jointly advancing.

LIKE CONNECTICUT'S Burpee Post, the roughly seven thousand individual GAR posts across the country required as many designated community spaces for members to conduct their fraternal business. The location of these quarters varied widely and was determined by a number of factors: comrade preferences, resources and revenue of the local post, and the magnanimity of nonveterans, to name a few. For many posts, especially those in small towns and rural areas where members were usually fewer and poorer, comrades were likely to rent humble quarters with just enough space for basic fraternity functions. Leasing a spare room at a nearby business was a common option for many posts. Others might make arrangements to share space with their communities' better-established fraternities like the Odd Fellows or Freemasons (often, GAR members belonged to these orders too, helping facilitate the negotiations). Some particularly enterprising posts—especially larger, wealthier, and more urban ones—pooled resources to purchase their own accommodations outright. Still others petitioned their fellow citizens and local officials to grant them suitable quarters in public spaces. Many community courthouses and town halls, for example, complemented their traditional functions by serving as the local GAR post's meeting place.[10]

This demand for GAR quarters, coupled with a wider community impulse to commemorate the Civil War, produced a veritable eruption of Grand Army memorial halls constructed across the North in the years surrounding the turn of the twentieth century. When a town sought to erect a tribute to its defenders, preference for a memorial hall often centered on the belief that such a gesture was a more permanent and touching testimonial to the war generation. "Monuments erected to the memory of the brave become defaced with the lapse of years," reasoned one commentator. "In a memorial hall their names might be kept green in memory, as long as time itself shall last."[11] For other advocates, these structures better preserved additional aspects of Civil War history besides solely the memory of a town's war heroes. One supporter, for instance, suggested that "in a [memorial] hall could be placed relics, documents and portraits bearing upon the rebellion. Here they would be carefully preserved for all time for the use of those that might be interested in the study of the history of a great struggle."[12] Still others touted memorial hall projects because they proved more practical for the benefit of all citizens. Indeed, promises of "usefulness" and "utility" pepper the many building proposals advanced by both GAR veterans and other advocates. In this vein, one hall promoter stated that such a structure in his town "would be a monument in every sense of the word and one that while commemorating the heroic deeds of the dead would also prove of benefit to the living."[13]

To be sure, not everyone—veteran or nonveteran—welcomed the prospect of a memorial hall in his or her community. When, for instance, the Iowa General Assembly deliberated in the late 1880s and early 1890s over erecting a commemorative structure on the capitol grounds "for the purpose of perpetuating an expression of the patriotism, courage and distinguished soldiery" of its defenders (funded in part by a refunded federal war tax), a designated commission appraised the merits of a memorial hall. One hall supporter asked the state's Grand Army posts to consider whether they wanted to invest the funds in a traditional monument of "'dead marble' with its proverbial iron fence and notice to 'keep off the grass'" or a memorial hall that would be "in keeping with a progressive practical people in that which is useful and instructive and consequently more pleasing to the eye."[14] Ultimately, however, it was decided that a memorial hall risked devolving into a "patriotic storage room" for war relics where "flags decay and turn to dust, and arms lose interest as years roll on."[15] When put to a vote by the Grand Army posts of the state, veterans ultimately agreed with the monument commission's assessment (though some posts spurned using the funds for either a monument or a memorial hall, preferring instead that the money go to disabled veterans in the state's soldiers' home at Marshalltown).[16] The result was the raising of the $150,000 Iowa Soldiers' and Sailors' Monument, completed in 1896.[17]

In other instances, citizens felt memorial halls were an unwarranted expense or an improper commemorative offering. The GAR veterans of Kalamazoo, Michigan's, Orcutt Post were repeatedly stymied in their attempts to construct a memorial hall with public funds for many years before the realization of a building in 1908. One reason for the delay was the indignation of the citizens residing on the county's periphery who saw no value in building up the county seat. "There are but few old soldiers in the county outside of Kalamazoo who are physically and financially qualified to take advantage of the benefits of such an institution," one community complained, "and the whole matter is looked upon as a 'graft' on the part of Kalamazoo people to beautify their city at the expense of the county."[18] Relying instead on friendly area businessmen, civic-minded citizens, and their own post funds, Orcutt Post secured the $8,000 for the building without reaping public financing.[19] During the fund-raising phase for a memorial hall in New York, some disgruntled citizens editorialized about their displeasure at the community's transfer of public funds from a monument to a memorial hall. One rankled critic asked whether it was "right for us to give our money to build a monument to perpetuate the memory of the 'gallant dead,' and then have the money diverted to build a hall?" Another, citing the types of public activities that might threaten the sanctity of a memorial structure feared that "the memory of the gallant dead will be perpetuated by holding high carnival in the monumental hall."[20]

Despite these qualms from some quarters, the construction of memorial halls nonetheless received widespread backing and became a cultural phenomenon across the North. In several states, legislators passed bills empowering county commissioners or other local entities to appropriate money for commemorative Civil War markers. Grand Army veterans were active both in petitioning for these taxation measures and, occasionally, for widening the scope of these laws to include memorial halls. In Iowa, for instance, the state's General Assembly approved a law in 1884 authorizing each county to levy a tax (not to exceed $3,000 in revenue) to erect a soldiers' monument to that county's Union dead. Two years later, the efforts of state representative and Union veteran Rufus S. Benson amended the law to permit counties to collect the tax for the construction of a monument or a memorial hall. Grand Army veterans in rural Franklin County responded immediately, petitioning the county to put the taxation question on the ballot. The Board of Supervisors conceded, and in the 1887 spring election, voters authorized a tax to finance a memorial hall at the county seat of Hampton. Supplemented by donations gathered by the veterans and aided by the town council's donation of land for the building, Franklin County's Grand Army men moved their post meetings to the brick structure after its 1890 dedication.[21]

Indiana veterans were also active in establishing a memorial hall in Porter County, working to extend the intent of the state's law on commemorative building. After the war, the Indiana legislature empowered boards of county commissioners to appropriate funds for soldiers' monuments. As early as 1885, veterans and civilian allies of Valparaiso's Chaplain Brown Post organized to establish a monument to the town's defenders, aided by a $500 contribution collected by the post's Women's Relief Corps (WRC) auxiliary. By this point, public opinion had shifted toward using the funds to create a more impressive memorial hall. Former Brown Post commander A. Lytle Jones drew up an amendment to the existing state law, and members of the post journeyed to Indianapolis to press their case in person. During the 1891 legislative session, Jones's amendment passed, and Brown Post was free to solicit subscriptions for the memorial hall, assign a building committee to plan construction, and hire an architect and contractors to erect the $15,000 structure. Assisted by the Board of County Commissioners, who leased the building's site free of charge, the dedication took place in November 1893. Besides housing Brown Post's fraternal hall and quarters for the WRC, Valparaiso's newest civic center included a twelve-hundred-seat auditorium, stage, and ticket office for community events.[22]

Elsewhere, GAR veterans proved exceptionally proficient in tailoring their memorial hall advocacy strategies to the specific needs of their communities. In rural areas across the North, for instance, GAR members recognized that commemorative structures could double as their regions' first centers for entertainment or civic functions. The southwest corner of sparsely populated Livingston County, New York, is illustrative. Here, three memorial halls cropped up within a ten-mile radius in the span of a quarter century. The village of Portage raised the first in 1880 to pay tribute to the thirty-five area soldiers who had died during the Civil War. As early as 1865, the community's Soldiers' Monument Association began collecting money for a marble monument. Earning contributions from individual donors and various fund-raisers, the association amassed nearly $2,000 by the late 1870s.[23] By that time, however, many veterans and civilians suggested that a memorial hall was "the most sensible way to expend the money" as it "would be of some use to the living and as honorable to the dead."[24] Portage ultimately constructed a modest brick structure, which became the new GAR headquarters of the William C. Hall Post.[25] Eight years later in nearby Dalton, members of the local GAR post worked with citizens in erecting their own memorial hall. Comparable in size and expense to the Portage structure, Dalton's hall was similarly lauded as "a building that will be found very useful for general gatherings of the people."[26]

The memorial hall at Nunda was the last in the region to be constructed, largely due to the villagers' comparative apathy about raising a commemorative testament to its defenders. Despite the fund-raising efforts of the local Craig W. Wadsworth Post in the 1880s, the local newspaper reported that citizens did "not appear . . . very anxious to contribute" even though "they concede that it should be done."[27] Efforts hibernated for the next two decades until native son John J. Carter gifted $20,000 to erect a stately memorial hall in the middle of town.[28] Carter, a Congressional Medal of Honor recipient who earned his wealth in the Pennsylvania oil fields after the war, intended the building to serve Nunda's GAR and other patriotic organizations for the benefit of "the old soldiers and citizens of Nunda and the rising generation—the hope of the future."[29] Completed in 1906 and transferred to the Nunda Memorial Hall Corporation, the building became the headquarters of Wadsworth Post and its auxiliaries.

Livingston County's memorial halls quickly assumed broad functionality. To be sure, the structures played important roles in commemorating the soldier dead, providing meeting places for Grand Army veterans, and serving as focal points for Decoration Day observances. However, perusal of the local newspapers reveals the overlooked roles of the halls—that is, as sites for the activities of nonveterans who molded the facilities into vital civic centers. Portage's memorial hall, for example, served as the headquarters of the town's chapter of the Women's Christian Temperance Union, the local Grange, the Red Cross sewing circle, and even as a storage facility for area farmers' produce. During one particularly active span between 1895 and 1896, the structure hosted a temperance lecture sponsored by a local Baptist church, an oyster supper for the benefit of the local cornet band, a maple sugar social for the junior missionary society of an Episcopal Church, and voter registration for the fall elections.[30] Nunda's hall became the site of the American Legion's public fairs and a consultation clinic for nearby Mt. Morris's pulmonary treatment facility.[31] In Dalton, the memorial hall became the villagers' venue for square dances and moving picture shows during the 1910s and 1920s.[32] All told, Livingston County's memorial halls served not just as sites of memory or preserves set aside solely for GAR use. They were also centers for rural entertainment and civic assembly for all citizens.

Meanwhile, in many small towns across the postwar United States, residents came together in improvement associations to promote municipal planning and public works projects. Enterprises were broad—ranging from civil or sanitary engineering undertakings, village beautification schemes, and the establishment of libraries or other public institutions—all of which markedly enhanced provincial life.[33] Through their advocacy of memorial halls, small-town GAR posts became part of this movement to bring new amenities to their communities. They advertised the civic and educational benefits of their projects, secured donations from interested backers, appealed to public officials and voters for appropriations and tax support, and cultivated grassroots civic engagement.[34] The post at Paw Paw, Michigan, demonstrated this spirit of improvement. Initially seeking to erect a soldiers' monument, the veterans "upon mature consideration" opted to build a memorial hall "which would be of greater benefit to the community at large and would serve equally well as a memorial to the veterans of the Civil War."[35] Upon its completion in 1912, the post advertised its new home as a place for the public at large—"bright, clean, light and warm—a place to congregate with your brothers and sisters, feast and visit and commune."[36] The front room of the memorial hall was equipped as a public "rest room" with seating and reading material for all comers to enjoy, a mark of the post's "appreciation of the help [they] received from the community in building their new hall."[37] In a short time, the memorial hall not only served as the headquarters of the GAR post but also became a regular meeting place for the local branches of the Grange, the Knights of Pythias, the Lady Maccabees, and the Royal Neighbors.[38]

Similarly, in Windsor Locks, Connecticut, the members of Joseph H. Converse Post No. 67 coordinated to bring their small town a useful building. The veterans bought a tract of land from their own funds in 1889 and then united with wealthy local mill owner Charles E. Chaffee, a "warm sympathizer with the veterans" who donated the money to erect a two-story memorial hall that included a library, meeting rooms, and the post quarters.[39] One town elder deemed the new structure, dedicated in 1891, "an education to future generations" in that it would teach "how much a free people thought of their government and that men found something beyond themselves worth dying for."[40] Jealous of the valuable amenities the memorial hall offered, some citizens of neighboring Thompsonville feared Windsor Locks was now the more attractive community. Noting that there was always "some rivalry between the towns as to public improvements," one commentator suggested that Thompsonville compete with its adversary to erect a similar building that would serve "partly for the Grand Army and largely furnish accommodations for public institutions."[41] Although the town never erected such a structure, interest in doing so illustrates how small communities sought to improve livability with these useful GAR-backed structures.

GAR members in larger towns advocated commemorative tributes too but had the resources to propose bigger and costlier structures. These veterans proved particularly adept at leveraging their influence to coordinate carefully planned municipal-building endeavors designed to enhance civic life.[42] In Rockford, Illinois, for instance, members of the Garret L. Nevius Post placed a proposition on the 1900 ballot advocating the construction of a testament to the county's Union veterans. After voters overwhelmingly backed the measure, post commander Thomas G. Lawler presented a petition before the Winnebago County Board of Supervisors. Signed by some two hundred area veterans, the petition proposed that the board "make their appropriation for a Memorial Hall, believing that such a building, where the records and relics of the different wars could be preserved, would be more useful than a monument."[43] The county's investigative committee approved the memorial hall scheme the following year, insisting "that if a hall was built it be made large enough to be used for county purposes as well as for ornament and for keeping of records."[44] Rockford's Soldiers and Sailors Memorial Hall—which included a GAR post room, a large library, and an auditorium—was dedicated in 1903 (with President Theodore Roosevelt in attendance) at a cost of nearly $60,000. Insistent that the memorial hall remain widely accessible, Nevius Post directed the hall's custodian to observe liberal operating hours for the public's benefit (8:00 a.m. to 6:00 p.m. on weekdays).[45]

In large cities, efforts to construct memorial halls often corresponded with broader community efforts to improve, beautify, and reform urban spaces. Participating in this trend, veterans negotiated with powerful state legislatures, city councils, planning boards, estimators, and architects to raise structures that not only consecrated the Union dead and accommodated GAR veterans but also promoted urban artistry and utility. The establishment of Toledo, Ohio's, Soldiers Memorial Building fit these criteria. In 1879, fifteen individuals (five GAR veterans, five women's auxiliary members, and five "citizens in civil life") created the Toledo Soldiers Memorial Association to raise money "to erect a memorial building in the City of Toledo, in which the records of our soldiers and relics of the war may be suitably kept, and to make the same building answer a practical purpose."[46] To meet that end, the memorial association envisioned that the building would include ample space for a city armory, national guard drill hall, banquet hall, and quarters for an artillery battery. Through the efforts of the memorial association and funds authorized by the state legislature, the building was completed in 1886. At the dedication services, GAR veteran J. Kent Hamilton proclaimed, "At last we have a Soldiers' Monument worthy of the name. Not of useless marble or bronze, but a structure which commemorates the valor, the sacrifices, the triumphs, and glories, of the soldiers of the Republic, and is also a temple where is to be taught all civic virtues."[47]

In neighboring Michigan, GAR officials appointed a committee in 1891 to research the feasibility of a memorial hall at Detroit that would serve area posts as a meeting place and records repository. Mindful of a time when the GAR would cease to exist, the building would "then be devoted to the preservation of the records, museum and library of the Grand Army of the State of Michigan for ever, and it shall thereafter be an armory and War Museum."[48] The five veterans on the committee received great latitude to solicit and handle funds, choose and purchase a site, canvass architectural designs, and select cost-effective construction proposals. The GAR took to the newspapers to gain public support for the project, which would "stand for all time, as an educator . . . [so] the young may gather inspiration from the object lesson it would teach."[49] Despite difficult negotiations with tight-fisted city officials, the project at last received the approval of the city council and board of estimates in 1898, which issued $38,000 in bonds (complemented by a $6,000 donation from the state GAR department). Completed in 1900, Detroit's Grand Army of the Republic Building was, according to one comrade, "a monument . . . of more practical value to present and to coming generations than any stately shaft or simple pile of stone."[50]

Meanwhile in turn-of-the-century Pittsburgh, the Allegheny County Grand Army Association—a select committee of prominent GAR veterans representing the region's roughly three dozen posts—began promoting a plan for an enormous memorial hall where local posts' scattered records, battle flags, and relics could "be gathered together and placed in a building . . . [where] they would be an incentive to patriots and to generations yet unborn."[51] Besides serving as a GAR repository, veterans imagined a vibrant civic space complete with a library, spacious meeting rooms, and a five-thousand-seat auditorium. The veterans' crusade for what would become Soldiers and Sailors Memorial Hall occurred within Pittsburgh's larger urban renewal movement designed to bring moral uplift, aesthetic grandeur, and public amenities to the teeming industrial city. These efforts centered on Oakland, a district situated some three miles east of the downtown commercial area, where city leaders (perhaps most conspicuously, the steel magnate Andrew Carnegie) fashioned a true civic center to showcase Pittsburgh's culture and provide citizens with opportunities for entertainment, education, and self-improvement. Here, a cluster of colleges, museums, galleries, theaters, and places of worship cropped up thanks to a considerable investment in coordinated planning and construction.

It was amid Oakland's cultural profusion that Allegheny County's GAR veterans and their allies determined to flaunt their memorial hall. Starting in 1902, they undertook an eight-year campaign of concerted advocacy and negotiation to bring about their vision. Beginning with a massive petition drive, veterans persuaded the county's commissioners and courts to support the endeavor. By 1905, the state legislature—under steady GAR pressure—authorized the project, permitting Pittsburgh's veterans to select ten of their own to form an oversight committee to work alongside the commissioners. Veterans next mobilized to garner the support of the county's voters, whose approval was needed to fund the endeavor. GAR flyers and other literature circulated through the city in the weeks ahead of the fall vote, and on election day post commanders ordered their men to stake out the polling places to encourage a favorable referendum. With the ballots tallied, 47,902 voters supported the project and just 5,487 came out against—a stunning 90 percent approval rate. "It is especially gratifying," GAR members concluded, "that this Memorial has not been accorded grudgingly, but by an overwhelming favorable vote by our fellow Citizens."[52] With taxpayer funding secured, Pittsburgh veterans assisted the county commissioners in the arduous consultations with the city planners, county officials, architects, and construction teams needed to make the memorial hall a reality. After more than two years of construction and a final price tag exceeding $1.7 million, Allegheny County's imposing testament to its Civil War defenders was complete.

From the start, Pittsburgh's veterans intended Soldiers and Sailors Memorial Hall to serve the public at large. For the three-day dedication in October 1910, they cajoled area schools and businesses to close in order to permit as many people to join in the proceedings as possible. Governor Edward S. Stuart attended and lauded the versatility of the memorial hall, noting that it had "been constructed with a view to practicability" all the while standing "as a monument to the valorous deeds of the brave men who went to the front when they heard the call of duty."[53] Meanwhile, the GAR insisted that the dedication be an integrated celebration, with careful references made to the war's emancipatory outcome.[54] One white GAR veteran urged his African American compatriots to attend, stating "that no distinction could be made between Comrades of the Grand Army, and inasmuch as the Memorial building was erected by the people of this county, colored citizens have the same rights as others."[55] Within weeks, many of the county's GAR posts (including Pittsburgh's all-black Robert G. Shaw Post No. 206) shuttered their meeting halls and moved their monthly events to the specially designated post rooms set aside for GAR members rent free.[56] GAR auxiliaries like the WRC and Sons of Veterans of the Civil War also frequented the facilities.

Soldiers and Sailors Memorial Hall demonstrated its civic utility to civilians too, as droves of nonveterans made use of the venue for years afterward. To benefit the public, the veteran-led Board of Managers approved ample visitation hours—"week days from 9:00 A.M. to 5:00 P.M. and on Sundays and holidays from 1:00 P.M. to 5:00 P.M."[57] Fraternal groups, ladies' societies, commercial and civic clubs, and professional organizations all utilized the capacious facilities in the months following the dedication. Meanwhile, an examination of the memorial hall's guest register reveals that the hall enjoyed seasonal visitation cycles from a wide variety of groups. During the spring, school field trips brought hundreds of students in to see the magnificent structure with its relics to a bygone war. Summer attracted high volumes of out-of-state travelers vacationing in Pittsburgh, as well as troops of the newly established Boy Scouts. Autumn months at the hall most frequently attracted the regimental reunions of Pittsburgh-area veterans. And in winter, a brief rush of pre-Christmas holiday field trips in early December gave way to well-attended January and February programs for McKinley's, Lincoln's, and Washington's birthdays complete with lectures, songs, and hymns. One New York veteran doubtless captured the sentiment of many of the hall's visitors as he scrawled his concise praise in the guest book: "This is the best Memorial to the GAR I have seen."[58]

AS THE TWENTIETH CENTURY progressed and more and more Grand Army veterans answered "the last roll call," their once-powerful organization faced ultimate extinction. But many of the memorial halls they had a hand in creating survived and even thrived. To be sure, some strayed from the commemorative intent for which they had been conceived. Valparaiso's memorial hall, for instance, passed into the hands of a community theater guild in the 1950s and currently hosts theatrical performances and other entertainments. Detroit's Grand Army of the Republic Building fell into extreme disrepair for much of the last century but has become a cornerstone of the city's downtown renewal, with trendy restaurants now populating its ground floor. Others remain closer to their foundational roots. Pittsburgh's Soldiers and Sailors Memorial Hall, while still protective of its GAR heritage, now functions as a memorial and museum to all military veterans. The Rockville Memorial Building in Connecticut now hosts its own museum and research center with Burpee Post's records and relics at the heart of its collection. Beyond the Civil War sesquicentennial, these useful structures honor the Union's defenders with their very vitality, quite apart from the solemn granite shafts or stone sentinels standing forever on guard atop their fixed pedestals. Living on with civic purpose long after the passing of the Civil War generation, these memorial halls uphold the belief that many GAR veterans shared—that war commemoration need not be a somber venture.

NOTES

1. "Rockville Memorial Hall," *Springfield Republican,* November 18, 1888, 6.

2. On Burpee Post, see Harry Conklin Smith, ed., *A Century of Vernon, Connecticut, 1808–1908* (Rockville, CT: T. F. Rady, 1911), 19–20.

3. Burpee Post resolutions, September 24, 1890, box 7, folder 9, Thomas F. Burpee Post No. 71 Collection, New England Civil War Museum and Research Center, Rockville, CT. Special thanks to museum director Matthew Reardon for sharing his knowledge and research on the construction of the Rockville Memorial Building.

4. Kirk Savage addressed the proliferation of the common-soldier monument in the postwar United States. These commemorative tributes typically featured an infantryman standing at parade rest atop a pedestal listing the names of the community's defenders and their wartime achievements. These monuments, spurred by a niche industry that churned out the marble or granite soldier figures en masse, spread across public spaces in both the North and the South. Little attention, however, has been paid to the commemorative trend or function of the memorial hall. See Savage, *Standing Soldiers, Kneeling Slaves: Race, War, and Monument in Nineteenth-Century America* (Princeton, NJ: Princeton University Press, 1997), especially chapter 6.

5. For instance, Lynn Dumenil discusses the Masonic temple's status as a privileged space that "set a man apart from the outside world." Mary Ann Clawson argues that fraternalism used exclusion to derive its power and the fraternal lodge as the social space by which men cultivated that power through bonds of solidarity. Mark C. Carnes asserts that the secretiveness of the lodge protected it from "threatening" women and other forces that sought to weaken male bonds. See Dumenil, *Free-*

masonry and American Culture, 1880–1930 (Princeton, NJ: Princeton University Press, 1984), 18–19; Clawson, *Constructing Brotherhood: Class, Gender, and Fraternalism* (Princeton, NJ: Princeton University Press, 1989), 178–80; and Carnes, *Secret Ritual and Manhood in Victorian America* (New Haven, CT: Yale University Press, 1989), 81–89. See also Nicholas L. Syrett, *The Company He Keeps: A History of White College Fraternities* (Chapel Hill: University of North Carolina Press, 2009).

6. Recent studies that have emphasized the separateness of Civil War veterans from nonveterans, and the challenges returning soldiers faced in postwar society underscore this view. See, for example, Eric T. Dean, *Shook over Hell: Post-Traumatic Stress, Vietnam, and the Civil War* (Cambridge, MA: Harvard University Press, 1997); James Marten, *Sing Not War: The Lives of Union and Confederate Veterans in Gilded Age America* (Chapel Hill: University of North Carolina Press, 2011); and Brian Matthew Jordan, *Marching Home: Union Veterans and Their Unending Civil War* (New York: Liveright, 2014).

7. *Address of Department Commander Samuel S. Burdett, at the 16th Annual Encampment of the Department of the Potomac, G.A.R., Washington, D.C., Jan. 30, 1884* (Washington, D.C.: n.p., 1884), 14.

8. Stuart McConnell, for instance, briefly addresses memorial halls as places that "serve[d] as meeting rooms during the lives of the members and as shrines after their deaths." Moreover, the study suggests that GAR commemorative structures, including memorial halls, frequently "fell victim to meager funding, disinterest, or more-pressing civic priorities." This conclusion is reached after assessing the loss of one Wisconsin post's investment in a failed memorial hall project and another Massachusetts post's inability to convince residents to use funds to build a memorial hall. These limited examples must not overshadow the myriad GAR successes in a wide range of other locations across the country. For quotes, see McConnell, *Glorious Contentment: The Grand Army of the Republic, 1865–1900* (Chapel Hill: University of North Carolina Press, 1992), 89–90, 201.

9. Lynn Dumenil notes that during the late nineteenth century, Freemasons constructed their own temples for lodge meetings with greater frequency. These structures, like GAR memorial halls, were often monumental in size and effect, were built to imply the permanency and stability of the local lodge, and stood in architectural juxtaposition to their community's courthouses, town halls, and other public buildings. Unlike the record of many GAR memorial halls, however, Dumenil notes that Masonic temples were built to be imposing and inaccessible to nonmembers. See Dumenil, *Freemasonry*, 18–19.

10. On GAR post rooms, see McConnell, *Glorious Contentment*, especially chapter 4.

11. "A Memorial Building," *New Haven Evening Register*, April 14, 1884, 4.

12. *Democrat and Chronicle*, January 1, 1886, 4.

13. *Huntington Democrat*, June 20, 1895, 2.

14. "The Iowa Soldier's Monument," *Grand Army Advocate*, May 2, 1889.

15. *Journal of the House of Representatives of the Twenty-Fourth General Assembly of the State of Iowa, Which Convened at the Capitol in Des Moines, Iowa, January 11, 1892* (Des Moines: G. H. Ragsdale, 1892), 197.

16. See, for instance, the resolutions of Dubuque's Hyde Clark Post, which favored directing the war tax refund toward "the building of cottages at the soldiers' home at Marshalltown to which the disabled veterans, with their wives, and widows of veterans shall be admitted and provided for at the expense of the state." Quoted in "Want Cottages for the Veterans," *Postville Graphic*, January 14, 1892, 2.

17. On the dedication of Iowa's Soldiers' and Sailors' Monument, see Cora Chaplin Weed, *Hand Book for Iowa Soldiers' and Sailors' Monument* (n.p., 1897).

18. "Galesburg Objects to Grand Army Memorial Hall in Kalamazoo," *Grand Rapids Press*, January 11, 1904, 5.

19. On the dedication of Kalamazoo's memorial building, see "Honor Bestowed on War Veterans," *Kalamazoo Gazette*, April 10, 1908, 5.

20. For quotes, see "Portage," *Livingston Republican*, March 11, 1880, 3, and "Another View of the Soldier's Monument or Memorial Hall in Portage," *Nunda News*, April 10, 1880, 3; accessed in compiled documents folder entitled Livingston County Military, Monuments, Memorials, and Organizations, vol. 2, Office of the Livingston County Historian, Mt. Morris, NY. Despite the criticisms, the memorial hall at Portage, New York, was nonetheless erected. The history of its construction is recounted later in this essay.

21. I. L. Stuart, ed., *History of Franklin County, Iowa: A Record of Settlement, Organization, Progress and Achievement* (Chicago: S. J. Clarke, 1914), 1:167–68.

22. "In Memory of Heroes," *Chicago Tribune*, November 27, 1893, 3; *History of Porter County, Indiana: A Narrative Account of Its Historical Progress, Its People and Its Principal Interests* (Chicago: Lewis, 1912), 1:124–25. Despite hosting many GAR-related events, Chaplain Brown Post could not overcome the indebtedness derived from the expensive structure, and the building was turned over to the county in 1901. Post members continued to enjoy use of their second-story hall for the remainder of the post's life, however, and the building continued to host concerts, minstrel shows, and other entertainments; attracted speakers including William Jennings Bryan and Theodore Roosevelt, and by the 1920s,, the facility showed motion pictures.

23. "The Soldier's Fund in Portage," *Nunda News*, March 27, 1880, 3; accessed in compiled documents folder entitled Livingston County Military; Monuments, Memorials, and Organizations, vol. 2, Office of the Livingston County Historian, Mt. Morris, NY.

24. *Nunda News*, March 13, 1880, 3, in ibid.

25. For further history of the construction of Portage's memorial hall, see James H. Smith, *History of Livingston County, New York with Illustrations and Biographical Sketches of Some of Its Prominent Men and Pioneers, 1687–1881* (Syracuse: D. Mason, 1881), 272–73.

26. *Nunda News*, April 20, 1888, 3, May 5, 1888, 3; accessed in compiled documents folder entitled Livingston County Military; Monuments, Memorials, and Organizations, vol. 2, Office of the Livingston County Historian, Mt. Morris, NY.

27. "Soldiers' Monument Fund," *Nunda News*, February 4, 1888, 2, in ibid. The newspaper shamed stingier citizens by printing the names of those who *had* contributed to the fund.

28. On the Carter Memorial Hall and the military career of John J. Carter, see H. Wells Hand, ed., *Centennial History of the Town of Nunda, 1808–1908* (Rochester, NY: Rochester Herald Press, 1908), 606–10.

29. "Memorial Hall Corporation," *Nunda News*, July 4, 1908.

30. See *Dalton Enterprise*, March 15, October 18, and November 15, 1895, and April 10, 1896.

31. "Tonight Is the Big Night," *Nunda News*, December 6, 1929, 1; "Briefs from Rochester Neighbors," *Rochester Times-Union*, July 5, 1938, 3.

32. "Not Ready to Give Up Identity," *Genesee County Express*, May 9, 2002; accessed in compiled

documents folder entitled Livingston County Military; Monuments, Memorials, and Organizations, vol. 2, Office of the Livingston County Historian, Mt. Morris, NY.

33. Miles Orvell, *The Death and Life of Main Street: Small Towns in American Memory, Space, and Community* (Chapel Hill: University of North Carolina Press, 2012), especially chapter 3.

34. Kirin J. Makker analyzed the history of these village improvement associations, their links to small-town municipal works projects, and the development of social capital among its otherwise provincial members. See Makker, "Village Improvement and the Development of Small Town America, 1853–1893," *Journal of Planning History* 13 (February 2014): 68–87. See also Makker, "Mary G. Hopkins and the Origins of Village Improvement in Antebellum Stockbridge, Massachusetts," *Landscape Journal* 34, no. 1 (2015): 1–14.

35. "New Memorial Hall Nearing Completion," *Kalamazoo Gazette,* December 6, 1912, 10.

36. "The Home of the Brave," *True Northerner,* January 17, 1913, 1.

37. "Paw Paw G.A.R. Men Provide Rest Room in Memorial Hall," *Kalamazoo Gazette,* February 15, 1913, 2.

38. *True Northerner,* February 19, February 26, March 5, and August 6, 1915.

39. For the quote, see "The Grand Army Memorial Hall," *Springfield Republican,* February 14, 1890, 3. On the construction of Windsor Locks' memorial hall, see Henry R. Stiles, *The History and Genealogies of Ancient Windsor, Connecticut; Including East Windsor, South Windsor, Bloomfield, Windsor Locks, and Ellington, 1635–1891* (Hartford, CT: Case, Lockwood, and Brainard, 1891), 1:528–31.

40. "Dedication at Windsor Locks," *Springfield Republican,* June 11, 1891, 4.

41. For quote, see "Thompsonville Needs a Hall," *Springfield Republican,* June 14, 1891, 2.

42. For more on urban building projects in modest-sized cities, see Maureen Ogle, "Beyond the Great City: Finding and Defining the Small City in Nineteenth Century America," in *American Cities and Towns: Historical Perspectives,* ed. Joseph F. Rishel (Pittsburgh: Duquesne University Press, 1992), 48–66.

43. Quote from digitized page of the 1903 minutes of the Winnebago County Board, in possession of curator of Rockford's Veterans Memorial Hall. See also "Memorial Hall History," *Rockford Republic,* June 3, 1903, 2.

44. "Memorial Hall History," *Rockford Republic,* June 3, 1903, 2.

45. "Post Meets in New Home," *Rockford Daily Register-Gazette,* June 9, 1903, 8.

46. John R. Osborn, *An Historical Sketch of the Rise and Progress of the Toledo Soldiers Memorial Association* (Toledo, OH: Barkdull, 1883), 8, in box 1, folder 19, Toledo Soldiers Memorial Association collection, Toledo-Lucas County Public Library, Toledo, OH.

47. *Soldiers' Memorial Building, Toledo, Ohio, in Honor and in Memory of Those Who Fought and Those Who Fell in Defense of Our Country during the War of the Rebellion* (Toledo, OH: B. F. Wade, 1886), 46.

48. Report of Committee on Ex-Senator Palmer's Proposition, June 1892, William Herbert Withington Papers, microfilm reel 1, Bentley Historical Library, University of Michigan, Ann Arbor, MI.

49. "Realty and Building," *Detroit Free Press,* July 5, 1896, 19.

50. "History of Memorial Hall," *Detroit Free Press,* December 12, 1900, 8.

51. Allegheny County Grand Army Association minute book entry, July 26, 1902, box 3, Allegh-

eny County Grand Army Association Records, Soldiers and Sailors Memorial Hall and Museum, Pittsburgh, PA.

52. Report of the Allegheny County Grand Army Association Monument and Memorial Committee, November 25, 1905, pasted in minute book, box 3, Allegheny County Grand Army Association Records, Soldiers and Sailors Memorial Hall, Pittsburgh, PA.

53. "Veterans of the Civil War March to Memorial Erected in Their Honor," *Pittsburgh Press,* October 11, 1910, 1.

54. On white and black GAR veterans' pride in fighting for emancipation, see Barbara A. Gannon, *The Won Cause: Black and White Comradeship in the Grand Army of the Republic* (Chapel Hill: University of North Carolina Press, 2011), especially chapter 11.

55. Report of H. H. Bengough, August 24, 1910, record and minute book of the Soldiers' Memorial Hall Committee, Soldiers and Sailors Memorial Hall, Pittsburgh, PA. Special thanks to curator Michael Kraus and the staff of Soldiers and Sailors Memorial Hall and Museum, who made available rare and fragile manuscript materials.

56. For coverage of Shaw Post's first use of Soldiers and Sailors Memorial Hall to hold its meetings, see "G.A.R. to Meet," *Pittsburgh Press,* November 6, 1910, 27.

57. Rules of Government for Hall, October 1910, record and minute book of the Soldiers' Memorial Hall Committee, Soldiers and Sailors Memorial Hall and Museum, Pittsburgh, PA.

58. Guest register entry of John T. Roberts, October 19, 1915, Soldiers and Sailors Memorial Hall visitor's register (February 1915–May 1917), Soldiers and Sailors Memorial Hall and Museum, Pittsburgh, PA.

Veterans at the Footlights

*Unionism and White Supremacy in the Theater
of the Grand Army of the Republic*

TYLER SPERRAZZA

EN RANKS OF eight men in blue uniforms come into view, strutting as if
on parade. The troops approach an appointed place and halt, lifting their
rifled muskets as their commanding officer calls for them to "make ready."
Opposite their formation, a line of men in butternut and gray are poised to
meet them. A Union commander gives the order to fire, the guns roar, and the
men in gray fall. The blue-coated troops then rush forward, breaking formations as they crash into the Confederate line; the ranks comingle, and smoke
rises above the din of small arms fire and the cries of dying men. When the
engagement is over, only men in blue remain standing. A curtain falls, and the
crowd whoops and cheers. The second act of *The Volunteer at Sedgwick Post
No. 1* in Norwich, Connecticut, has concluded. The play, written in 1871 by an
anonymous group of Connecticut veterans, was just one of the hundreds of
plays written by or for the benefit of the Grand Army of the Republic in the
years following the US Civil War.

In an 1868 speech, John Alexander Logan, commander in chief of the
Grand Army of the Republic (GAR), called on his comrades to "preserve and
strengthen" the fraternal feelings of the "late rebellion."[1] The members of the
GAR—the largest fraternal organization of Union veterans, composed of over
two thousand posts across thirty states—heeded Logan's call to memorialize
the Civil War in a variety of ways, but one of their most popular means of
commemoration was through theatrical representations. Union veterans wrote
and produced hundreds of plays, performance pieces, and "grand exhibitions"
dedicated to the GAR, often centering on the real events of the war with titles

like "Shiloh," "Gettysburg," and "Appomattox." Union veterans performed these plays in GAR halls throughout the North during the 1880s, 1890s, and into the twentieth century. Not surprisingly, all of these plays, while championing the Union cause, took a very harsh stance toward the Confederacy—depicting southern villains as murderers, rapists, and abhorrent, lust-filled slaveowners. The plays often gave important roles to African American characters and highlighted their contributions to Union victory. Yet while African Americans received prominent roles, they were depicted as simple-minded and childlike, always speaking in dialect and clearly unprepared for freedom after slavery. This essay argues that these plays help illuminate both the ideologies and day-to-day realities of the postwar North in two distinct ways: first, they provide compelling evidence that northern veterans were interested in perpetuating anti-southern rhetoric well into the twentieth century, countering the narrative of a harmonious reunion between North and South occurring as early as 1880. Second, these plays underscore strong racial prejudices entrenched in northern society even after emancipation. Through its theatrical presentations, the GAR helped reaffirm stereotypes about African Americans while nodding to the segregated audiences and stages where the plays were performed.

The first argument expands on work that casts the first fifty years of Civil War memory as a contest between "reconciliationists," who made a tragic postwar alliance with white supremacists, and "emancipationists," who preserved the memory of the war as an abolition crusade and continued to demand social, civil, and political rights for African Americans.[2] David W. Blight's *Race and Reunion: The Civil War in American Memory* offers compelling evidence that despite the best efforts of some Republican politicians in the North (a large number of whom were veterans), sectional reconciliation took hold of the nation by 1877, coinciding with the end of the federal military occupation of the southern states.[3] Blight argues that the popular culture of Reconstruction was a major factor in creating and perpetuating the ideology of reunion. The anti-southern "bloody shirt" rhetoric in GAR plays amends Blight's argument; that while the dominant narrative among veterans was one of reunion, there was still a significant population, both white and black, unwilling to forgive the South and reconcile. Thus, Blight's claims that the "reconciliationist vision . . . stood triumphant" by 1877 overlooks the cultural work done by Union veterans to combat such a vision for at least another three decades. Numerous GAR posts performed these plays well into the early twentieth century. In fact, most of these plays were written after 1880. The anti-southern rhetoric of these plays complicates a clean narrative from military occupation's end in 1877 to veterans clasping hands across the bloody chasm.

Caroline Janney's work responds to Blight's claims and aligns more closely with the evidence found in these veteran-penned plays. Janney asserts that reconciliation did not occur as easily as Blight suggests. Union veterans in particular were hesitant to "bind the wounds" of the late war due to the trials suffered on the battlefield and in Confederate prison camps. While former Union soldiers were by no means a monolithic group during Reconstruction, the popularity of the plays written by GAR men point to a significant number of veterans who enjoyed viewing evil portrayals of Confederates well into the twentieth century.[4]

The second argument complicates recent arguments made by historians of the GAR, who take the organization to be proof of racial harmony in the North—at least among veterans. Barbara A. Gannon argues in her book *The Won Cause: Black and White Comradeship in the Grand Army of the Republic* that "black and white veterans were able to create and sustain an interracial organization in a society rigidly divided on the color line because the northerners who fought and lived remembered African Americans' service in a war against slavery."[5] Stuart McConnell counters this argument in *Glorious Contentment: The Grand Army of the Republic, 1865–1900,* stating that "the Grand Army conception of the war was pivotal: because members viewed the conflict primarily as a battle to preserve an existing Union rather than as a crusade to free slaves or establish social equality, they felt no compulsion to change their views of blacks once the war ended."[6] This essay supports Gannon's claim that some veterans of the GAR understood the war as fought to free the slaves and thus created bonds with black veterans who shared a common cause. Nevertheless, GAR plays represent a much more segregated racial hierarchy within the GAR itself. Despite the presence of some integrated posts, white GAR members did not view black veterans or free blacks in the North as social equals and did not attempt to establish social equality once the war had ended.[7] In fact, as the final third of this essay reveals, the GAR became embroiled in a scandal when it refused to allow black patrons to attend a theatrical performance sponsored by both white and black GAR posts. This followed similar patterns typical of theater in northern cities during the postwar period.

Northern theater boomed in the postwar years. The waves of immigration that swelled northern cities demanded more and more popular entertainments to keep the burgeoning urban working classes happy, drunk, and somewhat out of trouble—though theaters had a less than stellar reputation of aiding sobriety and civility. In the early part of the century, theater was predominantly the realm of working-class actors who scrounged and scraped to make their way performing on circuits throughout the major East Coast cities (only sometimes venturing to the Midwest). However, wartime expansion of the railroads and western development forged the creation of the theatrical and vaudeville circuits that became mainstays of early twentieth-century popular entertainment. Space for African American performers in these major entertainment ventures was limited, however, and most African American theater artists of this time were forced to stomp the boards in their local communities in churches, living rooms, and schoolhouses in order to eke out a living. Amateur playwrights, actors, and producers, white and black, needed to find outlets for their work; white playwrights found a much easier road to publishing their work, and some even opened their own publishing houses at war's end.[8]

One of these veteran playwrights, A. D. Ames, chose to return to his native Ohio following the war, after serving in the 19th New York Cavalry from 1863 to 1865. Ames and his compatriots were not mustered out of the army until June 30, 1865, and they participated in the Grand Review of the Armies in May 1865. This event was so important in the formation of veteran memory that Stuart McConnell began his history of the Grand Army of the Republic with a retelling of its ritual and pageantry. The Grand Review "offered a startling and unprecedented vision of national unity." It was the last time veterans would be immersed in the rigidity and discipline of the army. After the Grand Review, there would be no more camp meetings, no more daily drill, and no more camaraderie around the campfire. The men of the northern army sought to reconcile their time served in the war with their lives back home. Veterans' organizations like the GAR, the Sons of Union Veterans, and the aptly named Union Veterans Union, gave them the means for that reconciliation. A. D. Ames did so by opening a publishing house in Clyde, Ohio, and spent the years between 1870 and 1917 printing over four hundred plays and other materials written by veterans, radical Republican sympathizers, and GAR members. A. D. Ames Publishing Company was just one cog in the great Republican propaganda machine, and one that served an important cultural purpose by creating constant, vivid reminders of what the North sacrificed in order to put down the southern rebellion.[9]

Each GAR play compelled audience members to make a moral judgment on the war. The playwrights championed the virtues of the northern soldiers and the Union war effort, while depicting every southern character as evil, immoral, and godless. Republican propaganda during Reconstruction spread throughout the North and the South, and these plays became a crucial part of the propaganda mission.[10] Northern newspapers called for a successful Reconstruction in order to strengthen the national economy and viewed the freed slaves as a potential boon of labor and resources. Liberal Republicans embraced reconciliation, but Radical Republicans saw themselves as protecting the legacy of the war. They used any means necessary to protect the significant gains made in the Thirteenth, Fourteenth, and Fifteenth Amendments. Democrats attacked Radicals as too interested in the creation of a radical oligarchy and too eager to subvert the constitution by insisting upon the military occupation of the South. Among others, Andrew Johnson embraced these sentiments, and during the late 1860s and 1870s, Republicans boosted their propaganda efforts in order to meet these challenges. Republicans championed veteran organizations like the GAR and used materials like the veteran plays to bring their message to a wider audience in some of the rural areas of the North. While it is impossible to track the cultural influence of these productions, they are nonetheless important portals into the ways in which veterans attempted to construct a memory for a northern audience.[11]

The plays always centered on the events of the Civil War, though the actual names, dates, and battlefields referenced in the dialogue were often slightly anachronistic and inconsistent. The plots were structured like melodramas of the early nineteenth century but with added elements of tableau, battle reenactment, and musical interludes. These melodramas mimicked the preferred theatrical form during the late nineteenth century while incorporating elements of Greek tragedy and Shakespearean comedy. The plays often centered on one of three plot lines: the villain tricks the hero's fiancée into marriage by convincing her that the hero has died, culminating in a final showdown between the villain and the hero; the hero's father is killed by the villain and needs to be avenged before the final curtain; or a hero is forced to go against his family's wishes in order to protect his fiancée and his righteous cause, often sacrificing himself in the end.[12] The Civil War was the perfect backdrop for these melodramatic portrayals because the plots often rested on deception and espionage, families torn apart by the war, and a villain embodied by a slave-beating, wife-raping, father-killing Confederate soldier.

Convoluted plots of disguise and deception moved the story along, but the sections of the plays mentioned most often by reviewers were the tableaus and reenactments. These tableaus and interludes were common theatrical techniques that complemented the actions of the plot and allowed for symbolic representations of war memory. In the 1879 play *The Spy of Atlanta*, written by A. D. Ames, a stage direction depicts a "Tableau of Secession." The direction reads: "In the center is placed the Goddess of Liberty with sword and shield. . . . The seceding states are upon the left, South Carolina nearest the Goddess . . . at a signal South Carolina raises a dagger to strike the Goddess."[13] The deliberate theatrical choices made by Ames, particularly in placing the seceding states on the left-hand side and the northern states on the right while depicting South Carolina as attempting to stab the Goddess of Liberty, offer a blatant anti-southern message. The placement of the North on the right also seems to suggest the North at "the right hand" of Liberty, clearly the more powerful and morally righteous of the two positions. Some playwrights chose to choreograph tableaus in a specific way, while others left the staging up to the actors. These tableaus served as effective transitions between the scenes of the plays and depicted symbolic representations of critical events in the war.[14]

Like tableau, the use of battle reenactments was crucial to the plots of the veteran memory plays. The casts of these performances sometimes numbered in the hundreds due to the need for reenactors and the desire of many GAR members and their families to take part in the proceedings. The reenactments routinely lasted for over thirty minutes and involved live animals, real uniforms, and in some cases—inexplicably—live ammunition. A journalist from Baraboo, Wisconsin, reported that a woman was accidentally shot and killed during one of the reenactment scenes in a theatrical presentation of the GAR melodrama *Winchester* in 1893.[15] These battle scenes attempted to represent the harsh reality of the war and combat to civilian audiences and gave the members of the GAR a chance to drill again. The plays offered multiple opportunities for the GAR member actors to perform their drills and battle formations for their audiences. They often involved an early scene depicting Union troops mustering and being put through drill, taking the time for comic relief to make fun of Irish or black enlistees and their lack of military knowledge, while including skirmishes and a massive final battle in the play's penultimate act.[16]

According to eyewitness reports, these plays were incredibly effective and received rave reviews from audiences. An 1870 review of Samuel Muscroft's *The Drummer Boy* performed at Bosworth Post No. 2 in Portland, Maine, stated, "It is sufficient to say that the house was crowed in every part. The success of this drama has been most remarkable; for we believe there is no record of any similar performance ever taking place in this city where such immense audiences have gathered to witness it for four nights running."[17] The article continued with a rave review of the "gentlemen of the G.A.R." responsible for handling the business arrangements, and the men and women of the post who served as actors and ultimately raised over $700 in profits.

An article celebrating veteran and GAR member J. N. Culver's production of *Loyal Mountaineers* in the *St. Albans Daily Messenger* in April 1874 similarly gushed: "For the benefit of charity in the G.A.R. . . . the war drama Loyal Mountaineers has been so much improved that those who saw it here before will hardly recognize the play and we predict that it will afford more delight than any of its predecessors."[18] An 1896 review of Samuel Muscroft's *The Drummer Boy: or Battlefield of Shiloh,* performed in Reading, Pennsylvania, stated, "The members taking part acquitted themselves very creditable, and the performance of Thursday evening in the town hall was by far the best of the week [they] kept the audience in an almost continuous roar of laughter. . . . A large audience is expected to be present to-night and tomorrow evening."[19] *The Drummer Boy* was one of many popular entertainments centered on the life of Johnny Clem, the "Drummer Boy of Shiloh." In the play, the title character—named Johnny Howard—is swept up in the wave of patriotism and enlists in the Union army as a drummer boy. He continues to serve admirably until he is captured and brought to Andersonville. The ending of the play, however, is Muscroft's own creation. He concludes the story with a dramatic scene of Johnny the drummer boy being shot down in the infamous prison camp while trying to scrounge for food in order to feed his fellow prisoners.[20] This tale was far removed from the real story of John Clem, but for the audiences in the North, this was the type of entertainment they clamored to see: Union men anxious to enlist, who served bravely, and who were almost always heroically sacrificed for the good of their fellow soldiers.

The reviews highlight one of the major benefits of these plays: their ability to adapt to any performance venue. They would often be performed in spaces that occupied important positions in the public sphere, such as churches, town halls, and local schoolhouses. A review of *The Spy of Atlanta*'s 1885 performance in Great Barrington, Massachusetts, highlighted the positive experience of seeing the play performed in the town with members of the local community participating:

> The troupe made a fine appearance as they came into the place, marching down from the station headed by the Forest band, which did its 'level best,' rendering some of the finest music we have heard on our streets for some time, and when we saw the familiar faces of Dr. Wilcox, Capt. Shannon and Horton, with others as well known, we went to the hall expecting to be pleased, and were not disappointed.[21]

The GAR melodramas consisted of large casts of characters, huge battle scenes, and many different locations, often necessitating community involvement in order to be performed. Thus these plays became central to municipal Decoration Day celebrations throughout the North, creating a space for Civil War memory to enter the lives of white northerners. These plays satisfied a strong northern demand for plays about the recent war that celebrated Union soldiers and the survival of the Union, while casting the Confederates as the ultimate villains. Most of these plays did not, however, garner praise for their literary elements. The same critic from Great Barrington who celebrated *The Spy of Atlanta*'s community involvement noted, "The play may not possess as much literary merit as many others"; however, he qualified that statement by describing its "thrilling scenes and well-acted parts."[22] The reviews of the performances raved about the acting and the cameo appearances by community leaders, but more importantly, they reflected the audience's enthusiastic support of the GAR and its anti-southern rhetoric.[23] An 1883 review of a performance of *The Drummer Boy* in Akron, Ohio, details the lengths to which Samuel Muscroft and playwrights like him sought to involve Civil War veterans and other prominent community members in their performances. The review states, "Capt. H. H. Brown, of the Akron City Guard concluded arrangements with Mr. Muscroft for a production of 'The Drummer Boy' to be played in this city."[24] Muscroft, like many theatrical producers of the veteran plays traveled into cities with GAR posts and other fraternal organizations and enlisted their help in disseminating his plays to the public. They also reveal that the GAR's main goal was an interpretation of the war as fought to preserve the Union, not emancipate enslaved people. This becomes clearer when examining depictions of African American characters in these plays.

Northern veteran playwrights clearly waved the "bloody shirt" well into the twentieth century, but their depictions of African Americans as simple-minded, dialect-speaking comic relief reveal the darker side of these memorials—the entrenched racial prejudice among northern white veterans that did not dissipate after emancipation. Both antebellum and postwar theater in the United States treated black performance in similar ways, save for one major difference. The blackface minstrel tradition that flourished in the mid-nineteenth century North was reinvigorated by the integration of "authentic darkies" into the minstrel casts. Black performers were prized for their "realness," and companies like Christie's Minstrels traveled the country performing for white and black audiences. Minstrelsy exploded in the post–Civil War years, and the interpretations of African Americans in the GAR plays follows a similar trajectory.[25] For these veteran-penned plays, free black characters served incredibly important roles: they always signed up to fight alongside the Union soldiers and were often portrayed as the unwitting heroes who accidentally uncovered the Confederates' evil plans or stumbled into scenes and witnessed the rebel villains in the act of torturing or attempting to rape a virtuous white northern woman. These characters would have been played, certainly in all-white posts, by white GAR members in blackface. Northern soldiers marching through the South used antebellum popular culture like minstrel shows and blackface "to render an alien land and people familiar."[26] Minstrel shows were a comfortable form of entertainment that conjured feelings of home for Union men, and they took advantage of the newly freed people that flocked to their lines. Union soldiers called on southern blacks to perform for them in camp and demanded that they ascribe to tropes the soldiers had seen in the antebellum minstrel shows. Thus blackface was deeply entrenched not only in northern society but also in veteran society and veterans' memories of camp life.

In the GAR plays the black characters always speak in some form of dialect. There are no instances where a free black character, whether born in the North or a runaway from the South, speaks in the same style of English as the white characters.[27] This use of dialect implicates white veteran playwrights in the continuation of negative racial stereotypes throughout the North. The language used by the black characters is important because it demonstrates how the same white Union veterans who embraced the emancipationist vision of Civil War memory nonetheless wrote minstrel like dialogue for African American characters in GAR plays.[28]

Most of these plays presented free blacks and runaway slaves as joining the Union cause in various capacities, although rarely as typical regimental soldiers. The character of the contraband runaway Pete in the 1891 drama *After Taps*, written by white veteran George Baker, willingly helps in other ways: "I can brack yer boots massa. An' oh, massa Colonel, I do so lub a horse! Le me take care ob yours. I can handle 'em massa. If dey be eber so debblesome. Please jes try me; an I do eberytin yer axes me, sho's yer born."[29] Unfortunately the colonel has no horse, so Pete settles for the position of the colonel's personal bodyguard and receives a uniform and sword to defend his new charge. Here, the African American character is only granted a uniform and a weapon when his initial request to simply "brack boots" and "handle horses" is denied. The white colonel grants Pete responsibility he did not ask for, a common trope in many of these plays that rendered black men as unwitting—but always loyal—followers to a compassionate and trusting white Union officer.

Depictions of black characters in these plays point to a common narrative throughout the North following the war and one that was competing with reconciliation as a possible national memory: the emancipated, humble slave proving himself by taking up the Union cause and fighting the wicked Confederacy. But despite the anti-southern rhetoric found in the veterans' plays and their celebration of emancipation, many of them borrowed their depictions of black characters directly from plays written by Confederate playwrights during the Civil War. The southern plays rely heavily on the use of dialect and the loyal southern slave unwilling to accept freedom, who choses instead to remain a slave and care for his loving masters. Evidence suggests that these Confederate plays were written throughout the war and performed widely throughout the South but were particularly popular among the southern political elite of Richmond and other major southern cities.[30]

The introduction to *The Guerrillas*, written by Virginian J. D. McCabe in 1863, reads: "Our enemies have discarded every feeling of pity and humanity and have carried death and desolation wherever they have been. . . . Dark and fearful are the tales of woe that are brought across the mountain by those who have fled from the fierce hordes of the North."[31] The slaves in McCabe's drama echo these sentiments toward the North, and they speak in the same rough dialect as the free black characters in the GAR plays. When the slave, Jerry, acts particularly heroically in defending his white mistress's honor from the raiding Union soldiers, his benevolent master offers him his freedom. Jerry responds thus:

> I don't want to be free . . . I tank de good Lord I 'siders myself heap better dan any abulishuner dat eber libed. What I want to be free for, and leave you? . . . I bin in yer family eber since I bin born. . . . I carried you in my arms. . . . I lub you jis like you was my own son. If you'se tired of old Jerry, jis take him out in de field and shoot him, but don't send him away from you; don't set him free.[32]

This scene made sense in the context of the Confederate mentality toward slavery and their thoughts concerning the loyalty of their slaves. However, a similar scene written by a northern playwright highlights the common themes present in Union and Confederate plays. In *The German Volunteer,* written with the express endorsement of the Pennsylvania and Kansas departments of the GAR, the word comes down to the slaves on a Virginia plantation that they are free. While some of the slaves eagerly run away, others like Uncle Jeff, the patriarch of the slave community, elect to remain behind. Uncle Jeff states: "I was born'd on dis ole plantation: when Masser Kurnel was a little boy I toted him around in my arms, an' now dat he is dead an' gone, does yea 'spose I'se going to leave de ole missus? . . . I'se going to stick by de ole plantation."[33] Once all the other slaves leave, Uncle Jeff ominously portends what the future will bring for those who leapt too eagerly for their freedom; "One day," he says, "'ll jast bet a fip dem darkies 'll wish day was bac' on de ole planatation again."[34] The similarities between the plays written by Union and Confederate veterans highlights the potentially difficult place of white Union veterans in the Reconstruction North. On the one hand, many fought alongside black soldiers and understood their loyalty and service to the Union. However, their prewar prejudices were not easily forgotten. The depictions of black characters in these plays serve as a reminder that allowing black veterans to become members of the GAR did not necessarily mean recognizing social equality.

An 1871 play, *The Volunteer,* commissioned by members of GAR Sedgwick Post 1 in Norwich, Connecticut, exposes the complicated and often contradictory ways GAR playwrights dealt with African Americans and their service.[35] The play features, as one of the central characters, an escaped contraband named Pete who speaks in dialect. Pete does not enlist as a soldier but fulfills an important role as a spy for the Union troops. Pete often provides comic relief: during a scene in the Union camp he is compelled to dance for the white troops and is incapable of performing a jig, prompting ridicule from white onlookers.[36] The character of Pete is very clearly a racist depiction, and his is the only black face in the entire cast. Thus this play reads like every other GAR play—save for a single moment in the final act where the anonymous playwright includes a passage that makes explicit reference to the sacrifices made by black soldiers. The Confederate commander states that he expects "no mercy" from the "savage" Union troops. The Union commander responds:

> Savages are we? No mercy from us? Did your butcher Quantrel show mercy to our troops when at Fort Pillow he mercilessly butchered two hundred men after they had surrendered? We savages? I tell you lieutenant, the shrieks and groans of our wounded as they lie on the battlefield robbed and bayoneted by your cowards, rise hourly to the throne of Eternal Justice— calling for Divine vengeance upon men whose cruelty in this war finds no parallel in history![37]

This passage is referring to the 1864 Fort Pillow Massacre. Following a successful assault on Union troops—many of whom were African American—at Fort Pillow, Tennessee, Confederate troops under the command of Nathan Bedford Forrest killed over two hundred black troops rather than taking them prisoner in what historians have deemed a "mass lynching."[38] This play, in which the sole African American character is considered a bumbling fool by the rest of the cast, nonetheless points to one of the most horrific acts committed against black soldiers as a testament to southern cruelty. Rather than focusing on the horrors suffered by white men in Confederate prisons, as many GAR plays did, this play by an integrated post asserted the heroism and sacrifice of black men.[39] This hypocritical juxtaposition of depictions of bumbling freedmen with assertions of black heroism and sacrifice was repeated in the winter of 1886 when two GAR posts in New York City, one all-white and one all-black, battled over the physical segregation of theatrical audiences.

African American organizations and societies had been fixtures of cities like New York, Philadelphia, and Boston prior to the Civil War, but with the equal opportunities promised during Reconstruction, those organizations grew exponentially. The presence of these organizations and the newspapers and pamphlets they produced contributed to the creation of black counterpublics in the heart of many northern cities. Counterpublics are networks of institutions and individuals existing both within and outside of the larger public sphere.[40] Those institutions and individuals can, when externally pressured or internally motivated to do so, rise up into the larger sphere to spur political change. All-black GAR posts were constituent parts of black counterpublics but merely one small piece of a much larger network bolstered by the power of the emerging black press. Indeed, African American newspapers became the engine that drove the black counterpublics in northern cities like New York and Philadelphia.[41] These newspapers—in New York, the *New York Age, New York Freeman,* and *New York Amsterdam News*—were the primary organs of the major African American organizations and acted as community billboards where local clubs and groups could advertise events, discuss politics, and engage with the mainstream public sphere. The Brooklyn Literary Union was one such African American organization, and in 1886 it used the *New York Freeman* as its main weapon to fight against an act of discrimination by white veterans toward the all-black William Lloyd Garrison GAR Post 207.

The attacks were launched in December of 1886 against Colonel Sinn, a former Confederate who had moved to the Democratic Party stronghold of New York after the war and took over management of the Park Theatre. The members of Brooklyn's all-white GAR post planned a joint event with the members of the William Lloyd Garrison Post 207 for the benefit of the GAR Employment Bureau. Colonel Sinn, in his position as manager of the Park Theatre, stated that any black patron attending the benefit performances would be seated in the third-level balcony, regardless of what section was printed on his or her ticket. Sinn defended his discriminatory seating practices by stating to the *Brooklyn Daily Standard* that he "would have no objection to sell reserved seats at all times to colored persons. I have found, however, that public sentiment is against such a step. I regret it, but I can't help it."[42] On December 14, a week after Sinn's public statement, the Brooklyn Literary Union, in conjunction with the William Lloyd Garrison Post, published a series of resolutions that condemned both Sinn and the members of Brooklyn's white GAR post. The resolutions attacked Sinn's claims that he was merely catering to public sentiment by citing other locales in New York, such as the Academy of Music, that allowed black patrons to circulate and sit "among the wealthiest and most cultured of their white neighbors, and receive such courtesies from them as the offer of their opera glasses, etc."[43] The final resolution took aim at the white men of the GAR while also celebrating the response to Colonel Sinn made by members of the William Lloyd Garrison Post. "We repudiate the apologies made by distinguished officers of the Grand Army for Colonel Sinn, and approve of the manly position taken by the representatives of the colored race—who denounced to their comrades this unjust discrimination, and who, because of it, declined to sell tickets."[44] The Literary Union elected a committee who met with Colonel Sinn on December 17 and presented their resolutions. The meeting was documented as "polite and courteous . . . but achieving no result."[45] A final editorial on the matter appeared in the *New York Freeman* a week later, and while it spent some time attacking Sinn, it took greater issue with the actions of the white GAR in not standing up to his discriminatory rule:

> The Brooklyn white members of the Grand Army of the Republic . . . showed themselves more cowardly in the atmosphere of peace than in the presence of rebel cohorts in the atmosphere of war . . . and demonstrated that they were capable of greater baseness than we gave them credit for. . . . [They] should blush themselves into an honest state of shame and repentance, and their colored brothers in arms should wear crape for thirty days in token of the baseness and the treachery which have been shown by their white comrades.[46]

The African American community in Brooklyn painted a picture of the white members of the GAR as cowardly and saw their defense of Sinn as backward and against the tide of history. "The doom of such unjust intolerance is written on the wall," stated the editorial's epigraph, "and it is futile for the mossbacks to defy the ultimatum of Fate."[47] Unfortunately for the Literary Union this prediction would not be fulfilled for decades to come, as the discriminatory actions of Sinn and others like him continued throughout the postwar North.[48]

What do these memories of the Civil War, stereotypical depictions of African Americans, and physical segregation in theater houses tell us about the Grand Army of the Republic and the larger culture of Civil War memory in the North? First, the particular type of war memory that was performed onstage suggests that in many northern communities, a deep-seated resentment of the South persisted into the 1890s and beyond. Such "bloody shirt" memories compel us to rethink previous conclusions about the ubiquity of reconciliation as the dominant narrative of Civil War memory after 1880. Second, the depictions of African Americans in GAR plays, as well as the physical segregation of theater houses endorsed by the GAR, reveal how deeply entrenched white supremacy was throughout the northern states in the years following the Civil War. Even white men who fought and died alongside African American soldiers, lived with them in camp, and welcomed them into their veterans' organizations could not always move beyond prewar prejudices about the subordinate place of African Americans in society. Instead, they reinforced the point that shouldering a musket in an emancipation army did not consistently lend itself to an embrace of racial equality after the war.

NOTES

1. John Alexander Logan, "G.A.R. General Order 11," May 5, 1868, box 42, John Alexander Logan Family Papers, Manuscript Division, Library of Congress.

2. See David Blight, *Race and Reunion: The Civil War in American Memory* (Cambridge, MA: Harvard University Press, 2001), 2–5. See also Eric Foner, *Reconstruction: America's Unfinished Revolution 1863–1877* (New York: Harper and Row, 1988); Heather Cox Richardson, *The Death of Reconstruction: Race, Labor, and Politics in the Post-Civil War North, 1865–1901* (Cambridge, MA: Harvard University Press, 2001); and Caroline E. Janney, *Remembering the Civil War: Reunion and the Limits of Reconciliation* (Chapel Hill: University of North Carolina Press, 2013).

3. Blight, *Race and Reunion*, 90.

4. Janney, *Remembering the Civil War*, 128–29.

5. Barbara A. Gannon, *The Won Cause: Black and White Comradeship in the Grand Army of the Republic* (Chapel Hill: University of North Carolina Press, 2011), 5.

6. Stuart McConnell, *Glorious Contentment: The Grand Army of the Republic, 1865–1900* (Chapel Hill: University of North Carolina Press, 1997), 4.

7. Janney, *Remembering the Civil War*, 52.

8. On the development of theater in the antebellum period see Bruce A. McConachie, *Melodramatic Formations: American Theater and Society, 1820–1870* (Iowa City: University of Iowa Press, 1992).

9. For more on the Grand Review of the Armies on May 23 and 24, 1865, see McConnell, *Glorious Contentment*, 1–17.

10. Janney, *Remembering the Civil War*, 126–30.

11. For more on Radical Republicans during Reconstruction see Heather Cox-Richardson, "A Marshall Plan for the South? The Failure of Republican and Democratic Ideology during Reconstruction," *Civil War History* 51, no. 4 (2005): 378–87; William Blair, "The Use of Military Force to Protect the Gains of Reconstruction," *Civil War History* 51, no. 4 (2005): 388–402; Stephen K. Prince,

"Legitimacy and Interventionism: Northern Republicans, the 'Terrible Carpetbagger,' and the Retreat from Reconstruction," *Journal of the Civil War Era* 2, no. 4 (2012): 538–63; James L. Huston, "An Alternative to the Tragic Era: Applying the Virtues of Bureaucracy to the Reconstruction Dilemma," *Civil War History* 51, no. 4 (2005): 403–15; Richard H. Abbot, *For Free Press and Equal Rights: Republican Newspapers in the Reconstruction South*, ed. John Quist (Athens: University of Georgia Press, 2004); and Andrew, L. Slap, *The Doom of Reconstruction: The Liberal Republicans in the Civil War Era* (New York: Fordham University Press, 2006).

12. For more on the types of melodrama present in the nineteenth century see David Grimsted, *Melodrama Unveiled: American Theater & Culture, 1800–1850* (Berkeley: University of California Press, 1987); Jeffrey Mason, *Melodrama and the Myth of America* (Bloomington: University of Indiana Press, 1993); and McConachie, *Melodramatic Formations*.

13. A. D. Ames and C. G. Bartley, *The Spy of Atlanta, a Grand Military Allegory, in Six Acts* (Clyde, Ohio: A. D. Ames, 1879), 14.

14. For specific instances of tableau, see *The Spy of Atlanta*, 12–14; Samuel Muscroft, *The Drummer Boy, or, the Battlefield of Shiloh, A New Military Allegory in Five Acts and Accompanying Tableaux. Arranged from Incidents of the Late War, and Respectfully Dedicated to the Grand Army of the Republic* (Worcester, MA: Charles Hamilton, 1868), 11; and J. N. Culver, *Loyal Mountaineers; or, the Guerrilla's Doom, A War Drama, Descriptive of the Hardships, Sufferings, and Brave Endurance of the Unionists of East Tennessee, Founded on Facts* (St. Albans, VT: E. A. Morton, 1872), 9.

15. *Broad Ax*, March 23, 1893.

16. Sidney Sanders, *Post of Honor, A Military Drama in Four Acts* (Springfield, MA: Clark W. Bryan, 1872), 6, 22, 27–29, 31–32.

17. "G.A.R.," *Portland Daily Press*, August 12, 1870.

18. "The G. A. R. Theatricals," *St. Albans Daily Messenger*, April 7, 1874, 3.

19. *Reading Eagle*, December 18, 1896.

20. Muscroft, *The Drummer Boy*, 24.

21. Quoted in Roger E. Stoddard and Hope P. Litchfield, "A. D. Ames, First Dramatic Publisher in the West," *Books at Brown* 21 (1966): 98.

22. Quoted in ibid..

23. "The War Drama," *St. Albans Daily Messenger*, April 9, 1874, 3. A complete list of the amateur plays published by northern veteran playwrights following the war does not exist. For an incomplete but well-researched list, see Mason, *Melodrama and the Myth of America*, 239–41. For more on the importance of performance and the rise of melodrama during Reconstruction, see Thomas Postlewait and Bruce A. McConachie, eds., *Interpreting the Theatrical Past: Essays in the Historiography of Performance* (Iowa City: University of Iowa Press, 1989); Benjamin McArthur, *Actors and American Culture, 1880–1920* (Iowa City: University of Iowa Press, 2000); Grimsted, *Melodrama Unveiled*, 1–16; and McConachie, *Melodramatic Formations*, 28–38.

24. "City Guard in 'The Drummer Boy,'" *Summit County Beacon*, February 28, 1883.

25. Eric Lott has written the definitive book on blackface minstrelsy both before and after the Civil War. His analysis alongside those of Robert C. Toll and W. T. Lhamon Jr. reveals that throughout the postwar years blackface remained a common practice, often juxtaposing white actors in blackface with "troupes of authentic Negros" to provide musical accompaniment. See Robert C. Toll,

Blacking Up: The Minstrel Show in Nineteenth-Century America (New York: Oxford University Press, 1974); Eric Lott, *Love and Theft: Blackface Minstrelsy and the American Working Class* (New York: Oxford University Press, 1993); and W. T. Lhamon Jr., *Raising Cain: Blackface Performance from Jim Crow to Hip Hop* (Cambridge, MA: Harvard University Press, 1998).

26. Peter C. Luebke, "'Equal to Any Minstrel Concert I Ever Attended at Home': Union Soldiers and Blackface Performance in the Civil War South," *Journal of the Civil War Era* 4, no. 4 (2014): 509.

27. For a fantastic article on the use of dialect and its understanding by white authors see Jeffrey Hadler, "Remus Orthography: The History of the Representation of the African American Voice," *Journal of Folklore Research* 35, no. 2 (May–August 1998): 99–126.

28. For more complete histories on the depictions of African Americans onstage during the antebellum and postbellum years see Heather S. Nathans, *Slavery and Sentiment on the American Stage, 1787–1861: Lifting the Veil of Black* (Cambridge: Cambridge University Press, 2009), and Hazel Waters, *Racism on the Victorian Stage: Representations of Slavery and the Black Character* (Cambridge: Cambridge University Press, 2007).

29. Rachel E. Baker, from the notes and unfinished manuscript of George Baker, *After Taps: A Drama in Three Acts* (Boston: Walter H. Baker, 1891), 20.

30. Mary DeCredico, *Mary Boykin Chesnut: A Confederate Woman's Life* (Lanham, MD: Rowman and Littlefield, 1998), 60–65.

31. James D. McCabe Jr., *The Guerrillas: A Domestic Drama in Three Acts* (Richmond: West and Johnson, 1863), 1.

32. McCabe, *The Guerrillas*, 25.

33. *The German Volunteer: A Military Allegory and Comedy Drama in Four Acts* (Philadelphia: Will D. Saphar, n.d.), 20.

34. *The German Volunteer*, 20.

35. *The Volunteer: A Military Drama in Six Acts, and Accompanying Tableau. Arranged from Incidents of the Late War, and Dedicated to the Grand Army of the Republic* (Norwich, CT: n.p., 1871).

36. *The Volunteer*, 16.

37. *The Volunteer*, 25. This is one of the many anachronistic moments found throughout these plays. The playwright has conflated the Lawrence Massacre with the Fort Pillow Massacre. William Clarke Quantrill (correct spelling) and his men murdered two hundred civilians in Lawrence, Kansas, in August of 1863. See Matthew Christopher Hulbert's essay in this volume.

38. Richard Fuchs, *An Unerring Fire: The Massacre at Fort Pillow* (Mechanicsburg, PA: Stackpole, 2002), 14. See also John Cimprich, *Fort Pillow, a Civil War Massacre, and Public Memory* (Baton Rouge: Louisiana State University Press, 2005), and Andrew Ward, *River Run Red: The Fort Pillow Massacre in the American Civil War* (New York: Penguin, 2005).

39. Many of the GAR plays concluded with scenes set in Confederate prisons in order to show the incredible cruelty inflicted on northern soldiers by Confederates. This theme was not unique to GAR plays: David Blight argues that "no wartime experience . . . caused deeper emotions, recriminations, and lasting invective than that of prisons." Most veteran literature and memoirs contained descriptions of prison conditions as the harshest part of the war. Blight, *Race and Reunion*, 152; Janney, *Remembering the Civil War*, 129.

40. Michael Dawson, *Black Visions: The Roots of Contemporary African-American Political Ideolo-*

gies (Chicago: University of Chicago Press, 2003), 4. For more on Dawson's conception of the black counterpublic sphere see Michael Dawson, *Not in Our Lifetimes: The Future of Black Politics* (Chicago: University of Chicago Press, 2011), vii–xvi.

41. Barbara Gannon argues that African American newspapers were fundamental to the success of black GAR posts because they helped connect the black community as a unified entity—an "essential element that shaped the world African Americans made in the G.A.R." Gannon, *The Won Cause*, 53.

42. "The Color-Line in Theatres," *New York Freeman*, December 18, 1886.

43. "Brooklyn Literary Union—On Account of Color," *New York Amsterdam News*, December 1, 1886.

44. Ibid.

45. "Shuffling Colonel Sinn," *New York Freeman*, December 25, 1886.

46. "Col. Sinn, the Theatres and the Grand Army of the Republic," *New York Freeman*, December 25, 1886.

47. Ibid.

48. For more on discrimination in northern theaters see Errol Hill and James Hatch, *History of African American Theater* (New York: Cambridge University Press, 2008). There were multiple movements throughout the northern states during and after the war to end segregation on public transit and in public spaces like theaters. While some were successful, the overall success of these movements and their link to the larger African American freedom struggle and the civil rights movement are topics of debate among historians. See Allen C. Guelzo, *Fateful Lightning: A New History of the Civil War and Reconstruction* (New York: Oxford University Press, 2012), 382–84; Beth Tompkins Bates, *Pullman Porters and the Rise of Protest Politics in Black America, 1925–1945* (Chapel Hill: University of North Carolina Press, 2001); and Judith Giesberg, *Army at Home: Women and the Civil War on the Northern Home Front* (Chapel Hill: University of North Carolina Press, 2012).

III

THE MULTIVOCALITY

OF

CIVIL WAR

VETERANHOOD

"Our Beloved Father Abraham"

African American Civil War Veterans and Abraham Lincoln in War and Memory

MATTHEW D. NORMAN

S ALEXANDER AUGUSTA attempted to travel by train from Baltimore to Philadelphia in the spring of 1863, he was assaulted by a gang of men who swore at him and ripped one of the shoulder straps from his uniform. A recently appointed army surgeon, Augusta wore the rank of a major, and the sight of a black man in an officer's uniform was too much for some of the white men aboard the train to bear. A few months after he was assaulted, Augusta was ejected from a Washington streetcar due to his skin color. Within weeks of this latest indignity, Augusta attended a reception at the White House. Wearing his army uniform with the shoulder straps laureled with golden leaves, Augusta met President Lincoln who "kindly received" him. Augusta's brief encounter with the president was covered in the press. A Detroit newspaper claimed that the ladies present were "very much disgusted" by the spectacle, while a Syracuse, New York, paper warned that mixing an "odorous" person like Augusta with white people was clear evidence of the sorry state of affairs under the Lincoln administration. It was apparent to these Democrat editors that Lincoln was determined to bring about the social equality of the races.[1]

While black men in blue uniforms faced great peril on the battlefield from an enemy who threatened to treat them as criminals engaged in servile insurrection rather than as soldiers, Augusta's experiences vividly demonstrate some of the serious obstacles they confronted on the home front. In a society where the ascribed status of African Americans was lower than the lowliest of white Americans, the mere sight of black men in uniform provoked violent outbursts. Augusta escaped with his life, but Lieutenant Anson Sanborn of the 1st US Colored Troops (USCT) was not as fortunate. Dr. David Wright of Norfolk, Virginia, became so enraged when he saw Sanborn leading black soldiers through the city that he shot and killed the white officer. Despite pleas for clemency from Virginia Unionists, Lincoln refused to commute Wright's death sentence once a physician certified that he was not insane. Joseph T. Wilson, a veteran of the 54th Massachusetts who had been wounded at the Battle of Olustee, recalled this incident over twenty years later and contrasted it with the joy felt in celebrating the anniversary of Lincoln's "immortal Proclamation of Emancipation." For Wilson, Sanborn's murder was a memory from "darker days," and by invoking the "spirit of 1863," he hoped African Americans would be inspired to continue the "battle" for "recognition and equality in the ranks of mankind."[2]

By associating the Emancipation Proclamation with his military service and the ongoing struggle for equality, Wilson was acting in a manner that Lincoln had predicted. Regardless of what motivated him to issue the Emancipation Proclamation and call for the recruitment of black soldiers, Lincoln realized that these men were exhibiting great courage, playing a vital role in the war effort, and had every reason to expect their service would pave the way for political and civil rights. Nevertheless, Lincoln was severely criticized for expanding the war aims to include freedom for the enslaved and enlisting black men to help fulfill this objective. In an August 1863 letter to James C. Conkling that was published to defend these policies, Lincoln noted that black soldiers were making an important contribution toward vindicating the democratic principle that "among free men, there can be no successful appeal from the ballot to the bullet." Well aware of the hostility these men faced on the battle front and the home front, Lincoln presciently foresaw the struggle that would occur once the rebels were defeated. He predicted that "there will be some black men who can remember that, with silent tongue and clenched teeth, and steady eye, and well poised bayonet, they have helped mankind on to this great consummation; while, I fear, there will be some white ones, unable to forget that, with malignant heart, and deceitful speech, they have strove to hinder it."[3]

In these few well-chosen words, Lincoln encapsulated one of the central issues pertaining to the legacy and memory of the Civil War. African Americans would not forget the vital role they had played in preserving the Union and abolishing slavery. Black veterans were especially keen to keep this memory alive in order to advance the cause of racial equality. As Sergeant Henry J. Maxwell of the 2nd US Colored Light Artillery made clear to a convention of black men at Nashville, Tennessee, in the summer of 1865: "We want the rights guaranteed by the Infinite Architect. For these rights we labor, for them we will die. We have gained one—the uniform is its badge. We want two more boxes, beside the cartridge box—the ballot box and the jury box. We shall gain them." Just as African American soldiers had made an important contribution in winning the war, African American veterans were activists and symbols in the struggle for equal rights.[4]

In his seminal work *Lincoln and the Negro*, Benjamin Quarles states that "Lincoln became Lincoln because of the Negro." Quarles details a special relationship between Lincoln and African Americans, and he concludes that they came to know Lincoln "by heart." Clearly, the Emancipation Proclamation made Lincoln a venerated symbol and earned him a special place in the hearts of African Americans. Black veterans were central figures in commemorating Lincoln and remembering the war, but the narrative of emancipation that they offered was more nuanced and complex than either the "folklore Lincoln" that Quarles emphasizes or what became the dominant popular image of black passivity. While black veterans participated in reunions, organized Memorial Day ceremonies, and joined organizations such as the Grand Army of the Republic (GAR) that were specifically associated with military service, they were also prominent in African American celebrations of Emancipation Day and Lincoln's birthday. These commemorative activities all provided opportunities to assert the vital contribution that black soldiers had made in winning the war. The story of emancipation at these events was far more than a single moment when a benevolent Lincoln bestowed the gift of freedom upon grateful, kneeling slaves. Rather, black soldiers had stood at Lincoln's side as indispensable partners, for their bravery and sacrifices had made the Emancipation Proclamation a reality. Sergeant Maxwell, Joseph Wilson, and other black veterans were determined to enjoy the same rights as white citizens, and they were also resolute in constructing a civic memory of the war in which African Americans were essential participants. "Father Abraham" had a special place in not just the hearts but also the heads of African American Civil War veterans as they appropriated the memory of Lincoln as a symbol of racial equality in the ongoing struggle for political and civil rights. Unsuccessful in their efforts to erect a permanent monument to black soldiers, African American veterans functioned as living monuments whose presence served to remind the nation of their role in helping Lincoln preserve the republic and abolish slavery.[5]

Before Lincoln became a symbol of freedom and racial equality, some African American soldiers viewed him with suspicion. Prior to being able to don blue uniforms, Martin Delany, Joseph Barquet, and H. Ford Douglas were so discouraged by the state of race relations in the 1850s that they seriously considered leaving the United States, just as Alexander Augusta had become an exile when racial prejudice prevented him from attending medical school. An abolitionist who had advocated emigration to Haiti, H. Ford Douglas met Lincoln during his campaign for the US Senate in 1858 and asked him to sign a petition that urged the Illinois legislature to repeal the law that prohibited African Americans from testifying against whites in court. Lincoln refused to sign the petition. Throughout the Senate campaign and for the remainder of his political career, Lincoln was hounded by the unrelenting charge that he sought to elevate African Americans to a position of social and political equality. In 1858, Lincoln attempted to make his position clear by arguing that while African Americans were entitled to natural rights as enumerated in the Declaration of Independence, it did not necessarily follow that they should have civil or political rights. Although Lincoln's Democratic opponents did not find this argument credible, Douglas concluded that Lincoln was no friend and his antislavery convictions were insincere. After Lincoln received the Republican nomination for president in 1860, Douglas actively campaigned against him. Pointing to Lincoln's willingness to enforce the Fugitive Slave Act, his apparent support for the Illinois Black Laws that severely limited the freedom of African Americans, and his belief that slavery could only be abolished through gradual means, Douglas condemned Lincoln "for his pro-slavery character and principles."[6]

Once Lincoln became president, there was little to encourage African Americans during his first two years in office, as he initially conceived of the war as a limited conflict whose sole purpose was to preserve the Union. The army turned away black men willing to volunteer to fight, and Lincoln revoked emancipation decrees issued by his generals. He further provoked the ire of many African Americans when he met with a delegation of black men in August 1862 and urged them to leave the United States and form a colony in Central America. Frederick Douglass condemned Lincoln's colonization scheme as evidence of his "contempt for negroes and his canting hypocrisy," but not everyone agreed with him. Joseph Barquet was an Illinois abolitionist who fought against the Black Laws and had joined with Douglass in 1853 to condemn colonization during the state's first convention of African American men. However, in the wake of the Dred Scott decision, Barquet came to the conclusion that "the time has arrived in our dark history for us to choose between exile and slavery." Barquet therefore urged African Americans to emigrate, and in 1862 he expressed a willingness to accept Lincoln's offer to move to Central America.[7]

Lincoln's final Emancipation Proclamation not only altered Barquet's plans but had a profound impact upon how African Americans perceived him. Barquet was unable to fulfill a commitment to speak at a celebration of the Emancipation Proclamation in Chicago on January 1, 1863, but a veteran from another war—Osborne Anderson, the sole African American to survive John Brown's raid on Harpers Ferry—addressed the meeting and praised Lincoln. For Anderson, Lincoln's proclamation vindicated Brown. Less than a week after Lincoln issued the proclamation, Alexander Augusta wrote to the president from Toronto, Canada, and offered to serve as an army surgeon, for he wished to return from exile and "be of use to my race." In a letter to Frederick Douglass, H. Ford Douglas stated that Lincoln's "one simple act of Justice to the slave" effectively "links his memory with immortality." For Douglas, the Emancipation Proclamation portended a new era and a new Lincoln, as he believed the "war will educate Mr. Lincoln out of his idea of the deportation of the Negro quite as fast as it has some of his other proslavery ideas with respect to employing them as soldiers." Douglas was confident that African Americans would "be educated and lifted to a higher and nobler life," and in anticipation of this turn of events, he had enlisted in an Illinois regiment, where his skin color was not an issue. He eventually became one of the few African American commissioned officers. Like Douglas, John Proctor of the 34th USCT believed Lincoln's proclamation was the impetus for revolutionary change. The Emancipation Proclamation freed Proctor from slavery in South Carolina, and he wasted little time in enlisting and expressing to the president his desire to exact revenge on his former master. Proctor's one regret was that he was unable to see Lincoln "with mine own eyes," but he hoped Lincoln would remember him to his "felow cittysons of the united states."[8]

Barquet did not speak in Chicago on January 1, 1863, but a year later he was a sergeant in the 54th Massachusetts and the featured orator at the regiment's Emancipation Day celebration. In scarcely more than a year, Barquet had gone from being ready to leave the United States to risking his life as a noncommissioned officer. Lincoln's proclamation promised freedom and an opportunity for black men to assert their manhood. When Barquet, Douglas, Proctor, and thousands of other African Americans volunteered and seized the chance to have a leading role in this revolution, they did so with expectations regarding their military service. Some became disillusioned and condemned the Lincoln administration for failing to act accordingly. George E. Stephens, a fellow sergeant with Barquet in the 54th Massachusetts, criticized the Emancipation Proclamation for exempting slaveholders in the loyal border states and portions of the occupied states in rebellion. Stephens believed this "false and indefinite policy" indicated that Lincoln had not abandoned plans for colonization and was more interested in protecting slavery than advancing the cause of racial equality.[9]

Black soldiers were most upset by the government's failure to treat them as the equals of white soldiers. The president's allegedly slow response to rebel threats that black soldiers taken captive would either be enslaved or summarily executed was naturally a source of grave concern to the soldiers and prompted urgent responses from luminaries such as Frederick Douglass, Senator Charles Sumner, and the father of Colonel Robert Gould Shaw of the 54th Massachusetts. On the day that Lincoln issued an order that authorized retaliation for any mistreatment of soldiers taken prisoner, the mother of a soldier in the 54th Massachusetts wrote to him: "Dont you think you oght to stop this thing and make them do the same by the colored men[?]" Equally galling was the policy of paying black soldiers less than their white comrades. As John H. Morgan of the 86th USCT wrote to Lincoln, "All we ask for is Justist Bestowed on ous." With the approach of the 1864 election, Sergeant Barquet wished that someone other than Lincoln would be the Republican nominee because "we cannot look for justice from the present Administration." A soldier in the 5th Massachusetts Cavalry agreed and claimed that while "many of our intelligent colored men believe in Mr. Lincoln," black soldiers "know him better" and realized he did not deserve their support. After the Democrats nominated George B. McClellan, the soldier admitted Lincoln was preferable but also made clear that "we abhor him when we consider the many injustices he has allowed to be practiced on colored men."[10]

These harsh words of criticism stand in stark contrast to accounts of encounters that occurred between Lincoln and black soldiers. Lincoln had treated Alexander Augusta with respect and when Martin Delany went to the White

House to discuss his plan to alleviate prejudice against African Americans in the army by raising a force of black men commanded by black officers, Lincoln listened to the proposal with such an open mind that Delany felt he "was not content that my color should make its own impression." Following this meeting, Delany was commissioned a major in the 104th USCT and became the first African American field officer. Black soldiers cheered so enthusiastically when they saw Lincoln reviewing them from the balcony of Willard's Hotel in April 1864 that many observers wept at the sight. Lincoln made a point of reviewing black troops during his visits to General Grant in Virginia in 1864 and 1865. A witness recalled that on one of these occasions black soldiers greeted Lincoln with such fervor that it brought tears to his eyes and he could barely speak to acknowledge them. When the president reviewed black soldiers in the 25th Corps during the spring of 1865, he was met with "repeated cheers." Years later, in his history of black soldiers, veteran George Washington Williams concluded that this incident was "one of the most magnificent military spectacles of the civil war." African American soldiers were the first to occupy Richmond, Virginia, in April 1865, and Lincoln visited the city shortly after it fell. Alexander Newton of the 29th Connecticut was present and recalled that the vast number of black people who welcomed Lincoln to the city presented "a sight never to be forgotten." Chaplain Garland H. White of the 28th USCT was also an eyewitness to Lincoln's visit, and after seeing newly freed people shouting praises to "father" Abraham, White "became so overcome with tears" that he "could not stand up under the pressure of such fulness of joy in my own heart."[11]

The joy in Chaplain White's heart and the anger of the soldier from the 5th Massachusetts Cavalry reflect the ambivalence of African Americans regarding Lincoln and capture the tension between what he did and what he failed to do. The question of whether Lincoln's views on racial equality had changed since he refused to sign H. Ford Douglas's petition in 1858 is central to his legacy. With Lincoln's sudden death from an assassin's bullet, much of this ambivalence was replaced with sorrow. As the war ended, black soldiers and veterans did not hesitate to seize the terrain in a new contest in which Lincoln's memory and the struggle for civil and political rights were inseparable. As Lincoln predicted, malignant-hearted whites opposed these efforts.

Black soldiers led Lincoln's funeral procession through Washington, but once his body arrived in New York, local officials resisted African American efforts to march in the procession, and only a directive from the War Department made it possible for them to participate. A sergeant in the 43rd USCT could hardly believe Lincoln was gone, as it had been only a few weeks since the president had reviewed his regiment and the men had "looked upon him with that holy awe and reverence which was due him." Even though Lincoln was dead, the sergeant believed he continued to live in the hearts of soldiers and in the "millions of those whom he by his love of justice, liberty, and his well known belief in the rights of man, redeemed from the curse of slavery." George Le Vere had met Lincoln at the White House prior to becoming chaplain of the 20th USCT, and in his eulogy of the "much beloved president," he praised Lincoln for being "unalterable in his purposes for justice and the right." While the sergeant in the 43rd USCT believed Lincoln continued to live in the hearts of African Americans, Chaplain Le Vere went a step further and suggested that Lincoln had become a member of all their families, and he urged his audience to go home and "write upon the records of [their] family Bible the name of Abraham Lincoln."[12]

As the nation focused on the task of reconstruction under the leadership of Lincoln's successor, Andrew Johnson, African American soldiers and veterans wasted no time invoking Lincoln's memory to advance the cause of racial equality. Writing from the US-Mexican border in the summer of 1865, a soldier made the connection between Lincoln's legacy and African American political rights unequivocal when he suggested that "our beloved father" continued to live in their actions and words. Black men had proven themselves in battle, and by using the "freedom of speech" that Lincoln had given them, the soldier was confident that "we will get our rights as men and citizens." Meeting at Davenport, Iowa, in the fall of 1865, a convention of soldiers from the 60th USCT honored Lincoln as a "martyr" and "devoted friend of our race." The soldiers called on the Iowa legislature to enable them to vote since "he who is worthy to be trusted with the musket can and ought to be trusted with the ballot." President Johnson proved to be no friend to African Americans, despite his pledge to be their "Moses," and as the power struggle between Johnson and the Republican-controlled Congress intensified, black veterans organized a convention where their voices could be heard. The convention met at Philadelphia in early 1867, and one of the speakers, Sergeant A. W. Handy, asserted that a "black man who could tell a loyal man from a traitor was entitled to vote." Handy believed it was the duty of all black veterans to seek the franchise, and though their "present political Moses" was a failure, he sensed "the spirit of Lincoln" was with them and they would soon enjoy all the rights of citizenship.[13]

While President Johnson proved to be anything but a Moses, African American veterans bolstered their claim to Lincoln as an ally in the cause of civil and political rights by pointing to a letter that he wrote to Governor Michael Hahn of Louisiana in March 1864. In this confidential letter, Lincoln suggested that some black men, namely those who were either "very intelligent" or had "gallantly fought in our ranks," be allowed to vote. By giving these men the franchise, Lincoln believed they would help "keep the jewel of liberty within the family of freedom." Hahn published the letter shortly after Lincoln's death, and it was cited to support voting rights and draw a clear distinction between Lincoln and Johnson. Following his discharge from the army, Sergeant Barquet returned home to Illinois and continued to advocate for equality. In 1866, he helped organize a statewide convention of black men and assisted in drafting the convention's address to the American people. The convention emphasized the sacrifices of black soldiers as evidence that they were entitled to the same rights as white citizens. The address that Barquet helped write invoked the memory of Lincoln and his letter to Hahn in making the case for voting rights: "A voice from the tomb of the martyred Lincoln seems now to reach the national ear, saying, 'The hour is come in which to enfranchise the colored American people, that they may help you keep the jewel of liberty in the family of freedom.'" Lincoln's spirit remained very much alive throughout the country, as a speaker at the 1866 New York convention of African American men also quoted from the Hahn letter and listed some of the key battles where black soldiers had fought to support his argument for equal rights. Lincoln's letter to Hahn continued to resonate even after the ratification of the Fifteenth Amendment. To mark the second anniversary of the amendment's ratification, black veterans in Philadelphia organized a celebration that included a portrait of Lincoln and a banner that proclaimed: "We helped to keep the jewel of freedom in the family of nations."[14]

Given this inextricable association between military service, Lincoln's legacy, and the effort to secure equal rights, black veterans sought to keep the memory of their sacrifices alive through participation in a variety of commemorative activities. The GAR emerged as the leading fraternal organization for men who had worn blue in the Civil War, and it assumed the responsibility for organizing the observance of Memorial Day. Although not without some controversies, black veterans were able to become GAR members, and each year on May 30 they reminded the public that they too had fought and died for freedom and Union. Whether in racially integrated or all-black posts, African American veterans marched in Memorial Day parades and participated in services at cemeteries where addresses were made and the graves of their fallen comrades were decorated. Speeches at these ceremonies gave meaning to the sacrifices of the dead by emphasizing the progress that had been made and exhorting the audience to overcome remaining obstacles. In 1869, a speaker at a ceremony organized by an African American post from Philadelphia recalled how black volunteers were "indignantly rejected" at the start of the war. Without mentioning Lincoln by name, the orator alluded to the Gettysburg Address when he observed that the black soldiers who died in the war "did not die in vain" because their deaths brought "liberty, citizenship, and participation in the government." All-black posts in New York City made the connection to Lincoln more explicit by organizing services at the Lincoln statue in Brooklyn's Prospect Park and inviting a speaker to deliver an address on Lincoln. John Mercer Langston had helped recruit black soldiers during the war, and in 1874 he accepted an invitation from the African American post in Baltimore to be the keynote speaker. With a civil rights bill pending in Congress, Langston made it clear that the men who gave their lives must not be forgotten. Jim Crow practices dishonored their memory, and Langston demanded "in the name of our dead colored soldiers that there be given to us complete and constant equality everywhere." After a black GAR member read the Gettysburg Address at the 1907 observance held at an African American cemetery in Washington, DC, the featured orator listed the principal engagements where African American soldiers had fought, praised their manhood for refusing to accept unequal pay, and concluded that "all the Negro had accomplished as citizens was made possible by the heroism of the Negro soldier."[15]

Such a statement reveals the power associated with African American military service, and two veterans, George Washington Williams and Joseph Wilson, not only participated in commemorative activities but also wrote books about African Americans soldiers in an effort to further solidify their place in history and memory. Wilson's *The Black Phalanx* (1887) and Williams's *A History of the Negro Troops in the War of the Rebellion* (1888) appeared a decade after federal troops had been withdrawn from protecting the remaining Republican governments in the South. With Democrats firmly in control of the "Solid South," and as more white Americans embraced sectional reconciliation on terms largely dictated by the side that had lost the war, African Americans saw many of the advances that had been made during Reconstruction disappear. Alarmed by what he had witnessed on a visit to the Deep South, Frederick Douglass denounced emancipation as a "stupendous fraud" in the same year that Williams's history was published. Douglass made it clear that this was not Lincoln's fault, and he worried that people were becoming forgetful of the past. Williams and Wilson were determined to keep the memory of black military service alive when such memories complicated the whitewashing of the Civil War.[16]

Wilson and Williams detailed a complex relationship between Lincoln and African Americans soldiers. Both made it clear that Lincoln was a reluctant emancipator who initially opposed the enlistment of African Americans. However, Lincoln eventually came to embrace emancipation and the recruitment of black soldiers. In doing so, he redeemed himself and provided an opportunity for blacks to prove themselves worthy of citizenship. Reprinting Lincoln's July 30, 1863, Order of Retaliation verbatim, Williams and Wilson made it clear that Lincoln was on the right side in dealing with atrocities committed against black soldiers. At a time when African Americans were being lynched and the federal government essentially turned a blind eye, neither Wilson nor Williams would allow Fort Pillow and other similar incidents to be forgotten. Such memories might prove inconvenient in light of the increasing desire for reconciliation, but as Williams forcefully asserted, "The Southern conscience of to-day may seek, like Cain, to hide from the bar of public sentiment, but like the first murder, neither the Confederate Congress nor its hired assassin, the Confederate army, can ever escape the fierce light of impartial history." Williams and Wilson also emphasized the emotional bond that developed between Lincoln and black soldiers. In recounting scenes of Lincoln reviewing black troops, Wilson noted the mutual affection that existed between the commander in chief and his men, while Williams wrote that Lincoln was "deeply moved at the sight of these Negro troops, against whose employment he had early and earnestly protested." In a conflict filled with many dramatic events, Williams concluded that few matched the sight of Lincoln meeting with black soldiers on the James River in March 1865.[17]

To further preserve the memory of their role in the war and their special relationship with Lincoln, black veterans sought to erect monuments as permanent tributes that would endure long after they departed. In the days following Lincoln's assassination, Major Martin Delany submitted a detailed proposal for an abstract monument depicting "Ethiopia stretching forth her hands unto God." He thought this would be a "just and appropriate tribute of respect and lasting gratitude from the colored people of the United States to the memory of President Lincoln, the Father of American Liberty." Lincoln was of such significance that Delany urged every African American to contribute just one cent so that all could participate in the project. Black veterans contributed money for the construction of Lincoln's tomb in Springfield, Illinois, and Joseph Wilson took pride in the fact that black soldiers donated thousands of dollars for Thomas Ball's Emancipation Group in Washington, DC. Frederick Douglass delivered the dedication address for this controversial monument in 1876, which depicts Lincoln freeing a kneeling slave. George Washington Williams believed the "surest way to teach national history is in monumental marble" and his proposal for a monument to black Civil War soldiers in Washington would have been a counterpoise to the image of black passivity represented in Ball's monument. In Williams's view, a black soldier monument in the nation's capital "would have a beneficent influence upon the entire people for all time to come." At its national encampment in 1888, the GAR refused to endorse Williams's monument proposal for fear that it would detract from a pension bill in Congress. George W. Bryant, a veteran from St. Louis, sought to erect a monument in Chicago that commemorated black soldiers, emancipation, and Lincoln. He began raising funds in 1891 with the hope that the monument would be completed in time for the 1893 World's Fair. The monuments that Delany, Williams, and Bryant proposed were unrealized, and one is left to wonder what impact these sculptures might have had upon the memorial landscape.[18]

While efforts to erect permanent monuments to black soldiers failed, African American veterans were conspicuous in civic celebrations of Emancipation Day and Lincoln's birthday. Their presence at these events was both symbolic and substantive, for they acted as living monuments to remind people what the war was really about and demonstrate that African Americans were not merely passive recipients of Lincoln's Emancipation Proclamation but instead had fought to secure their freedom and citizenship. Prior to the Civil War, African Americans and white abolitionists celebrated the anniversary of the emancipation of slaves in the British West Indies. After the war, the commemoration of Emancipation Day occurred either in the late summer to coincide with both the earlier tradition and the anniversary of Lincoln's preliminary proclamation on September 22 or on January 1 to mark the date of the final proclamation. These festive social occasions typically included a parade, music, food, and speeches. In 1886, navy veteran William B. Derrick delivered an Emancipation Day address at New Bedford, Massachusetts, that captured all of the key themes. He praised Lincoln as the "great Emancipator" and also made it clear that the "epoch of our emancipation" was not Lincoln's work alone, for "none did more to maintain the integrity of the nation and preserve the Union than the negro soldiers." In reflecting on how much progress had been made since "those dark and disastrous times" under slavery, Derrick cautioned that much work remained. Citizenship, he proclaimed, "should not be considered as a favor or concession, but simply as an inalienable and legal right," and for those who wondered how they should go about obtaining all the rights and privileges they were entitled to, his advice was "to agitate, agitate, agitate."[19]

For as long as they were able, black veterans organized and participated in Emancipation Day activities throughout the country. The 1867 celebration in Springfield, Illinois, included a procession to Lincoln's tomb, a picnic, and speeches from Joseph Barquet and William Herndon, Lincoln's law partner and biographer. In 1894, the all-black Fort Pillow GAR post in Topeka, Kansas, issued a call urging Kansans to celebrate September 22 as Emancipation Day and participated in a parade with white veterans. In 1903, a member of the Fort Pillow post was one of the featured speakers at the Topeka celebration, while the Abraham Lincoln GAR post at New Albany, Indiana, organized Emancipation Day festivities with veterans from Louisville, Kentucky. African American residents of the soldiers' home in Dayton, Ohio, were regular participants in the annual Emancipation Day parade. In 1910, the veteran at the head of their procession carried a banner with Lincoln's portrait and another veteran, William Steele, delivered the keynote address, "Abraham Lincoln at Gettysburg." While over a hundred black veterans from the Dayton home marched in the 1910 parade, the ranks quickly diminished. By September 1912, the fiftieth anniversary of Lincoln's preliminary Emancipation Proclamation, only twenty were able to march, and the local newspaper commented that "every soldier in the small band was gray, every one was enfeebled with years."[20]

The celebration of Lincoln's birthday had become so closely associated with

African Americans that an editorial published in a leading black magazine in 1909, the centennial year of Lincoln's birth, ironically noted not only the increasing prevalence of white celebrations of Lincoln's birthday but also the tendency of these events to prohibit black participation. African American veterans took leading roles in organizing and participating in Lincoln birthday commemorations. In urging his fellow members of the New Jersey GAR to approve a resolution requesting the state legislature to make Lincoln's birthday a legal holiday, William Murrell indicated that he was a beneficiary of the Emancipation Proclamation and declared that black people "love the name" Lincoln. He would therefore be "be false to my God" if he "did not stand in the defense of Abraham Lincoln." Black veterans organized Lincoln Day celebrations in New York, Washington, and Marion, Indiana, where residents of the soldiers' home wore buttons with Lincoln's image. An African American newspaper reported that the veterans "never forget their Moses, the martyred Lincoln." A 1905 commemoration of Lincoln's birthday in Buffalo, New York, featured a portrait of Lincoln along with two "bloodstained" flags that black soldiers had carried in the war. Two African American veterans, one of them with an "empty sleeve" and the other on crutches, paused before Lincoln's portrait and saluted it. When the speaker discussed Lincoln's assassination, it was reported that they began to weep.[21]

The tears that these veterans shed forty years after Lincoln was assassinated are further evidence of the strength and depth of feeling that they had for their commander in chief. By the early twentieth century, the spirit of Lincoln remained alive and was a source of hope in a time of increasing despair. As blacks were systematically disfranchised, placed under rigid Jim Crow laws, and lynched, southern whites increasingly came to view Lincoln as a friend because they believed his opposition to black social and political equality in 1858 reflected his true convictions, and if he had lived to complete his second term as president, he would have saved the South from the alleged horrors of Reconstruction. This embrace of Lincoln dovetailed with a desire for sectional reconciliation that sought to minimize the importance of emancipation. In 1909, amid much fanfare, white GAR members in Atlanta celebrated the centennial of Lincoln's birth with their former foes, including the commander in chief of the United Confederate Veterans. In Lincoln's hometown of Springfield, Illinois, organizers of the centennial celebration excluded blacks. A white Indiana veteran observed, "While people are celebrating the birth of Lincoln they are repudiating the great cause on which his fame rests." Though the white veteran favored reconciliation, he noted that "where the blue and the gray have met, the blues have had to go far over the line of truth to keep the peace."[22]

African American veterans refused to bow to these trends. During annual national GAR encampments, they conducted their own campfire meetings that took on the tone of civil rights rallies as they condemned lynching, denounced disfranchisement, and praised the efforts of Ida B. Wells. At the 1901 campfire gathering in Cleveland, veterans "relieved their pent up feelings with tears and shouts" as they listened to stirring speeches, including one from General O. O. Howard, who called for Congress to pass an antilynching law. Veteran Charles Douglass, a son of Frederick Douglass, addressed the campfire meeting at Rochester in 1911 and emphasized the obstacles that black soldiers had overcome in the war and the progress that had been achieved since Lincoln issued the Emancipation Proclamation. Though their ranks were thinning, black veterans celebrated the fiftieth anniversary of the Emancipation Proclamation in 1913. The commander of the John Brown GAR post in Chicago spoke at an emancipation celebration, William Murrell helped organize an event in New York, and Henry McNeal Turner penned a warm reminiscence that paid tribute to the "Immortal" Lincoln. Though recent events had made the former army chaplain embittered to the point of advocating emigration to Africa, Turner fondly recalled being in Washington on January 1, 1863, when he fought for one of the first copies of the newspaper that contained the text of the Emancipation Proclamation and ran to the White House to catch a glimpse of Lincoln. While some might prefer to forget the Emancipation Proclamation, for Turner it could only be matched by "our entrance into heaven," and he urged every African American minister to mark the anniversary by delivering a speech that reflected on the proclamation's significance.[23]

As African Americans commemorated the semicentennial anniversary of the Emancipation Proclamation, thousands of veterans from both sides gathered at Gettysburg to mark the fiftieth anniversary of the battle. To many, including President Woodrow Wilson, who addressed the assembled veterans, the event symbolized how the warring sections had resolved their differences and reunited as a nation. John H. Murphy Sr., a veteran and editor of the *Baltimore Afro-American*, looked askance at the Gettysburg reunion and all the talk of goodwill between the Blue and Gray. The South, according to Murphy, was "in the saddle" and with the notable exception of preserving slavery, southerners had accomplished everything they had fought for during the Civil War. As the Wilson administration proceeded to segregate the federal government, this was even more evident. For Murphy, the words Lincoln spoke at Gettysburg in November 1863 had become perverted. Lincoln had spoken of persevering "government of the people, by the people, for the people," yet when one looked at conditions for African Americans in the South, Murphy deemed it a government "by the WHITE people" and only for white people. Murphy and thousands of other black men had taken up Lincoln's call to bear arms, their "blood consecrated almost every battlefield," and fifty years later their blood was "crying from the ground in every Southern State." The only solution, in Murphy's view, was for the nation to live up to the words of the "immortal Lincoln."[24]

Perhaps the angry soldier in the 5th Massachusetts Cavalry was right in claiming black soldiers understood Lincoln better than anyone else, and H. Ford Douglas was correct that the war educated Lincoln. African American soldiers proved to be excellent teachers who made Lincoln a better president. In taking up his call to enlist, they made the most of the opportunity to prove themselves equal to white soldiers. They certainly convinced the man who shook hands with Alexander Augusta and became emotional upon hearing their cheers that they should be treated as equals. While Lincoln did not act as fast as some wanted, he eventually believed black soldiers should have equal pay with white soldiers, that their marriages required legal recognition so their widows and orphans could receive veterans' benefits, and he ordered retaliation if black prisoners were mistreated. Just days before his assassination he publicly advocated what he had privately recommended to Governor Hahn when he endorsed voting rights. This was the Lincoln that continued to live in the hearts and minds of black veterans as they struggled for equal rights. Rueben McCleland was a survivor of the Fort Pillow Massacre who revered the memory of Lincoln and refused to allow people to forget what he had endured. In 1939, one of the oldest surviving veterans was 104-year-old James Brown, a veteran of the 29th Connecticut who proudly kept a portrait of Lincoln in his home. The following year, the GAR held its national encampment in Springfield, Illinois. Among those in attendance were five African Americans, including one-hundred-year-old James H. Lewis and ninety-two-year-old George W. Johnson, who wanted to visit the tomb of "our beloved Father Abraham" one last time. When they tried to get something to eat at the Abraham Lincoln Hotel, they were refused service. Lewis and Johnson signed a resolution protesting their treatment that was presented to the encampment, and a member from Texas responded in a malignant-hearted fashion by claiming, "You cannot amalgamate the two races.... We don't put them on an equality with us, and we cannot do it and we will not do it." Over seventy-five years after Major Augusta had been assaulted on the train, the cause for which these men fought had not been fully won.[25]

NOTES

1. "The Late Outrage upon Surgeon Augusta, in Baltimore," *Liberator,* May 29, 1863; *Congressional Globe,* 38th Cong., 1st Sess., 553–55; "The Reception at the White House," *Evening Star,* February 24, 1864; "Negroes at the President's Levee," *Detroit Free Press,* March 4, 1864; "Negro Equality Socially," *Syracuse Daily Courier and Union,* February 15, 1864.

2. Lucius H. Chandler to Abraham Lincoln, August 1863; Lincoln to John P. Gray, September 10, 1863; Norfolk, Virginia Citizens to Lincoln, October 17, 1863, Abraham Lincoln Papers, Library of Congress; Joseph T. Wilson, *Twenty-Two Years of Freedom. An Account of the Emancipation Celebration by the Freedmen of Norfolk, Va.* (Norfolk: Thomas F. Paige, 1885), 8, 11, 13.

3. Lincoln to James C. Conkling, August 26, 1863, Lincoln Papers.

4. *Proceedings of the State Convention of Colored Men of the State of Tennessee* (Nashville: Daily Press and Times Job Office, 1865), 6.

5. Benjamin Quarles, *Lincoln and Negro* (1962; New York: Da Capo, 1991), page 3 of unpaginated foreword. For studies of African American soldiers see George W. Williams, *A History of the Negro Troops in the War of the Rebellion* (New York: Harper and Brothers, 1888); Dudley Taylor Cornish, *The Sable Arm: Black Troops in the Union Army, 1861–1865* (Lawrence: University Press of Kansas, 1956); Donald R. Shaffer, *After the Glory: The Struggles of Black Civil War Veterans* (Lawrence: University Press of Kansas, 2004); John David Smith, *Lincoln and the U.S. Colored Troops* (Carbondale: Southern Illinois University Press, 2013); Ian Michael Spurgeon, *Soldiers in the Army of Freedom: The 1st Kansas Colored, the Civil War's First African American Combat Unit* (Norman: University of Oklahoma Press, 2014); Kelly D. Mezurek, *For Their Own Cause: The 27th United States Colored Troops* (Kent, OH: Kent State University Press, 2016); and Douglas R. Egerton, *Thunder at the Gates: The Black Civil War Regiments That Redeemed America* (New York: Basic Books, 2016).

6. "Speech of H. Ford Douglass," *Liberator,* July 13, 1860. For more on Douglas and Lincoln's position on race in 1858, see Matthew D. Norman, "The Other Lincoln-Douglas Debate: The Race Issue in a Comparative Context," *Journal of the Abraham Lincoln Association* 31 (2010): 1–21.

7. Frederick Douglass, "The President and His Speeches," *Douglass' Monthly,* September 1862; "The Illinois Slave Law," *Western Citizen and Chicago Weekly Times,* March 8, 1853; "Colonization," *Galesburg Free Democrat,* February 1, 1855; Philip S. Foner and George E. Walker, eds., *Proceedings of the Black State Conventions, 1840–1865* (Philadelphia: Temple University Press, 1980), 2:54–67; "Haytien Emigration," *Galesburg Semi-Weekly Democrat,* May 11, 1859; "Colored People Moving," *Rock Island Argus and Daily Union,* August 25, 1862.

8. "Rejoicing Over the Emancipation Proclamation," *Anglo-African,* January 17, 1863; Alexander T. Augusta to Abraham Lincoln, January 7, 1863, compiled military service record, Alexander T. Augusta, surgeon, 7th US Colored Infantry, M1820, Record Group 94, National Archives, Washington, DC; H. Ford Douglas to Frederick Douglass, January 8, 1863, in *Douglass' Monthly,* Feb. 1863; John Proctor to Abraham Lincoln, April 18, 1863, Abraham Lincoln Papers, Library of Congress.

9. Luis F. Emilio, *History of the Fifty-Fourth Regiment of Massachusetts Volunteer Infantry, 1863–1865* (Boston: Boston Book, 1891), 144; G[eorge] E. S[tephens], "From the 54th Regiment Massachusetts Volunteers," *Anglo-African,* June 18, 1864.

10. Charles Sumner to Abraham Lincoln, May 20, 1863, Francis George Shaw to Lincoln, July 31, 1863, Lincoln Papers, Library of Congress; Hannah Johnson to Lincoln, July 31, 1863, Record Group 94, Entry 360, Letters Received by the Colored Troops Division, National Archives, Washington, DC; John H. Morgan et al. to Abraham Lincoln, January 16, 1864, Record Group 94, Entry 360, Letters Received by the Colored Troops Division, National Archives, Washington, DC; Joseph Barquet, "From the Fifty-Fourth Regiment Massachusetts Volunteers," *Anglo-African,* June 4, 1864; "Africano," to the Editor, *Anglo-African,* August 6, 1864; "Africano" to the Editor, *Anglo-African,* September 24, 1864.

11. Frank A. Rollin, *Life and Public Services of Martin R. Delany* (Boston: Lee and Shepard, 1883), 166–71; "Military Review," *Daily National Republican,* April 25, 1864; "The President's Visit to the Army," *National Republican,* June 24, 1864; Horace Porter, *Campaigning with Grant* (New York: Century, 1906), 219–20; "The Army of the James," *New York Daily Herald,* March 29, 1865; Williams, *A History of the Negro Troops,* 293; Alexander H. Newton, *Out of the Briars: An Autobiography and Sketch of the Twenty-Ninth Regiment Connecticut Volunteers* (Philadelphia: A.M.E. Book Concern, 1910), 65–67; "Letter from Richmond," *Christian Recorder,* April 22, 1865.

12. *Anglo-African,* May 13, 1865; "Funeral Ceremonies of Abraham Lincoln in Washington," *Christian Recorder,* April 22, 1865; "Death of the President," *Christian Recorder,* May 6, 1865; "Discourse Delivered by Rev. Geo. W. Levere," *New Orleans Tribune,* May 7, 1865.

13. "Letter from Brownsville, Texas," *Christian Recorder,* September 23, 1865; "Convention of Colored Iowa Soldiers," *Christian Recorder,* November 18, 1865; "National Convention of Colored Soldiers and Sailors," *Christian Recorder,* November 3, 1866; "Colored Soldiers' and Sailors' Convention," *Christian Recorder,* January 12, 1867.

14. Lincoln to Michael Hahn, March 13, 1864, Lincoln Papers, Library of Congress; "The Late President Lincoln on Negro Suffrage," *New York Times,* June 23, 1865; *Proceedings of the Illinois State Convention of Colored Men, Assembled at Galesburg, October 16th, 17th, and 18th.* (Chicago: Church, Goodman and Donnelley, 1867), 36; "State Convention of Colored Men," *National Anti-Slavery Standard,* October 27, 1866; "Jubilee. Ratification of the Fifteenth Amendment," *Philadelphia Inquirer,* March 31, 1871.

15. *National Memorial Day: A Record of Ceremonies over the Graves of Union Soldiers, May 29 and 30, 1869* (Washington, DC: Headquarters of the Grand Army of the Republic, 1870), 920; "At the Lincoln Statue," *Brooklyn Daily Eagle,* May 28, 1888; "Memorial Services in Brooklyn," *Sun,* May 25, 1891; "Colored Soldiers' Memorial Day," *Baltimore Sun,* June 2, 1874; "At Harmony Cemetery," *Washington Bee,* June 8, 1907. For a discussion of African American involvement in the GAR, see Barbara A. Gannon, *The Won Cause: Black and White Comradeship in the Grand Army of the Republic* (Chapel Hill: University of North Carolina Press, 2011).

16. "The Colored Veterans," *Monongahela Valley Republican*, August 19, 1880; *Twenty-Two Years of Freedom;* Philip Foner and Yuval Taylor, eds., *Frederick Douglass: Selected Speeches and Writings* (Chicago: Lawrence Hill Books, 1999), 712–24.

17. Williams, *A History of the Negro Troops*, 86, 88, 105–6, 293, 313, 319; Joseph T. Wilson, *The Black Phalanx* (Hartford, CT: American Publishing, 1887), 104, 249, 319–20, 349, 382, 384.

18. "Monument to President Lincoln," *Anglo-African*, May 13, 1865; "Monument to President Lincoln," *Anglo-African*, June 10, 1865; "Lincoln's Monument in Danger," *National Tribune*, June 4, 1885; Wilson, *Black Phalanx*, 512–14; Williams, *A History of the Negro Troops*, 23, 328–30; "Proposed Emancipation Monument," *Chicago Tribune*, July 10, 1891; *Inter Ocean*, August 7, 1891.

19. "Emancipation Day," *Messenger-Inquirer*, September 22, 1897; "South Carolina Negroes," *Austin American-Statesman*, January 2, 1901; William B. Derrick, "An Oration," *A.M.E. Church Review* 2, no. 4 (April 1886): 445–51.

20. "Celebration by the Colored Population of this City," *Illinois State Journal*, September 24, 1867; "Emancipation Day Is Observed at Dayton, O.," *Freeman*, October 1, 1910; *Horton Headlight-Commercial*, August 30, 1894; "Emancipation," *Topeka Daily Press*, September 22, 1894; "The Dawn of Freedom," *Topeka Plaindealer*, September 25, 1903; "New Albany News," *Freeman*, October 3, 1903; *Dayton Herald*, September 23, 1895; "Negro Veterans Will Head Emancipation Day Parade," *Dayton Herald*, September 8, 1910; "Colored People Celebrate Holiday with Big Street Demonstration," *Dayton Daily News*, September 23, 1912.

21. "Lincoln Day and the White Folks," *Colored American Magazine* 15, no. 3 (March 1909): 135; *Proceedings of the Twenty-Third Annual Encampment of the Department of New Jersey, Grand Army of the Republic* (Camden, NJ: Democrat Book and Job Print, 1890), 147–48; "Anniversary of Lincoln's Birthday," *Sun*, February 13, 1892; "Tributes by Veterans," *Evening Star*, February 12, 1912; "Soldiers' Home Notes, Marion, IND," *Freeman*, March 11, 1916; "Lincoln Day Honored by Negroes," *Buffalo Courier*, February 13, 1905.

22. *Services in Commemoration of the Anniversary of the One Hundredth Anniversary of the Birth of Abraham Lincoln Arranged by Union and Confederate Veterans* (Atlanta: Blue and Gray Veterans, 1909); "One View of the Negro Problem," *National Tribune*, August 5, 1909; *National Tribune*, September 27, 1900. For more on how white southerners appropriated Lincoln, see Matthew D. Norman, "'Had Mr. Lincoln Lived': Alternate Histories, Reconstruction, Race, and Memory," *Journal of the Abraham Lincoln Association* 38, no. 1 (Winter 2017): 43–69.

23. *Huntsville Gazette*, September 29, 1894; "Wipe Out Anarchy and Lynch Law," *Washington Bee*, September 21, 1901; "Camp Fire for Negro Veterans," *Democrat and Chronicle*, August 25, 1911; "Emancipation Celebration," *Chicago Defender*, September 27, 1913; "Observe Emancipation," *Indianapolis Star*, September 23, 1913; "Col. Wm. Murrell Writes," *Washington Bee*, June 21, 1913; Henry McNeal Turner, "Reminiscences of the Proclamation of Emancipation," *A.M.E. Review* 29, no. 3 (Jan. 1913): 211–14.

24. "A Government for the People," *Baltimore Afro-American*, July 5, 1913.

25. "The Fort Pillow Massacre," *Emporia Daily Republican*, September 7, 1901; "Oldest Living Vet Recalls Slavery, War," *Pittsburgh Courier*, July 4, 1939; "Men Who Fought to Preserve Union Jim Crowed at Lincoln's Home Town," *Chicago Defender*, September 21, 1940; *Journal of the Seventy-Fourth National Encampment of the Grand Army of the Republic* (Washington, DC: Government Printing Office, 1941), 110–11.

"The Colored Veteran Soldiers Should Receive the Same Tender Care"

Soldiers' Homes, Race, and the Post–Civil War Midwest

KELLY D. MEZUREK

N MAY 1912, Congressman Seaborn Roddenbery unsuccessfully proposed an amendment to the Sherwood Pension Bill, legislation that sought to increase payments to Civil War veterans and dependent survivors. With "his face flushed with anger," he proposed that pensions for black veterans cease until the federal government built a new facility for the National Home for Disabled Volunteer Soldiers (NHDVS) system that was "distinctly separate" and "maintained exclusively" for aged soldiers of "African descent." The Georgia representative, who also failed in his attempts to create an antimiscegenation constitutional amendment, demanded that black inmates should be "consolidated, removed, and domiciled in a national soldiers' home at a place separate and apart from any other such home occupied by other soldiers and veterans of the Civil War or other wars."[1] Roddenbery's plea came not from a fear of what might happen. Rather, he was reacting to the fact that African Americans, who had de jure equal rights to the benefits provided to Union veterans and their families, had been actively pursuing government-funded assistance since the end of the US Civil War.

One of those benefits included admittance into and care at state and federal domiciliary institutions. Despite the systemic racism that pervaded society during the postbellum years, the requirements for entrance into the state and federal facilities were not defined by race. The homes were open to all Union men regardless of service or color, even if in practice African Americans faced potential segregation. The inclusion of black veterans who lived in soldiers' homes, and the African American community's interactions with the facilities, expands and complicates interpretations about the diverse ways in which citizens of the United States, depending on their race, region, and status as veterans, understood and sought to use their wartime experiences. African American men who served in the US Colored Troops (USCT) or Union navy, and their communities, often cited military service as evidence of their loyalty to and support for the nation as they sought equal access to education, suffrage, public accommodations, and other civil and political rights. They especially did so when they actively claimed part of the postwar public spaces by residing in government-funded homes, participating in military ceremonies and reunions connected to the domiciliary institutions, and through visits to the facilities and from the facilities back to the communities.[2]

Although not carved from a single piece of granite or marble, soldiers' homes are monuments to the nation's military past. Who lived there, what occurred there, and how the larger citizenry interacted with the sites provides additional evidence for how people understood the US Civil War. Black veterans who resided in state and national facilities challenged narratives of reminiscence and commemoration along with the men who participated in reunions and parades, joined Grand Army of the Republic (GAR) posts, were buried in soldiers' circles and government cemeteries, and were included in the histories penned in the postwar years. Their inclusion in the soldiers' homes during the late nineteenth and early twentieth centuries attests to the visible presence of their past military service and is one example of how, as W. Fitzhugh Brundage argues, "Black veterans emerged as both participants and symbols in the struggle to determine the meaning and legacy of the Civil War."[3] As competition over the memory of the war grew more contested, the presence of African American men in government-sponsored domiciliary facilities helped make the claim for a permanent place for black Union soldiers and sailors alongside the white martial citizens who sacrificed to preserve the United States.

Almost every state and federal soldiers' home had African American residents in the late nineteenth and early twentieth centuries, but the largest number of black veterans lived in facilities located in the Midwest. The earliest black settlers came into the Old Northwest during the first years of the nineteenth century. Although they faced significant challenges and experienced overt racism, small but committed black communities persevered in rural midwestern towns before the Civil War. After their service in the Union armies and navies, most surviving soldiers returned to the Midwest. Still, this does not account for the larger percentage of black veterans in midwestern homes, as those states received the least credit for the number of black troops furnished during the Civil War. The Midwest contributed just under 12 percent of the USCT, compared to almost 20 percent from the Northeast and Mid-Atlantic states and just over 65 percent from Kentucky and the Confederate states.[4] A growing number of other African Americans, during and after the war, though, relocated to the region. Many of these emigrants were black Union soldiers and sailors whose wartime experiences (meeting African Americans from other geographic regions, gleaning knowledge from travels to unfamiliar places, and earning pay that gave them the financial ability to relocate) contributed to their willingness to move to the Midwest after their muster out of service.[5]

Many USCT and navy veterans who moved into the Midwest before the Great Migration of the early twentieth century settled in or near the established antebellum black communities. The presence of these African American veterans contributed to the shaping of a midwestern identity, one in which "race and racial thinking . . . played a crucial role in the formation and articulation of a foundational Midwestern regional consciousness." Focusing on this cultural and geographic location moves analysis away from the now outdated regional dichotomy of the North versus the South. The Midwest had a larger combination of southerners and northerners living together than any other area in the nineteenth-century United States; as a result, a variety of ideas about the meaning of freedom and citizenship (as well as the relationship between race and democracy) competed there. The experiences in the postwar Midwest are therefore an important area of analysis for African American Civil War history, one that historian Christopher Phillips concludes is a "yet unreconciled intraregional contest over the meanings and broader outcomes" of the Civil War.[6]

Black midwestern citizens realized the importance of challenging the growing Lost Cause narrative and the Unionist and reconciliationist ideologies that later dominated postwar reminiscences, histories, and commemorations. They did so despite attempts by many white midwesterners, often through violent means, to "maintain white supremacy over the long term" and relegate African Americans to a precarious second-class status. Black citizens persisted in their efforts to keep African American soldiers and sailors, and therefore the issues of slavery, emancipation, and the three constitutional amendments that came as a result of the Civil War, as part of the national narrative.[7] During the late nineteenth and early twentieth centuries, black veterans from all geographic regions in the country proudly displayed their Civil War contributions in midwestern public spaces, including the use of and interactions with state and local soldiers' homes.

Even before the last soldiers mustered out, civilians recognized the burden that returning veterans might place on families and taxpayers. When creating facilities for soldiers on furlough, organizational leaders did not turn a blind eye to the USCT and black sailors. Soldiers' Depots, also called rests, homes, or lodges, popped up along various routes followed by homeward-bound soldiers. The facilities provided meals, a place to sleep or recuperate, and often medical care. In April 1862 the Soldiers' Aid Society of Northern Ohio, a branch of the US Sanitary Commission, began operating a Depot Hospital in Cleveland. By December 1863 the women obtained enough donations to open the Cleveland Soldiers' Home. They announced their service on printed cards shared throughout the city and on a sign above the door that read, "Sick and wounded soldiers, discharged soldiers, awaiting pensions and back pay, or furloughed soldiers without money, will find lodging, a resting place and food, free of charge." They continued the service after the war ended, until the Union army had discharged almost all the midwestern troops.[8]

Over a thousand soldiers from the 102nd United States Colored Infantry (USCI), the only black regiment recruited in Michigan, stopped at the Cleveland Soldiers' Home. The regiment had mustered out of service in September 1865 while in Charleston, South Carolina; soon afterward the soldiers left for Detroit to receive their final discharge. Over a hundred sick men who needed additional care remained at the Cleveland facility until well enough to travel again. Those who survived the journey found another soldiers' rest in Detroit. In the spring of 1865 board members of the Northwest Sanitary Commission and Soldiers' Home Fair vowed to "provide for every soldier, WITHOUT DISTINCTION OF STATE OR COLOR" when they asked Chicagoans to support the North-Western Sanitary Fair, a fund-raiser to help returning troops at both the home and the Soldiers' Rest. There were also depots in the midwestern cities of Cairo, Illinois; Cincinnati and Columbus in Ohio; and Jeffersonville and New Albany in Indiana.[9]

Federal officials, under pressure to provide for the men too ill or injured to transition back to civilian life, recognized the need for government-funded institutional care. Before the guns fell silent, Congress created a federal system for incapacitated Union soldiers. In 1866 the NHDVS, originally named the National Asylum for Disabled Volunteer Soldiers, opened the Eastern Branch, in Togus, Maine. The next year the first facility to house black veterans, the Central Branch in Dayton, Ohio, accepted its first patients. Initially, political leaders intended to furnish residence only for those men who suffered from war-related wounds or disease that prevented them from supporting themselves and their families. Within two decades, however, the cumulative effects of nineteenth-century soldiering led to an increasing number of Union veterans who could no longer provide or care for themselves, so in 1884 Congress amended the requirements to allow any honorably discharged veteran to enter one of the facilities.[10]

Martial citizens held a special status and, as a result, many people believed veterans should receive treatment that recognized them as honorable protectors of the Union, not helpless members of society. To further mark their distinction, the federal government created facilities and grounds for former soldiers that resembled domestic settings rather than the institutions that provided support for the elderly or the poor. In addition to living quarters, dining halls, and hospital facilities, the branches of the NHDVS included libraries, performance halls, parks, and chapels. The men could attend classes, complete occupational training, and work for small wages. The *National Tribune* defended the expanse of amenities when editors explained to readers in 1883 that residence in one of the homes was "not a charity, but is a reward to the brave and deserving, and it is their right." By 1900 there were ten veterans' homes across the country; black veterans resided in every one of the five located in the Midwest. In addition to Dayton, the federal government opened branches in Milwaukee, Wisconsin (Northwestern Branch, 1867); Leavenworth, Kansas (Western Branch, 1885); Marion, Indiana (1888); and Danville, Illinois (1898).[11]

During the same period, under mounting pressure from the GAR, many state governments appropriated funds to build homes for needy former soldiers. Members were alarmed by the growing number of their "fellows-in-arms" who sought refuge in almshouses or found overcrowded NHDVS branches unable to accept new inmates. They often had to defend their claims to nonveteran citizens who had grown wary of the expense and who argued that such benefits created a class of men who would become apathetic, prone to immoral behavior, or unwilling to work. Despite the contested atmosphere, when the GAR advocated for veterans' rights to state-supported domiciliary care, federal pensions, and local burial funds, it included the black men who served in the USCT and Union navy.[12]

State-funded institutions offered basically the same domestic settings and services as the NHDVS branches. Once officials opened the homes, the GAR leadership shifted its focus to aiding former soldiers who needed help with the admissions process. Midwestern states that provided domiciliary care for Union veterans in the late nineteenth and early twentieth centuries include Illinois (Chicago, 1864, and Quincy, 1887); Indiana (West Lafayette, 1896); Iowa (Marshalltown, 1887); Kansas (Fort Dodge, 1890); Michigan (Grand Rapids, 1886); Minnesota (Minneapolis, 1888); Missouri (St. James, 1896); Nebraska (Burkett and Grand Island, 1888, and Milford, 1895); North Dakota (Lisbon, 1893); Ohio (Sandusky, 1888); South Dakota (Hot Springs, 1889); and Wisconsin (King and Waupaca, 1887).[13]

Historian Patrick J. Kelly argues that "the willingness of the federal government to shelter African-American veterans is testimony to the force of the martial citizenship status granted to Union veterans." But access to domiciliary care in state and federal facilities came equally from the actions of the USCT and Union navy veterans who pursued their due recognition and rewards; they did not have to be "lucky enough to live in the right Northern community" to enter one of the soldiers' homes. Yet historians have all but ignored the black men who resided in the facilities. The accounts that do include USCT and Union navy residents have downplayed the significance of their residence and the connections between African American communities and the homes. Aside from Barbara Gannon's pivotal scholarship on the GAR, almost all other works on African American Civil War veterans have overwhelmingly placed more focus on the discrimination and unequal treatment former black soldiers confronted in the postwar years.[14]

The most repeated justification for the lack of research on the experiences of black Civil War veterans who sought domiciliary care is the claim that "only two or three at any time" lived in any of the residences, or "few were admitted to national and state soldiers' homes." Estimates of how many black men lived in soldiers' homes range widely, from "around 1 percent of the residents of NHDVS homes between 1876 and 1905" to "By 1899 . . . only 2.5 percent (or 669) of the veterans assisted in the NHDVS were African-American," or "at least sixty-seven veterans from the 27th USCT . . . living in Ohio government homes. . . . This number represented 5.2 percent" of the regiment. In part, the ability to provide accurate numbers is a matter of unclear or unavailable administrative records. Not all federal documentation has been preserved, and there is no central or consistent means of researching state home records. Nevertheless, as Larry Logue, a leading Civil War veterans historian, warns, "Understanding the experience of those who lived in the homes requires looking beyond official statements."[15]

While it is misleading to claim that references to African American veterans who resided in government domiciliary care "barely appear in documents related to the homes" or in other primary records, it can be extraordinarily difficult to locate black servicemen in accessible primary sources. For example, NHDVS and most state home registers indicate the veteran's unit of service, which means that the USCT designation for soldiers in the Union army marks their race. But for former black sailors, the name of the ship they served on does not. It therefore requires extensive research to determine just how many and which African American men are included in many of the surviving records.[16]

Black veterans made the choice, sometimes with the help of family members, to enter soldiers' homes because it was a benefit earned and because they had health or financial problems that left them disabled or destitute. For many of the men, severe injuries or protracted illnesses reduced their ability to earn a self-sustainable living, already made difficult by the changing economy and population shifts that impacted African Americans more severely than other midwesterners during the postwar years. The physical and psychological turmoil, from battle wounds, extensive fatigue duty, and disease, only increased for former soldiers as they aged. The attempts, and often the failures, of Civil War veterans who tried to deal with the repercussions of their service have been well documented. These issues were magnified for black soldiers who received inferior medical treatment during the war and for those men who had once been enslaved and had to deal with the additional physical and emotional hardships wrought by lives of servitude.[17]

The same issues that qualified men for acceptance into one of the state or federal soldiers' homes could also hinder their attempts. Lack of funds to relocate or the inability to travel hampered some of the veterans, especially those who still resided in the former Confederate states. More significantly, though, the additional physical hardships of wartime service had a greater effect on black veterans, who died earlier and at a higher rate than white Union soldiers.

By 1890, close to 50 percent of all white men who soldiered in the war were still alive, while only approximately 30 percent of African Americans still survived. Although black men composed almost 10 percent of the Union forces, 20 percent of the soldiers died in service. By 1890, they made up only 2 percent of the surviving veterans. One has to one wonder how the number of black veterans in soldiers' homes could have been much higher in the late nineteenth and early twentieth centuries.[18] While black veterans suffered from physical and psychological hardships similar to those experienced by white men who served, they faced additional and often daunting challenges that continued from their prewar lives. Furthermore, racial discrimination and segregation often threatened access to their earned governmental benefits.

As the war came to an end, though, some evidence existed that black military participation might contribute to real change. Once Congress equalized soldier pay in 1864, all future federal legislation provided Civil War veteran benefits equally to all who served and received an honorable discharge, with no exclusions or differences based on race. Their shared experiences of war, as men who sacrificed for the preservation of the Union, even led some white veterans to rally "to the defense of their disabled black comrades" in the decades after the war. African American men who served with white Union soldiers and sailors also died alongside them in the state and federal homes and lie next to them in cemeteries with the same government-issued headstones. Yet life for black veterans who resided in soldiers' homes rarely lived up to the claim of president and treasurer of the Board of Managers General Benjamin Butler that domiciliary care and inmate relations would be "without thought of each other except as soldiers disabled." The belief in a brotherhood of soldiers over pervasive racial attitudes went only so far. Massachusetts senator George Frisbie Hoar received a "touching and impressive letter" in 1900 from an inmate who shared that black residents "find their life rather hard, as not finding it agreeable to the white soldiers in all cases to treat them on terms of entire equality."[19]

In addition to issues with other inmates, black men often experienced discrimination from administrators. The policies differed for each soldiers' home, often depending on the number of African American residents. Sleeping and eating areas might be segregated, and at some homes the black veterans had to use different barbers. In 1901, the new commandant at the Sandusky Soldier's and Sailors' Home in Ohio, Thomas M. Anderson, moved African Americans from their assigned integrated rooms to a separate cottage. This outraged prominent black Clevelanders, who claimed that veteran George K. Nash's acceptance of the policy was "ill-coming a patriotic Republican governor and an attempt to revive the distinctions the war was supposed to have wiped out." The well-connected African American barber George A. Myers sent a missive to Nash to find out if it was a state-sanctioned policy. Although the local newspaper reported on the new rule in July, the governor's secretary replied to Myers's October letter that the governor had "never heard such a charge made before and does not believe it is true." The gubernatorial office followed up with an investigation, and Anderson denied the charge. Myers persisted, using his contacts within the Republican Party. Senator Joseph B. Foraker, who was also a veteran and advocate of black veteran's pensions, claimed that he had just been to the Sandusky home and had spoken to a crowd that had "both colored and white soldiers and they mingled indiscriminately and there was no indication of any separation of any kind on account of color," thus refusing to confront the issue of segregated sleeping quarters.[20]

When it appeared to some of the residents in the Iowa Soldiers' Home in March 1907 that officials had started to systematically reassign all black men to one specific seating area, several veterans claimed that the facility leadership "had drawn the color line in the dining room" and "had refused to recognize them as American citizens." The men were so upset that three of the inmates threatened to refuse their meals. For the most part, administrators downplayed the event. Nicholas Swenson, who supervised Company K, or the "old men's building," declared, "If I wanted to draw a color line, I would separate the men in the rooms, and that has not been done, neither is it contemplated." Swenson claimed that the "white men would just as soon have . . . good negroes . . . as table companions as any of their own race." Some of the black veterans interviewed suggested that meals would be "more congenial" at a table with mostly African American men. "Tom" Scott acknowledged that "they do that way in other homes," possibly referring to the black residents in the NHDVS branch in Leavenworth, who reportedly asked for separate seating where they could "enjoy one another's company better." The "threatened disturbance" at the Marshalltown facility abated by the next morning. With less than a dozen African American men in the home at the time, there were few other recorded complaints from either group.[21]

In the spring of 1915, the Alpha Suffrage Club demanded an investigation into the segregation of facilities at the Illinois branch of the NHDVS. The Chicago-based organization, the first dedicated to the voting rights for black women, sought assistance from Illinois congressman Martin B. Madden, who helped black veterans and their dependents receive equal access to pensions. Madden responded to Ida B. Wells-Barnett, "I have already taken up the matter of segregation in the Danville Soldiers' Home, and I will let you know what I get from it." Three years earlier, Madden vehemently opposed Congressman Roddenbery's attempt to create "jim crow soldiers' homes throughout the country." He declared, "No men fought more bravely than the black men. . . . Thank God the close of the war brought liberty alike to the north and to the south, to the whites and to the blacks." Madden addressed domiciliary care directly when he stated that "colored veteran soldiers should receive the same tender care in his declining years that we are proud to accord to the white men. . . . We should know no color in ministering to the wants of those who gave their all in defense of the country." He also espoused his commitment to the growing federal power over citizens when he warned, "Let the news spread into every home in this broad land of the free that congress will tolerate no discrimination in the treatment of the country's veteran soldiers on account of the color of their skin."[22]

Seaborn Roddenbery, the rabid Georgia representative, was not the first to formally seek separate domiciliary facilities for aging, ill, or disabled Civil War veterans. Politicians and civic leaders had been contemplating the idea almost as soon as governmental officials approved funds for the first homes. In a December 1870 meeting of the NHDVS Board of Managers, members reported that the "new asylum at Fortress Monroe will be ready for occupancy next February, when it is proposed to transfer thence the colored inmates" from the Dayton and Milwaukee homes. The branch in Hampton, Virginia, established earlier that year, was also intended to provide a healthier climate for aging veterans who suffered from pulmonary conditions. In 1889, the Illinois Encampment of the GAR tabled a request for the US Congress to build a "colored soldiers' and sailors' home" at Chicago, instead of in Washington. And, in 1892, the GAR Department of Louisiana and Mississippi discussed seeking support from Congress to convert an abandoned marine hospital into a home for Louisiana, Texas, Arkansas, Mississippi, and Alabama "colored survivors of the war or their widows." Members believed the national organization would provide additional aid to the local GAR posts affiliated with the Louisiana facility.[23]

Even those who had demonstrated support for black veterans entered the fray. In April 1900, Senator Hoar submitted a resolution that requested the secretary of war provide the US Senate with the number of "colored or Indian soldiers, or persons partly of African or Indian descent" residing in the NHDVS. Hoar wanted to know if there were enough of "that class of old soldiers" to "warrant some separate provision," although he carefully explained that his concern was for the comfort of minority veterans. Propositions came from across the political and geographic spectrum, but in 1910 a white Union veteran focused his angst on just one region of the country. John T. Campbell of Lafayette, Indiana, warned readers of an African American newspaper that "the Southern states have persistently worked over since to undo all that their disappointing war had done against them. They are insisting on the repeal of the war amendments. They have disenfranchised the Negro. . . . They will yet pension the rebel soldiers. They will yet drive the old Union veterans out of the soldiers' homes or put their own soldiers in them." In the early twenty-first century, one historian concluded that it was "remarkable . . . that black veterans were accepted into the same homes as white soldiers at all."[24]

Despite the probability of second-class racially based treatment, black Civil War veterans and their families used government-funded domiciliary care based on their own choices and individual needs. Their presence in the homes was proof of their military service and of the rights and benefits they had earned. White inmates had daily reminders, as did visitors and the communities where the facilities were located, of African American Civil War contributions, the related issues of slavery and emancipation, and the causes for the radical changes made to the US Constitution after the conflict subsided. The daily experiences of black veterans, once admitted, followed the same path as the white men who lived in the homes. Administrators and the public required that all former Union soldiers act in such a way that demonstrated their moral and patriotic superiority. As a result, officials ran soldiers' homes like military camps, complete with uniforms and daily schedules. The men could enter and leave at their own request, but they could also be dishonorably discharged. Despite the attempts to create a homelike setting, inebriated inmates proved a vexing problem. Alcohol abuse occurred on the grounds or in nearby towns, which also enticed the men with gambling and houses of ill repute.[25]

Government domiciliary care, despite aiding invalid, aging, and unemployable veterans, was often a lonely, isolated existence; life could be quite bleak for some inmates. In part, many men believed the public focused more attention on commemorating the Union dead. Black former soldiers and sailors sometimes felt even less appreciated, as they were rarely represented in the local, state, and national statuary erected after the war. Also, some African American veterans had little contact with family members due to the expense of travel or because formerly enslaved men had been unable to reconnect with family after the war. Some residents and their families experienced shame due to their inability to care for the former soldiers. Many wished they could be taken care of elsewhere by family or friends if not by themselves. Others suffered from painful health and psychological problems. Over time the federal facilities became more like nursing homes as the nation's veteran population aged.[26] For many men, including black veterans, the national facilities would be their last home and final resting place.

Because of these challenges, black veterans and the larger African American community had conflicting thoughts about residence in state and federal homes. They believed they deserved and had the right to the special status and recognition awarded citizen soldiers. Therefore, it was important for former soldiers and sailors, if they needed or wanted them, to claim the benefits not available to others in the United States, white or black, who had not served. At the same time, citizens increased their accusations that only weak, lazy, or deceitful men sought handouts. Those who dared take government assistance might threaten the black population's hard-earned, even if uneven or partially unfulfilled, gains.[27] Most of the first African Americans to enter domiciliary care, though, most likely focused more on their personal needs than the larger political and social issues that challenged midwestern communities in the immediate postwar years.

Like other Union veterans who sought care in the newly established soldiers' homes, the men who served in the USCT and Union navy entered the facilities because they had serious disabilities related to their wartime service. Protracted illness, battle wounds, or fatigue duty injuries and exhaustion left them unable to care for themselves, or their familial situations left them without support from relatives. While the USCT participated in fewer battles than white soldiers, black men suffered from a higher rate of disease, not to mention the inferior daily sustenance and medical care.[28] Such conditions led Dewitfield Anderson to enter the Central Home in Dayton in February 1870, where he remained for the next seven years. Anderson enlisted with the 102nd USCI in Detroit and served in the regimental band. Late in the war, the New Jersey–born man suffered an attack of cerebritis (inflammation of brain tissue) that left him almost completely blind. As a result, the musician left the army with a disability discharge and soon after received a pension. Once Anderson better adjusted to his loss of sight, he requested a discharge from the NHDVS and moved to Columbus with his wife and four children.[29]

Some men sought care in a soldiers' home while married; others did so when widowed, divorced, or estranged from a spouse. Clayborne Meacham joined the 59th USCI in March 1865 and served for ten months. Although raised in Tate County, Mississippi, he joined the US Army in Tennessee and moved to Oklahoma after the war. The farmer was married several times and had three children. In 1900, at the age of fifty-four, he lived with his seven-year-old son, Edwin, in Fort Smith, Arkansas. Three years later Meacham provided the name of his daughter Mattie as his next of kin when he entered the Western Branch in Leavenworth, Kansas. Although he had married Emma Shelton in 1898, he listed his marital status as separated. Suffering from several ailments, he could no longer care for himself, and his familial contacts no longer could or would care for him.

As Meacham's monthly pension rate increased from ten to thirty-two dollars, he continued to move from place to place. In March 1905, he transferred to the Mountain Branch in Johnson City, Tennessee, where he remained until he asked for a discharge in January 1906. Four months later, he reentered the Leavenworth home. After a year, he again sought a discharge. Five weeks later, Meacham entered the Pacific Branch in Sawtelle, California, where he remained until his death on October 9, 1919. After sixteen years of moving in and out of the Midwest he returned to Arkansas, where he is buried with a government headstone at the US National Cemetery at Fort Smith.[30]

Both black and white veterans made soldiers' homes their final residence, transferred between facilities, or resided for varying lengths of time over multiple stays. They did so for a variety of often unknown reasons, mostly on their own accord. Some of the men left the institutions and never returned. Henry Modlin entered the Central Branch in October 1901. Less than three months later, the veteran of the 28th USCI returned to his own home and place of his birth in Spiceland, Indiana. Kentucky-born Junius Alexander was a man on the move. During the Civil War he served in the 81st USCI, originally the 9th Regiment Infantry, Corps d'Afrique. He mustered out as a sergeant in New

Orleans in 1866. He then reenlisted into the short-lived 39th US Infantry for black soldiers. By the end of the nineteenth century, he resided in Bloomfield, Indiana, and while there entered the NHDVS for the first time. In 1900 he was admitted to the Marion Branch, but eventually he transferred to the Milwaukee Branch and then to the Battle Mountain Sanitorium in South Dakota. He left Hot Springs in 1913 and returned to the Marion home before moving to Washington, DC, where he died on August 9, 1915. His travels began in a quest to serve in the Union army and ended with his burial in the US Soldiers' and Airmen's Home National Cemetery.[31]

The ill-fated attempt of the NHDVS Board of Managers to place all black residents in the Southern Branch in Hampton, Virginia, may have affected other inmates. John Smith, who served in the 1st Kansas Colored Infantry, spent only one week at the Northwestern Branch in Milwaukee. Smith, born into slavery in Missouri, transferred to the Southern Branch in July 1871. Still, African American men were not deterred from their quest to remain in midwestern facilities, and other formerly enslaved men continued to move into midwestern, eastern, and western homes instead of those located in the South. Abraham Trice, who served as a private in the 136th USCT and lived in Hot Springs, Arkansas, after the war, entered the Western Home in Leavenworth, Kansas, in 1910. Twelve years later he transferred to the Pacific branch near Los Angles. Benjamin Davis transferred to the Central Branch in June 1874 after one year at the Wisconsin home. Although born in Leesburg, Virginia, Davis joined the 55th Massachusetts Infantry while in Boston during the war. Unlike the Northwestern Branch, a significant number of black veterans entered and stayed in Dayton. In 1870, when the NHDVS Board of Managers discussed sending black inmates to Virginia, there were at least thirty black veterans living at the Central Branch in Ohio. Only 20 percent of these men, all born in former slave states, eventually transferred to the Hampton Branch.[32]

Midwestern soldiers' homes served as the site of intersections between the recognition and commemoration of black martial service. They also provided evidence for the African American population's claim to public spaces and activities that shaped the region's remembrances and constructed meanings of the Civil War. Veterans who lived in one of the homes where administrators practiced segregation faced painful reminders of the second-class status they had endured as members of the Union army and navy during the war, but the domiciliary facilities also allowed for geographic proximity to other black men who lived in the Midwest, an area that had a low number of African Americans per capita in the late nineteenth century. The grounds also offered protection for African Americans who might otherwise be threatened by white citizens who used intimidation and force to limit public displays, especially when the activities focused on gains specific to the black population. Those who celebrated Emancipation Day often faced challenges to their planned commemorations, but it was less of a problem for the black inmates at the Marion Branch. In September 1913 they held a successful event to honor the anniversary of Abraham Lincoln's initial proclamation. The veterans presented attendees from the town and visitors from other communities with "boutonniere flag pins and small silk flags."[33]

The black community had much interest in the "Old Soldiers" homes. Families, friends, and groups interacted with the inmates, which helped keep veterans and their wartime service part of the larger African American Civil War narrative in the late nineteenth and early twentieth centuries. During the summer of 1881 the Springfield African Methodist Episcopal (AME) Church Sunday school took a trip to the Central Branch in Dayton. The next year, members of an Urbana, Ohio, AME Church Sunday school went there for an "annual excursion." When Sandusky citizens organized and installed the Abraham Lincoln Lodge of Good Templars at the soldiers' home in 1892, they selected resident William Miles, formerly of the 12th United States Colored Heavy Artillery (USCHA), as the lodge guard. African Americans in Leavenworth "celebrated the anniversary of the signing of the emancipation proclamation by President Lincoln by having a picnic" next to the NHDVS branch in 1896. When the Indiana Grand Lodge Knights of Pythias held its eighth annual convention in 1905, they arranged for members to take a "trolley ride" to the Marion Branch. After retiring from a railway company in 1909, Madison "Matt" White, formerly of the 12th USCI, took an "extensive trip in the North." One of the Nashville veteran's stops was the soldiers' home in Dayton. A year later another Nashville resident visited the Midwest. Julia Thompson spent time at the Danville Branch, where she tended to her husband, James, during his last days. The veteran, who had served in the 16th USCI, died in July 1910 and was laid to rest in the home cemetery. And Columbus, Ohio, resident Grant Johnson traveled with Thomas Hill of the 23rd USCI when Hill entered the Marion Branch in September 1913.[34]

African American state militias also interacted with inmates at the soldiers' homes during the postwar period, demonstrating to the larger midwestern population that black men continued to actively participate in military service in local, state, and national units. In April 1880 the Columbus-based Palmer Guards and Coronet Band went as guests of the Butler Guards in Dayton to visit the Central home. Along with other black militia from Xenia and Springfield (Duquesne Blues), they attended the address of prominent African American politicians, George W. Williams and Solomon Day, who spoke to the integrated Veteran Post 5, honoring the "fifteenth anniversary of the assassination of Abraham Lincoln." In September 1881, the Ohio National Guard, 9th Battalion, from Springfield, the only "colored" troops in the state guard, visited the Dayton home. The commander, Robert R. Rudd, later announced that "the boys report a good time."[35]

Residents were free to take furlough from the state and national homes to visit their family and friends; others interacted with the black communities near the domiciliary facilities. Their activities, arrivals, and departures were often noted in the local press, which further reminded African Americans of their collective Civil War past. In March 1908, Jacob Morehead traveled from the Marion home to spend several days in Indianapolis. The elderly man, who had moved into the facility two years before, was one of the first black men to enter Union service when he enlisted in December 1862 into the 3rd Louisiana Native Guards. Also, in the city that month was Basil Vancleave, who had resided at the Marion Branch since 1900. The veteran of the 107th USCI spent twelve more years in the Indiana State Soldiers' Home before he moved to the Danville Branch. Gabriel B. Manuel, formerly of the 28th USCI, visited his daughter in Rockville, Indiana, in May 1912. He had lived in the Danville, Illinois, home since 1903.[36]

Reverend Charles Carter left the home grounds to participate in a rally, where he "preached an able sermon" as a guest at the Allen Temple AME in Marion. The veteran from the 102nd USCI transferred between the Central Branch in Dayton and the Indiana home multiple times between 1908 and 1919, with a one-month stay at the Hampton Branch in Virginia in early 1920. "Chaplain" William Miles gave the benediction at the Decatur Street Baptist Church in Sandusky, Ohio, in a May 1902 service. Before moving to the Sandusky Soldiers' and Sailors' Home, where he was a founding member of the Abraham Lincoln Lodge of Good Templars, Miles had resided in Toledo, where he had joined the integrated Ford Post 14. Members elected him chaplain in 1889, and he presided over Memorial Day services that year. In 1904 Miles returned to Lucas County in death, where he is buried in the GAR section of the North Oregon Cemetery, thus ending his role in connecting communities with veterans in domiciliary care.[37]

GAR posts affiliated with or near a soldiers' home were one of the most important ways that African American inmates demonstrated their rightful place in the NHDVS. Black men who served in the Union army or navy joined all-black and integrated posts. Their membership helped keep their roles in the war, and more importantly their martial contributions to the Union victory, visible and part of public Civil War commemorations. It also validated their status as veterans. Although the organization established rules that treated all members equally, the practice in local posts and in national events often reflected the second-class status African Americans men faced in civilian life and often in the homes. But as Barbara Gannon has convincingly demonstrated, black veterans had a recognized role in the GAR. In the Midwest they had more opportunities to join integrated posts than anywhere else in the country.[38]

This is evident in the activities connected to the posts near or established by residents in soldiers' homes. In 1886, the inmates at the Western Branch in Leavenworth, Kansas, organized Thomas Brennan Post 380. In October 1890, some of the men attended the "grand reunion and mass meeting of the surviving colored soldiers of the First and Second Kansas" regiments held in the hall of the Col. R. G. Shaw Post 208, which received its charter in 1883. One of the officers of the African American post, John Mathews, moved into the home in 1892, but the former corporal from the 83rd USCI did not transfer to the integrated Brennan Post until 1909 when the Shaw Post closed because it no longer had enough members. At least four midwestern national homes had integrated GAR posts within the same city. In addition to the Brennan Post in Leavenworth, there was the Veteran Post 5 in Dayton, Bennett Post 546 in Marion, and Lawton Post 792 in Danville. There were the same number near state homes, including Lewis Post 394 in Dodge City, Sheridan Post 452 in Marshalltown, Shepard Post 628 in Quincy, and Toland Post 695 in Sandusky. In addition to the Shaw Post in Leavenworth, at least two other communities had all-black organizations: Shaw Post 233 in Quincy and Delaney Post 615 in Dayton.[39]

Living in a midwestern soldiers' home made it possible for many black men to attend integrated veteran reunions, often connected to the GAR. Their participation reflected their recognition that they had a legitimate claim to domiciliary care and the right to commemorate their service in the Civil War. The Inter-state Reunion in Kansas City, Kansas, boasted over four thousand veterans in attendance, including members of George Taylor Post 212, an all-black GAR post from Missouri, and the integrated Brennan Post from the Western Branch of the NHDVS. In total, an estimated two hundred black veterans marched in the Grand Review on September 11, 1891. Organizers did not relegate the African Americans to the back; the former soldiers marched in the middle of the parade in front of an "estimated . . . forty thousand people." Men who lived too far away from events or lacked the financial resources to travel before they entered one of the state or national homes had more opportunities to attend national proceedings, like the gathering of ex-prisoners of war at the Central Branch for two days in June 1882.[40]

While soldiers' homes afforded African American veterans the opportunity to organize, the public often conflated the alarm over the growing disreputable aspects of government domiciliary facilities with preconceived views about black men. Citizens certainly learned about veterans who failed to live up to societal expectations that required them to demonstrate their patriotic and moral superiority. Such news threatened the status of local black communities. When William Whittaker at the Marion home opened a letter addressed to W. C. Whittaker given to him in error by the facility staff, he removed a two-dollar bill before delivering the envelope to the correct inmate. Although he initially claimed he did nothing wrong, a week after his arraignment he pleaded guilty. When the judge sentenced the elderly US navy veteran to a one-year term in the state penitentiary, the newspaper mocked Whittaker's supposed claim that he looked forward to the stay. When describing a previous imprisonment in Philadelphia Whittaker explained that they kept him in the hospital, where they treated him "pow'-ful nice."[41]

The *Sandusky Star Journal*, like many other newspapers near soldiers' homes, had a special section for news about inmates at the local facility. In January 1916 the editor printed an article on Isaac Johnson, who had served in the 15th USCI, that questioned Johnson's valor and bravery. Johnson sought a discharge from the home because "evil spirts tickled the bottoms of his feet." The story ridiculed Johnson, who had been a slave "befoh de wah." It noted that even though Johnson slept with a walking stick and a knife, nothing could ward off the evil spirits. He had "been done conjured," his pain so "unendurable" that he was forced to leave. Within three months he entered the Central Branch of the NHDVS in Dayton, where he died in August 1917 with his daughter by his side. Charles Bertrand Lewis, a midwestern journalist and satirist, represented African Americans with similar language and insinuations of inferiority. He created a series of sketches, printed in the *Detroit Free Press* and in a book, *Brother Gardner's Lime-Kiln Club*, about the meetings of a fictitious society. Lewis had his characters address the issue of black veterans and domiciliary care when Sir Isaac Walpole requested that the secretary write to Washington, DC, to "ascertain if there was a colored soldiers' home in this country; if so, where it was? If not, why had this element of the war been overlooked and uncared for?"[42]

More serious and sometimes violent stories also spread across the Midwest. Any behavior deemed inappropriate could antagonize local whites and provided those who lived near soldiers' homes with evidence that inmates were troublesome nuisances and potentially dangerous. This was particularly hazardous for black veterans, as racial violence was ever present across the Midwest. White residents unwilling to accept the changes wrought by the Civil War attacked and sometimes lynched African Americans, especially in areas such as Leavenworth, Kansas, where black men who enlisted after the Civil War lived on military posts.[43]

Jack Smith, an inmate at the Western Branch, pleaded guilty in federal court to assault. After Smith injured another resident with a razor, a local judge fined him fifty dollars and sent the veteran of the 72nd USCI to the US military prison at Leavenworth until he could pay. Alcohol and a political disagreement led to the fight between Peter Thomas and James Johnson, residents at the Michigan soldiers' home. Johnson knocked Thomas to the floor and repeatedly kicked the man. In retaliation, Thomas stabbed Johnson in the groin. Johnson, formerly of the 102nd USCI, died on March 13, 1892, and is buried in the Grand Rapids Veterans' Home Cemetery; Thomas, a New Yorker who had served in the 31st USCI, spent three years in the state prison for manslaughter. In January 1916, Isaac N. Williams, a black Spanish-American War veteran, took the life of fellow Dayton Branch inmate Ennis McGuffin, who had served as a sergeant in the 114th USCI during the Civil War and then in the 9th US Cavalry during the Indian Wars. Williams claimed that he had acted in self-defense when he cut the older man's throat.[44] These actions threatened the black community's tenuous access to the rights promised by the Fourteenth and Fifteenth Amendments born in part out of African American Civil War martial contributions.

However, these were not the only stories about black veterans who resided in state and federal homes. While it is true that by the early twentieth century too many accounts came from "white-authored portrayals of African Americans in the Midwest that trivialized slavery" or focused on issues that reinforced preconceived notions that black men suffered from racial inferiority or detrimental character, other narratives were available to the larger midwestern populations, white and black. Sometimes they came from white Union veterans, who, as M. Keith Harris argues in *Across the Bloody Chasm: The Culture of Commemoration among Civil War Veterans,* did not all sentimentalize, sanitize, or ignore slavery, emancipation, or the role of their black comrades.[45] Newspaper editors across the Midwest printed these types of accounts as well. White midwesterners, especially those who lived near one of the national or state homes, therefore encountered or heard about black veterans during the postwar years. Combined with GAR activities and community interactions, the recognition of the black veterans who lived in domiciliary facilities challenged narratives that shifted the focus away from the martial contributions of African American men and the war's connections to enslavement and its abolition.

In a 1905 feature, "In The Cheerful City of Peace: How Battle-Scarred Inmates of the Marion Soldiers' Home . . . Spend Their Declining Days . . . ," under a section entitled "The Good Gray Ghosts," the author included the photograph and story of the 104-year-old African American veteran Edward Dorsey. The oldest man in the home, he "brims with anecdotes of slavery days and stories of his glory-winning in the uniform he loves." At the age of fifty-four, Dorsey had enlisted as a corporal in the 123rd USCI at Camp Nelson, Kentucky. O. W. Grimes presented proof of his ownership of Dorsey and then signed a pledge of his own loyalty to the Union. Another black inmate, who had just died, made the feature, although left unnamed. "Within the last month the last shredded raveling of an old-time romance of two worlds was buried with the body of a colored member. . . . What mystery, what lineage, what undiscovered passage of racial history was wrapped in the silence of the sick man no one knew."[46]

Between 1891 and 1906, newspapers across the Midwest shared the story of Cyrus Greenleaf, a resident in the Illinois Soldiers' and Sailors' home who had served in the 61st USCI. Most focused on his age, "anywhere between 109 and 128" years, but many of the editors also shared the experiences of his long eventful life. Born enslaved in North Carolina, "Uncle Cyrus" told how he had been "sold and resold a number of times," that his parents had been born in Africa, and that when a child he had the "proud honor of having held" George Washington's "horse for a few moments." Greenleaf claimed to have served in the Mexican War, and when the Civil War broke out, at age sixty-six joined the Union army in Tennessee, where he had been taken by his most recent owner. Although the veracity of his stories was questioned, the reports lauded his hardworking, God-fearing, and honorable status as a US veteran.[47]

Several Indiana newspapers recounted Mansfield Smith's harrowing experience with the Ku Klux Klan in Tennessee after the war, in which he had the "sensation of having a rope tied about his neck." The veteran escaped by lying; he swore that he had not served in the Union army, his supposed crime, and then turned over the only money he had, ten dollars. The article concluded with the Marion Branch inmate's background, explaining that he had been "born a slave . . . determined to run away." He and his mother went to Norfolk, where he joined the 2nd USCI. "He never saw his mother after the day of his enlistment, learning later that she died at Fortress Monroe."[48]

A story out of Carlinville, Illinois, began with the announcement that Martin Taylor had moved to the "Quincy Soldiers' Home" in August 1916. Although the writer left Taylor's experiences as a Union soldier out of the news report, his role in the Civil War and the centrality of slavery were clear. The black veteran garnered attention because "the faithful Colored man" had taken care of former governor, senator, and 1896 candidate for president John H. Palmer, who had become ill during the war while leading the 14th Illinois Volunteer Infantry. Despite his later service in the 3rd USCHA, Taylor is identified as Palmer's "body servant."

The focus of the article is on how Palmer defied state black laws and brought Taylor home with him while on leave. When the brigadier general returned to duty, Taylor remained behind and worked as a servant to Palmer's family. This angered the local community, and "one night a party of horsemen was organized to mob the lad." The newspaper claimed that the incident inspired Abraham Lincoln's secretary, John Hay, to compose his postwar poem "Banty Tim." Although Palmer's daughter thwarted the kidnapping, "a patriotic Copperhead gave information to the Grand Jury and had the General indicted for the offense of bringing a free negro into the State of Illinois."

Palmer, home again in mid-October 1864, gave a speech in Springfield. He chastised the man who offered evidence against him, remarking that the Democrat had changed tack after being drafted. Palmer claimed that "the first person to whom" the "meddlesome copperhead" asked "to go as a substitute for him was the General's servant." Two weeks earlier, Martin Taylor had enlisted in Springfield—as a substitute for Jacob Frey Davis of Woodford County.

There is no doubt that the intended hero of the 1916 article is James M. Palmer, who prevailed when "force was met with force and slavery in Illinois was driven forth forever." Yet in death, Taylor is remembered as a soldier, not as a formerly enslaved man from Missouri or a general's servant. He is buried in the Carlinville City Cemetery with a government headstone that reads: "Martin Taylor, Illinois, PVT 3 US CLD HV ARTY, May 18, 1842–Aug 21, 1917."[49]

Newspapers shared similar accounts of black veterans with less sensational lives as well. When Martin Hammonds died in 1907, the *Quincy Daily Herald* recognized his military valor with the headline "Old Colored Veteran . . . Succumbs to Wound Received in War." The Missouri-born man, who joined the 29th USCI and was injured on Cemetery Hill during the Battle of the Crater on July 30, 1864, was laid to rest in the "Soldiers' Home cemetery." Southern-born Richard Elliott joined the Union army as a substitute for an Illinois farmer. After his regiment mustered out in Kentucky at the end of the war, he settled in Iowa, and in 1908 he entered the soldiers' home in Marshalltown. When he died in 1913, the *Daily Gate City* reported that Elliott was a "well known old colored citizen of Keokuk, a veteran of the civil war." The *Evening Times-Republican* shared that the ninety-four-year-old had "spent his boyhood and the years of his young manhood as a slave" before joining the 13th USCHA. He is buried with a government headstone in the Iowa Veterans Home Cemetery. The shared stories of the black men, like Hammonds and Elliott, who were recognized along with thousands of other Civil War soldiers who went to their final resting place in the late nineteenth and early twentieth centuries further challenged the multitude of adverse narratives shared throughout the Midwest and the nation.[50]

The recognition and benefits earned by veterans of the USCT and the Union navy were extended to their wives, widows, and children who could seek residence in some of the midwestern state homes. This contrasted with the NHDVS, which considered the issue only until 1866, when board members decided that the care of soldiers' family members fell under the auspices of local communities. But the GAR and its auxiliary, the Women's Relief Corps, pushed for state governments to provide additional assistance to veterans' families. The Wisconsin Veterans' Home in Waupaca was the first to admit women, and the Kansas State Soldiers' Home in Fort Dodge was the first to provide cottages for families. Administrators at the Iowa Soldiers' Home began to accept women in 1893, as did the Indiana State Soldiers' Home in 1896. GAR members in Illinois pressed for the Quincy facility to include wives when it opened in 1887; instead the state opened a separate home for women in Wilmington. In 1902 Illinois veterans continued to pressure state leaders to follow the example set in Indiana. Supporters declared, "It seems hard that where a man and his wife have lived together all their lives they should, when disabled, be compelled to separate." The next year, state legislatures changed the residency requirements to allow wives, if they had married a veteran before January 1, 1900, to join their husbands. But once the former soldier died, women who wanted to continue to live in state-sponsored domiciliary care had to move to the Soldiers' Widows Home in Wilmington. An attempt by Michigan veterans failed to convince legislatores in their state to allow the men and women to live together in Grand Rapids, but in 1894 officials had a separate building erected on the grounds for wives and widows.[51]

Sarah Clark moved into a cottage at the Kansas State Soldiers' Home with her husband and daughter sometime before 1900. Edmond Clark lived in Cheneyville, Louisiana, when the Civil War broke out, served in the 70th USCI, and later moved to Kansas. They were the only black residents at the facility in 1900. That same year, two African American women lived in the Indiana State Soldiers' Home: Clara Douglas, who lived with her husband of eighteen years, George, formerly of the 29th USCI, and Mary Carmichael, the widow of John Carmichael. Alone and with only a survivor's pension, John's service with the 28th USCI provided Mary access to state-sponsored care. In 1914, Martha Pepper moved into the Illinois Soldiers' and Sailors' Home. Her husband, Edmond, had been a sergeant in the 65th USCI. They married in 1890, after Martha's first husband died. After Edmond's death in 1896, she worked full time as a house cleaner and cook. For a time, Pepper had the assistance of her son and his family, who lived with her in a home that she owned in Quincy. He was the only child of eleven from her first marriage that still survived. Although the widow received a pension based on Edmond's service, by 1914 she no longer had familial support and could no longer care for herself.

Martha Pepper utilized her widow's benefits obtained through her husband's Civil War military service to obtain domiciliary care during the last decade of her life.[52]

Although African Americans made up over 5 percent of the population at the Illinois Soldiers' and Sailors' Home between 1887 and 1916, Martha Pepper was one of only a small number of black women who entered the facility. Other midwestern homes also housed only a few African American wives and widows. In part it was because so many of the black veterans were widowers. It also could have been because many of the homes, like the NHDVS, had waiting lists in the late nineteenth century, and African American women found themselves passed over for white widows. But if the women who became inmates are any indication, even with their husband's pensions, they desperately needed assistance. Like Martha Pepper, few had family who could help them. By 1900, Sarah Clark in Kansas had outlived twelve of her thirteen children; in Indiana, none of Mary Carmichael's five progeny survived. In 1910, twelve of the fourteen black women who resided at the Indiana State Soldiers' Home had borne children. Only nine of the thirty-nine offspring were still alive.[53]

Even after death, wives and widows of black veterans still might share the benefits of their husbands' service. When Martha Pepper died at the soldiers' home, officials buried her near Edmond in the Illinois Veterans' Home Cemetery in Quincy. In April 1909, editors of the *Evening Times Republican* printed notice of Catherine Conner's death at the Iowa Soldiers' Home. Her husband, Isaac, who had served in the 29th USCI, died only the year before. Catherine's funeral was held at the facility, and she is buried in the grave next to Isaac's in the Iowa Veterans' Cemetery. At least two of the couples who resided in the West Lafayette home in 1910 were later laid to rest together in the Indiana Soldiers' Home Cemetery, Clara and George W. Douglas and Evaline and Eli Outland, a veteran of the 28th USCI.[54]

Like Douglas and Outland, some black women buried in military cemeteries have headstones that designate their marital connection to Civil War veterans, even when they are buried in different locations than their husbands. Queen Givens, age fifty-seven, died at the Indiana home in 1915. From Chicago, she moved to the Hoosier State when her husband, Ambrose Gordon Givens, entered the NHDVS in Marion. He had served in the 13th USCHA, and after the war he joined the 24th US Infantry and went to Texas. Ambrose lived in both the Danville Branch, between 1902 and 1906 and again from 1927 to 1929, and the Marion Branch, from 1908 to 1909. Queen Givens is buried in the Indiana Soldiers' Home Cemetery; Ambrose survived his wife by almost fifteen years and is buried in Danville National Cemetery.[55]

It is in the burial plots with government headstones at veterans' homes, national cemeteries, and local soldiers' circles where the black veterans make their final and most enduring stand. Most of the men died with the belief, or at least the hope, that the "promissory note" owed to them by the government and the white populace had value; the many printed death notices indicated that at least they were recognized for their service. A Fort Wayne correspondent reported to the *Indianapolis Recorder* that "Uncle Abe Williams" of the Marion Branch died in late December 1902. The Ross County, Ohio, native was injured at the battle of Honey Hill while serving in the 55th Massachusetts. He left his daughter Anna and friends in both Columbus and Fort Wayne. The paper printed another obituary when Aaron Ward, "an old veteran known as 'uncle' died" at the Indiana home. Ward, who joined the 27th USCI during the war, entered the facility in 1904 but requested a discharge after two years. A month later he returned and remained at the NHDVS until his death in April 1907. Both he and Williams are buried in the Marion National Cemetery with government headstones. The Red Oak community learned of Benjamin F. Everhart's death from an article, "Old Veteran Passes Away," in the *Iowa State Bystander*. Everhart, who had been a sergeant in the 60th USCI, resided at the Leavenworth Branch, and on June 6, 1906, was buried there with military honors. His family sent for his body, and he was reinterred in his hometown cemetery in Iowa a few days later. When Frances A. Spencer passed away in 1910 while a resident at the Iowa Soldiers' Home, the *Evening Times Republican* noted that she was "the widow of the late James Spencer, who served in Company D, Thirteenth Colored Infantry." They had moved to Grinnell, Iowa, sometime before 1880; James died there in 1887 and is buried in the GAR section of the Hazelwood Cemetery with a government headstone.[56]

Although black-owned newspapers printed the obituaries of African American veterans and their wives, white newspaper editors who covered the communities where soldiers' homes were located (and the hometowns of deceased veterans) collectively printed more death notices. These midwestern purveyors of information, the main source of news for late nineteenth- and early twentieth-century US citizens, may have held reconciliationist or Unionist beliefs. But their decision to draw attention to the loss of an "old colored soldier," especially when they included specific information on the black man's service or life before the war, provides evidence that the emancipationist view had strong roots in many midwestern communities. Furthermore, the inclusion of stories on black Union army and navy veterans in African American newspapers provides evidence that the Civil War military role continued to hold more importance with the larger black community into the twentieth century than some have recognized.[57]

Despite the active engagement between the soldiers' homes and African American communities, midwestern black citizens faced a daunting challenge in the late nineteenth and early twentieth centuries. As people across the nation reshaped how they remembered and commemorated the Civil War in modes that suited their regional purposes, African Americans lost "the struggle over which kind of soldiers' memory would prevail in the public culture."[58] Abetted by historians, the role of black soldiers and sailors became less visible, and therefore over time less respected or appreciated by the larger populace. The segregated aspects of domiciliary care contributed to the implicit federal and state approval of a continued structural racism and helped to normalize such practices in the government and by US citizens in the decades after the Civil War. While race played a significant role in the public's dismissal of black Civil War veterans, scholars have for far too long contributed to the void. Both have helped to shape the societal systemic patterns in which late nineteenth- and early twentieth-century black voices have been ignored, dismissed, or silenced. The history of the black Civil War veterans who chose to live in state and federal solders' homes, despite the yet unfulfilled realization of equal treatment, provides a glimpse of the African American citizenry's fortitude on their long journey to obtain rights earned by martial deeds.

If we want to better understand the consequences of nineteenth-century black military service, especially how war and race impacted US society, then we need to analyze the entire spectrum of experiences. What we leave out of our local, state, and national histories most certainly hinders our current attempts to deal with racism and inequality. The recognition of what was earned and utilized by African American veterans, albeit often unequal or incomplete, will continue to occupy "only the margins of history" only if historians leave it there.[59] Black Civil War veterans who lived in the midwestern soldiers' homes, and their community's interactions with the facilities, are an important part of the African American experience in the postwar United States. Their stories challenge long-held assumptions, not only about the contributions of and benefits gained by African Americans during the Civil War and Reconstruction, but about their own role in the formation of a midwestern identity.

NOTES

1. *Pittsburgh Courier,* May 25, 1912; *Indianapolis Recorder,* November 2, 1912; *Washington Post,* January 31, 1913.

2. Patrick J. Kelly, *Creating a National Home: Building the Veterans' Welfare State, 1860–1900* (Cambridge, MA: Harvard University Press, 1997), 98, 154. Kelly refers to the homes as "open" institutions in which the veterans were encouraged to "interact with the outside world."

3. W. Fitzhugh Fleche, "Race, Memory, and Masculinity: Black Veterans Recall the Civil War," in *The War Was You and Me: Civilians in the American Civil War,* ed. Joan E. Cashin (Princeton, NJ: Princeton University Press, 2002), 137–38. See also Brundage, "'Shoulder to Shoulder as Comrades Tried': Black and White Union Veterans and Civil War Memory," *Civil War History* 51, no. 2 (June 2005): 175–201.

4. In addition to the numbers provided, almost 6,000 black men were credited to "other areas," and 5,052 of the men credited to Union nonslave-holding states came from Confederate states. See Ira Berlin, Joseph P. Reidy, and Leslie S. Rowland, eds., *Freedom: A Documentary History of Emancipation, 1861–1871,* Series II, *The Black Military Experience* (New York: Cambridge University Press, 1982), 12, and Chulhee Lee, "Military Positions and Post-Service Occupational Mobility of Union Army Veterans, 1861–1880," *Explorations in Economic History* 44 (2007): 682.

5. I define the Midwest based on Jon K. Lauck's definition in *The Lost Region: Toward a Revival of Midwestern History* (Iowa City: University of Iowa Press, 2013), 8. Lauck includes Indiana, Illinois, Iowa, Kansas, Michigan, Minnesota, Missouri, Nebraska, North Dakota, Ohio, South Dakota, and Wisconsin. The African American population in the Midwest grew from 69,291 in 1860 to 495,751 in 1900. See Richard Sisson, Christian Zacher, and Andrew Cayton, eds., *The American Midwest: An Interpretive Encyclopedia* (Bloomington: Indiana University Press, 2007), 200. For discussions about African American movements into the Midwest see Darrel E. Bigham, *On Jordan's Banks: Emancipation and Its Aftermath in the Ohio River Valley* (Lexington: University Press of Kentucky, 2006); Brent M. S. Campney, *This Is Not Dixie: Racist Violence in Kansas, 1861–1927* (Urbana: University of Illinois Press, 2015); Anna-Lisa Cox, *The Bone and Sinew of the Land: America's Forgotten Black Pioneers and the Struggle for Equality* (New York: Public Affairs, 2018); Christopher Robert Reed, *Black Chicago's First Century, 1833–1900* (Columbia: University of Missouri Press, 2005); Leslie A. Schwalm, *Emancipation's Diaspora: Race and Reconstruction in the Upper Middle West* (Chapel Hill: University of North Carolina Press, 2009); Matthew E. Stanley, *The Loyal West: Civil War and Reunion in Middle America* (Urbana: University of Illinois Press, 2017); and V. Jacque Voegeli, *Free but Not Equal: The Midwest and the Negro during the Civil War* (Chicago: University of Chicago Press, 1967).

6. Susan E. Gray, "Stories Written in Blood: Race and Midwestern History," in *The American Midwest: Essays on Regional History,* ed. Andrew R. L. Cayton and Susan E. Gray (Bloomington:

Indiana University Press, 2001), 124; Christopher Phillips, *The River Ran Backward: The Civil War and the Remaking of the American Middle Border* (New York: Oxford University Press, 2016), 334.

7. Campney, *This Is Not Dixie*, 208; Stanley, *The Loyal West*, 122–28; Bigham, *On Jordan's Banks*, 91; David W. Blight, *Race and Reunion: The Civil War in American Memory* (Cambridge, MA: Harvard University Press, 2001), 192–98. Blight identifies three major "visions" of competing national Civil War memory: reconciliationist, white supremacist, and emancipationist (2). Gary W. Gallagher argues that there are four "traditions": the Lost Cause, the Union cause, the Emancipation cause, and the Reconciliation cause. The Union cause includes those who remembered and commemorated the preservation of the nation. Although slavery and emancipation could be included in the Unionist ideology, the concept of African American equality was not part of the larger focus. Gallagher, *Causes Won, Lost, and Forgotten: How Hollywood and Popular Art Shape What We Know about the Civil War* (Chapel Hill: University of North Carolina Press, 2008), 2. Robert J. Cook refers to the "Unionist, emancipationist, southern, and reconciliatory" narratives that he claims were "fashioned largely by those who lived through the sectional conflict," in *Civil War Memories: Contesting the Past in the United States since 1865* (Baltimore: Johns Hopkins University Press, 2017), 4.

8. Mary Clark Brayton and Ellen F. Terry, *Our Acre and Its Harvest: Historical Sketch of the Soldiers' Aid Society of Northern Ohio* (Cleveland: Fairbanks, Benedict, 1869), 278–79, 293–95, 313.

9. Brayton and Terry, *Our Acre and Its Harvest*, 381–83; *Quad-City Times*, May 22, 1865; *Soldiers' Journal* (Rendezvous of Distribution, VA), June 21, 1865.

10. Kelly, *Creating a National Home*, 5, 54–55, 98, 104, 128.

11. Kelly, *Creating a National Home*, 7, 94–95, 115–20; Thomas H. Patten, "Health and Behavior in Homes for Veterans: Some Old and New Patterns," *Journal of Health and Human Behavior* 2, no. 1 (Spring 1961): 47–49; Brian Matthew Jordan, *Marching Home: Union Veterans and Their Unending Civil War* (New York: Liveright, 2014), 178–79; *National Tribune*, July 5, 1883. Eventually the number of branches grew to include a total of thirteen homes. In addition to those listed, they include Southern Branch, Hampton, Virginia 1870; Pacific Branch, Sawtelle, California, 1888; Roseburg Branch, Roseburg, Oregon, 1894; Mountain Branch, Johnson City, Tennessee, 1903; Battle Mountain Sanitarium, Hot Springs, South Dakota, 1907; Bath Branch, Bath, New York, 1929; and St. Petersburg Home, St. Petersburg, Florida, 1930. "Branches of the National Home for Disabled Volunteer Soldiers," *Prologue Magazine* 36, no. 1 (Spring 2004), n.p.

12. Stuart McConnell, *Glorious Contentment: The Grand Army of the Republic, 1865–1900* (Chapel Hill: University of North Carolina Press, 1992), 142–43; Andre Fleche, "'Shoulder to Shoulder as Comrades Tried': Black and White Union Veterans and Civil War Memory," *Civil War History* 51, no. 2 (May 2005): 177; Jordan, *Marching Home*, 169, 182–83. Both Caroline E. Janney and Andre Fleche argue that most white northern veteran groups did not celebrate a reconciliationist ethos based on race and that white former soldiers' references to emancipation in writings and speeches increased in the late nineteenth century. Janney, *Remembering the Civil War: Reunion and Limits of Reconstruction* (Chapel Hill: University of North Carolina Press, 2013), 230–31, 340n43, 374n74; Fleche, "Shoulder to Shoulder as Comrades Tried," 177–81.

13. McConnell, *Glorious Contentment*,129; "US Military Old Soldiers Home Records," *Family Search*, Research Wiki. For a description of a state home see Henry Howe, *Historical Collections of Ohio in Two Volumes: An Encyclopedia of the State* (Norwalk, OH: Laning, 1888), 2:286.

14. Kelly, *Creating a National Home,* 99; Blight, *Race and Reunion,* 195; Barbara A. Gannon, *The Won Cause: Black and White Comradeship in the Grand Army of the Republic* (Chapel Hill: University of North Carolina Press, 2011). In addition to Gannon, see Fleche, "Shoulder to Shoulder as Comrades Tried." The importance of the history of discrimination and the unequal treatment of African Americans in the post–Civil War era cannot be overstated. Over the last several decades historians have made significant contributions to those areas and have rightly helped to place the story of the USCT and black sailors on preserved battlefields, incorporated black men and women into historical site and museum interpretations, challenged the Lost Cause historiography, placed slavery at the center of historical causation, and have contributed to difficult discussions about Confederate flags and monuments.

15. James Marten, "Exempt from the Ordinary Rules of Life," in *The Civil War Veteran,* ed. Larry M. Logue and Michael Barton (New York: New York University Press, 2007), 120; James Marten, *Sing Not War: The Lives of Union and Confederate Veterans in Gilded Age America* (Chapel Hill: University of North Carolina Press, 2011), 3; Donald R. Shaffer, *After the Glory: The Struggles of Black Civil War Veterans* (Lawrence: University Press of Kansas, 2004), 137, 239n50; Kelly, *Creating a National Home,* 99; Kelly D. Mezurek, *For Their Own Cause: The 27th United States Colored Troops* (Kent, OH: Kent State University Press, 2016), 232–33; Larry M. Logue, "Union Veterans and Their Government: The Effects of Public Policies on Private Lives," *Journal of Interdisciplinary History* 22, no. 3 (Winter 1992): 415.

16. Marten, *Sing Not War,* 3. Surviving NHDVS registers have been scanned from the microfilmed collections of the Records of the Department of Veterans Affairs, Record Group 15, National Archives and Records Administration, Washington, DC. They are available along with Indexes, Admissions, Applicants, Hospital Indexes, Deaths and Burials on "US National Homes for Disabled Volunteer Soldiers, 1866–1938," Ancestry (hereafter NHDVS registers).

17. Historians have also claimed that one of the reasons there were fewer black veterans in the homes was because the African American community shunned institutional care. Yet NHDVS registers and newspaper articles clearly show family interactions with the inmates and the facilities. See Shaffer, *After the Glory,* 16, 138; Kelly, *Creating a National Home,* 225n33; and Sven E. Wilson, "Prejudice and Policy: Racial Discrimination in the Union Army Disability Pension System, 1865–1906," *American Journal of Public Health* 100, no. S1, Supplement 1 (September 1, 2010): S59. For soldier health care see Margaret Humphreys, *Intensely Human: The Health of the Black Soldier in the American Civil War* (Baltimore: John Hopkins University Press, 2008). For the adjustments of the formerly enslaved, see Jim Downs, *Sick from Freedom: African-American Illness and Suffering during the Civil War and Reconstruction* (New York: Oxford University Press, 2012). By 1890 almost 75 percent of the black men who served in the USCT or Union navy resided in the former Confederate or border slave states. Brundage, "Race, Memory, and Masculinity," 138. If they were healthy enough and had the financial ability to travel, veterans who were formerly enslaved sought admittance into midwestern as well as other state and federal homes.

18. Lee, "Military Positions and Post-Service Occupational Mobility," 695; Shaffer, *After the Glory,* 16, 55–56, 137–38; Blight, *Race and Reunion,* 193–94. Between 1870 and 1900, the average white male lived to age fifty, whereas the average age for black males was just over forty years. Elizabeth A. Regosin and Donald R. Shaffer, *Voices of Emancipation: Understanding Slavery, the Civil War and Re-*

construction through the U.S. Pension Bureau Files (New York: New York University Press, 2008), 106.

19. Blight, *Race and Reunion,* 194; Fleche, "Shoulder to Shoulder as Comrades Tried," 176; Jordan, *Marching Home,* 120–22; Butler quote in Kelly, *Creating a National Home,* 98; *Congressional Record,* 56th Cong., 1st Sess., vol. 33, pt. 5: 4356. Hoar was an anti-imperialist who used his political position to support Native and African Americans.

20. Shaffer, *After the Glory,* 139; Kelly, *Creating a National Home,* 98, 148; *Sandusky Star Journal,* July 13 and November 5, 1901; Kenneth L. Kusmer, *A Ghetto Takes Shape: Black Cleveland, 1870–1930* (1976; repr., Urbana: University of Illinois Press, 1978), 122.

21. *Evening Times Republican,* March 21, 1907.

22. *Broad Ax,* March 27, 1915; Reed, *Black Chicago's First Century,* 462; *Indianapolis Recorder,* November 2, 1912.

23. *New York Herald,* December 20, 1870; Shaffer, *After the Glory,* 140; *Indianapolis Journal,* February 22, 1889; *Democrat Northwest,* August 8, 1892.

24. *Congressional Record,* 56th Cong., 1st Sess., vol. 33, pt. 5: 4356; *Broad Ax,* May 7, 1910; Shaffer, *After the Glory,* 140. The *Taney County Republican* informed readers on May 17, 1900, that the secretary of war reported there were 30 men of color in the DC home and 699 in the other facilities around the country.

25. Logue, "Union Veterans and Their Government," 414, 416–18; Kelly, *Creating a National Home,* 140–42, 154–55, 176–78; Patten, "Health and Behavior in Homes for Veterans," 50–51; Jordan, *Marching Home,* 185–88. For the process of applying and admittance to the homes, see Jordan, *Marching Home,* 176–77. For issues with alcohol, see James Marten, "Nomads in Blue: Disabled Veterans and Alcohol at the National Home," in *Disabled Veterans in History,* ed. David A. Gerber (Ann Arbor: University of Michigan Press, 2000).

26. Jordan, *Marching Home,* 177–79; James Marten, "Not a Veteran in the Poorhouse: Civil War Pensions and Soldiers Homes," in *Wars within a War: Controversy and Conflict over the American Civil War,* ed. Joan Waugh and Gary W. Gallagher (Chapel Hill: University of North Carolina Press, 2009), 211, 214. For a summary of the unsavory aspects of institutional experiences, see James Marten, "Exempt from the Ordinary Rules of Life."

27. Marten, *Sing Not War,* 190–96; Janney, *Remembering the Civil War,* 104; Marten, "Not a Veteran in the Poor House," 214–18.

28. For a perceptive discussion of disease, sustenance, and medical care experienced by many black soldiers see Humphreys, *Intensely Human.*

29. Dewitfield Anderson, Dayton, NHDVS registers; DeWitfield Anderson, 102nd USCI, "Civil War Service Records," Fold3 (hereafter CWSR); Dewittfield Anderson, Co. H, 102nd USCI, "Civil War Pension Index," Fold3; Franklin County, Ohio, "1880 United States Federal Census," Ancestry. Due to the variations in the spelling of some of the veterans' names, in the text I have used the spelling in home records; references in notes are spelled according to the source.

30. Clayborne Meachom, 59th USCI, CWSR; Oklahoma and Indian Territory, Oklahoma, "1890 Veterans Schedules," Ancestry; Case Files of Approved Veterans Who Served in the Army and Navy in the Civil War and the War with Spain, 1861–1934, Records of the Veterans Administration, Record Group 15, National Archives and Records Administration, Washington, DC, Clayborn Meacham, 59th USCI, Certificate 1,001,763; Clayborn Meacham and Emma Shelton, "Arkansas, County Mar-

riages Index, 1837–1957," Ancestry; Clayborne Meacham, Leavenworth, Johnson City, and Sawtelle, NHDVS registers; Clayborn Meacham, "U.S. National Cemetery Interment Control Forms, 1928–1962," Ancestry.

31. Henry Modlin, Dayton, NHDVS registers; *Indianapolis Recorder,* January 18, 1902; Junius Alexander, 81st USCI, CWSR; Junius Alexander, Co. F, 9th Louisiana, "Civil War Pension Index," Fold3; Junius Alexander, Marion, Milwaukee, and Hot Springs, NHDVS registers; *Evening Star,* August 10, 1915.

32. Colored John Smith, Milwaukee, NHDVS registers; John Smith, Hampton, NHDVS registers; John Smith, 79th USCI, Co. C, CWSR; Abraham Trice, Leavenworth and Sawtelle, NHDVS registers; Benjamin Davis, Milwaukee and Dayton, NHDVS registers; Benjamin Davis, 55th Massachusetts Infantry, CWSR; Montgomery County, Ohio, "1870 United States Federal Census," Ancestry; Dayton and Hampton, NHDVS registers. The 79th USCI organized originally as the 1st Kansas Colored Infantry.

33. Schwalm, *Emancipation's Diaspora,* 223–33; *Indianapolis Recorder,* September 27, 1913. For a discussion of violence in Kansas see Campney, *This Is Not Dixie.*

34. *Indianapolis Leader,* July 16, 1881, and June 24, 1882; *Sandusky Daily Register,* November 21, 1892; William Miles, "Ohio, Soldiers Grave Registration Cards," Fold3; William Miles, Ohio Soldiers and Sailors Home, Erie County, Ohio, "1890 Veterans Schedules," Ancestry; *Kansas City Daily Journal,* September 23, 1896; *Indianapolis Recorder,* July 15, 1905, and September 27, 1913; *Nashville Globe,* May 10, 1907, September 17, 1909, September 9, 1910, and September 20, 1912; Madison White, 12th USCI, CWSR; Thomas Hill, 23rd USCI, CWSR; Thomas Hill, Danville, NHDVS registers.

35. *Indianapolis Leader,* April 3 and 24, 1880, and September 24, 1881; *Cincinnati Enquirer,* April 15, 1880; *Cincinnati Daily Start,* April 13, 1880; John Hope Franklin, *George Washington Williams: A Biography* (1985; repr., Durham, NC: Duke University Press, 1998), 169–70; T. G. Steward, *Buffalo Soldiers: The Colored Regulars in the United States Army* (1904; repr., Mineola, NY: Dover, 2014), 283.

36. *Indianapolis Recorder,* March 7, 1908, and May 4, 1912; Jacob Morehead and Basil Vancleave, Marion, NHDVS registers; Jacob Moorehead, 75th USCI, CWSR; Basil VanClieve, 107th USCI, CWSR; Gabriel Manuel, 28th USCI, CWSR; Basil Vancleave and Gabriel B. Manuel, Danville, NHDVS registers. The 3rd Louisiana Native Guards was later renamed the 75th USCI.

37. *Indianapolis Recorder,* December 5, 1914; Charles Carter, Marion, Dayton, and Hampton, NHDVS registers; *Sandusky Star Journal,* May 5, 1902; *Sandusky Daily Register,* November 21, 1892; Gannon, *The Won Cause,* 218; *National Tribune,* December 15, 1892; William Miles, "Ohio, Soldiers Grave Registration Cards," Fold3.

38. Gannon, *The Won Cause,* 92.

39. "Kansas, Grand Army of the Republic Post Reports, 1880–1940," Leavenworth (National Military Home), Thomas Brennan Post 380 (1886–1926), Ancestry; *Leavenworth Times,* October 8, 1890; "Kansas, Grand Army of the Republic Post Reports, 1880–1940," Leavenworth, Col. R. G. Shaw Post 208 (1883–1909), Ancestry; John Mathews, Leavenworth, NHDVS registers; Gannon, *The Won Cause,* 202–20. The 1st Kansas Colored Infantry was later renamed the 79th USCI, and the 2nd Kansas Colored Infantry became the 83rd USCI.

40. *Barton County Democrat,* September 17, 1891; *Indianapolis Leader,* June 24, 1882.

41. *Indianapolis Journal,* November 24 and 29, part one, 1903; William Whittaker (no. 2), Marion, NHDVS registers.

42. *Sandusky Star Journal,* January 11, 1916; Isaac Johnson, Dayton, NHDVS registers; Charles Bertrand Lewis ("M. Quad"), *House of Beadle and Adams Online,* part IV, The Authors and Their Novels; *Sunday Leader,* February 14, 1886.

43. Campney, *This Is Not Dixie,* 26, 30, 33–34, 53, 61–62, 121; Brundage, "Race, Memory, and Masculinity," 139.

44. *Topeka State Journal,* April 10, 1901; Jack Smith, Leavenworth, NHDVS registers; *Grand Rapids Herald,* March 8, April 1, 2, and 5, 1892; *Herald Advance,* March 18, 1892; State Soldiers Home, Kent County, Michigan, "1890 Veterans Schedules," Ancestry; James Johnson, March 13, 1892, Grand Rapids, Michigan, "Headstones Provided for Deceased Union Civil War Veterans, 1861–1904," Ancestry; *Dayton Herald,* March 11, 1916; Isaac N. Williams and Ennis McGuffin, Dayton, NHDVS registers.

45. Schwalm, *Emancipation's Diaspora,* 219; M. Keith Harris, *Across the Bloody Chasm: The Culture of Commemoration among Civil War Veterans* (Baton Rouge: Louisiana State University Press, 2014), 6, 7, 13, 14, 92–96, 112–13; Janney, *Remembering the Civil War,* 104–5.

46. *Indianapolis Morning Star,* May 5, 1905; Edward alias Ned Dorsey, Marion, NHDVS registers; Ned Dorsey, 123rd USCI, CWSR.

47. *Times Herald,* July 8, 1891; *Appleton Post,* July 9, 1891; *Daily Times,* March 29, 1905; *Rock Island Argus,* March 29, 1905; *Jasper Weekly Courier,* March 31, 1905; *Potos Journal,* March 29, 1905; *Morgan County Democrat,* March 31, 1905; *Iron County Register,* March 30, 1905; *Quincy Daily Journal,* February 20, 1901; *Quincy Weekly Whig,* February 7, 1901; *Quincy Daily Whig,* March 31, 1901; *Quincy Daily Herald,* March 12, 1906; Cyrus Greenlee, 61st USCI, CWSR. Although it was common for men to give an inaccurate number, either because they did not know their actual age or they wanted to seem younger or older, Greenleaf's enlistment papers state that his age at muster in was twenty-nine years, much different than his claims later in life.

48. *Richmond Palladium and Sun-Telegram,* November 20, 1911; *Indianapolis News,* November 17, 1911.

49. *Broad Ax,* August 5, 1916; *New York Times,* September 26, 1900; Martin Taylor, 3rd USCHA, CWSR; Jessie Palmer Weber, "Editorial," *Journal of the Illinois State Historical Society* 10, no. 3 (October 1917): 441; *Alton Telegraph,* October 21, 1864; Martin Taylor, August 21, 1917, City Cemetery, Carlinville, Illinois, "US, Headstone Applications for Military Veterans, 1925–1963," Ancestry; Martin Taylor, Carlinville City Cemetery, *Find A Grave.* The August 1916 article mistitled the poem "Banty Jim." Indictments were brought against Palmer in both Illinois and Kentucky.

50. *Quincy Daily Herald,* January 25, 1907; Martin Hammons, 29th USCI, CWSR; Martin Hammond/Hammonds, Sunset Cemetery, *Find A Grave;* Richard Elliott, 13th USCHA, CWSR; *Daily Gate City,* February 2, 1913; *Evening Times-Republican,* February 1, 1913; Richard Elliott, Iowa Veterans Home Cemetery, *Find A Grave.*

51. Kelly, *Creating a National Home,* 99–100; Jordan, *Marching Home,* 183; McConnell, *Glorious Contentment,* 143; Judith Gladys Cetina, "A History of Veteran's Homes in the United States, 1811–1930" (PhD diss., Case Western Reserve University, 1977), 227–34; *Report of the Commissioners of the Iowa Soldiers' Home* (Des Moines: G. H. Ragsdale, 1894), 3–5; *Decatur Herald,* September 5, 1902; *Moline Dispatch,* January 17, 1903.

52. Ford County, Kansas, "1900 United States Federal Census," Ancestry; Edmond Clark, 70th USCI, CWSR; Tippecanoe County, Indiana, "1900 United States Federal Census," Ancestry; George

Douglass, 29th USCI, CWSR; John Carmichael, 28th USCI, CWSR; Edmond Pepper, 65th USCI, CWSR; Martha Pepper, "Soldiers and Sailors Home Residents from Adams County Illinois," *Adams County IL Gen Web;* Mrs. Martha Marble and Edmon Pepper, "Illinois, Compiled Marriages, 1851–1900," Ancestry; Adams County, Illinois, "1900 United States Federal Census," Ancestry; Edmund Pepper, Co. G, 65th USCI, "Civil War Pension Index," Fold3.

53. Jordan, *Marching Home,* 182; *Palatine Enterprise,* January 18, 1907; *Fort Wayne News,* December 20, 1912; Ford County, Kansas, "1900 United States Federal Census," Ancestry; Tippecanoe County, Indiana, "1900 United States Federal Census," Ancestry; Tippecanoe County, Indiana, "1910 United States Federal Census," Ancestry. A few of the African American men in the Illinois Soldiers' and Sailors' Home were veterans of the Spanish American War. Adams County, Illinois, "1900 United States Federal Census," Ancestry; Adams County, Illinois, "1910 United States Federal Census," Ancestry.

54. Martha Pepper, Sunset Cemetery, *Find a Grave;* Edmond Pepper, Sunset Cemetery, *Find A Grave; Evening Times Republican,* April 21, 1909; Isaac Conner, Co. H, 29th USCI, "Civil War Pension Index," Fold3; Catharine Conner, Iowa Veterans Home Cemetery, *Find A Grave;* Isaac Conner, Iowa Veterans Home Cemetery, *Find A Grave;* Clara R. Higgins Douglas, Indiana Soldiers' Home Cemetery, *Find A Grave;* George W. Douglas, Indiana Soldiers' Home Cemetery, *Find A Grave;* Evaline Outland, Indiana Soldiers' Home Cemetery, *Find A Grave;* Eli Outland, Indiana Soldiers' Home Cemetery, *Find A Grave.*

55. Queen Givins, Indiana Soldiers' Home Cemetery, *Find A Grave;* Ambrose Givens, Marion and Danville, NHDVS registers; Ambrose Gordon Givens, Danville National Cemetery, *Find A Grave.*

56. "Promissory note" is from Martin Luther King Jr.'s "I Have a Dream" speech on the Lincoln Memorial steps in Washington, DC, on August 28, 1963. *Indianapolis Recorder,* January 17, 1903, and April 13, 1907; Abner A. Williams, Marion, NHDVS registers; Abner A. Williams, 55th Massachusetts Infantry, CWSR; Aaron Ward, Marion, NHDVS registers; Aaron Ward, 27th USCI, CWSR; Aaron Ward, Marion National Cemetery, *Find A Grave;* Abner A. Williams, Marion National Cemetery, *Find A Grave; Iowa State Bystander,* July 6, 1906; Benjamin F. Everheart, 60th USCI, CWSR; Leavenworth County, Kansas, "1900 United States Federal Census," Ancestry; *Evening Times Republican,* December 8, 1910; James Spencer, 13th USCHA, CWSR; Poweshiek County, Iowa, "1880 United States Federal Census," Ancestry; James Spencer, Hazelwood Cemetery, *Find A Grave;* James Spencer, March 21, 1887, Grinnell, Iowa, "Headstones Provided for Deceased Union Civil War Veterans, 1861–1904," Ancestry. Spencer served in the 13th USCHA, not the 13th USCI.

57. See for example, John A. Casey Jr., who argues that the African American communities and their leadership found little value in the meaning of Civil War veterans by the end of the nineteenth century. Casey, *New Men: Reconstructing the Image of the Veteran in Late-Nineteenth Century American Literature and Culture* (New York: Fordham University Press, 2015).

58. Blight, *Race and Reunion,* 198.

59. Blight, *Race and Reunion,* 192.

Lost to the Lost Cause

Arkansas's Union Veterans

REBECCA HOWARD

THE 1ST ARKANSAS Cavalry of the US Army was organized beginning in June 1862, in Cassville, Missouri, a town on the physical border between North and South but in a region where that divide was much less defined.[1] That the first of the Arkansas units was formed in a liminal space is apt. Starting with their time in uniform, later as they claimed their status as Union veterans, and even as they passed into memory, these Arkansas men were always caught between, until the ambiguity of their very existence necessitated they be erased. During the war, suspicious northern officers knew some enlisted out of patriotism but others out of desperation, fear, or pragmatism. As soldiers, they served almost exclusively in Arkansas, the very ground on which they stood, making them simultaneously loyal and disloyal, depending on the affiliation of the observer. After the war, Arkansas's Union men expected their patriotism and sacrifice to be rewarded, only to see most of the state's government and the leadership of the newly formed Republican Party land in the hands of former northern officers. By the 1880s and 1890s, however, it seemed Arkansas's Union veterans solidified their visibility and influence. They settled into a functional, if not necessarily enthusiastic, relationship with their comrades from the North, received pensions for their service, and supported the Republican Party. They also wore proudly their status as US veterans and participated in public events wearing their Grand Army badges and regalia. As the years and decades wore on, though, the Lost Cause myth's reluctance to recognize internal dissent in the Confederate South led to their erasure from the historical narrative. That said, they did not surrender without a fight.[2]

Approximately ten thousand men served in the Arkansas units of the US Army during the Civil War.[3] Under Colonel Marcus La Rue Harrison, the

1st Arkansas Cavalry was originally organized in Missouri, but many Arkansas men enlisted later, as Union troops haltingly progressed across the state. Arkansas is divided into distinct regions. Along a rough diagonal from southwest to northeast, the state is split between the upcountry of the Ozark and Ouachita Mountains to the north and west and delta cotton country to the south and east. Fayetteville anchored the northwest corner, and, in 1860, was seat of the county with the largest white population in the state.[4] The mountains held the typical upcountry South mix of yeoman farmers and a few old Whigs. In the decade before the war, as the population of the state doubled, power shifted to the cotton-rich delta counties along the Mississippi River. The northern counties still held enough control to contest secession until Lincoln's call for troops forced the state off the fence.[5] Union forces arrived almost ten months later, and, on March 8, 1862, defeated rebels at the Battle of Pea Ridge, less than three miles south of the Missouri border and less than thirty miles east of the border with Indian Territory.[6] With this toehold gained, Union troops spent the next three years attempting to quell the state and recruiting loyal men to their ranks.

In Arkansas, no federal African American units organized until the location of Union troops, political sensibilities in Washington, DC, and the sheer numbers of self-freed refugees forced the issue. This occurred in mid-1863, with the first black units formed at Helena, on the Mississippi River.[7] However, some African American Arkansans went north to enlist in the 1st Kansas Colored Infantry. The origin of the unit along the Kansas/Missouri border, roughly 150 miles north of Fayetteville, makes it possible there were northwest Arkansas fugitive slaves in its ranks. Organized at Fort Scott, Kansas, in August 1862, the 1st Kansas sparked controversy and was not officially recognized for five months. Mustered into service in January 1863, it was later redesignated as the 79th United States Colored Infantry (New).[8] Tantalizingly, there were a handful of men in the unit with surnames in common with Arkansas slaveholders, most notably a group of men with the surname Bean, who listed their birthplace as "Cherokee Nation."[9] Given the extensive history of the slaveholding Bean family in the northwest Arkansas / Cherokee Nation region, the men had some connection to northwest Arkansas, whether or not they were enslaved there in 1860.[10] Some men, like their white counterparts, had to wait until federal troops drew closer. Ran Maxey, enslaved in Crawford County at the start of the war, enlisted with the 2nd Kansas when they arrived in Fort Smith, on the western border of the state, from Fort Gibson in Indian Territory. "At the beginning of the rebellion," he remembered in 1871, "I sympathized with the Union cause, because I thought they was my friends, and if anybody would take me out of bondage, they would."[11]

Federal troops maintained an unsteady occupation of the Ozark and Ouachita Mountains for most of the war, controlled Little Rock and the paths to the Mississippi River, and destabilized the Confederate rebellion in the southern portions of Arkansas. Whether white or black, Arkansas's Union soldiers served mostly inside the state. The 1st and 2nd Arkansas Cavalries and 1st and 2nd Arkansas Infantries barely left the Ozarks. Poorly trained and inexperienced when it came to pitched battle, Arkansas recruits did not acquit themselves well in formal engagements. Their strength, and utility to the US military, however, lay in their knowledge of the rough and poorly mapped physical terrain. In addition, as the Arkansas Ozarks descended into guerrilla war in 1863, the Arkansas soldiers' familiarity with neighbors who remained affiliated with the Confederate cause became invaluable. A man captured in northwest Arkansas by local guerrilla leader Tuck Smith (and the father of two Union soldiers) testified after the war, "My Boys were on the fight and the Rebels knowd that if I was killed some of their old men would have to answer for it, for the last time I was a prisoner my boys sent the Rebels word that if I was killed certain old rebels in the country would go under the sod certain."[12] The war was personal for Arkansas's fighting men.

Caught between oaths, obligations to family, and the dawning reality of a war more brutal and protracted than expected, many members of the US Arkansas units were intimately familiar with who was in the Confederate Army because many of them had recently left it. Elisha McGinnis of Madison County in the northwest corner of the state, for example, enlisted with the Confederate army in December 1861. He signed up for a year.[13] During that time, the Confederate army lost the battle of Pea Ridge, retreated to Fort Smith, burned Fayetteville, and left his widowed mother and younger siblings to the whims of Union occupation and general lawlessness. When his year of service to the Confederate army ended, he did not reenlist. He departed the army at Fort Smith and a few days later enlisted with the Union army at Fayetteville, just in time to fight his former comrades at the Battle of Prairie Grove.[14] By the end of the war, at least 50 percent of white men serving in the federal Arkansas units had previous Confederate service.[15] The personal knowledge and experience Arkansas men brought to the table, no matter how they acquired it, helped US military commanders and insured that the tenuous hold Union troops maintained in the region never completely broke.

At war's end, Arkansas was economically and physically devastated, as well as nearly depopulated. Arkansas's new veterans found themselves in a no-man's-land. There was no homecoming for them, no parades. In late summer 1865, as the Arkansas units were mustered out, many veterans actually left their home region, following family that had refugeed in Kansas or Missouri.[16] Of those who stayed, many in western Arkansas spent the fall and winter in for-tified post colonies created by General M. La Rue Harrison to protect local civilians—a "secure hamlet system" predating Vietnam by a century. Nothing drives home the gravity of the situation in Arkansas more than the fact that people gathered for protection on communal farms only a few miles from their own land.[17] In 1866, veterans began to return to Arkansas, especially if they or their families owned land. In contrast to the awkward homecoming their northern comrades endured as they came home to communities disconnected from their experiences, virtually everyone in Arkansas lived the war in some way, usually to a devastating degree.[18] The suspicion Arkansas's veterans expe-rienced concerned their decisions about loyalty and the opinion their neighbors might hold of them.

Veterans took an active role in rebuilding their communities and expected their wartime choices to yield political rewards as Reconstruction unfolded. Instead, the "carpetbagger" governor Brigadier General Powell Clayton pushed Arkansas veterans out of power. Clayton preferred appointing his fellow Union army comrades rather than local Arkansans. Reconstruction politics in Arkan-sas were volatile and violent.[19] Most of Arkansas's Union veterans retreated to their home communities, or, in the case of many African American veter-ans, built new ones from scratch by making land claims near one another.[20] Once resettled, they cultivated networks of veterans that backed one another as needed and ignored messy state politics in favor of leveraging their status in any way they could with the federal government.

In the first two and half decades after the war, Arkansas's Union veterans benefited from financial compensation offered by the Southern Claims Com-mission and the ever-expanding federal soldiers pension system, but not with-out scrutiny. When federal officials came to investigate claims and applications, Arkansas's veterans often found themselves caught in the sectional divide once again: fighting the same suspicions about loyalty that dogged them during their service, compounded by the postwar reality that returning to their communities necessitated interacting with former Confederates at a level some outside investigators found concerning. Ironically, investigators opposed to southerners of any stripe receiving benefits might actually side with negative testimony supplied by former Confederates to deny some Union veterans' claims. For loyal Arkansans who had stuck with the Union during the war only to see their hopes for power in the postwar period dashed, the cash payments offered by the commission were cold comfort—and late, considering that some claims were not paid until 1878—but at least it was something.

While the one-time payments from the Southern Claims Commission helped, other families received monthly compensation for the loss or disability of a family member through the federal pension system. Fulfillment of Lincoln's second inaugural vow "to care for him who shall have borne the battle and for his widow and his orphan" rested in the hands of Bureau of Pensions.[21] The bureau, which began caring for the Civil War's disabled veterans, widows, and children well before the war ended, was housed in the Department of the Interior during the lives of most Civil War veterans and their dependents. The size and scope of the bureau expanded dramatically from the beginning of the Civil War until the deaths of all those involved. Initially, pensions were granted, upon application, to men disabled during their service—for nearly any reason—and dependents, including wives, children, and mothers of men who perished during their service. Important legislation passed in 1862, 1873, 1874, and 1877 modified and expanded benefits, adjusted amounts, defined and redefined grades of disability, and gave the commissioner of pensions additional power to determine pension rates in unusual circumstances.[22] These provisions, however, applied to all veterans of service in the US Army and Navy, no matter the conflict; the Bureau of Pensions served all veterans equally. The first act that created special provisions for Civil War veterans was passed in 1879. The Arrears Act stated that pensions were payable to Civil War veterans from the date of death or disability, even if the application for pension was not filed until years later.[23] In Arkansas and across the country, this led to a surge in applications, especially among the disabled, who sought to prove that their current troubles originated during their service.

The Arrears Act transformed the pension system into a program that affected the country on a number of levels. For many people, it brought the federal government into their private lives in ways never before experienced. Widows, orphans, and injured soldiers across Arkansas, if willing to endure the application and investigation process, could receive substantial benefits. Much of this relied upon the testimony of friends and neighbors. Length of service, onset of disability, or, if the soldier was dead, marriage or paternity were easier to prove with witnesses. The testimony of witnesses on issues ranging from health details and romantic liaisons to work ethic and moral character proved useful to Elisha McGinnis, the former rebel who entered Union service just before the Battle of Prairie Grove. He served until he was discharged with a disability in the summer of 1864. He made a disability claim in 1877, which was denied, but challenged the denial in the wake of the Arrears Act. He was eventually successful—after multiple agents from the Pension Office investigated and interviewed dozens of witnesses—and received a pension in 1886.[24]

McGinnis's experience illustrates the challenges faced by many Arkansas veterans who sought compensation for wartime injuries between the end of the war and 1890, as well as the level of visibility Union veterans had in their communities. As only injuries obtained during service in the federal army were initially eligible for compensation, the Bureau of Pensions relied on the testimony of those acquainted with the soldier prior to the war to establish the timeline of his injury. This was a fairly simple prospect for northern men but more complicated in states like Arkansas, where potential witnesses often fought for the other side. Furthermore, the issue of previous Confederate service, while not officially grounds for denial of benefits, usually merited scrutiny and may have tainted the opinions of investigators. Previous service could complicate the timeline of an injury. Examiners often had their own opinions of the character of someone who switched sides. Though Arkansans were no longer burning down each other's barns, stealing livestock, or shooting at one another from behind trees, they were still perfectly willing to disparage an individual to federal officials. Many such issues come together in Elisha McGinnis's pension application. First, his discharge records from March 1864 indicated he was probably dying of "lung disease" (likely tuberculosis) and, based on the surgeon's notes, was not long for this world.[25] However, when McGinnis made his claim in 1877, he said it was for a disability of the eyes. Examiners discussed whether or not he even was the same Elisha McGinnis, as the surgeon's comments on his discharge records were so dire. In the end, as McGinnis was still with the living, they appear to have dismissed the surgeon's wartime diagnosis. Proving the onset of the vague eye disease, however, proved difficult. Agents called on a variety of both Confederate-affiliated and Union-affiliated persons. As a result, McGinnis had witnesses who changed their stories or feigned ignorance, and all had different memories. Many of them directly contradicted one another. One man indicated that McGinnis had a debilitating childhood disease, while someone else minimized this as just the usual childhood illnesses. Another person said McGinnis had perfect eyesight at enlistment, while still another remembered red, sore eyes at enlistment. Those who especially disliked McGinnis alleged his sore eyes were the result of drunkenness or venereal disease.[26]

With hard feelings from the war so obvious, the discretion of special examiners played an important role in determining whether a pension received approval. McGinnis's first examiner was strangely willing to give equal weight to Confederate testimony, and he may have had a problem with McGinnis's year spent in Confederate service. McGinnis's first claim was denied. In a letter requesting a second investigation into his pension claim, in 1884, McGinnis alleged that the special examiner was biased against him. Rather than directly challenging the character of the examiner, however, he alleged the man had been misled by "Confederate Captain Samuel G. Phillips, Samuel Lane, and Martin Fritts, all of them notoriously opposed to the Pension law or Federal soldiers, and especially to me because I had deserted the Confederate service."[27] McGinnis received a new special examiner for the second investigation into his claim. This investigator, much more thorough than the first, deposed three times as many individuals and paid careful attention to the political landscape of the community. When interviewed by the second special examiner, Phillips maintained his stance that McGinnis did not deserve a disability pension, stating, when asked by McGinnis directly about his feelings toward veterans receiving pensions, "I am willing for them to have it, if entitled."[28] The second special examiner dismissed Phillips's testimony on that point and stated in his notes, "Reputation of deponent [Phillips] good, but he is known as a man opposed to any soldiers drawing a pension, and there is no doubt in my mind but that he is prejudiced against claimant [McGinnis], because he deserted his company." Furthermore, the examiner noted the prejudices of both Lane and Fritts: "This witness [Lane] has the reputation of being bitterly opposed to Union soldiers drawing a pension" and "from his [Fritts's] manner of testifying and talking, I think his evidence ought not to have *any* [emphasis his] weight either way in the case."[29] This second investigation also included the county officials requested by McGinnis and more than ten brothers-in-arms from the 1st Arkansas Calvary. All the Union veterans deposed, many of them childhood friends or relatives, supported McGinnis's ultimately successful second claim.

Connections between veterans proved critical, as the status of Union men in a rebel state often worked against them. However, it became especially important in the wake of the passage of the act of June 27, 1890, that drastically changed pension eligibility. The real turning point for pension law, veterans, their dependents, and the country came when all the survivors of the war became eligible for pensions. Veterans needed only prove a current disability; the reason for their incapacity did not have to have been caused by their service. Simply put, the act created an old-age pension system for Union veterans. Anyone who had served more than ninety days, was honorably discharged, and currently suffered a permanent physical or mental disability became eligible for anywhere from six to twelve dollars of support from the federal government each month.[30] Numerous advertisements by lawyers offering guidance in the application process appeared in Arkansas newspapers for months after the passage of the legislation.[31] Nearly every man on the muster rolls for the Arkansas units of the Union army, as well as most Arkansas men in the US Colored Troops outfits, eventually applied for pensions. In still largely rural Arkansas, they collected their checks for years at the hub of rural life, the post office. Credit for the massive pension system that transformed the lives of many of Arkansas's Union men goes to the national organization that represented them, the Grand Army of the Republic (GAR).

The Grand Army first attempted to organize posts in Arkansas in 1867, but they failed to flourish. According to an 1871 report, the organization may have fallen victim to Reconstruction-era quarrels of the Republican Party: "Five posts were organized in the state. A difficulty with the Department Commander resulted in the disbandment of these Posts late in the year 1868. Efforts have since been made to reorganize the Department but without much success, owing, I believe, to the disturbed condition of political affairs in that State."[32] By 1873, the organization had all but given up on Arkansas and the southern states in general. After declaring recruiting in Arkansas hopeless, the adjutant-general of the GAR commented, "I am inclined to the opinion that in nearly all the Southern States the Order cannot become strong for two reasons." The first was the low population of veterans, the second "because public prejudice against the Order is very bitter. In many localities membership in the Grand

Army is deemed a sufficient reason even for withholding patronage from a businessman. . . . Those who do join are compelled to keep their membership as secret as if it were a capital crime." He lamented the damage done by campaigning during the election of 1872, implying that the perception the Grand Army was involved in politics was detrimental to the organization. "It was thought best to allow matters to remain in status quo, rather than risk any repetition of the story of politics and the Grand Army, which has heretofore affected the Order so disastrously." In short, "Liability to political complications would be particularly great in the Departments where the work was a work of re-organizing Departments killed by politics."[33] The same political environment that drove native Arkansas Republicans back to their home communities during the same time period likely inhibited growth of the Grand Army as a state organization in the first decade after the war. Stuart McConnell has argued that "the partisan character of the early GAR most likely had already deterred potential recruits who were not sympathetic to Radical Republicanism."[34] In a state as politically divided as Arkansas these considerations were particularly acute.

With time, the GAR came to emphasize fraternity and charity over fidelity to radical republicanism. This shift in tone likely made membership among Arkansas veterans more attractive. The GAR finally organized the Department of Arkansas on July 11, 1883.[35] By the time the last Union veteran passed away, Arkansas boasted over one hundred posts, although not all in operation at the same time. Though posts formed across the state, the individuals driving the formation of the Department of Arkansas resided in Little Rock and Fort Smith, both hubs of postwar settlement by northern Union veterans, as well as Republican appointees to the federal court system monitoring lawlessness along the border between Arkansas and Indian Territory. These men dominated department leadership, but representatives from posts across the state show up in department-level leadership positions as well.

Though post membership rolls are scarce, the locations of the posts often reflected wartime locations of Unionists. For example, more posts existed north of the Arkansas River than south of it. Posts also indicated where Union veterans settled after the war and provided clues as to how the Grand Army made a resurgence in Arkansas in the 1880s. The railroads that arrived in northern Arkansas early in that decade brought an influx of people, many of whom were Union veterans.[36] For example, of the sixteen posts in northwest Arkansas, about half sprang up in railroad towns that formed or grew substantially only after the Civil War.[37] Two of those, the Curtis Post in Siloam Springs and the Grant Post in Springdale, have extant membership rolls. The rolls contained few members from Arkansas's Union units; most members served out of state.[38] The Grand Army returned to Arkansas in 1883, not only because of a more settled political situation but also because reinforcements had arrived.[39]

The existence of the posts demonstrated the visibility of Arkansas veterans in daily life, and the names of some of the posts were quite bold. Posts could be named after veterans, but only if they were deceased.[40] The J. M. Clayton Post at Pine Bluff (Jefferson County), Phillip Sheridan Post at Aurora (Madison County), and the Sherman Post at Judsonia (White County) would have been provocative to the veterans' Democratic neighbors. Sheridan and Sherman need no explanation. Clayton, the brother of Governor Powell Clayton was assassinated in early 1889 in Conway County (central Arkansas) during an investigation of fraud against Republicans during the election of 1888.[41] Some of the names were more personal to Arkansas. The Noel G. Rutherford Post at West Fork (Washington County) honored a man raised in Arkansas who became an officer in the 1st Arkansas Cavalry. Guerrillas captured and executed Rutherford near Ozark in 1863.[42] Rutherford's Arkansas-native brothers, cousins, and childhood friends filled the ranks of that post, which was active for decades. The Confederate guerrilla who captured his father and threatened to kill him during the war, and may have been connected to Rutherford's death, lived less than ten miles away.[43]

Arkansas's Union veterans were publicly visible in local society and politics in the 1880s and 1890s in ways that would surprise many Arkansans today. They posed in their Grand Army regalia on city streets. An image of the entire membership of the Phillip Sheridan Post at Aurora in the 1880s shows thirty-nine men.[44] Another photograph from roughly the same time shows twenty men of the Rowan Mack Post at Sulphur Springs, in Benton County, dressed up for Decoration Day and supported by a large band.[45] Local newspapers included notices of Grand Army post meetings regularly, in the same lists as the Masons, Odd Fellows, Knights of Pythias, Knights of Labor, and even Wheelers.[46] In Goodspeed's *Histories*, which were sold in a number of counties across Arkansas, many men claimed membership in Grand Army posts or listed themselves as US veterans and proud Republicans. City and town profiles often included local Grand Army posts with the Masons and other secret societies so popular in the era.[47] Arkansas's Union veterans were a part of the fabric of their communities.

The public claiming of veteran status was not limited to white veterans. African American veterans organized at least five Arkansas posts. The Grand Army officially viewed all who served as equal, no matter their skin color, and thus did not explicitly identify in their records when a post was African American. The known African American posts were located in Little Rock, Fort Smith, Hot Springs, Brinkley, and Marianna, with the Anderson Post, later renamed J. M. Clayton Post, at Pine Bluff a likely sixth.[48] Department of Arkansas encampments were integrated affairs, at least until laws passed in the 1890s requiring segregated accommodations and meeting spaces. An 1884 general order about the second annual state encampment to be held in Hot Springs in April included members of African American posts on committees and closed with a notice that "all members of the Grand Army of the Republic are invited to visit the encampment during its session."[49] A photograph from the 1890 Department of Arkansas encampment held at Eureka Springs in northwest Arkansas, at former Republican governor Powell Clayton's recently opened Crescent Hotel, included at least two African American veterans.[50] They are mixed in with the group, with one of the men standing in the front row and the other a few rows back. There may have been African American veterans welcome at some of the other Arkansas posts, but there are no known records of any integrated posts.[51]

Post records and newspaper accounts reveal especially passionate support for the three national cemeteries at Fayetteville, Fort Smith, and Little Rock. In northwest Arkansas, the U. S. Grant Post in Springdale organized processions and church services every year for Memorial Day in the 1890s. On the Sunday before the holiday, the entire post gathered at a patriotically decorated church, likely dressed in full regalia, to hear a sermon. They then gathered at 6:00 a.m. on Memorial Day, with family and flowers, and formed a procession for the ten-mile journey from their Grand Army hall in downtown Springdale to the national cemetery in Fayetteville. In 1891, they concurred with Fayetteville's Travis Post on extending an invitation to no less than William Clayton to speak on the occasion.[52] Clayton was a US attorney, brother to former governor Powell Clayton, and twin of John Clayton, the Republican martyr to violent Redeemer politics less than three years earlier. Inviting Clayton hardly affected a conciliatory note. However, the posts did not succeed in securing

Clayton as their speaker. According to the *Washington County Review*, Judge John M. McClure, a vocal Republican leader who served as lieutenant colonel of an African American regiment during the war, delivered "a masterful address."[53] McClure's invitation may have been even more provocative than Clayton's. Characterized by one scholar as "the only [carpetbagger judge] Southern conservatives truly reviled," even among a group largely disliked, McClure's uncompromising speech appeared in its entirety in the *Review*.[54] It provided a snapshot of early 1890s sentiment among Arkansas veterans.

For more than two decades, Arkansas's Union veterans, both native and northern transplants, navigated peace with rebels on their own terms. They arrived at their own place of coexistence, separate from national trends, that in various ways gave each side their due without altering the facts of the war. Intermarriage between former Unionists or former Confederates was quite common, especially in rural communities. In the 1870s and 1880s, most adult Arkansans had experienced the war firsthand, which made mythologizing about it more difficult. It is no coincidence that the Lost Cause gained traction after the people who led the Civil War generation passed away. Many Arkansas veterans may have seen the emerging national movement toward reconciliation, which obscured the facts of the war and seemed to accept significant portions of the Lost Cause myth, as not just rewriting history but challenging what Arkansas veterans on both sides had built for themselves. The rise of the Lost Cause, however, divided Arkansans—Union and Confederate, carpetbagger and native, black and white—once again. There was no place in that myth of tragic southern honor and nobility in the face of defeat by an outside invader for southerners who fought alongside the Yankees. The issue of slavery, as well as the idea of African Americans soldiers for the Union, was subsumed by the new idea of the war as a tragic fight between brothers. Former Confederates and former northern Union men—though minor characters in the South—were the honorable heroes of the story.[55] Arkansas's Union veterans, white or black, had no role at all.

Judge McClure's speech reflected the backlash to these national trends, and he clearly indicated he did not support reconciliation. Although ostensibly a carpetbagger himself, McClure's role in negotiating peace in the state for decades and his commitment to African American legal rights made him resistant to the changes of the 1890s. His brand of "unyielding partisanship" fairly blasted from the Fayetteville National Cemetery that day in 1891.[56] Far from an emphasis on heroism divorced from impact, he intoned, "We come not here to extol, or eulogize their personal valor and bravery, although it is recorded on many a bloody field, but to tell our children, so they may teach their children's children, that these dead died for the right, for God, and their native land."[57] Repeatedly, McClure emphasized the glory of the Union dead and the rightness of their cause. He noted the end of slavery and gloated over the lowered status of the former aristocracy: "Slavery, in its old form, has passed away. The cavalier, who fed and fattened on it and who imagined because of the food on which he lived, he was greater than another, now treads the same ground as you and I do."[58] McClure was well aware of the changing tide in the country and refused to give Confederates the grace of separating their personal honor from the dishonor of their cause, with the cutting observation, "We bear no animosity toward any man who did his duty as a confederate soldier. We are willing to concede he thought he was fighting for the right, and that he was conscientious in thinking so. They who forced Christ to crucifixion were conscientious. They who crushed liberty, in Poland, did not lack bravery." McClure proved unwilling to accept the new spirit of reconciliation: "It will be time enough to talk of letting bygones be bygones, when our adversaries cease relighting the fires on the altars of the lost cause."[59]

Not everyone in Arkansas could push back against shifting perceptions of the Civil War in widely viewed and published speeches, but some men took small, if no less decisive actions. In the 1890s, veterans and their kin in Arkansas saddled sons with names that signaled an unwillingness to accept the mythology of the Lost Cause. Alexander Dorsey, late of the 1st Arkansas Cavalry, named his sons, born in 1888, 1890, and 1897, Sherman, Sheridan, and Lincoln, respectively. Dorsey's sons with his other wife, born in the 1870s and 1880s, had more politically benign names like "Hunter." Across the state, in fact, the 1890s saw a surge in Shermans. Between 1870 and 1880, less than seventy-five Arkansas boys were named Sherman. The 1890s, by contrast, saw nearly 250 boys receive the name. There were also more young Lincolns and Grants in that decade. A neighbor of the Dorsey children was Sherman McGinnis, grandson of Elisha, born in 1897. Perhaps reflective of his grandfather's dual service, but definitely indicative of power of reconciliation, his middle name was Lee.[60]

Despite their efforts, the national message of reconciliation and the Lost Cause eventually overwhelmed Arkansas's Union veterans, especially after 1900. External forces played an important role, but the Grand Army itself ultimately failed to understand and preserve the unique position and experiences of Arkansas's veterans, both black and white. This failure appeared in another speech, that of commander in chief General A. D. Shaw. In a tour of southern Grand Army departments in 1900, he addressed the Arkansas encampment at Little Rock. His speech pleaded for cross-regional reconciliation, though leisure tourism—"we can invade the health resorts of the South"—and intermarriage, with the suggestions "in the summer, send your wives and daughters and babies to the North and we will return all but the daughters; those our sons will keep. In the winter we will send our wives and daughters . . . and give your sons the same chance of keeping our daughters." Shaw exhibited no understanding that Union veterans in the South had been doing the work of local reconciliation since the 1860s.[61] Many veterans present had likely followed the lead of Powell Clayton, Grand Army member and former Republican governor, who married a daughter of the South back in 1865.[62] The chances of anyone in the audience without at least one southern daughter- or son-in-law were negligible. Furthermore, what of the southern men of Arkansas who, in the tumultuous sixties, remained loyal to the United States and dealt with the consequences of their decision for decades? Those veterans appeared to be completely invisible in Shaw's remarks. Instead of attempting to understand the well-established form of reconciliation and coexistence that already operated in Arkansas, the leadership of the Grand Army of the Republic participated in ignoring if not outright upending it.

Even worse, the Grand Army abandoned some of its own in accepting the Lost Cause. In 1903, the African American Judson Post in Little Rock made front-page news for refusing to march behind the carriages in the annual Memorial Day parade and attempting to cut in line and join in the parade with the other Grand Army men as it progressed.[63] The Judson Post veterans were upset because they had been marching in line with the white Grand Army veterans every Memorial Day for nearly twenty years. Parade announcements in 1885, 1887, 1897, 1898, 1899, 1900, and the year before, 1902, all included the Judson Post with the other Grand Army men in the procession to the national cemetery. No one lined up behind the carriages.[64] In 1888, they led the white posts in the parade.[65] In 1904, they were again left out, told they had applied for a place too late to be included. They marched on their own.[66] In 1905, they were once again included in the parade, although separated from Little Rock's white McPherson Post via their placement in the "Second Division" of the parade, a new designation.[67] That was likely the last time the posts marched in the same parade. In 1906, the McPherson Post "made no allowances for the negroes or the negro members of the Judson post, but the post took matters into their own hands and arranged a parade, which was formed at the corner of Ninth and Gaines streets [in the black business district of Little Rock] and was then marched to the gate of the National cemetery to await the arrival of the parade arranged by the McPherson post." When the "white parade arrived," the Judson Post marched in behind the currently serving US troops, not the carriages.[68] In 1907, the local newspaper referred to the "McPherson Post Memorial Program," which included no mention of the Judson Post in the parade line up.[69] As late as 1937, Memorial Day activities were still organized "under the auspices of the McPherson Post No. 1, Department of Arkansas, G.A.R." with no mention of the Judson Post.[70] In the 1880s, the Grand Army stood strong for the inclusion of all veterans, but in their twilight years, abandoned their comrades.

Even white Union veterans eventually disappeared from popular memory and were largely removed from historical preservation efforts of the twentieth century in Arkansas. Complicity with the Lost Cause did not save them, although a combination of factors led to this disappearance. Most importantly, they had no enduring advocates—no daughters intent upon preserving their legacy and no younger veterans united in their organization to champion their memory. One northwest Arkansas Grand Army post officially passed the torch of Memorial Day commemoration to the local chapter of the Women's Christian Temperance Union.[71] Rejecting veterans of the Spanish-American War at least partly out of fear former Confederates could join if they served in both conflicts left the Grand Army with no clear heirs to their legacy. This was no small issue, because the Confederates did have custodians of their legacy. In 1905, the Arkansas state historian for the United Daughters of the Confederacy admonished members that only "ten chapters (and no camps)" responded to a call to collect data and historical material that had gone out to every camp and chapter in the state. She followed this by outlining her goal, "to embalm the memory of the Confederate soldier, private as well as officer, and we mean to do it lovingly and well." She also targeted education, in a manner that likely gave Judge McClure an apoplexy, with a call to fight "principals of public schools, teachers in so-called colleges" who sought to cover up the glory of the Confederacy.[72] Women often formed local historical societies in Arkansas in the early twentieth century. As Arkansas's Union veterans passed away, their papers, diaries, and letters were rarely collected.

Arkansas's Union veterans did not completely disappear when reconciliation and the Lost Cause took hold in Arkansas, but they ceased to matter. The Grand Army posts of Arkansas lingered on. Where they had been active community organizations, the twentieth century posts seemed to meet mainly to discuss who had died. They steadfastly continued to publicly perform patriotic rituals in support of Memorial Day. References to Grand Army commemorations of the holiday appear in area newspapers well into the twentieth century, especially in the three cities with national cemeteries. A notice of "Federal Memorial Day Services," for example, ran in the *Fayetteville Democrat* on May 29, 1916. Hosted by Fayetteville's Travis Post, the traditions of the 1890s continued as "in addition to locals, many people from nearby cities and towns and rural sections are expected to attend the exercises." Colonel Thomas J. Hunt, who had organized one of the first companies of the 1st Arkansas Cavalry at Cassville, delivered the opening remarks. Speeches, song, prayer, and a reading of Abraham Lincoln's Gettysburg Address followed him.[73] The only thing that silenced Arkansas's Union veterans was their last reveille. Reflective, however, of the strange space in which Arkansas's veterans had always existed, upon his death, Hunt's body was "surrounded by Confederate and G.A.R. veterans." As he was "consigned to the earth, the Stars and Stripes under which he had fought more than fifty years ago was lowered into the grave with him."[74]

NOTES

1. Frederick H. Dyer, *A Compendium of the War of the Rebellion* (Dayton: National Historical Society, 1908, 1979), 2:997. For more on the war in the Ozarks, see Brooks Blevins, *Hill Folks: A History of Arkansas Ozarkers and Their Image* (Chapel Hill: University of North Carolina Press, 2002); Michael Fellman, *Inside War: The Guerrilla Conflict in Missouri during the American Civil War* (New York: Oxford University Press, 1989); Matthew M. Stith, *Extreme Civil War: Guerrilla Warfare, Environment, and Race on the Trans-Mississippi Frontier* (Baton Rouge: Louisiana State University Press, 2016).

2. Recent interest in guerrilla warfare during the Civil War has led to a number of examinations of Unionism in border states. Much of this focuses on Appalachia. However, work on North Carolina, Kentucky, and Tennessee offers insights relevant to Arkansas. See Carl H. Moneyhon, *The Impact of the Civil War and Reconstruction on Arkansas: Persistence in the Midst of Ruin* (Baton Rouge: Louisiana State University Press, 1994); Noel C. Fisher, *War at Every Door: Partisan Politics and Guerrilla Violence in East Tennessee, 1860–1869* (Chapel Hill: University of North Carolina Press,

1997); John C. Inscoe and Gordon B. McKinney, *The Heart of Confederate Appalachia: Western North Carolina in the Civil War* (Chapel Hill: University of North Carolina Press, 2000); John C. Inscoe and Robert C. Kenzer, *Enemies of the Country: New Perspectives on Unionists in the Civil War South* (Athens: University of Georgia Press, 2001); Brian Dallas McKnight, *Contested Borderland: The Civil War in Appalachian Kentucky and Virginia* (Lexington: University Press of Kentucky, 2006); Mark K. Christ, *Civil War Arkansas, 1863: The Battle for a State* (Norman: University of Oklahoma Press, 2010); and Steven E. Nash, *Reconstruction's Ragged Edge: The Politics of Postwar Life in the Southern Mountains* (Chapel Hill: University of North Carolina Press, 2016). Few scholars trace Unionism into the postwar years, but a study of Unionists in Alabama, grounded in Southern Claims Commission claims rather than US military service, reveals relevant patterns. See Margaret M. Storey, *Loyalty and Loss: Alabama's Unionists in the Civil War and Reconstruction* (Baton Rouge: Louisiana State University Press, 2004).

3. Dyer, *A Compendium of the War of the Rebellion*, 1:11. This total does not include men from Arkansas who went north before 1862 and joined units in other states.

4. "U.S. Demography 1790 to Present," Social Explorer, US Census Bureau, socialexplorer.com.

5. Mark K. Christ and Michael B. Dougan, *The Die Is Cast: Arkansas Goes to War, 1861* (Little Rock: Butler Center Books, 2010); James M. Woods, *Rebellion and Realignment: Arkansas's Road to Secession* (Fayetteville: University of Arkansas Press, 1987).

6. William L. Shea and Earl J, Hess, *Pea Ridge: Civil War Campaign in the West* (Chapel Hill: University of North Carolina Press, 1992).

7. For more on African American enlistment at Helena, see Mark K. Christ, "'They Will Be Armed': Lorenzo Thomas Recruits Black Troops in Helena, April 6, 1863," *Arkansas Historical Quarterly* 62 (Winter 2013): 366–83.

8. See Dudley Taylor Cornish, *The Sable Arm: Black Troops in the Union Army, 1861–1865* (Lawrence: University Press of Kansas, 1956); Robert W. Lull, *Civil War General and Indian Fighter James M. Williams* (Denton: University of North Texas Press, 2013); and Ian Michael Spurgeon, *Soldiers in the Army of Freedom: The 1st Kansas Colored, the Civil War's First African American Combat Unit* (Norman: University of Oklahoma Press, 2014).

9. George Arthur and John Bean, 79th United States Colored Troops, Carded Records Showing Military Service of Soldiers Who Fought in Volunteer Organizations during the American Civil War, compiled 1890–1912, documenting the period 1861–1866, Records of the Adjutant General's Office, Record Group 94, National Archives and Records Administration, Washington, DC (hereafter NARA), reproductions at Fold3.com (accessed September 20–27, 2015) (hereafter Union Service Records, Fold3.com).

10. Land originally settled by the Bean brothers was part of Arkansas territory but ended up in Indian Territory when they failed to bend the placement of the final state border to their advantage. Petition of Mark and Richard H. Bean (to accompany H.R. no. 454), July 19, 1856, Committee on Public Lands, 34th Cong., 1st Sess., US House of Representatives, Congressional Edition, vol. 870 (Washington, DC: US Government Printing Office, 1856), Report no. 210.

11. Deposition of Ran Maxey, Ran Maxey (Crawford County, AR) claim no. 16328, Settled Case Files for Claims Approved by the Southern Claims Commission, 1871–1880, Records of the Accounting Officers of the Department of the Treasury, 1775–1978, Record Group 217, NARA, reproductions at Fold3.com (accessed January 1–7, 2013) (hereafter Settled Case Files, SCC, Fold3.com).

12. John Rutherford deposition, John Rutherford (Washington County, AR) claim no. 20497, Settled Case Files, SCC, Fold3.com (accessed January 1–7, 2013).

13. Elisha McGinnis deposition, Elisha McGinnis, Soldier's Certificate no. 366430, Case Files of Approved Pension Applications of Veterans Who Served in the Army and Navy Mainly in the Civil War and the War with Spain (Civil War and Later Survivors' Certificates), 1861–1934, Civil War and Later Pension Files; Records of the Department of Veterans Affairs, Record Group 15, NARA (hereafter Pension Files).

14. Elihu [Elisha] McGinnis, Seventeenth (Griffith's) Infantry, Compiled Service Records of Confederate Soldiers Who Served in Organizations from the State of Arkansas, Record Group 109, NARA, reproductions at Fold3.com (accessed June 10–15, 2014); Elisha McGinnis, First Arkansas Cavalry, Union Service Record, Fold3.com (accessed June 10–15, 2014).

15. For more on Union enlistment in Arkansas, see Georgena Duncan, "Uncertain Loyalties: Dual Enlistment in the Third and Fourth Arkansas Cavalry, USV," *Arkansas Historical Quarterly* 72 (Winter 2013): 305–32, and Brian K. Robertson, "Men Who Would Die by the Stars and Stripes: A Socio-Economic Examination of the Second Arkansas Cavalry (US)," *Arkansas Historical Quarterly* 69 (Summer 2010): 120–37.

16. Kansas State Historical Society, 1865 Kansas State Census, Schedule I (Free Inhabitants), Anderson, Douglas, Linn, and Franklin Counties, KS. Reproduced online at Ancestry.com (Accessed October 1, 2015).

17. Michael A. Hughes, "Wartime Gristmill Destruction in Northwest Arkansas and Military-Farm Colonies," *Arkansas Historical Quarterly* 46, no. 2 (Summer 1987): 167–86. See also Matthew M. Stith, *Extreme Civil War: Guerrilla Warfare, Environment, and Race on the Trans-Mississippi Frontier* (Baton Rouge: Louisiana State University Press, 2016).

18. For quantitative analysis of the negative effects of the Civil War on the population and economic output of Arkansas, see Moneyhon, *The Impact of the Civil War and Reconstruction on Arkansas.*

19. For more on Reconstruction in Arkansas, see Thomas A. DeBlack, *With Fire and Sword: Arkansas, 1861–1874* (Fayetteville: University of Arkansas Press, 2003).

20. For discussions of the importance of veterans living near each other see Barbara A. Gannon, "'She Is a Member of the 23rd': Lucy Nichols and then Community of the Civil War Regiment," in *This Distracted and Anarchical People: New Answers for Old Questions about the Civil War–Era North,* ed. Andrew L. Slap and Michael T. Smith (New York: Fordham University Press, 2013), 184–99, and Susannah J. Ural, *Hood's Texas Brigade: The Soldiers and Families of the Confederacy's Most Celebrated Unit* (Baton Rouge: Louisiana State University Press, 2017).

21. Abraham Lincoln, "Inaugural Address," March 4, 1865.

22. Gustavus Weber, *The Bureau of Pensions: Its History, Activity and Organizations* (Baltimore: Johns Hopkins Press, 1923), 4–5.

23. Ibid., 16.

24. Elisha McGinnis, Soldier's Certificate no. 366430, Pension Files.

25. As it is nearly impossible to prove onset of TB, men with the condition were almost never awarded a pension. Elisha McGinnis, First Arkansas Cavalry, Union Service Record, Fold3.com (accessed June 10–15, 2014).

26. Elisha McGinnis, Soldier's Certificate no. 366430, Pension Files.

27. Elisha McGinnis to William W. Dudley, January 15, 1884, ibid.

28. Phillips deposition, ibid.

29. A. M. Sproesen, Special Examiner to Honorable O. P. G. Clark, Commissioner of Pensions, December 21, 1884, ibid.

30. Weber, *Bureau of Pensions*, 7.

31. *Washington County Review,* July 1890.

32. *Proceedings of the First to Tenth Meetings 1866–1876 (Inclusive) of the National Encampment Grand Army of the Republic with Digest of Decisions, Rules of Order and Index* (Philadelphia: Samuel P. Town, 1877), 116.

33. Ibid., 211.

34. Stuart McConnell, *Glorious Contentment: The Grand Army of the Republic, 1865–1900* (Chapel Hill: University of North Carolina Press, 1992), 33.

35. *Unofficial Proceedings in Connection with the Twenty-Fourth National Encampment, Grand Army of the Republic, Held in Boston, Week August 11–16, 1890* (Boston: E. B. Stillings, 1890), 273.

36. Blevins, *Hill Folks*, 71–73.

37. GAR Records project, Sons of Union Veterans of the Civil War, www.garrecords.org.

38. "U. S. Grant Post Minute Book," Paul Dolle Collection, Shiloh Museum of Ozark History, Springdale, Arkansas; "Handwritten Roster Members of the Curtis Post, No. 9, Siloam Springs," GAR Collection, Siloam Springs Museum Society, Siloam Springs, Arkansas.

39. One of the most complete and reliable listings of posts in Arkansas has been gathered from various historical sources over the last ten years by the Sons of Union Veterans of the Civil War. Unfortunately, there are very few known sources for the Arkansas posts, so the records are largely incomplete. See www.garrecords.org.

40. *Ritual of the Grand Army of the Republic* (Philadelphia: Headquarters of the Grand Army of the Republic, 1903).

41. For more on Clayton's assassination, see Kenneth C. Barnes, *Who Killed John Clayton? Political Violence and the Emergence of the New South* (Durham, NC: Duke University Press, 1998).

42. Noel G. Rutherford, First Arkansas Cavalry, Union Service Records, Fold3.com (accessed September 20–27, 2015).

43. *Fayetteville Democrat,* November 23, 1909.

44. S-2002-1-127, Shiloh Museum of Ozark History, Springdale, Arkansas.

45. S-85-60-7, ibid.

46. See the surviving 1890s issues of the *Eureka Springs Echo,* the *Springdale News,* the *Fayetteville Democrat,* the *Pine Bluff Commercial,* and the *Arkansas Gazette.*

47. The profile of Drake's Creek in Madison County, Arkansas, is an example. *Goodspeed's History of Benton, Washington, Carroll, Madison, Crawford, Franklin, and Sebastian Cos, Ark.* (Chicago: Goodspeed, 1889), 461.

48. Barbara A. Gannon, *The Won Cause: Black and White Comradeship in the Grand Army of the Republic* (Chapel Hill: University of North Carolina Press, 2011). The Pine Bluff post is mentioned in a short notation about a parade as "John M. Clayton Post: G.A.R., (colored)," *Daily Arkansas Gazette* (Little Rock), August 7, 1890.

49. *Arkansas Gazette,* March 2, 1884.

50. Photograph, Department of Arkansas Encampment 1890, Eureka Springs, AR, Paul Dolle Civil War Collection, Butler Center for Arkansas Studies, Arkansas Studies Institute, Little Rock.

51. Gannon, *The Won Cause*, 210.

52. Ibid.

53. "McClure Speech," *Washington County Review*, June 11, 1891.

54. Joseph A. Ranney, *In the Wake of Slavery: Civil War, Civil Rights, and the Reconstruction of Southern Law* (Westport, CT: Praeger Publishing, 2006), 24.

55. For more on the rise of these ideas, see David W. Blight, *Race and Reunion: The Civil War in American Memory* (Cambridge, MA: Harvard University Press, 2001). For a challenge to Blight's interpretation, see Caroline E. Janney, *Remembering the Civil War: Reunion and the Limits of Reconciliation* (Chapel Hill: University of North Carolina Press, 2013).

56. See Blight, *Race and Reunion*, 198.

57. "McClure Speech."

58. Ibid.

59. Ibid.

60. I made comparisons between names appearing in the US Bureau of the Census, Tenth Census of the United States, 1880, Population Schedule, and US Bureau of the Census, Twelfth Census of the United States, 1900, Population Schedule, both for Arkansas only. The Dorsey and McGinnis children are listed in 1900 census population schedules for Madison County, Arkansas.

61. *Arkansas Gazette*, March 28, 1900.

62. For a discussion of northern men marrying southern women see Nina Silber, *The Romance of Reunion: Northerners and the South, 1865–1900* (Chapel Hill: University of North Carolina Press, 1993).

63. *Arkansas Gazette*, May 31, 1903. The Judson Post was in Little Rock and is not the same as the Sherman post in Judsonia, Arkansas.

64. *Arkansas Gazette*, May 30, 1885, May 29, 1887, May 28, 1897, May 29, 1898, and *Arkansas Democrat*, May 29, 1899, May 29, 1900, May 29, 1902.

65. *Arkansas Gazette*, May 30, 1888.

66. *Arkansas Gazette*, May 31, 1904.

67. *Arkansas Gazette*, May 29, 1905.

68. *Arkansas Gazette*, May 31, 1906.

69. *Arkansas Gazette*, May 29, 1907.

70. "Memorial Day Program," series I, box 2, folder 23, Manuscript Collection MSS 03-18, Butler Center for Arkansas Studies, Little Rock, Arkansas.

71. "In Memory of Former Local G.A.R.," *Journal-Advance*, May 29, 1930.

72. *Arkansas Gazette*, Feb 19, 1905. For additional discussion of the importance of education see Steven E. Sodergren's essay in this volume.

73. *Fayetteville Democrat*, May 29, 1916.

74. "Military Honors Accorded Col. Hunt," *Fayetteville Democrat*, April 24, 1922.

Loyal Deserters and the Veterans Who Weren't

Pension Fraud in Lost Cause Memory

ADAM H. DOMBY

I
N APRIL 1865, as the Confederacy took its last breath, Union troops finally arrived in Davidson County, North Carolina. The war, of course, had been there for much longer. Since 1861, Confederate loyalists and those opposed to the Confederacy periodically fought each other in the North Carolina Piedmont. Characterized by robberies, arsons, death threats, and bushwhacking, violence steadily increased over the course of the war. Local citizens covertly fed deserters and hid escaped Union prisoners, while bands of deserters, recusant conscripts (the nineteenth-century equivalent of draft dodgers), and other dissenters openly resisted Confederate authority. In 1863, a regiment of Confederate regulars sent to suppress resistance scoured the region's woods hunting for deserters.[1] Over the course of two months, the unit captured at least three thousand deserters, and others died resisting. In March 1865, Lee dispatched a battalion of sharpshooters from his already-strained Army of Northern Virginia to suppress dissension. The unit, consisting of local men, summarily executed five dissenters and sent fifty more back to the front lines.[2]

As Union cavalry passed through Davidson County in 1865, southern dissenters' self-proclaimed loyalty to the Union did not protect their property from federal forces. Samuel Yokley had his horse taken by several cavalrymen when he ran into them in northern Davidson County. Left with no horse—and not even a receipt or a greenback to show for it—Yokley walked home. A decade passed before he received any compensation for his horse. In 1878, Yokley finally submitted a claim to the Southern Claims Commission for the horse taken by federal troops in the waning days of the war. Created in 1871, the commission allowed loyal southerners to receive compensation for any property taken by federal forces during the war. Commissioners examined written testimonies as well as wartime documents to determine if a claimant really remained loyal to the Union throughout the entire war—a key condition for compensation.

The laws that authorized the claims commission shaped how dissenters crafted their narratives and recalled wartime experiences, as claimants tried to gain compensation for their sufferings. The focus on loyalty to the Union that appears in the testimony is as much as product of the questions asked as the experiences of the claimants. The federal government set the standard for loyalty extremely high, and any aid given to the Confederacy, even if the alternatives were death or bodily harm, could result in rejection. Fortunately for the Yokley family, the federal government approved Samuel Yokley's claim in 1878, and he entered the history books as a certified Unionist. Within a generation, however, the family largely rejected their Unionist roots and portrayed themselves as staunch Confederates.

Today, few people recall the widespread dissent in the Piedmont. The reason North Carolinians have forgotten dissent is tied partially to Confederate pensions and their role in crafting the Lost Cause narrative. Pushed by southern elites after the war, the Lost Cause encompassed how many white southerners recollected the conflict. It disconnected slavery from the Civil War's cause, presenting chattel slavery in a positive light and blaming Jim Crow–era racial tensions on the meddling of outsiders during Reconstruction. Premised on the retelling of valiant efforts against unbeatable odds, Lost Cause advocates usually acted as if nearly all whites were Confederate loyalists who remained unwaveringly devoted to the cause throughout the war. The belief that nearly all Confederates willingly fought and fought well was crucial to the Lost Cause myth and continues to appear across the South in flag-waving neo-Confederate activists wanting to celebrate their ancestors' "heroic deeds."[3] But what if those deeds were not so heroic after all, or if they never even occurred? Pensions helped encourage the forgetting of dissent and replaced memories of desertion with remembrances of valor, but in the immediate aftermath of the war, a memory of dissent endured in part because being a "Unionist" had monetary rewards.

Neither the most transparent opportunists nor most self-effacing claimants, Samuel Yokley and his family provide a window into the motives, means, and memories of dissent during the postbellum era. The Yokley family's history also hints at why no lasting Unionist counter narrative to the Lost Cause took root in the North Carolina Piedmont or elsewhere in the South. The complexity of wartime dissent hampered efforts to create a lasting shared memory of opposing the Confederacy. Ultimately, however, the collective amnesia experienced by North Carolinians, including the Yokley family, was not solely a product of former Confederates chiefly writing their history; rather, former dissenters actively contributed to the erasure of dissent from the dominant narratives of the Civil War.[4]

Pensions, war claims, and other means of monetizing wartime experience served as driving forces in the creation of postwar memory, including a Lost Cause myth that presented a solid South where there was no internal dissent or "loss of will." As Marita Sturken observes about Vietnam, "Remembering is in itself a form of forgetting"; so it was with the formation of the Lost Cause.[5] Access to pensions and other rewards open to former Confederates helped create this memory of an idealized solid Confederacy by discouraging dissenters from speaking out publicly against the Lost Cause. Some former deserters who previously depicted themselves as Unionists began supporting a narrative that celebrated Confederate veterans, going so far as rewrite their own past to appear as if they had been staunch Confederates when in fact they had deserted or taken up arms against the rebellion.

Confederate pension applications not only reflect how white southern memories of the war changed over the years; pensions actively helped shape those very changes. The monetary and social capital available to former Confederate soldiers encouraged forgetting any events that contradicted the Lost Cause. Where once it paid to recall desertion as an act of loyalty to the Union, in the early twentieth century, pensions began to provide a monetary incentive to forget one's desertion. The end of the Southern Claims Commission followed by the expansion of pension eligibility helped shape how people remembered the war. The role of pensions in celebrating the Confederacy further provided social incentives to recall one's wartime experience within the confines of the Lost Cause mythology.

Confederate pensions could even encourage healing within communities divided by war: in part by motivating dissenters to forget, at least publicly, their anti-Confederate experiences and embrace the Lost Cause myth long after the Confederacy lost the war. Historian Jeffery Vogel argues that the very "meaning of the Civil War" was central to debates around Union pensions.[6] The same can be said about Confederate pensions; they reinforced the Lost

Cause narrative within the South. It is not surprising, as Jeffery McClurken points out, that the largest expansion of Virginia's pension program came in the same period "often associated with the rise of the Lost Cause movement." Furthermore, pensions "allowed white Conservative Democratic leaders to celebrate Confederate veterans" at the same time they instituted Jim Crow.[7] Pensions became more than just welfare for aging veterans or celebration of the Confederacy. They helped make ex-Confederates from former Unionists. At the turn of the century, monuments, reunions, textbooks, and pensions for ex-Confederates cemented the Lost Cause as a dominant narrative of the past. This essay aims to understand how pensions helped erase the memory of white dissenters and desertion in the Confederacy. Understanding the role of these sources in shaping the memory of the past may help historians use them more critically.

At first glance, one might expect Samuel Yokley and his family to have been secessionists from the start of the war. Already a prosperous famer in 1860, Yokley owned multiple farmsteads along the border between Davidson and Forsyth Counties. With fourteen slaves, he was heavily invested in the South's peculiar institution.[8] Nevertheless, Yokley, a prewar Whig, vocally opposed secession because he believed, correctly, that it would result in the end of slavery. Thus, the Yokley family was never enthusiastic about the Confederacy. They belonged to that substantial portion of the Piedmont's population that remained unconvinced of the need for a new nation. As the war progressed, their opinion of the Confederacy only diminished.[9]

Dissenters' approaches to resisting the Confederacy were as varied as their motivations. Members of the Yokley family, for example, dissented and avoided military service in a variety of ways. During the first year of the war, many families like the Yokleys, less supportive of the Confederacy, went about their lives with relatively few major disruptions. The advent of conscription in 1862, however, pushed even the most ambivalent citizen into taking a stance on the war. Too old to serve himself, Samuel Yokley watched as the Confederacy conscripted two of his six sons as well as his younger brother. Within a month, all three had deserted and returned home to hide in the woods. One of them, David Pinkney Yokley, eventually fled to northern lines. Another of Samuel's sons, who had left home for Missouri before the war, died in federal service, killed by guerrillas. In the latter part of the war, a fourth son became a recusant conscript, joining his brothers hiding in the woods. Samuel's younger brother,

Andrew, initially hired a substitute to avoid service, but when the Confederate Congress repealed the rule allowing substitutes, he arranged for himself "a detail to haul wood for the Rail Road." Only when that exemption became too costly did Andrew join his nephews in the woods. The Yokley family included deserters, recusant conscripts, and a federal volunteer. All of these individuals considered themselves and each other "Union men" and their community largely agreed during and after the war.[10]

Samuel Yokley's testimony to the Southern Claims Commission after the war reveals a wartime experience that exacerbated his initial disaffection for the Confederacy. First, Confederate loyalists threatened to burn his farm "because [his] boys would not fight for the Confederacy and [he] protected them." In addition to these threats of arson, Confederate troops arrested Yokley three times. Each time, the authorities eventually freed him, but these traumatic incidents bred additional resentment toward the rebels. In the fall of 1863, Captain John Gilmer of the 21st North Carolina arrested Yokley hoping to force his sons to return to service. When Yokley refused to cooperate, the twenty-two-year-old captain "ordered a portion of his men to shoot me; they immediately surrounded me and presented their guns at me." Yokley called his bluff and told the brash young officer, "If you kill me you will only have one old man out of the way." After a few moments, the officer and his men marched away, leaving Yokley behind. Yokley was lucky; the 21st North Carolina killed multiple dissenters during the unit's sweep of the Piedmont. Yokley's experiences clearly engendered no affection for the Confederacy and instead intensified his allegiance to the Union. As Samuel Yokley's case suggests, conscription, and the subsequent Confederate harassment of recusant conscripts and deserters, may have created more "Union men" than any other act of the Confederate government, including secession.[11]

In his claim, Samuel Yokley detailed his third arrest for hiding his sons, which resulted in a revealing conversation regarding the roots of his resistance. Samuel was dragged before an enrolling officer, who announced his intent to enroll one of Yokley's sons. Yokley declared that his son "did not belong to the Confederate service [as] he was 16 years of age," and threatened to "spend the last dollar, the last nigger & the last horse before they should have him." As Yokley made clear to the officer, protection of his family was central to his resistance. Upon learning that Yokley owned slaves the enrollment officer asked the farmer why he failed to support the Confederacy. Yokley indignantly replied "that I had lived under the Government of the United States; & it's Constitution & Government had always protected me and my property."[12] His resistance thus appears to have largely evolved not from blind patriotism but from family loyalty.

Although Samuel would give anything for his son's safety, he was less willing to give his last dollar, slave, or horse to the Union. In fact, the day after the federal cavalrymen took his horse, Yokley attempted to protest to the unit's commander and retrieve his animal, but the troops left the area before he reached their encampment.[13] Still, the constant harassment and mistreatment by Confederate authorities ensured that by 1865 Yokley identified more strongly with the Union than the Confederacy. Ideology and loyalty are always fluid, and there were limits to the Yokleys' love of the flag as well as tangible reasons for their allegiance to the Union. For Samuel Yokley, his wartime political loyalties remained first and foremost about protecting his sons and secondly preserving his property. That said, Yokley was not without some sense of loyalty to the Union and surely preferred their victory to a Confederate one. When two escaped Union prisoners arrived at his house, he hid them, gave them shelter for three days, and provided civilian clothing and provisions for their escape.[14]

A sense of patriotism almost certainly contributed additional motivation to the Yokleys' opposition to the Confederacy, but self-interest determined the manner of dissent and level of resistance. Unlike some dissenters who attacked the farms of secessionists and officers in the Home Guard to intimidate them, the Yokleys sought to avoid conflict.[15] For most of the war, their resistance consisted of avoiding service and helping others. The family never attacked the Confederate war effort directly by cutting a rail line, burning a bridge, or attacking a supply wagon. That changed in 1864, however, when the Home Guard captured one of Samuel's sons and the Yokley boys took up arms.

As a Confederate squad escorted three prisoners "tied with their hands behind them" about a dozen dissenters ambushed the rebel soldiers and freed the prisoners. Leading the rescue party was none other than Samuel Yokley. Other rescuers included neighbors and at least one of Samuel's sons; the group likely included two or three more family members as well.[16] The goal of this attack was not to bring about the fall of the Confederacy, though their perpetrators eagerly awaited its demise. Rather, Yokley went to rescue his kin.[17] Dissenters like the Yokleys often avoided conflict with Confederates and only took up arms to protect themselves and their family members.

In the immediate aftermath of the war, numerous reasons existed to maintain the memory of dissent and create a cohesive Unionist identity. The Southern Claims Commission, bitterness over wartime mistreatment, and political fights pitting former Confederates against the Republican Party all encouraged the creation of a Unionist identity inclusive of all dissenters. This identity, premised upon a myth of principled Unionism, flourished in the North Carolina Piedmont during the 1870s.[18]

Powerful external forces also encouraged dissenters to remember their dissent as a product of patriotism. Though stronger Unionist sentiment developed out of resentment toward the Confederacy, the patriotism and uncompromising opposition to the Confederacy expressed in Southern Claims Commission claims were partially a product of the legal standards for proving loyalty. The enabling legislation for the Claims Commission ensured that claimants framed the retelling of their resistance around their love of Union. The commission's standardized list of questions highlighted specific motivations and actions of claimants. Because the government defined true Unionist resistance as being a product of patriotism, the applications' questions and claimants' answers stressed rigid political allegiances. Samuel Yokley testified using the language of patriotism, but close examination of his testimony reveals that family and self-interest were equally if not more important to his resistance. Encouraged by newspapers, politics, and pecuniary interests, a narrative of uncompromising Unionism, principled dissent, and patriotism became the standard means for describing dissenters' resistance during Reconstruction.[19]

Unlike former Confederate soldiers who shared memories of battle and fighting for the Lost Cause, dissenters had trouble fashioning an analogous shared memory, since any narrative based on uncompromising Unionism ignored the complexities of dissent and failed to fit the wartime reality many dissenters experienced.[20] Basing an identity on a myth of uncompromising principle required extreme massaging of individual memories for many dissenters. In this context, it was often easier to forget the myriad reasons for dissent than to remember their complexities. Still, the efforts were made, especially when money was offered.

The Yokley family vividly demonstrates how a narrative of uncompromising Unionism ultimately failed to adequately describe their experiences. When Andrew Yokley, Samuel's brother, submitted a claim to the Southern Claims Commission, he declared, "I did all that I could for the cause. I kept out of the army." Keeping out of the army was apparently about all he felt he could do, as Andrew first hired a substitute and hauled wood for the railroad before eventually hiding in the woods with a small band of dissenters. Even Andrew's reasoning for joining the anti-Confederate secret society the Heroes of America seems passive and self-defensive in nature. He later recalled how the Piedmont-wide organization "was a protection for Union men, there was nothing bad or murderous about it." The Heroes never actively attacked the Confederate war effort as a guerrilla organization. Indeed, it seems many members of the Heroes opposed conscription far more than the actual Confederacy.[21] Andrew's contention that not fighting and helping others on the run proved his loyalty was unconvincing to the commissioners, who felt Andrew could have taken to the woods earlier.

What role memories of wartime dissent played in the postwar lives of individual dissenters frequently remains unclear. It seems likely Samuel remained a lifelong Republican. His hatred for the Confederacy may well have been constitutive of his postwar sense of self. Or his anti-Confederate past may have played only a minor role in his postbellum life, appearing only when useful in some manner, for example when he testified before the Claims Commission for compensation for the commandeered horse. Given all Samuel suffered at the hands of Confederates, we might assume he took great pride in his resistance, proudly identifying as a Unionist into old age. Yet apparently his family quickly forgot their Civil War travails.

The experiences of Samuel's family are suggestive of why a robust memory of dissent failed to survive alongside the Lost Cause. Samuel's son David Yokley was conscripted in August 1862 but deserted a month later with his brother and uncle. It was either David or his brother Charles Jefferson Yokley whom the Home Guard captured in 1864. Whether as captive or rescuer, David almost certainly participated in the rescue mission his father led. It seems likely it was David who was rescued since he and his uncle left the county shortly after and fled across Union lines.[22] After taking up arms against the Confederacy and fleeing to Indiana one might expect David to vocally oppose efforts to celebrate the Confederacy.[23] Indeed, he appears to have dabbled, at least a little, in Republican politics.[24]

Despite his wartime experiences, however, David Yokley does not appear to have been especially tied to the Union. David's second marriage—to a sixteen-year-old, born a decade after the war—endured until his death. What David told his young bride of the war remains unknown; however, he may have failed to mention his wartime resistance. In her 1930 application for a pension based on David's Confederate service, his widow answered the question "Was your late husband a deserter?" with a one-word answer: "No." The application was denied but only because her age—fifty-five instead of the minimum sixty—made the young widow ineligible.[25]

David's widow was hardly the most insincere member of the family when it came to pension applications. David's aunt, Cordelia Yokley, actually received a pension for her late husband's entire month of loyal Confederate service before he deserted and escaped to Union lines. Unlike David's wife, Cordelia definitely knew her husband's status as a deserter, having married him in 1864 while he was on the lam and shortly before he fled to the North.[26] Cordelia received a pension from 1924 until her death in 1927.[27] More striking still, David's wartime dissent had failed to deter even him from applying for a Confederate pension. Though in theory ineligible due to his desertion—not to mention lack of service—David claimed to have been a loyal Confederate and received a pension for three years until his death in 1926. For sixty dollars a year, David erased his past.[28]

Even if they did not believe their own lies, Confederate pensions like those received by David and other former dissenters helped strengthen the Lost Cause as the primary means of understanding the war among white southerners. There was little questioning of his credentials because an assumption existed by 1923 that Confederates rarely deserted. The applications for Confederate pensions were just part of the erasure of a Unionist identity for the family. Upon his death in 1926, an obituary noted David had been "a brave old Confederate soldier."[29] This stands in sharp distinction from his appearance sixty-four years earlier in a Raleigh newspaper as a deserter within five weeks of being conscripted.[30]

One of David's cousins presents an even more striking example of an attempt to garner a pension when undeserving, while also providing a caution in how historians use pension applications. Looking at Jacob Yokley's pension application is misleading. The digitized application clearly has "approved" written across the front of it, which might lead one to believe that he was a devoted Confederate and that he received a pension. In reality, Jacob never received any money for one very good reason: he had not served at all. Upon investigating deeper, checking the still undigitized payment lists and letter files within the state archives reveals that he was actually a recusant conscript who took up arms against the Confederate Home Guard.[31]

North Carolina's pension bureau rarely investigated attempts to defraud the state, a topic heretofore overlooked by scholars. Jacob Yokley, however, was one of those rare cases where an investigation occurred. The results of these investigations often do not appear in the digitized pension application files on which many scholars and genealogists have relied. The complexities of wartime loyalties were rarely reflected accurately in administrative records made by the pension bureau, and the application files are often incomplete to begin with.

In his application Jacob swore he had been in the 70th North Carolina State Troops (1st Junior Reserves) beginning in 1864. Jacob's attempt to twist, rewrite really, the past and create an economically useful narrative did not go unchallenged. His application to get a pension was initially approved, but his neighbors challenged his eligibility before he ever received a payment.[32] In many ways, what made Jacob unique was that he got caught. To understand how surprising it is that he was challenged, we must look to how atypical that made him. To put Jacob's fraud in perspective, it is necessary to have a sense of how the pension system evolved and how prevalent fraud was.

The 1901 law that expanded pension eligibility beyond wounded veterans banned deserters from getting pensions, which some veterans saw as a flaw in the law. In a 1901 letter to a Greensboro newspaper about who should be entitled to pensions, as well as membership in the United Confederate Veterans, Thomas Rhodes argued that some deserters were better than others. Rhodes felt those who deserted to the Union and those who "violated their furloughs by remaining at home over time for starving wives and children," were two distinct categories of deserters.[33] He argued the latter group, which included himself, should not be penalized because they had deserted to help their families as opposed to betraying the Confederate experiment. Many former rebels agreed, and by the turn of the century this became a standard way of dividing deserters into two classes: loyal Confederates who "laid down their arms out of an overpowering sense of duty to their families at home" and those who "turned their guns on their former comrades."[34] This ignored the fact that deserters at home were far more likely to literally point guns at their former comrades than those Union enlistees sent out West to garrison forts and face Native American uprisings. Whether accurate or not, historians of the Confederacy have latched on to this heroic depiction of desertion and often fail to consider it critically.[35]

In 1903, the legislature agreed and clarified, "No soldier who was honorably discharged or who was in service at the surrender shall be considered a deserter, even though he may have deserted at some time during the war."[36] Befitting North Carolina's reputation for absenteeism, going absent without leave (AWOL) was no longer grounds for losing a pension. This new definition of desertion made it easier for individuals who previously might have been labeled dissenters to obtain pensions.

Comparing wartime records with pension lists allows historians to estimate how frequently deserters received pensions. At least 15 percent of the post-1900 applicants in Davidson County would have been ineligible due to their service record by the 1901 standard. These ninety-five applications, which provide a useful sample for examining how one county's board dealt with desertion, can be split into two groups. Of these applications, forty-five were for individuals who were absent without leave or deserted but returned to their units before the surrender; they were thus eligible for pensions after 1903. The other fifty applications (8 percent of all Davidson County applicants) should still have been denied based on the established standard set in 1903, as the soldier never returned from his absence.[37]

Efforts to cull pension lists of deserters were rarely effective. In 1901 papers across the state reported that a wartime list of deserters from western North Carolina had been found and that at least twenty names on it were already drawing pensions![38] Some newspapers claimed fifty deserters had already been found.[39] When further investigation revealed two deserters were in the old soldier's home, outrage ensued. Newspapers around the state published the local pension list, so any undeserving soldier might be spotted.[40] Instructions were sent to county pension boards to carefully investigate each claim, though this does not appear to have led to much change.[41] A system of county advisory boards was even established to try to address the issue, but it did little to stop deserters from applying and receiving pensions.[42] Deserters remained on the books in most communities.

Though estimates of how many pensions were undeserved statewide ranged as high as 20 percent, little was actually done in Davidson County.[43] In 1902 Davidson County's new advisory board discovered only one deserter, Thomas Smith, whose pension had been approved the year before. Yet those estimates of 20 percent were not too far off: at least 17 percent (eighteen individuals) of approved soldiers' applications in Davidson County for 1901 were not eligible based on the stricter standard. Similar occurrences can be found within the widows' applications, as at least eight out of eighty-six Davidson County widows receiving pensions that year should not have been eligible. Indeed, at least thirteen of the Davidson County pensioners in 1901 would not even have met the service requirements of the more lenient 1903 rules.[44] Not that either standard was enforced. In other words, the new advisory committee detected less than 4 percent of ineligible pensioners.[45] Other counties found similar numbers.[46]

Even when someone spoke up, keeping deserters off the pension rolls proved nearly impossible. By 1904, Thomas Smith's widow was receiving a pension for his service, presumably as the new rules propagated in 1903 made her eligible.[47] After the 1903 changes, the number of North Carolinians who deserted or went AWOL applying for pensions increased. By 1909, 10.7 percent (twenty-nine) of Davidson County pensioners would not have been eligible without the law change. The new lenient standards were not the only reason an increased numbers of Davidson County deserters and their widows received pensions. In addition to the twenty-nine pensioners made eligible by the 1903 law change, another twenty-one pensioners should still have been ineligible, having never returned to their units, but they nevertheless received pensions.[48]

The efforts undertaken in 1901 and 1902 appear to be the last major attempt to systematically clear deserters from the pension lists. After 1903, as part of the reworking of the pension system, the advisory board was combined with the county pension board, decreasing the number of people examining each application.[49] Throughout the early twentieth century, technically ineligible men continued to receive pensions. In 1909, all of the surviving pensioners in Davidson County who undeservedly slipped by the board in 1901 still received pensions. In fact, the roll had more deserters than it had previously. Unless they made the mistake of outing themselves, an investigation was unlikely to be undertaken, let alone catch a deserter.

The fact that Jacob Yokley got caught so quickly set him apart from other deserters who applied for pensions. In fact, of fifty identified applications by Davidson County veterans who should have remained ineligible due to desertion, only three can be definitively shown to have been rejected due to their service records: Jacob Yokley, Thomas Smith, and Alfred Gordon. Gordon, who deserted to the enemy in the war's last winter, took the oath, and spent the last months of the war safely in Illinois, had his pension "disallowed" in 1901 for "not a good record." Yet when his disability progressed in the 1920s from "somewhat disabled," to "ruptured and unable to do any work," his pension application was approved. Like Smith's, Gordon's widow also received a pension after her husband's death.[50]

The pension system acted as an early statewide welfare system and incentivized county boards to recommend approval of pensions for disabled citizens for whom the county would otherwise be responsible.[51] One way or another, men like Alfred Gordon needed support, and the pension laws were designed specifically to keep counties from having to support indigent veterans. Instead of examining their service record, those concerned about eligibility focused on wealth. Per the 1903 pension act, pensioners had to have an accumulated wealth of less than $500.[52] Denials because of a person's wealth appear far more frequently than rejections for unsatisfactory war records. Scholar Elna Green argues that Florida's pension system served as an early "Confederate welfare system." North Carolina's operated similarly, thus lionizing the Confederacy while also providing for the aged and infirmed.[53] Many North Carolinians saw the pension system as first and foremost about providing for the aged.[54] Elderly former Home Guard members, those who had served on work details, and even people who had hired substitutes all inquired about pensions for their "service" in the 1920s.[55] As the veterans grew older and grayer, there was less concern about service eligibility, and more focus shifted to ensuring needy members of the community did not suffer.

The leniency and lack of investigation in most cases allowed many wartime dissenters, and even some enlisted men who voted with their feet and deserted their cause, to instead be welcomed into the pantheon of Confederate heroes. On February 18, 1864, Henry Newby deserted to a Union gunboat off Wilmington and was brought to Fortress Monroe. There he signed his oath of allegiance, before being sent to Pennsylvania for the rest of the war.[56] Yet five decades later, the seventy-three-year-old veteran claimed he had received wounds to his foot and heel in 1863, an injury of which no record exists.[57] In his obituary, which recognized him as one of the last veterans in Thomasville, North Carolina, there was no mention that he deserted over a year before the war ended. Indeed, in the years before his death he regularly attended Confederate reunions as well, where apparently no one awkwardly mentioned his acquittal in an 1863 court-martial or subsequent desertion to Union troops.[58]

Pensions gave Newby more than just a monetary reason to hide his desertion, as doing so also provided him an identity that carried with it valuable social capital. These pensions served not only to provide needed cash to impoverished veterans; they also legitimized individuals as respectable members of society. A pension served as evidence of an individual deserving respect within the community. Even the poorest veteran was still seen as honorable. At annual reunions, both local and national, veterans were feted by members of the community. Newby, for example, attended reunions in Richmond and Washington, DC.[59]

Pensions facilitated a specific memory of the war by ensuring that being known as a loyal Confederate enhanced one's social and economic standing. Perhaps the most surprising example of a Davidson County pension was John Crouch. Crouch and his brother Augustin were drafted into the 48th North Carolina Infantry in 1862.[60] In May of the next year, after both had received wounds, they deserted and returned home. They were arrested and returned to Virginia, and Augustin was executed in January 1864.[61] John deserted to Union lines shortly thereafter, took the oath of allegiance, and was sent to Philadelphia for the rest of the war.[62] Years later he applied for and received a pension for which he should not have been eligible.[63] Yet altering his own personal history for a pension may have been part of a broader rewriting of the past by his family. His brother's gravestone recounts Augustin as a volunteer, though sources from the war make clear he was drafted. No mention of his execution can be found on the stone, though it does note that he "died near Orange Co. VA."[64]

What likely undid Jacob Yokley, as opposed to his cousins, uncle, and neighbors—besides never having served—was that he was a braggart. Shortly after submitting his application in 1925, Jacob boasted to his neighbors about his dissent, going so far as to recount how he "drew a gun on the home guard" when they tried to capture him.[65] Jacob apparently took great pride in his ability to avoid capture, and bragged, "He was too sharp for the home guard." He was not too sharp for the pension board, though. His repeated telling to neighbors of how he had never served was exacerbated by using an "oath and curseword in his remarks about the home guard."[66]

Jacob's blatant refusal to even pretend he had been loyal to the South was as unacceptable as his actual lack of service. He vocally undermined the Lost Cause narrative with tales of resistance, so much so that eventually it could not be overlooked. Had he kept quiet, he might conceivably have been able to get away with it. Tasked to investigate the case, the local pension board, likely embarrassed to have passed his application in the first place, found that Jacob was not just a deserter but in fact did not serve in the Confederate army at all. They informed the state pension office that Jacob had admitted to the county pension board itself that he had not served and that he hid by wearing "women's clothes."[67] Yokley's critics attempt to emasculate him with accusations of dressing as a woman served to reassert the masculinity of loyal Confederates. While his crossdressing may have happened—indeed, deserters and recusant conscripts occasionally dressed as women to avoid Home Guard patrols—it also functioned to show Jacob was not the masculine, honorable Confederate hero he presented himself as.[68] Jacob's application contradicted the Lost Cause narrative in just too many ways.

Pensions lionized Confederate service while encouraging the forgetting of dissent even among those who spent the war challenging Confederate authority. Thus, former dissenters who had first shaped a Unionist identity into a political allegiance during Reconstruction actively participated in the erasure of dissent from popular memory by the turn of the century. The same emerald-tinted glasses that had encouraged deserters to see dollar signs in espousing staunch devotion to Union in the 1870s now helped some forget their past devotion to the Stars and Stripes. In time, often even before a recipient's death, a pension came to be seen as a badge of loyalty and devotion to the Confederacy. Making conscripts and deserters who returned to their unit eligible, and rarely enforcing the ban on desertion, are just some of the ways veterans with questionable service records became war heroes in postwar retellings of the war.

Seen vividly in the Southern Claims Commission records and Reconstruction-era election campaigns where opposing the Confederacy played a major role, the myth of the solid South did not take hold immediately after Appomattox. It had to be created after the war. Communities remained divided. Wartime loyalties and memories of the war shaped a disordered society during Reconstruction, and many southerners, black and white, refused to be labeled as supporters of the Confederacy. But by the turn of the century, pensions helped nearly every old veteran to be remembered heroically. The monetary incentive as well as the social capital veteran status supplied proved more powerful than a memory of dissent.

According to the Lost Cause narrative many dissenters had not even dissented: deserters only left to provide for their family, details provided important material support against overwhelming odds, and even fighting for the Union proved one's manhood.[69] Even former slaves could receive payment for their work in the 1920s (thus leading in part to the creation of a myth of black Confederates). Recusant conscripts (and perhaps galvanized Yankees) remained the only category that failed to have a place in the Lost Cause narrative.

In the end, Unionist memory failed to sustain a usable counter narrative to the Lost Cause. The postwar Unionist identity had been built with unstable foundations. A dependency on patriotic motivations and divided communities instead of shared experiences, skin color, or geographic location created inherent weaknesses within Unionist memory. Almost all southern whites were welcome to share in the glories of the Lost Cause, but to be a white Unionist required uncompromising devotion to the flag and persecution by other white southerners.

As many historians have pointed out, the resurgence in Confederate memory from 1890 to 1920—visibly demonstrated by the erection of Confederate monuments across the South—corresponded with the rise of Jim Crow. So too did the expansion of Confederate pensions in North Carolina. Instead of just rewarding their past heroics, pensions helped create living heroes to stand alongside the marble ones that remain controversial today.

Unionist memory simply failed to remain useful. Increasingly, Confederate memory worked to unite whites along racial lines by celebrating the honor and bravery of the white race. In contrast, Unionist memory continued to depend upon a memory of division and persecution, thus dividing neighbors and even families. As the number of former dissenters decreased due to death and emigration, Democratic politicians, too young to have fought, presumably became more politically acceptable than their Confederate predecessors whom Unionists refused to vote for. With the end of the Southern Claims Commission and the introduction of Confederate pensions, even the earlier monetary incentive to celebrate dissent was replaced by new motivation to proclaim a Confederate affiliation.

The Yokley family entirely forgot their anti-Confederate roots. The memory of Samuel's eldest son, Andrew J. Yokley, may be the most striking example of forgetting. Andrew had moved west in 1860, entered federal service in 1862, and was killed in an ambush by Confederate guerrillas while carrying dispatches in Arkansas two years later. The family did not learn of Andrew's enlistment or death in US service until after the war, as they were unable to communicate across the lines. After the war, Samuel collected his son's back pay, and his wife applied for her son's pension in 1884, at which time loyalty still paid. She proclaimed that her family had been "loyal to the union through the war."[70] Initially denied, it took six years' worth of correspondence and additional evidence to receive twelve dollars a month. Yet once the monetary incentive to remember Andrew's service disappeared with his mother's death in 1904, so did any incentive to remember Andrew's sacrifice for his nation.

Today, the Yokley family apparently has no memory of how their ancestors fought against the Confederacy. By 1982 an amateur genealogist tracing her family's heritage recalled that Andrew supposedly died "of a pistol wound reportedly inflicted by Jesse James while working with the Pony express." The Pony Express ceased operation in 1861, four years before Andrew actually died, and Jesse James was barely fourteen at the time. Instead of celebrating Andrew's devotion to the Union and his military service within the US Army, the family created a heroic story that disconnected his death from the war entirely.[71]

Just as using speeches given at the dedication of monuments is a problematic approach to understanding the war, using pension records can be a risky proposition for scholars wanting to interrogate the actual war. Indeed, looking at pension fraud forces us to question wartime levels of support for the Confederacy. As historians increasingly analyze the history of Unionism, desertion, and dissent, studies of historical memory present a unique opportunity to understand the nature of dissent. Historians of the "inner war" should not neglect the creation and ultimate failure of Unionist counter narratives. The Yokleys embraced the identities of both Unionist and Confederate when convenient and when it paid. Dissenters did not remain passive in the creation of an amnesia of dissent. Understanding how dissent was forgotten may also help us understand the nature of wartime dissent. Examining the Yokley's memory of the war not only provides insight into why Unionism was forgotten but also displays the complexity of competing wartime loyalties. In the end, as was often the case with southern dissenters, above all other devotions, the Yokleys were loyal to family.

NOTES

1. Because of the complexity of wartime loyalties, I choose to use the term "dissenter," where others might use "Unionist." "Dissenter" encompasses anyone who resisted Confederate authority at any point during in the war. "Dissenter" as a term does not presume to define motivations. "Unionism," in

contrast, implies a political ideology as the basis for the dissenters' resistance to the Confederacy. I use the term "Unionist" to refer to the postwar identity claimed by many wartime dissenters. Though love of Union surely played a role in many dissenters' decisions, patriotism was only one of many motives. Religion, family obligation, kinship links to the North, as well as pragmatic self-interest all influenced dissenters' decisions and actions. Samuel Yokeley, "Claim of Samuel Yokeley (#10959)" Davidson County, *Southern Claims Commission Approved Claims, 1871–1880,* National Archives Microfilm Publication, RG 217, National Archives and Records Administration, Washington, DC (hereafter Claim of Samuel Yokeley). For examples of Home Guard fleeing, see "Another Good Haul," *Western Sentinel,* November 3, 1864. For more on deserters see also Joseph T. Glatthaar, *General Lee's Army: From Victory to Collapse* (New York: Free Press, 2008), 408–20.

2. See William T. Auman, "Neighbor against Neighbor: The Inner Civil War in the Central Counties of Confederate North Carolina" (PhD diss., University of North Carolina at Chapel Hill, 1988), especially 83, 243–44, 258–60, 380–81, 390, 395, 449, and 460. See also *People's Press* and *Western Sentinel* during the war for newspaper accounts of the community. For an account of the killing of one Forsyth County dissenter, see "Your Affectionate Mother" to "My Dear Son," October 29, 1863, Jarrett-Puryear Family Papers, Duke Manuscript Department. On the murder of five dissenters see David C. Williard, "Executions, Justice, and Reconciliation in North Carolina's Western Piedmont, 1865–1867," *Journal of the Civil War Era* 2, no. 1 (March 2012): 31–57. See also Victoria Bynum, *The Long Shadow of the Civil War: Southern Dissent and Its Legacies* (Chapel Hill: University of North Carolina Press, 2010).

3. Jim DeArman, "I Am Your Confederate Ancestor," *Virginia Flaggers,* November 30, 2013, http://vaflaggers.blogspot.com/2013/11/i-am-your-confederate-ancestor.html.

4. For more on Unionism and memory in North Carolina see Steven E. Nash, "The Immortal Vance: The Political Commemoration of North Carolina's War Governor," in *North Carolinians in the Era of the Civil War and Reconstruction,* ed. Paul D. Escott (Chapel Hill: University of North Carolina Press, 2008), 269–94; Adam H. Domby, "'Loyal to the Core from the First to the Last': Remembering the Inner Civil War of Forsyth County, North Carolina, 1862–1876" (MA thesis, University of North Carolina at Chapel Hill, 2011); Brian K. Fennessy, "The Re-Construction of Memory and Loyalty in North Carolina, 1865–1880" (MA thesis, University of North Carolina at Chapel Hill, 2014); and Barton A. Myers, "'Rebels against a Rebellion' Southern Unionists in Secession, War and Remembrance" (PhD diss., University of Georgia, 2009), especially 221–56. An excellent recent discussion of the Sothern Claims Commission is Barton A. Myers, *Rebels against the Confederacy: North Carolina's Unionists* (Cambridge: Cambridge University Press, 2014). For more on dissent and memory see also Philip S. Paludan, *Victims: A True Story of the Civil War* (Knoxville: University of Tennessee Press, 1981), and John C. Inscoe, *Race, War, and Remembrance in the Appalachian South* (Lexington: University Press of Kentucky, 2008).

5. Marita Sturken, "The Wall, the Screen, and the Image: The Vietnam Veterans Memorial," *Representations* no. 35 (Summer 1991): 137.

6. Jeffrey E. Vogel, "Redefining Reconciliation: Confederate Veterans and the Southern Responses to Federal Civil War Pensions," *Civil War History* 51, no. 1 (March 2005): 74.

7. Jeffrey W. McClurken, *Take Care of the Living: Reconstructing Confederate Veteran Families in Virginia* (Charlottesville: University of Virginia Press, 2009), 144.

8. Claim of Samuel Yokeley; Confederate Citizens File for Samuel Yokeley, *Confederate Papers*

Relating to Citizen or Business Firms, National Archives Microfilm Publication M346, RG 109, National Archives and Records Administration, Washington, DC; 1860 US Federal Census—Slave Schedules, United States of America, Bureau of the Census, Eighth Census of the United States, 1860. National Archives Microfilm Publication M653: National Archives and Records Administration, Washington, DC, 1860; and Population Schedule, United States of America, Bureau of the Census. Eighth Census of the United States, 1860 National Archives Microfilm Publication M653National Archives and Records Administration, Washington, DC.

9. "Whig Convention," *Weekly Raleigh Register,* April 20, 1859. and Claim of Samuel Yokeley.

10. Claim of Samuel Yokeley; Claim of Andrew Yokeley (#10729) (hereafter Claim of Andrew Yokeley) Davidson County, in *Southern Claims Commission Barred and Disallowed Claims* (hereafter *Disallowed Claims*); Claim of Jacob Charles (#10957), Forsyth County, *Disallowed Claims;* Compiled Service Records (hereafter CSRs) for D. P. Yokley, Joseph Yokeley, and Jefferson Yokeley of the 48th North Carolina Infantry in "Compiled Service Records of Confederate Soldiers Who Served in Organizations from the State of North Carolina," National Archives Microfilm Publication M270, RG 109, National Archives and Records Administration, Washington, DC, accessed via Footnote. com; CSR for Andrew J. Yokley of the 7th Cavalry, Compiled Service Records of Volunteer Union Soldiers who Served in Organizations from the State of Missouri, National Archives Microfilm Publication M405, National Archives and Records Administration, Washington, D.C.; Claim of Jackson M Jones (#2797) Davidson County, and Claim of Charles Long (#2707) Davidson County, *Southern Claims Commission Approved Claims.* Some sources indicate another relative, John Yokley, was also in hiding. See Christopher M. Watford, *The Civil War in North Carolina: Soldiers' and Civilians' Letters and Diaries, 1861–1865* (Jefferson: McFarland, 2003), 116.

11. Claim of Samuel Yokeley and CSR for John Gilmer of 21st North Carolina.

12. Claim of Samuel Yokeley.

13. Ibid. Ibid.; see also Chris J. Hartley, *Stoneman's Raid, 1865* (Winston-Salem, NC: John F. Blair, 2010), 207–208.

14. Claim of Samuel Yokeley.

15. For an example of those attacking Confederates see the Dials in Forsyth County. The best account of them is in Auman, "Neighbor against Neighbor," 242–44, 407, 433. See also Wilse Dial Letter, #3143-z, Southern Historical Collection, Wilson Library, University of North Carolina at Chapel Hill.

16. Claim of Samuel Yokeley.

17. The Yokleys were not unique in their willingness to take up arms to protect their sons and brothers. In February 1865, another "band of brother deserters" released two prisoners from the stagecoach along the same road. In March of that same year a local paper reported, "It has become a common occurrence for the stagecoach, on the High Point Road, to be attacked, and any deserter that might be on transportation turned loose." "Rescued," *People's Press,* February 2, 1865; "Deserter Shot," *Western Sentinel,* March 2, 1865.

18. For more on the formation of a Unionist coalition and political organizing see, Domby, "'Loyal to the Core from the First to the Last'"; Adam H. Domby, "War within the States: Loyalty, Dissent, and Conflict in Southern Piedmont Communities, 1860–1876" (PhD diss., University of North Carolina at Chapel Hill, 2015), 229–53. For the creation of Unionist-based political collations see Steven E. Nash, *Reconstruction's Ragged Edge: The Politics of Postwar Life in the Southern*

Mountains (Chapel Hill: University of North Carolina Press, 2016). See also Fennessy, "The Reconstruction of Memory and Loyalty in North Carolina."

19. In 1876, Republican gubernatorial candidate Thomas Settle recognized two types of deserters: those who "deserted from bad motives" and those "who would rather have been shot than to have fought against the flag of our fathers." "The Great Contest" *Union Republican,* August 24, 1876.

20. "Unionist" became a negotiated postwar identity during Reconstruction. The debate over what made one a Unionist is easily seen in testimony and decisions of the Southern Claims Commission. My conception of identity is largely shaped by Malinda Lowery's argument that identity is best viewed as "conversation between insiders and outsiders; these categories themselves are not fixed, and the labels represent heterogeneous populations." Lowery, *Lumbee Indians in the Jim Crow South: Race, Identity, and the Making of a Nation* (Chapel Hill: University of North Carolina Press, 2010), xii.

21. Claim of Andrew Yokeley and Claim of Samuel Yokeley.

22. Samuel Yokeley, Claim of Samuel Yokeley; files for Joseph Yokley and D. P. Yokly, Union Provost Marshals' File of Papers Relating to Individual Civilians, M345, National Archives and Records Administration, Washington DC.

23. CSRs for D. P. Yokley, Joseph Yokeley, and Jefferson Yokeley of the 48th North Carolina and Claim of Samuel Yokeley.

24. "Davidson County," *Tri-Weekly Era,* April 18, 1872, 2–3.

25. Pension File for D. P. Yokley (Davidson County), Office of the State Auditor, North Carolina State Archives, Raleigh, North Carolina (hereafter NCSA). Additionally, she married David in 1890, which made her ineligible, as marriages had to have occurred before 1880 at the time (Baxter Durham to E. C. Byerly, January 23, 1931, Folder "Davidson, 1931–1932," Correspondence, Pension Bureau, State Auditor, NCSA). When her pension application was revisited, the issue of her age and her wealth were the only questions the county pension board asked about (see multiple letters in Folder "Forsyth 1931–1932," Correspondence, Pension Bureau, State Auditor, NCSA).

26. Davidson County Marriage Bonds, Series II, 161, in North Carolina County Registers of Deeds, microfilm, Record Group 048, NCSA, in *North Carolina, Marriage Records, 1741–2011.*

27. Forsyth County Pension Lists, 1924–1926, NCSA; Baxter Durgham to C. M. McKaughan, July 5, 1927, Folder "Forsyth, 1927–1928," Correspondence, Pension Bureau, State Auditor, NCSA; Pension Application File for Joseph Yokeley (Forsyth County), Pension Applications, NCSA.

28. "Soldiers Application for Pension" for D. P. Yokley, December 1923, and "Widow's Application for Confederate Pension" for Mrs. D. P. Yokley, August 6, 1926, filed in Davidson County, box 6.654, NCSA; "Widow's Application for Confederate Pension" for Cordelia Yokeley, July 7, 1924, filed in Forsyth County, box 6.654, NCSA; "Widows entitled to Forsyth County Pensions," reprinted in *Forsyth County Genealogical Society Journal* 23, no. 2 (Winter, 2005): 134–35. General Assembly of North Carolina, "Chapter 189: An Act to Amend and Consolidate the Pension Laws," in *Public Laws and Resolutions of the State of North Carolina Passed by the General Assembly* (Raleigh: Mitchell, 1921), 481–87.

29. "D. P. Yokeley Succumbs at Home Near Walburg," *Charlotte Observer,* August 8, 1926, 3.

30. "Headq's 48th Regt., Centerville Road, September 3, 1862," *Raleigh Register,* September 24, 1862, 1.

31. Pension File for Jacob H. Yokley (Davidson County), Office of the State Auditor, NCSA. For a full accounting of the investigation, see letters in Folder "Davidson, 1925–1927," Correspondence,

Pension Bureau, State Auditor, NCSA. Pension applications can be accessed online at http://digital
.ncdcr.gov/cdm/home/collections/1901-confederate-pension-applications. For this study, I mainly
focused on those from Davidson County.

32. Pension File for Jacob H Yokley (Davidson County), Office of the State Auditor, NCSA;
Folder "Davidson, 1925–1927," Correspondence, Pension Bureau, State Auditor.

33. Thomas Rhodes, "The Status of Veterans," *Greensboro Patriot,* July 10, 1901, 11. Interestingly,
although Rhodes claimed to have deserted, his military record did not reveal his desertion, demonstrating that relying on the CSRs used in this paper to determine the war record of pensioners may
undercount absence without leave and desertion. The only indicator of disciplinary trouble was that a
hospital record says, "This man was turned over to his captain." CSR for Thomas Rhodes of the 27th
North Carolina Infantry.

34. "State Press," *Semi-Weekly Messenger,* November 21, 1902, 7.

35. The depiction of men deserting to care for their families likely described many, perhaps even
the majority of deserters, but this depiction took on a mythic life of its own, which pervades the
historiography today. For the creation of the loyal deserters and how it remains in the historiography
see Adam H. Domby, "'Loyal to the Core from the First to the Last,'" 65–68.

36. "Regarding Pensions," *Union Republican,* June 25, 1903, 4.

37. Cross-referencing CSRs and Davidson County Pension Applications files, NCSA, allowed
me to uncover a sample of individuals who applied for pensions but who were ineligible. In eliminating individuals with good records, I was greatly aided by Christopher M. Watford, *The Civil War
Roster of Davidson County, North Carolina: Biographies of 1,996 Men before, during, and after the Conflict* (Jefferson, NC: McFarland, 2001). The percentages of ineligible men applying for and receiving
pensions is likely higher than I discovered. Record keeping fell apart in 1865 in almost every unit, so
late deserters often do not appear in the CSRs. Additionally, depending on the unit, record keeping
could be better or worse throughout the conflict. The CSRs likely underreport desertion. For example, in Bladen County a man who lost his pension in 1902 as a deserter does not show any sign of
desertion in his very brief CSR (Bladen County Pension list 1902, NCSA; CSR for John Tedder, 2nd
North Carolina Artillery). Among the Davidson records, I found ninety-five pension applications
from men whose CSRs would have raised questions in 1901. Fifty have CSRs that imply they would
have remained ineligible even under the more lenient standards after 1903. Out of fifty application
files based on service records that should have made the applicant ineligible even after 1903, forty-
six were approved (some were initially rejected before being approved later). Of those rejected and
never approved, two were rejected for insufficient disability and not their service record. The other
two were Delila Hill (whose husband joined the Union army) and Jacob Yokley. Why Hill's was rejected remains unknown, but her pension application for a federal pension was similarly denied. Mary
Hinkle (widow of Mathias Hinkle, whose service record should have made him ineligible) had her
record rejected in 1901 for unknown reasons; she died in 1902 and never had the chance to reapply
under the more lenient standards. The case of Susan Younts shows that even suspicions of desertion
were often overcome. She answered the question "Was your late husband a deserter?" with the cagey
answer "Not at close of the war." When her application raised suspicions, she successfully argued that
although the records kept in Washington said her husband had been AWOL, he had actually been
arrested and returned to the Army of Northern Virginia by the Home Guard before Appomattox.

38. "State News," *Progressive Farmer,* April 30, 1901, 3.

39. "The Prodigal's Return," *Dispatch,* March 27, 1901, 4.

40. "Wake Pension List," *North Carolinian,* July 11, 1901, 8. The article included the subheading "Are Any Names on It That Ought Not Be There?"

41. "Instructions to Pension Boards," *Asheville Daily Citizen,* April 16, 1901, 2; "Looking Up Deserters" *Daily Journal,* April 16, 1901, 1.

42. "The Pensions Are Here," *Dispatch,* December 17, 1902, 1.

43. "Instructions to Pension Board," 6.

44. Again, I used the data set of ninety-five pension files whose CSRs or other evidence implies they lacked eligibility. I compared these to the actual pension lists found at the state archives and in local newspapers to confirm a pension was received.

45. Davidson County Pension Lists, 1901, 1902, NCSA.

46. Bladen County for example discovered three deserters on the list in 1902 (none of which show desertion on their CSR). There is clearly a need for a larger study outside of just Davidson County.

47. Davidson County Pension Lists, 1901, 1902, 1904, NCSA and Pension File for Thomas Smith (Davidson County), NCSA.

48. "The Davidson Pensioners," *Dispatch,* December 1, 1909, 2; CSRs. My sample of fraudulent pensions is likely incomplete; to clear many Davidson pensioners of desertion I used secondary sources such as *The Civil War Roster of Davidson County.* Watford usually indicates if an individual deserted, but due to name duplication and confusion, some deserters may have been missed. Hence my estimates are likely low.

49. "Favor Anti-Cigarette Law," *Charlotte Observer,* February, 27, 1903, 3.

50. Pension File for Alfred T. Gordon (Davidson County), NCSA; CSR for Alfred Gordon, 44th North Carolina Infantry.

51. For more on how these pensions systems functioned as welfare see Kathleen Gorman, "Confederate Pensions as Social Welfare," in *Before the New Deal: Social Welfare in the South, 1830–1930,* ed. Elna C. Green (Athens: University of Georgia Press, 1999), 24–39. For more on how pensions connect to welfare see Theda Skocpol, *Protecting Soldiers and Mothers: The Political Origins of Social Policy in United States* (Cambridge, MA: Harvard University Press, 1992).

52. "The New Pension Law," *Union Republican,* April 16, 1903, 2. It was later increased to $2,000.

53. Elna C. Green, "Protecting Confederate Soldiers and Mothers: Pensions, Gender, and the Welfare State in the U.S. South, a Case Study from Florida," *Journal of Social History* 39, no. 4 (2006): 1079.

54. Some even wrote the pension board to ask if old age was enough to qualify for a pension.

55. The correspondence of the NCSA are flush with such letters arranged by county. See for example E .C. Byerly to Baxter Durham, April 9, 1924, Folder "Davidson, 1923–1924," Correspondence, Pension Bureau, State Auditor, NCSA; E. C. Byerly to Baxter Durham, July 7, 1925, Folder "Davidson, 1925–1927," Correspondence, Pension Bureau, State Auditor, NCSA; E. C. Byerly to Baxter Durham, December 31, 1923, Folder "Davidson, 1923–1924," Correspondence, Pension Bureau, State Auditor, NCSA; Baxter Durham to W. E. Church, August 6, 1931, Folder "Forsyth 1931–1932," Correspondence, Pension Bureau, State Auditor, NCSA; and Reece and Hall to Baxter Durham, June 20, 1931, Folder "Yadkin 1931–1933," Correspondence, Pension Bureau, State Auditor, NCSA.

56. CSR for Henry B. Newby, 10th Battalion, North Carolina Heavy Artillery.

57. Pension File for H. B. Newby (Davidson County), NCSA.

58. "Davidson Confederate Veteran Passes Away," *Winston-Salem Journal,* April 9, 1928, 10; "Thomasville U.D.C. Feasts Old Soldiers," *Greensboro Daily News,* December 8, 1927, 2; "Thomasville Department," *Dispatch,* June 22, 1922, 7; CSR for Henry B. Newby; Jack A. Bunch, *Roster of the Courts-Martial in the Confederate States Armies* (Shippensburg, PA: White Mane Books, 2002), 256.

59. "Thomasville Department," *Dispatch,* June 22, 1922, 7; "Thomasville Department," *Dispatch,* June 13, 1917, 8.

60. They were both drafted in 1862 in the county draft that occurred just before general conscription began. For more on the Crouch brothers see Domby, "War within the States," 36, 211.

61. For more on Augustin Crouch's death see Aldo S. Perry, *Civil War Courts-Martial of North Carolina Troops* (Jefferson, NC: McFarland, 2012), 96.

62. CSRs for Augustin Crouch and John C. Crouch, 48th North Carolina Infantry.

63. Pension file for John C. Crouch (Davidson Country), NCSA.

64. Domby, "War within the States," 36; "The Draft-Volunteering," *People's Press,* March 14, 2; Kathy Merris Mills and Dan Stevenson, "Augustin Crouch," *Find A Grave,* April 27, 2007, http://findagrave.com/cgi-bin/fg.cgi/http%22//fg.cgi?page=gr&GRid=19113724. Exactly when the gravestone was placed is unknown.

65. J. K. P. Thomas and J. A. Eller, affidavit, December 16, 1925, Folder "Davidson 1925–1927," Correspondence, Pension Bureau, State Auditor, NCSA.

66. W. E. Conrad, V. S. Briles, and H. H. Hodge, "In Re Pension Allowance for Jacob H. Yokley," affidavit, December 15, 1925, Folder "Davidson 1925–1927," Correspondence, Pension Bureau, State Auditor, NCSA.

67. E. C. Byerly et al. to Baxter Durham, "In Re Jacob H. Yokley Pension," December 30, 1925, Folder "Davidson 1925–1927," Correspondence, Pension Bureau, State Auditor, NCSA.

68. For an example of dressing as a woman, see Claim of Ransom Phipps (#10716), Guilford County, NC, *Disallowed Claims.*

69. For an excellent example of Lost Cause proponents welcoming deserters, see Julian S. Carr, Speech [fragment], folder 32, in the Julian Shakespeare Carr Papers #141, Southern Historical Collection, Wilson Library, University of North Carolina at Chapel Hill. The speeches in the Carr papers provide an amazing overview of efforts to create a white memory of the Civil War. For discussions of the Lost Cause, see David W. Blight, *Race and Reunion: The Civil War in American Memory* (Cambridge, MA: Harvard University Press, 2001); David W. Blight, *Beyond the Battlefield: Race, Memory, and the American Civil War* (Amherst: University of Massachusetts Press, 2002); Gaines M. Foster, *Ghosts of the Confederacy: Defeat, the Lost Cause, and the Emergence of the New South, 1865 to 1913* (New York: Oxford University Press, 1987); Carol Reardon, *Pickett's Charge in History and Memory* (Chapel Hill: University of North Carolina Press, 1997); Caroline E. Janney, *Remembering the Civil War: Reunion and the Limits of Reconciliation* (Chapel Hill: University of North Carolina Press, 2013).

70. Pension and CSR for Andrew J. Yokley, 7th Missouri Cavalry (USA), National Archives and Records Administration, Washington, DC.

71. Francis Y. Kestler, "Amos Yokley," in *The Heritage of Davidson County, 1982,* ed. North Carolina Genealogical Society of Davidson County (Lexington, NC: Genealogical Society of Davidson

County, 1982), 639. Claim of Samuel Yokeley; Andrew J. Yokley (Company E, 7th Missouri Cavalry), index card; imaged from *Organization Index to Pension Files of Veterans Who Served Between 1861 and 1900*, T289 (Washington, DC: National Archives). For an excellent biography of James see T. J. Stiles, *Jesse James: Last Rebel of the Civil War* (New York: Alfred A. Knopf, 2002). Nowhere in the biography does the Pony Express appear.

Veterans in New Fields

Directions for Future Scholarship on Civil War Veterans

BRIAN MATTHEW JORDAN

F OR DECADES, Civil War veterans lurked in the shadows of our histories. Despite the emergence of a rich scholarship on the wartime thoughts and deeds of Johnny Reb and Billy Yank, remarkably few scholars pursued them home from the battlefield.[1] To be sure, few Civil War veterans maintained the prodigious literary output they achieved during the war. Men no longer felt a sense of urgency to record the daily details of their lives. Contemporaneous accounts of Confederate veterans returning home are especially scarce, and the National Archives and Records Administration (NARA) destroyed the records of the National Home for Disabled Volunteer Soldiers, preserving only "randomly sampled" case files that are today scattered among NARA's regional branches in Boston, Chicago, New York, and Kansas City. Grand Army of the Republic archives are likewise decentralized.[2]

While the quantity of postwar manuscript material pales in comparison to the heaps of letters generated during the war, scholars have nevertheless discovered many portals through which to access the postbellum lives of Johnny Reb and Billy Yank. Veterans' newspapers are remarkable quarries of information about the social, cultural, and political lives of Civil War veterans.[3] Federal pension files have revealed much more than the obstacles that Union veterans surmounted in order to secure a pension claim. Among many other insights, pension files have betrayed intimate details about physical, psychological, and emotional wounds; veterans' domestic situations and economic conditions; relationships between and among veterans; the geographic mobility of ex-soldiers; the process by which veterans translated raw wartime memories into narratives of suffering or sacrifice; and the effects of postwar politics and policy making on the everyday lives of veterans and their families.[4]

Other sources are more infrequently used but no less rewarding. The records of the US House Committee on Invalid Pensions, for example, include pleas and petitions submitted to Congress by veterans' organizations and pension lobbyists. These sources not only identify what pensions meant to individual veterans but also show how Civil War soldiers developed a new "rhetoric of rights." Though decentralized, the administrative and post–relief fund records of the Grand Army of the Republic likewise afford an entry point into the postbellum experiences of Billy Yank, revealing that "charity" and relief were perhaps more significant than politics in the largest fraternal society for Union veterans. Indeed, these sources might prove essential to a much-needed history of poverty and penury among Lincoln's ex-soldiers.[5] When mined for more than tactical minutiae, as historian Lesley J. Gordon has recently demonstrated, regimental histories can illuminate how veterans made sense of their service, sterilized traumatic pasts, and developed a sense of history.[6]

Recent scholarship has afforded us a much richer, more nuanced picture of Civil War armies: one teeming with sharp political divisions, class tensions, and ethnic diversity.[7] Just as recent scholars of Civil War soldiers have embraced the notion that individuals experienced the war in radically different ways, abandoning archetypes for aberrations, scholars of the veteran experience now need to catalog diverse physical, psychological, and emotional responses to the war.[8] Homecoming demanded adjustments of all who served, but those adjustments were made in unique ways. How did soldiers' prewar lives or distinctive wartime experiences shape their veteranhood? What about the role of religion? To date, these remain oddly understudied questions.[9] Jason Phillips invited historians of Civil War soldiers to try their hand at biography; his suggestion seems no less promising for scholars working on Civil War veterans.[10] New databases and emerging digital tools will allow us to ask better questions: How did regimental itineraries, high casualty rates, and participation in high-intensity combat situations, for example, affect the trajectory of veteranhood and actual longevity? Did the men who shouldered muskets in one of William F. Fox's "Three Hundred Fighting Regiments" suffer psychological injuries with greater frequency than those whose units saw less combat? Can we draw any conclusions about how losses in the soldier's "primary group" affected post-war behavior?[11]

At the same time, we should ponder how domestic situations, perceived community support, and kin networks—real and fictive—dulled veterans' grief, despair, and guilt. We know much too little, for instance, about the vital roles played by wives, sweethearts, parents, and children in the process of reintegration. Former comrades and those who shared in the experience of war may have been even more important in this process. Though "students of Civil War battles have long recognized the primary place of the regiment in the hearts and minds of Civil War soldiers," remarkably few scholars have examined an obvious peculiarity of Civil War veteranhood: because the vast majority of fighting units were raised from adjoining towns and counties, those who survived the war quite frequently lived, worked, and worshipped with their former comrades.[12] In effect, as Susannah J. Ural points out in her recent study of Hood's Texas Brigade, many units never really "demobilized." This no doubt proved a boon for many men who relied on fellow veterans when gathering evidence for a pension claim or searching for that niggling detail necessary to complete a memoir or regimental history. To be sure, pension files testify to the frequency with which veterans visited after the war, looked after the ailing and distressed, horded information, and attended Grand Army meetings together. Barbara A. Gannon has written about the "community of the regiment" in a brilliant essay on the African American nurse Lucy Nichols. During the war, Nichols tended to the men of the 23rd Indiana Volunteer Infantry; those men regarded Nichols as a comrade after the war and saw to her welfare. More work along these lines will enhance our understanding of why some veterans returned to civilian life without difficulty even as others regarded reintegration as an impossible feat.[13]

At the same time, living among former comrades must have been a burden for some veterans. Certainly, the absence of the dead and missing was agonizingly tangible in many small towns and villages. Perhaps some veterans simply desired a fresh start or wished to grapple with the war alone; this may explain the allure of Iowa, Nebraska, and Kansas, three states where the population of Union veterans soared in the last decades of the nineteenth century. In his essay in this volume, historian Kurt Hackemer explores another cohort of ex-soldiers who migrated west—those who formed so-called "veteran colonies" in the Dakota Territory. These men desired to live with other veterans but clearly hunted new opportunities far removed from the scenes of their prewar lives. Did they understand the move west as an opportunity to improve their physical or mental health? If so, were they practicing what historian Kathryn Shively has called "self-care"?[14]

Hackemer's piece not only opens a window into the lives of veterans about whom we know very little but also invites new questions about veterans' health and the way that ex-soldiers thought about their aches, pains, and spells of melancholy. Indeed, while scholars have devoted much energy to the medical history of the war and consequences of amputation, the longitude and life-span of other wounds—together with the effects of chronic diseases, pulmo-nary ailments, sunstroke, and physical exhaustion—have not been adequately considered.[15] What did it mean, for instance, to live with an "invisible" illness in an age that regarded empty sleeves and pinned up trousers as "honorable scars"? Historian Brian Craig Miller has noted the gendered implications of amputation, but wounds that rendered soldiers incontinent were no less emas-culating. Most curiously, historians have all but neglected regimental surgeons, who continued to play significant roles in the lives of veterans by supporting their pension claims. We also know precious little about pension attorneys and pension claim agencies, upon whose services veterans and their widows neces-sarily relied when navigating the dense thicket of federal pension legislation, statues, and rules. Histories of the postwar years written from the perspective of either regimental surgeons or pension attorneys would almost certainly yield new insights into the meaning of Civil War pensions and the ordinary lives of those who survived the war.

Contemplating the ordinary lives of veterans might also revise our under-standing of the mechanics of Civil War memory. When we consider how aches and pains continued to annex their lives and routines, we might well reach the conclusion that "forgetfulness" about the war was practically impossible for many of its veterans. On that score, we might develop a more capacious definition of Civil War "memory work." "Sometimes," David Blight concedes, "the study of memory can seem like just one damned commemoration or rit-ual after another with no framework, as though history is really nothing more than competing parades and monuments." Similarly, Alon Confino observes, "There exists in memory studies the danger of reducing culture to politics and ideology, instead of broadening the field from the political to the social and the experiential, to an everyday history of memory."[16] Clearly, Civil War "memory" entailed more than attending a GAR meeting, contributing to a regimental history, delivering a monument dedication speech, or strutting past the court-house on Memorial Day; it was also the Ohio veteran, wounded by a Confed-erate artillery shell on the first afternoon at Gettysburg, who "always referred to [his] wound in the shoulder and pronounced curses upon the rebel who shot him."[17] In myriad and mundane ways, veterans remembered.

In much work on Civil War memory, Confederate veterans have emerged as the more determined custodians of the past. Historians routinely portray former rebels as "obdurate" and "unreconstructed" while depicting former Union soldiers as "pension obsessed" men wanting principle or conviction. Though recent scholars have offered correctives, the lamentable view persists that Union veterans were negligent at best or complicit at worst in the retreat from Reconstruction.[18] Here again, a more comprehensive depiction of the day-to-day realities of life for Union veterans might prove instructive. The overwhelming demands of Civil War veteranhood—not "purposeful forgetfulness" or some ill-timed "hibernation"—may have precluded the men who won the war from assuming a more active or public role in the course of Reconstruction. Perhaps even more important, the reconciliatory narratives peddled by northern elites left little room for the gritty memories of Union ex-soldiers, who as early as 1868 were scorned for their insistence that the war "was not yet over." What effect, in other words, did the "culture of conciliation" have on veterans who sought to make sense of a costly and deeply ideological war—one that, in many ways, the nation insisted never happened?[19]

When we discard the assumption that Union veterans willfully abandoned their cause, a fascinating line of questioning emerges. How did Union veterans respond to the horrors of Reconstruction? Did the course of Reconstruction prompt some veterans to wonder if the war had been worth it after all? If so, how did veterans wrestle with that question?

During the war, Union soldiers greeted expressions of copperheadism on the northern home front with sharply worded resolutions and vows of vengeance. Once home, how did veterans respond to the draft dodgers, deserters, and antiwar Democrats now in their midst? Historian John J. Hennessy has argued that among the men of the Army of the Potomac in 1863, the "fire in the rear" served to clarify what was at stake in the war. Manifestations of disloyalty welded fractious brigades together. Did the imperative to "forgive and forget" similarly unite ex-soldiers after the war? Or did a lack of consensus about the war's meaning among northern civilians render Union veteranhood especially difficult?[20]

Veterans are frequently studied as custodians of the war's memory, but remarkably little work has considered the place of the Civil War veteran in US memory. We need more scholarship on the depiction of Civil War veterans in both fiction and the visual arts—and on celluloid.[21] Furthermore, because histories of Civil War memory so rarely stray beyond the Gettysburg jubilee and into the mid-twentieth century, the veritable celebrity enjoyed by the "last veterans" has not been thoroughly explored.[22] By the mid-1940s, US citizens looked on with certain awe at the last surviving veterans, once spurned as "pension beggars" or "hand-organ grinders." Bruce Catton, one of the war's most beloved chroniclers, wrote elegiacally about the tottering veterans who passed their final days in his hometown of Benzonia, Michigan. "The Civil War veterans were men set apart," he began. "On formal occasions they wore blue uniforms with brass buttons and black campaign hats. . . . They gave an especial flavor to the life of the village. Years ago they had marched thousands of miles to legendary battlefields, and although they had lived half a century since then in our quiet backwater all anyone ever thought of was that they had once gone to the ends of the earth and seen beyond the farthest horizon."[23]

Not unrelated to memory, public historians have expressed little interest in Civil War veterans. While the recent addition of Reconstruction Era National Monument remedied the National Park Service's long lamented inattention to the post–Civil War years, no site in the NPS system is solely devoted to interpreting the lives of Civil War veterans.[24] The sprawling, tree-shaded campuses of the National Home for Disabled Volunteer Soldiers in Milwaukee, Wisconsin, or Dayton, Ohio, would be splendid places to interpret the postwar lives of Civil War soldiers.[25] And while its primary mission is to purchase, preserve, and interpret battlefield land, it is somewhat surprising that the Civil War Trust has paid little attention to crumbling Grand Army of the Republic halls and "living monuments" to Civil War veterans throughout the country.[26]

DESPITE A BLIZZARD of recent books about Civil War veterans, this essay suggests that historians have much to discover about the postwar lives of Johnny Reb and Billy Yank. Scholarship on Confederate veterans has hardly kept pace with that on Union veterans.[27] We still lack a social and cultural history of the major southern veterans' organization, the United Confederate Veterans. Local relief networks and charitable efforts on behalf of Confederate veterans have not been adequately mapped.[28] Ex-sailors, who formed their own fraternal societies, want for serious treatment, as do the veterans of the irregular war, who held their own reunions. A stunning array of veterans' organizations and survivors' guilds—the Society of the Army of the Tennessee, the National Association of Battle of Shiloh Survivors, the National Sultana Survivors Association, and the Sheridan's Veterans' Association—demand treatment, as do auxiliaries, such as the Ladies of the Grand Army of the Republic and the Women's Relief Corps. Work on black veterans, meanwhile, has settled into something of a holding pattern, though the essays in this volume suggest some promising new directions.[29]

Scholars have paid considerable attention to veterans' reunions and the Grand Army of the Republic (GAR); nonetheless, despite an emerging literature on the material culture of the Civil War era, we await serious scholarship on the materiality and commercial aspects of veteranhood. Civil War veterans trafficked in war relics, assembled reference libraries, and organized "battlefield excursions." The GAR relied on firms like M. C. Lilley & Company of Columbus, Ohio, to bedeck its members in brass pins and bronze badges. A study of these enterprises—together with a full accounting of the commercial windfall experienced by cities hosting Blue-Gray reunions and national encampments—would not only plug a gap in the literature, but might suggest one more important incentive for sectional reconciliation.[30] Yet another emerging subfield—the history of emotions—seems especially fertile soil to till with respect to Civil War veterans. Already, Martha Hodes has demonstrated the wrenching ambiguities of the immediate postwar months for ordinary men, women, and children, white and black, North and South. In particular, veterans greeted the war's end with a combination of relief, guilt, angst, and even fear. By more intently reading the emotions of Civil War veterans immediately after Appomattox and beyond, we might better understand the life cycle of memory, the question of "nostalgia," and the healing process itself. "Decoration Day" exercises—surprisingly little studied—might be a useful way to organize such a history and track changes over time. Work on veterans' emotions would take the field in a useful new direction, all the while avoiding the presentist—and ultimately unproductive—diagnosis of post-traumatic stress disorder (PTSD).[31]

Fifty years after Appomattox, the Reverend A. H. Nichols announced to the "rapidly thinning ranks" of the Grand Army of the Republic his pride in what they had achieved between 1861 and 1865: saving the Union, ending slavery, preserving self-government. The heft of those achievements persuaded many Union veterans that they were somehow exceptional men; in the twilight of their lives, this gave them confidence that even the thorniest of "civil questions and problems" at home and around the globe could be remedied. "It is true that most of us have passed the scriptural allotment, 'three score years and ten,' and are not as strong physically as we once were, yet we can make our presence in society of a mighty force," the bewhiskered Nichols began immodestly. "The past is on record and cannot be erased," he continued, but "the future is before us and we must not fold our hands and say 'the work is finished.' The work is not finished."[32] Nor is ours.

NOTES

1. The first scholars of Civil War veterans were almost exclusively interested in their influence on state and national politics. See, for example, Mary R. Dearing, *Veterans in Politics: The Story of the G.A.R.* (Baton Rouge: Louisiana State University Press, 1952); Frank H. Heck, *The Civil War Veteran in Minnesota Life and Politics* (Oxford, OH: Mississippi Valley, 1941); and George J. Lankevich, "The Grand Army of the Republic in New York State, 1865–1898" (PhD diss., Columbia University, 1967). More recent synthetic treatments of Civil War veteranhood include Stuart McConnell, *Glorious Contentment: The Grand Army of the Republic, 1865–1900* (Chapel Hill: University of North Carolina Press, 1992); Donald R. Shaffer, *After the Glory: The Struggles of Black Civil War Veterans* (Lawrence: University Press of Kansas, 2004); James A. Marten, *Sing Not War: The Lives of Union and Confederate Veterans in Gilded Age America* (Chapel Hill: University of North Carolina Press, 2011); Barbara A. Gannon, *The Won Cause: White and Black Comradeship in the Grand Army of the Republic* (Chapel Hill: University of North Carolina Press, 2011); Brian Matthew Jordan, *Marching Home: Union Veterans and Their Unending Civil War* (New York: Liveright, 2014); and Paul A. Cimbala, *Veterans North and South* (Santa Barbara, CA: Praeger, 2015).

2. For a rare contemporaneous account of a Confederate veteran's homecoming, see *A. B. Green's Diary: The Journey Home: Appomattox to Moscow, TX, April 13–July 11, 1865* (Austin: Hood's Texas Brigade Association Reactivated, 2015).

3. Steven E. Sodergren's essay in this volume suggests the potential dividends of the *National Tribune,* now fully digitized by the Library of Congress. The newspaper is now indexed as well. See Richard A. Sauers, *The National Tribune Civil War Index: A Guide to the Weekly Newspaper Dedicated to Civil War Veterans, 1877–1943,* 3 vols. (El Dorado Hills, CA: Savas Beatie, 2018). Beyond the *National Tribune* and its counterpart *Confederate Veteran,* dozens of less well known local, regional, and state veterans' newspapers remain to be mined systematically. These include the *Western Veteran* (Topeka, Kansas); *Veterans' Advocate* (Concord, New Hampshire); *Soldiers' Record* (Hartford, Connecticut); *Relief Guard* (St. Paul, Minnesota); *Soldier's Casket* (Philadelphia, Pennsylvania); *Soldiers' Record* (Madison, Wisconsin); and *American Tribune* (Indianapolis, Indiana).

4. See, for example, Megan J. McClintock, "Civil War Pensions and the Reconstruction of Union Families," *Journal of American History* 83, no. 2 (September 1996): 456–80. In addition to pension files, the "Records of the Veterans Administration Pertaining to the Issuance of Artificial Limbs" are especially revealing about the everyday lives of amputees. These records include applicants and correspondence (not infrequently complaints) regarding government-issued artificial limbs.

5. William Marvel, *Lincoln's Mercenaries: Economic Motivation among Union Soldiers during the Civil War* (Baton Rouge: Louisiana State University Press, 2018), broaches this subject with his consideration of the pecuniary motivations of northern volunteers. There is likewise room for a new, synthetic study of the Grand Army of the Republic; rather than focusing on "fraternity" and "loyalty," as Stuart McConnell and Barbara Gannon's excellent monographs do, this tome might take "charity" as its organizing theme. In 1883, for instance, the Bay State GAR reported that it had dispensed "over six hundred thousand dollars" in relief funds "during the last seventeen years." *Bivouac* 1, no. 11 (November 1883): 379.

6. Lesley J. Gordon, *A Broken Regiment: The 16th Connecticut's Civil War* (Baton Rouge: Louisiana State University Press, 2014).

7. See Jonathan W. White, *Emancipation, the Union Army, and the Reelection of Abraham Lincoln* (Baton Rouge: Louisiana State University Press, 2014); Zachery A. Fry, "Lincoln's Divided Legion: Loyalty and the Political Culture of the Army of the Potomac, 1861–1865" (PhD diss., Ohio State University, 2017); Lorien Foote, *The Gentlemen and the Roughs: Violence, Honor, and Manhood in the Union Army* (New York: New York University Press, 2010); Ryan W. Keating, *Shades of Green: Irish Regiments, American Soldiers, and Local Communities in the Civil War Era* (New York: Fordham University Press, 2017); Susannah J. Ural, *The Harp and the Eagle: Irish-American Volunteers and the Union Army, 1861–1865* (New York: New York University Press, 2006); and Christian Keller, *Chancellorsville and the Germans: Nativism, Ethnicity, and Civil War Memory* (New York: Fordham University Press, 2007). Most glaring among the gaps in the literature is work on ethnic Grand Army of the Republic posts and the veterans of ethnic regiments.

8. Jason Phillips, "Battling Stereotypes: A Taxonomy of Civil War Soldiers," *History Compass* 6 (2008). For examples of work on aberrations, see Gordon, *A Broken Regiment;* Stephen Berry, ed., *Weirding the War: Stories from the Civil War's Ragged Edges* (Athens: University of Georgia Press, 2011); and my own forthcoming work on the 107th Ohio Volunteer Infantry.

9. Cimbala, *Veterans North and South,* makes a sensible appeal for future historians to understand the life arc and trajectory of Civil War veterans.

10. James Marten's masterful biography of James Tanner, the veteran of the 87th New York who lost both legs at Second Bull Run and became well known on the Grand Army lecture circuit, is a good example of biography's promise. Marten's book is especially impressive because Tanner left only traces in the archives. See Marten, *America's Corporal: James Tanner in War and Peace* (Athens: University of Georgia Press, 2014). Elizabeth R. Varon is at work on a life of the African American veteran and historian Joseph Thomas Wilson. A number of other promising subjects—such as *National Tribune* editor George Lemon, Andersonville survivor John McElroy, and badly wounded Gettysburg veteran John F. Chase—await biographers. Finally, Mark H. Dunkelman, *War's Relentless Hand: Twelve Tales of Civil War Soldiers* (Baton Rouge: Louisiana State University Press, 2006), demonstrates the promise of work on less well-known individuals.

11. William F. Fox, *Regimental Losses in the American Civil War, 1861–1865* (Albany, NY: Albany Publishing, 1889). Essential to this work will be the Union Army Data Project, pioneered by the late economic historian Robert Fogel and the National Bureau of Economic Research. For more on this project and its enormous promise, see Earl J. Hess, "The Early Indicators Project: Using Massive Data and Statistical Analysis to Understand the Life Cycle of Civil War Soldiers," *Civil War History* 63, no. 4 (December 2017): 377–99.

12. Gerald Prokopowicz, *All for the Regiment: The Army of the Ohio, 1861–1862* (Chapel Hill: University of North Carolina Press, 2001), 5. Jay Winter's notion of "fictive kinship" may be especially useful here. See Winter, "Forms of Kinship and Remembrance in the Aftermath of the Great War," in *War and Remembrance in the Twentieth Century,* ed. Winter and Emmanuel Sivan (Cambridge: Cambridge University Press, 2000), 40–60. In what was very likely the first census of Civil War veterans, the adjutant general of Ohio recorded the number of men—by regiment—who lived in various Buckeye State counties and municipalities. While the extant records are woefully incomplete, the project itself is remarkable evidence of the attention paid by contemporary officials to veterans' networks. See "Numerical Returns of Civil War Veterans by County and Township, 1866," State Archives Series 2986, box 50, entry 640B, Ohio History Connection, Columbus, Ohio.

13. Susannah J. Ural, *Hood's Texas Brigade: The Soldiers and Families of the Confederacy's Most Celebrated Unit* (Baton Rouge: Louisiana State University Press, 2017); Barbara A. Gannon, "'She Is a Member of the 23rd': Lucy Nichols and the Community of the Civil War Regiment," in *This Distracted and Anarchical People: New Answers for Old Questions about the Civil War–Era North,* ed. Andrew L. Slap and Michael Thomas Smith (New York: Fordham University Press, 2013). See also Mark Dunkelman, *Brothers One and All: Esprit de Corps in a Civil War Regiment* (Baton Rouge: Louisiana State University Press, 2006).

14. Kathryn Shively Meier, *Nature's Civil War: Common Soldiers and the Environment in 1862 Virginia* (Chapel Hill: University of North Carolina Press, 2013).

15. On amputation, see Brian Craig Miller, *Empty Sleeves: Amputation in the Civil War South* (Athens: University of Georgia Press, 2015), and Megan Kate Nelson, *Ruin Nation: Destruction and the American Civil War* (Athens: University of Georgia Press, 2012). For recent work on the war's medical history, see Margaret Humphreys, *Marrow of Tragedy: The Health Crisis of the American Civil War* (Baltimore: Johns Hopkins University Press, 2013), and Shauna M. Devine, *Learning from the Wounded: The Civil War and the Rise of American Medical Science* (Chapel Hill: University of North Carolina Press, 2014). Barbara Gannon similarly urged greater attention to the effects of chronic disease and diarrhea at a roundtable on Civil War veterans at the Society for Civil War Historians Biennial Meeting in Chattanooga in 2016.

16. David W. Blight, "The Memory Boom: Why and Why Now?" in *Memory in Mind and Culture,* ed. Pascal Boyer and James V. Wertsch (Cambridge: Cambridge University Press, 2009), 242; Alon Confino, "Collective Memory and Cultural History: Problems of Method," *American Historical Review* 102, no. 5 (December 1997): 1386–1403, quote at 1402. For two recent, efficient syntheses of Civil War memory, see Barbara Gannon, *Americans Remember Their Civil War* (Santa Barbara, CA: Praeger, 2017), and Robert J. Cook, *Civil War Memories: Contesting the Past in the United States since 1865* (Baltimore: Johns Hopkins University Press, 2017).

17. Philip Seltzer Pension File, application no. 149,360, certificate no. 101,745, RG 15, National Archives and Records Administration, Washington, DC.

18. For recent correctives, see M. Keith Harris, *Across the Bloody Chasm: The Culture of Commemoration among Civil War Veterans* (Baton Rouge: Louisiana State University Press, 2014); Robert Hunt, *The Good Men Who Won the War: Army of the Cumberland Veterans and Emancipation Memory* (Tuscaloosa: University of Alabama Press, 2010); Andre Fleche, "'Shoulder to Shoulder as Comrades Tried': Black and White Union Veterans and Civil War Memory," *Civil War History* 51 (2005): 175–201; Gannon, *The Won Cause;* Caroline E. Janney, *Remembering the Civil War: Reunion and the Limits of Reconciliation* (Chapel Hill: University of North Carolina Press, 2013); and Jordan, *Marching Home.* With a few exceptions, Union veterans are mostly indistinguishable from northern "reconciliationists" in David W. Blight, *Race and Reunion: The Civil War in American Memory* (Cambridge, MA: Harvard University Press, 2001). Gerald Linderman, *Embattled Courage: The Experience of Combat in the American Civil War* (New York: Free Press, 1987) did much to cement this argument, contending that the war's veterans, wearied by the experience of combat, skulked into a state of "hibernation" for at least fifteen years after Appomattox.

19. Nina Silber, *The Romance of Reunion: Northerners and the South, 1865–1900* (Chapel Hill: University of North Carolina Press, 1993).

20. On soldiers' responses to copperheads during the war, see John J. Hennessy, "Evangelizing for Union, 1863: The Army of the Potomac, Its Enemies at Home, and a New Solidarity," *Journal of the Civil War Era* 4, no. 4 (December 2014): 533–58, and Mark E. Neely Jr., *The Union Divided: Party Conflict in the Civil War North* (Cambridge, MA: Harvard University Press, 2002). For an example of a Union veteran reflecting on these questions, see *What Did We Fight For? A Response by A. H. Mattox at the Second Annual Reunion of the* [Seventeenth Ohio Veteran] *Battery, at Springfield, Ohio, August 5, 1886* (Cincinnati: Robert Clarke, 1885).

21. Works of fiction dealing with Civil War veterans include Cyrus Cobb and Darius Cobb, *The Veteran of the Grand Army: A Novel* (Boston: Cyrus and Darius Cobb, 1870); Dennis McFarland, *Nostalgia* (New York: Pantheon, 2013); Howard Bahr, *The Judas Field: A Novel of the Civil War* (New York: Picador, 2006); John Hough Jr., *Seen the Glory: A Novel of the Battle of Gettysburg* (New York: Simon and Schuster, 2009); and Robert Hicks, *The Widow of the South: A Novel* (New York: Warner Books, 2005). For an excellent treatment of veterans in fiction (as well as their various contributions *to* fiction), see Craig A. Warren, *Scars to Prove It: The Civil War Soldier and American Fiction* (Kent, OH: Kent State University Press, 2009). Emmett Early, *The War Veteran in Film* (Jefferson, NC: McFarland, 2003) includes material on Civil War veterans, but a comprehensive analysis is necessary.

22. The last veterans received popular treatment in Richard Serrano, *Last of the Blue and Gray: Old Men, Stolen Glory, and the Mystery that Outlived the Civil War* (Washington, DC: Smithsonian Books, 2013). Building on the work of Jay Hoar, historian Frank Grzyb, in *The Last Civil War Veterans: The Lives of the Final Survivors, State by State* (Jefferson, NC: McFarland, 2016), provides capsule biographies of the war's last survivors.

23. Bruce Catton, *Waiting for the Morning Train: An American Boyhood* (1972; repr., Detroit: Wayne State University Press, 1987), 189–90.

24. See Jennifer Whitmer Taylor and Page Putnam Miller, "Reconstructing Memory: The Attempt to Designate Beaufort, South Carolina, the National Park Service's First Reconstruction Unit," *Journal of the Civil War Era* 7, no. 1 (March 2017): 39–66.

25. For a superb history of the National Home for Disabled Volunteer Soldiers, see Patrick J.

Kelly, *Creating a National Home: Building the Veterans' Welfare State, 1860–1900* (Cambridge, MA: Harvard University Press, 1997).

26. For one recent example, see Rick Miller, "Civil War Author Disappointed at County's Refusal to Preserve Monument," *Olean Times Herald,* October 6, 2014.

27. See, for example, Jeffrey W. McClurken, *Take Care of the Living: Reconstructing Confederate Veteran Families in Virginia* (Charlottesville: University of Virginia Press, 2009); David Silkenat, *Moments of Despair: Suicide, Divorce, and Debt in Civil War Era North Carolina* (Chapel Hill: University of North Carolina Press, 2011); Diane Miller Sommerville, *Aberration of Mind: Suicide and Suffering in the Civil War–Era South* (Chapel Hill: University of North Carolina Press, 2018); Miller, *Empty Sleeves;* Rusty Williams, *My Old Confederate Home: A Respectable Place for Civil War Veterans* (Lexington: University Press of Kentucky, 2010); and David C. Williard, "Confederate Veterans and the Reconstruction of Southern Society, 1861–1880" (PhD diss., University of North Carolina at Chapel Hill, 2012).

28. Deborah Cohen, *War Come Home: Disabled Veterans in Britain and Germany, 1914–1939* (Berkeley: University of California Press, 2001), argues that the "burdens" of the Great War "could not be met by states alone." Local charitable efforts played an essential role in the treatment of wounded veterans; further, by supplying evidence that the public at large acknowledged the war's costs, they "brought about a reconciliation between disabled veterans and those for whom they had suffered." After the Civil War (perhaps owing to the fact that Confederate veterans could not apply for federal pensions), local benevolent and religious networks took great interest in caring for ex-soldiers. Mapping these networks—work that Jeffrey W. McClurken ably began in *Take Care of the Living*—may permit future historians to draw sharper contrasts between the attitudes of Union and Confederate veterans. Cohen, *War Come Home,* 1, 7.

29. Two recent books, Kelly D. Mezurek, *For Their Own Cause: The 27th United States Colored Troops* (Kent, OH: Kent State University Press, 2016), and Douglas R. Egerton, *Thunder at the Gates: The Black Civil War Regiments That Redeemed America* (New York: Basic Books, 2016), consider the postwar experiences of black soldiers. Because black soldiers' experiences in the war and as veterans were so distinct, they are often excluded from sweeping national studies. Future historians must do a better job of explaining the differences between black veterans and black nonveterans, as well as the differences between black veterans and white veterans. But this work will depend upon a critical mass of state-based case studies on black soldiers and veterans. For an example of the latter, see Richard M. Reid, *Freedom for Themselves: North Carolina's Black Soldiers in the Civil War Era* (Chapel Hill: University of North Carolina Press, 2008).

30. For promising work along these lines see, in addition to Jonathan Neu's essay in this volume, C. Ian Stevenson, "Vacationing with the Civil War: Maine's Regimental Summer Cottages," *Civil War History* 63, no. 2 (June 2017): 151–80. On material culture in the period more generally, see Joan E. Cashin, ed., *War Matters: Material Culture in the Civil War Era* (Chapel Hill: University of North Carolina Press, 2018). On battlefield excursions, see C. O. Brown, *The Old Battlefields Revisited after 16 Years!,* copy in Edward Schewitzer Papers, Huntington Library, San Marino, California.

31. Martha Hodes, *Mourning Lincoln* (New Haven, CT: Yale University Press, 2015). On the "history of emotions," see Susan J. Matt's useful introduction, "The History of American Emotions," *American Historian* 9, no. 3 (August 2016): 22–27; and Susan J. Matt and Peter N. Stearns, eds., *Doing Emotions History* (Urbana: University of Illinois Press, 2014). On PTSD and Civil War soldiers, see

Eric T. Dean Jr., *Shook over Hell: Post-Traumatic Stress, Vietnam, and the Civil War* (Cambridge, MA: Harvard University Press, 1997).

32. Nichols as quoted in *Journal of the Thirty-Fourth Annual Encampment of the Department of Oregon, Grand Army of the Republic Held at McMinnville, Oregon, June 14–16, 1915* (Salem, OR: State Printing Department, 1915), 33.

CONTRIBUTORS

ADAM H. DOMBY is assistant professor of history at the College of Charleston. His article "Captives of Memory: The Contested Legacy of Race and Atrocity at Andersonville National Historic Site" won the 2018 John C. Hubbell Prize.

ZACHERY A. FRY is assistant professor of military history at the U.S. Army Command and General Staff College. His dissertation, "Lincoln's Divided Legion: Loyalty and the Political Culture of the Army of the Potomac, 1861–1865," won the Edward M. Coffman Prize.

KURT HACKEMER is interim provost and chair of History, Philosophy, and Native Studies at the University of South Dakota. He is the author of *The U.S. Navy and the Origins of the Military Industrial-Complex, 1847–1883*.

SARAH HANDLEY-COUSINS is associate director of the Center for Disability Studies at the University of Buffalo. She is the author of the forthcoming *Bodies in Blue: Disability in the Civil War North*.

REBECCA HOWARD is assistant professor of history at Lone Star College–Montgomery. Her dissertation, "Civil War Unionists and Their Legacy in the Arkansas Ozarks," won the James L. Foster and Billy W. Beason Award from the Arkansas Historical Association.

MATTHEW CHRISTOPHER HULBERT teaches history at Texas A&M University–Kingsville. He is the author of *The Ghosts of Guerrilla Memory: How Civil War Bushwhackers Became Gunslingers in the American West*, which won the 2017 Wiley-Silver Prize.

BRIAN MATTHEW JORDAN is assistant professor and director of graduate studies in history at Sam Houston State University. He is the author of *Marching Home: Union Veterans and Their Unending Civil War*, which was a finalist for the 2016 Pulitzer Prize in History.

KELLY D. MEZUREK is professor of history at Walsh University. She is the author of *For Their Own Cause: The 27th United States Colored Troops*, which was a finalist for the 2017 Ohioana Book Award in Nonfiction.

JONATHAN D. NEU received his PhD at Carnegie Mellon University in 2018. He is revising his dissertation, "From Civil War to Civic Reform: Grand Army Veterans in the Progressive Era, 1890–1920," for publication.

MATTHEW D. NORMAN is associate professor of history at the University of Cincinnati–Blue Ash. He is the coeditor of *Ohio Valley History*, and the author of many articles, essays, and reviews.

JONATHAN A. NOYALAS is the director of the McCormick Civil War Institute at Shenandoah University. He is the author or editor of eleven books and more than 100 articles, essays, and reviews.

ANGELA M. RIOTTO is historian at Army University Press. She received her PhD from the University of Akron and was editorial assistant for *Civil War History*.

EVAN C. ROTHERA is assistant professor in the department of history at Sam Houston State University. His first monograph, *Civil Wars and Reconstructions in America: The United States, Mexico, and Argentina, 1860–1880*, is under contract with Louisiana State University Press.

STEVEN E. SODERGREN is associate professor of history and coordinator of the Studies in War and Peace Program at Norwich University. He is the author of *The Army of the Potomac in the Overland and Petersburg Campaigns: Union Soldiers and Trench Warfare, 1864–1865*, which won the 2018 Colby Award.

TYLER SPERRAZZA is a doctoral candidate in history and African American Studies at The Pennsylvania State University. He was editorial assistant for *The Journal of the Civil War Era*.

INDEX

CPSIA information can be obtained
at www.ICGtesting.com
Printed in the USA
LVHW030540151221
706182LV00001B/84